ENSLAVEMENT AND GENDER *in the* NEW TESTAMENT

ENSLAVEMENT AND GENDER *in the* NEW TESTAMENT

Jesus, Slavery, and Unconventional Masculinity

CARYN A. REEDER

Baker Academic
a division of Baker Publishing Group
Grand Rapids, Michigan

Published by Baker Academic
a division of Baker Publishing Group
Grand Rapids, Michigan
BakerAcademic.com

Printed in the United States of America

Library of Congress Cataloging-in-Publication Data
Names: Reeder, Caryn A. author
Title: Enslavement and gender in the New Testament : Jesus, slavery, and unconventional masculinity / Caryn A. Reeder.
Description: Grand Rapids, Michigan : Baker Academic, a division of Baker Publishing Group, [2026] | Includes bibliographical references and index.
Identifiers: LCCN 2026025090 | ISBN 9781540969033 paperback | ISBN 9781493456338 ebook | ISBN 9781493456345 pdf
Subjects: LCSH: Masculinity in the Bible | Slavery in the Bible | Bible. New Testament—Criticism, interpretation, etc.
Classification: LCC BS2545.M34 R44 2026
LC record available at https://lccn.loc.gov/2026025090

Unless otherwise indicated, Scripture quotations and quotations from other ancient works are the author's own translations.

Cover image: Pompeii wall painting / Carlo Bollo / Alamy
Cover design by Stefan Killen, Red+Company

Baker Publishing Group publications use paper produced from sustainable forestry practices and postconsumer waste whenever possible.

26 27 28 29 30 31 32 7 6 5 4 3 2 1

Contents

Acknowledgments

I have been thinking about this book for years. I am very grateful to the many students, colleagues, and friends who have listened to me talk through the ideas here, asked thoughtful questions along the way, and stimulated my research and thinking. In particular, Helen, Patti, Kya, Meredith, Amanda, Christen, Aaron, and Emma provided sounding boards and reminders to take walks, drink good coffee, and eat every once in a while. John Walton's characteristically generous response to an early version of some of the work here (published in a Festschrift in his honor) encouraged me to turn that chapter into a longer study. Anna Gissing, Bryan Dyer, and Alex DeMarco guided the project through the publication process, and I'm thankful for their work (and the whole team at Baker Academic). I also want to acknowledge Westmont's fantastic interlibrary loan staff, who managed to find even the most obscure books and articles, and a summer research grant from the college, which facilitated work in major libraries and museums. My godson enlivened many museum visits with his curiosity and interest in Roman hairstyles. I am, as always, grateful for the support of my family.

Abbreviations

ANCIENT GREEK AND ROMAN SOURCES

Achilles Tatius
Leuc. Clit. *Leucippe and Clitophon*

Adamantius
Phys. *Physiognomy*

Aelian
Var. hist. *Varia historia*

Anonymous Latinus
Phys. *Book of Physiognomy*

Appian
Bell. civ. *Civil Wars*
Hist. rom. *Roman History*

Apuleius
Apol. *Apology*
Metam. *The Golden Ass*

Aristophanes
Ach. *Acharnians*
Av. *Birds*
Pax *Peace*
Vesp. *Wasps*

Aristotle
Eth. eud. *Eudemian Ethics*
Eth. nic. *Nicomachean Ethics*
Gen. an. *Generation of Animals*
[*Oec.*] *Economics*
Pol. *Politics*
Rhet. *Rhetoric*

Artemidorus Daldianus
Onir. *Onirocritica*

Athenaeus
Deipn. *Deipnosophistae*

Julius Caesar
Bell. gall. *Gallic War*

Cato
Agr. *Agriculture*

Chariton
Call. *Callirhoe*

Cicero
Amic. *De amicitia*
Att. *Epistulae ad Atticum*
Cat. *In Catalinam*
Clu. *Pro Cluentio*
Fam. *Epistulae ad familiares*
Leg. *De legibus*
Mur. *Pro Murena*

Off.	*De officiis*
Phil.	*Orationes philippicae*
Pis.	*In Pisonem*
Planc.	*Pro Plancio*
Prov. cons.	*De provinciis consularibus*
Rab. Perd.	*Pro Rabirio Perduellionis Reo*
Sen.	*De senectute*
Tusc.	*Tusculanae disputationes*
Verr.	*In Verrem*

Columella

Rust. *De re rustica*

Cornelius Nepos

Att. *Atticus*
Fr. *Fragments*

Digesta

Dig. *Digesta*

Dionysius of Halicarnassus

Ant. rom. *Antiquitates romanae*

Epictetus

Diatr. *Diatribai (Dissertationes)*

Euripides

El. *Electra*
Heracl. *Children of Hercules*

Florus

Epit. *Epitome of Roman History*

Gaius

Inst. *Institutiones*

Hesiod

Op. *Works and Days*

Homer

Il. *Iliad*

Horace

Carm. *Odes*
Ep. *Epistles*
Sat. *Satires*

Isocrates

Archid. *Archidamus (Or. 6)*
Paneg. *Panegyricus (Or. 4)*

Juvenal

Sat. *Satires*

Lucian

Merc. cond.	*Salaried Posts in Great Houses*
Prometh.	*Prometheus*
Sat.	*Conversation with Cronus*
Somn.	*The Dream*, or *Lucian's Career*
Symp.	*The Carousal*, or *The Lapiths*
Tim.	*Timon*

Macrobius

Sat. *Saturnalia*

Ovid

Am. *Amores*

Persius

Sat. *Satirae*

Petronius

Sat. *Satyrica*

Philostratus

Vit. soph. *Vitae sophistarum*

Plato

Gorg.	*Gorgias*
Leg.	*Laws*
Resp.	*Republic*
Symp.	*Symposium*
Theaet.	*Theaetetus*

Plautus

Asin.	*Asinaria*
Bacch.	*Bacchides*
Cas.	*Casina*
Men.	*Menaechmi*
Merc.	*Mercator*
Most.	*Mostellaria*
Pers.	*Persae*

Pliny the Elder

Nat. *Natural History*

Pliny the Younger

Ep. *Epistulae*

Plutarch

Aem.	*Aemilius Paullus*
Ag. Cleom.	*Agis et Cleomenes*
Ages.	*Agesilaus*
Alc.	*Alcibiades*
Alex.	*Alexander*
Amat.	*Amatorius*
Ant.	*Antonius*
[*Apoth. Lac.*]	*Apophthegmata laconica*
Art.	*Artaxerxes*
Cam.	*Camillus*
Cat. Maj.	*Cato the Elder*
Cat. Min.	*Cato the Younger*
Cic.	*Cicero*
Cim.	*Cimon*
Cleom.	*Cleomenes*
Cohib. ira	*De cohibenda ira*
Comp. Demetr. Ant.	*Comparatio Demetrii et Antonii*
Comp. Lyc. Num.	*Comparatio Lycurgi et Numae*
Conj. praec.	*Conjugalia Praecepta*
Cons. ux.	*Consolatio ad uxorem*
Cor.	*Marcius Coriolanus*
Crass.	*Crassus*
Curios.	*De curiositate*
Dem.	*Demosthenes*
Dion	*Dion*
Fab.	*Fabius Maximus*
Flam.	*Titus Flamininus*
Galb.	*Galba*
[*Lib. ed.*]	*De liberis educandis*
Marc.	*Marcellus*
Mor.	*Moralia*
Mulier. virt.	*Mulierum virtutes*
Oth.	*Otho*
Per.	*Pericles*
Phoc.	*Phocion*
Pomp.	*Pompeius*
Publ.	*Publicola*
Pyrrh.	*Pyrrhus*
Quaest. conv.	*Quaestionum convivialum libri IX*
Quest. rom.	*Quaestiones romanae et graecae*
Rect. rat. aud.	*De recta ratione audiendi*
Sept. sap. conv.	*Septem sapientium convivium*
Sol.	*Solon*
Sull.	*Sulla*
Ti. C. Gracch.	*Tiberius et Caius Gracchus*
Tim.	*Timoleon*
Virt. mor.	*De virtute morali*

Polemon

Phys. *Physiognomy*

Publilius Syrus

Sent. *Sentences*

Quintilian

Inst. *Institutio oratoria*

Sallust

Bell. Cat.	*Bellum catalinae*
Bell. Jug.	*Bellum jugurthinum*

Seneca the Elder

Controv. *Controversies*

Seneca the Younger

Ben.	*De beneficiis*
Clem.	*De clementia*
Const.	*De constantia*
Ep.	*Epistulae morales*
Helv.	*Ad Helviam*
Ira	*De ira*
Marc.	*Ad Marciam de consolatione*
Prov.	*De providentia*
Tranq.	*De tranquillitate animi*
Tro.	*Troades*
Vit. beat.	*De vita beata*

Soranus

Gyn. *Gynecology*

Suetonius

Aug.	*Divus Augustus*
Cal.	*Gaius Caligula*

Claud.	*Divus Claudius*
Dom.	*Domitianus*
Gramm.	*De grammaticis*
Jul.	*Divus Julius*
Nero	*Nero*
Tib.	*Tiberius*
Vesp.	*Vespasianus*
Vit.	*Vitellius*

Tacitus

Agr.	*Agricola*
Ann.	*Annales*
Dial.	*Dialogus de oratoribus*
Germ.	*Germania*
Hist.	*Historiae*

Varro

Rust.	*De re rustica*

Virgil

Aen.	*Aeneid*

Xenophon

Ages.	*Agesilaus*
Hell.	*Hellenica*
Lac.	*Respublica Lacedaemoniorum*
Mem.	*Memorabilia*
Oec.	*Oeconomicus*

ANCIENT JEWISH AND CHRISTIAN SOURCES

Augustine

Serm.	*Sermons*

Basil of Caesarea

Ep.	*Epistulae*

Clement of Alexandria

Paed.	*Christ the Educator*

Jerome

Comm. Phlm.	*Commentariorum in Epistulam ad Philemonem liber*
Vir. ill.	*De viris illustribus*

John Chrysostom

Hom. Col.	*Homiliae in epistulam ad Colossenses*

Josephus

Ag. Ap.	*Against Apion*
Ant.	*Jewish Antiquities*
J.W.	*Jewish War*

Mishnah and Talmud

b. Yebam.	Babylonian Talmud Yevamot
m. Avot	Mishnah Avot

Old Testament Pseudepigrapha

Jos. Asen.	Joseph and Aseneth
T. Ab.	Testament of Abraham
T. Job	Testament of Job
T. Zeb.	Testament of Zebulun

Philo

Contempl.	*De vita contemplativa*
Decal.	*De decalogo*
Det.	*Quod deterius poiori insidari soleat*
Ebr.	*De ebrietate*
Flacc.	*In Flaccum*
Fug.	*De fuga et inventione*
Her.	*Quis rerum divinarum heres sit*
Ios.	*De Iosepho*
Leg.	*Legum allegoriae*
Legat.	*Legatio ad Gaium*
Migr.	*De migratione Abrahami*
Mut.	*De mutatione nominum*
Opif.	*De opificio mundi*
Post.	*De posteritate Caini*
Prob.	*Quod omnis probus liber sit*
QG 1	*Quaestiones et solutiones in Genesin* I
Sobr.	*De sobrietate*
Somn.	*De somniis*
Spec.	*De specialibus legibus*
Virt.	*De virtutibus*

Tertullian

Nat.	*To the Heathen*
Ux.	*To His Wife*

PAPYRI

P.Fay. *Fayûm Towns and Their Papyri*
P.Mich. *Michigan Papyri*
P.Oxy. *The Oxyrhynchus Papyri*
P.Tebt. *The Tebtunis Papyri*
P.Yadin *Yadin Papyri*

TEXT COLLECTIONS

AE *L'Année Épigraphique*
BGU *Berliner Griechische Urkunden*
CEL *Corpus Epistolarum Latinarum*
CIG *Corpus Inscriptionum Graecarum*
CIL *Corpus Inscriptionum Latinarum*
CIRB *Corpus Inscriptionum Regni Bosporani*
FD *Fouilles de Delphes*
GDI *Sammlung der griechischen Dialekt-Inschriften*
IEph *Die Inschriften von Ephesos*
IG *Inscriptiones Graecae*
ILS *Inscriptiones Latinae Selectae*
InscrAqu *Inscriptiones Aquileiae*
ISIS *Le Iscrizioni Sepolcrali latine nell' Isola Sacra*
PSI *Papiri Greci e Latini*
SEG *Supplementum epigraphicum Graecum*
SGDI *Sammlung der griechischen Dialekt-Inschriften*
SIG *Sylloge Inscriptionum Graecarum*
TAM *Tituli Asiae Minoris*
UPZ *Urkunden der Ptolemäerzeit*

BIBLE TRANSLATIONS

CEB Common English Bible
ESV English Standard Version
KJV King James Version
NAB New American Bible
NASB 1995 New American Standard Bible 1995
NIV New International Version
NLT New Living Translation
NRSV New Revised Standard Version
NRSVue New Revised Standard Version Updated Edition

OTHER

LCL Loeb Classical Library
LXX Septuagint
PG Patrologia Graeca. Edited by J.-P. Migne. 161 vols. Paris, 1857–86
PL Patrologia Latina. Edited by J.-P. Migne. 217 vols. Paris, 1844–55

Introduction

The Intersections of Slavery and Masculinity in the New Testament

> Jesus got up from the meal, undressed, and wrapped a towel around himself. Then he filled a bowl with water and began to wash the disciples' feet, drying them with the towel he wore.
>
> —John 13:4–5

> At last we reclined on the couches. Some young Alexandrian slaves poured snow-cooled water over our hands, while others went for our feet and with great skill pared our hangnails. Even in this unpleasant duty they were not silent but sang while they worked.
>
> —Petronius, *Sat.* 31.3–4 (LCL)

In John 13:1–17, Jesus strips off his outer clothing, replacing it with a towel, and washes his disciples' feet. Interpreters sometimes identify the story as signifying Jesus's radical servant leadership. Alternatively, interpreters see the story as a message of sacrificial love. Footwashing acts as an object lesson to teach Jesus's followers to care for the needs of the people under their authority.[1] As Peter's reaction in verse 8 suggests, however, such interpretations minimize the tensions within the story. The social context of enslavement in

1. So Haenchen 1984, 107, 109; Okantey 2013; Crowther 2018, 84–85.

the Roman Empire and the rhetorical context of elite masculinity identify Jesus not as a humble servant but as a humiliated slave.

With respect to masculinity, gender throughout the Greco-Roman world was essentially a single-sex system with masculinity as the standard of evaluation.[2] An individual's degree of masculinity was determined on the basis of a complex of intersecting concerns, including biological sex, maturity, ethnicity, economic status, ancestral history, sexual activity, posture and movement, behavior, vocal range and speaking ability, clothing, familial and social relationships, moral virtue, and more. While specific definitions of masculinity varied, normative masculinity broadly centered on authority over self and others, expressed in self-discipline, emotional control, (sanctioned) violence, and ruling power within the household and community (e.g., involvement in the military or government). As these factors suggest, masculinity was a visible, audible performance, continually observed and evaluated by the public.

Dining rooms provided a stage for demonstrations of masculinity. The host's masculinity was made evident in the furnishings, the quality and quantity of food and drink, and the status of guests. Diners' behavior, including their posture, gestures, and speech, indicated their ability to enact masculinity.[3] At the beginning and end of the scene in John 13:1–17, Jesus and his followers (here, likely all men) recline to dine. Their posture and position in the spaces of dining indicate their manliness.[4] This implication is underscored by the terms that define Jesus in relation to his followers. He is their teacher, a title of honor and authority within Jewish and Greco-Roman philosophical contexts (vv. 13–14).[5] He is called "lord," κύριος, five times in the story (vv. 6, 9, 13, 14, 16). This term is variously used of the emperor, men who held political or social power, enslavers, and, in biblical texts, God. The authority of a lord/enslaver is evident in the correlation with a person who sends messengers (ἀπόστολος) in verse 16. These elements of the story place Jesus firmly on the spectrum of masculinity.

The framework of masculinity in John 13:1–17 is disrupted when Jesus stands, assumes the clothing of an enslaved server, and washes the diners' feet. His change of clothing and position identifies him with the enslaved servers

2. E.g., McDonnell 2006, 2; Boatwright 2011, 108–10; Myers 2017, 21. See further below, and in chap. 2.

3. See Booth 1991, 106; Roller 2001, 135–39; Dunbabin 2003, 11–13, 83–84; and chap. 4, below.

4. Cf. Aristophanes, *Vesp*. 1208–22; Livy 24.16.12–13; Valerius Maximus 2.1.3; Leyerle 1999, 30–31; Roller 2006, 16.

5. E.g., Aristotle, *Rhet*. 2.23.12; Philo, *Spec*. 1.59; Plutarch, *Conj. praec*. 48; m. Avot 4.12.

who bend, crouch, and move around dining rooms.[6] As in Petronius's story of Trimalchio's dinner party, the enslaved servers offer a visible contrast to the masculinity displayed by reclining guests.[7] Rome's system of slavery turned human beings into possessions, tools for their enslavers to use for their own advantage (note esp. Varro, *Rust.* 1.17.1). Within the range of definitions of gender in the first century, elite enslavers classified enslavement by the absence of the attributes of normative masculinity: the perceived (or rather, constructed) inability to control one's own emotions or desires; legal and social disenfranchisement; the permeability of bodily boundaries; and a lack of authority or control over others.[8]

The dishonor of enslavement is on display at Trimalchio's dinner party. Enslaved people do the work of cooking, serving, cleaning, and entertaining (e.g., Petronius, *Sat.* 31.3–5, 33.3–4, 36.7–8, 40.1). Their bodies are violated as they are beaten and fondled by their enslaver (34.2, 41.6–8, 74.8–9). They are demeaned as "disgusting slaves" (34.5). The representation of the enslaved people in the narrative distinguishes them from the "manly" diners (some of whom, including the host and enslaver Trimalchio, were formerly enslaved themselves).[9]

The work of footwashing in the scenes quoted at the beginning of this introduction is particularly gendered. At Trimalchio's dinner, enslaved boys (*puer*) carry out the work of footwashing (and, apparently, pedicures; *Sat.* 31.3–4). Footwashing is almost always the task of enslaved boys or men. In a very few traditions, non-enslaved women are associated with footwashing. Abigail and Aseneth are (metaphorical) slaves who wash the feet of potential husbands (or their households), a scene with echoes in Plutarch, *Mulier. virt.* 249d.[10] In *Life of Aesop* 61, a woman enslaver washes the feet of a low-status guest as part of the enslaved Aesop's plot to triumph over her. For Herodotus, the act of washing feet signifies free women's enslavement as wartime captives (6.19.2–3).

Stories in which freeborn men wash feet are rare. The clearest example comes from Plutarch, *Pomp.* 73.6–7.[11] The formerly great Pompey is sailing

6. In text and image, enslaved servers wear short tunics belted in at the waist, carry and use towels, and move through dining rooms (rather than reclining). See, e.g., Horace, *Sat.* 2.8.10; Petronius, *Sat.* 60.8, 91.1; Juvenal, *Sat.* 14.21–22; *SEG* 36.587; Roller 2006, 29, 85–87; Feník and Lapko 2021, 355.

7. See also Juvenal, *Sat.* 5.64–65; Dunbabin 2003, 11; Roller 2006, 19–22; and chap. 4, below.

8. E.g., Joshel and Murnaghan 1998, 9–11; Briggs 2003, 176–81; Cobb 2025, 121–23; and chap. 2, below.

9. See Ramsby 2012, 69–78, on the complexities of elite, freed, and enslaved status in Petronius's *Satyricon*.

10. 1 Sam. 25:41; Jos. Asen. 13.12, 20.2–3. See also women as footwashers in Aristophanes, *Vesp.* 607–9, and (reflecting early Christian practices) 1 Tim. 5:10; Tertullian, *Ux.* 2.4.2–3.

11. Note also the scene of Abraham washing the feet of an angelic guest in T. Ab. 3.

away from his (un-manly) defeat by Caesar. The absence of the enslaved attendants who would usually accompany an elite man evidences his humiliation (ταπεινός).[12] When the captain of the ship sees Pompey begin to remove his own shoes, he assumes the slavish work of washing Pompey's feet and serving him a meal. Plutarch emphasized that the captain, a person of lesser status than Pompey but nonetheless a man with a degree of status himself, only acted because no enslaved people were available; the characterization of his work as ἐλευθεριότης, a task done freely, maintains his identity as a free man. Plutarch's attention to the captain's action indicates how unusual it was. The association of footwashing with enslavement is otherwise consistent through antiquity.[13] As in Petronius's story, even for an enslaved person the work of washing feet was a troublesome or offensive (*molestus*) task.

Jesus's act of footwashing echoes Mary's act of anointing Jesus's feet in John 12:1–8. Along with the association of footwashing with enslavement, this narratival pairing makes gender a salient concern in 13:1–17. Jesus's actions in verses 4–5—changing his clothing and taking up the equipment of an enslaved server—represent his change of identity from a reclining diner to (in Petronius's description) a "disgusting slave."[14] The context clarifies Peter's reaction to Jesus's action (vv. 6–8). The narrative lacks the sorts of explanations that protect Plutarch's captain from the shame of slavery. By adopting the identity of an enslaved person at work in a humiliating task, Jesus also identifies with un-masculinity.

The affirmation of Jesus's authority as teacher and enslaver/lord in verses 13–16 comes only after Jesus resumes masculine identity (re-dressing himself and reclining). The affirmation of authority stands in tension with the humiliation of enslavement. Arguably, Jesus's assumption of the (un)dress, equipment, and work of enslavement redefines the status of teacher and lord/enslaver. The interpretation of the footwashing in John 13:12–17 marks Jesus's action as an example for his followers.[15] The disciples as "slaves" are not greater than their enslaver (v. 16), but if their enslaver washes their feet, his

12. Cf. Pliny, *Ep*. 3.16.8.

13. Plato, *Symp*. 175a, 213b; Plautus, *Pers*. 791–92; Petronius, *Sat*. 70.8; *Life of Aesop* 40; Athenaeus, *Deipn*. 9.409f; the dinner party scene in the House of the Triclinium, Pompeii; Thomas 2014, 40–47; Velden 2019, 299. Enslaved people are associated with other foot-related tasks in Catullus 64.160–63; Martial 14.65; and an enslaved person is compared with uncomfortable shoes in Dio Chrysostom 10.8. It does not seem that enslavers washed enslaved people's feet even at Saturnalia (unless footwashing is included in the dinner "services," διακονία, of Athenaeus, *Deipn*. 14.639b, 640a).

14. See Thomas 2014, 53, 83–84; esp. Feník and Lapko 2021, 352–55; and Powery 2025a, 37–38.

15. Thompson 2015, 298–90; Powery 2025a, 38.

own relative greatness becomes ambiguous. To be teacher or lord, the sorts of positions that demonstrate masculine status, requires giving up standard aspects of masculinity to wash the feet of enslaved people.[16]

In this respect, Jesus in John 13 models a different way for his followers to enact masculinity.[17] This message is also apparent in Mark 10:41–45; Luke 22:24–27; Philippians 2:1–11; and 1 Peter 2:18–25. Across these texts, the depiction of Jesus as an objectified, subordinated, humiliated, and abused slave defines Christology, discipleship, and the exercise of authority within the community of Jesus's followers. The development of a Christology and a discipleship informed by enslavement in the New Testament can be seen as a challenge to normative constructions of masculinity around status, honor, and authority over self and others. This book explores the un-gendering of enslavement in a first-century context as a framework for the interpretation of the embodied metaphors of enslavement that define Jesus's identity and mission, constrain the exercise of authority in the communities of Jesus's followers, and develop the values and characteristics of discipleship.

Masculinity and slavery are both major topics in New Testament studies. Chapters 1 and 2 explore each topic in greater detail through the lens of 1 Peter 2:18–25 to establish the parameters of the analysis of Philippians, Mark, and Luke in chapters 3 through 5. In what follows here, I will introduce several methodological concerns and hermeneutical approaches that frame the approach I take in this study.

Contextualizing Slavery in the New Testament World

A persistent conception in New Testament studies identifies enslavement in the Roman Empire as different from, and consequently better (or at least less oppressive) than, enslavement in the history of the United States.[18] Sometimes this approach highlights the social location of enslaved people within family households in ancient Rome. The inclusion of enslaved people in the extended *familia* of their enslavers, it is argued, encouraged decency on behalf of the enslavers. A related approach represents slavery in the Roman Empire as a system of social advance to the extent that impoverished people would sell

16. Velden 2019, 305–6, notes that Jesus's superior status enables his transgression of gender norms in the story.

17. See also Velden 2019, 298, 303–4.

18. See Callahan, Horsley, and Smith 1998, 2–7; Horsley 1998, 19–32; C. Martin 2005, 221–22; Hunt 2018, 29; A. Smith 2023, 177–83; McCoskey 2024, 64–74. For contemporary examples of this approach, see D. Martin 1990, 2–32; Nordling 2009; Arzt-Grabner 2010; Fairchild 2025, 39, 45–47. The discussion here reflects a variety of sources.

themselves into slavery in order to acquire status, education, and wealth. It is generally assumed that enslaved people were likely to gain freedom at a relatively young age, taking the advantages of professional training, citizenship, and association with their enslavers' family with them.

As developed in chapters 1 and 2 of this study, the interpretation of enslavement as an essentially fair system that allowed enslaved people to thrive and even succeed in society is not supported by the textual, visual, or archaeological evidence of first-century life. While some people were enslaved in households, close proximity to their enslavers facilitated denigration, abuse, and oppression as much as education, training, and social and emotional connections. Other enslaved people labored in poor conditions (with limited nutrition, inadequate clothing, and physical abuse) on large agricultural estates, in mills and mines, and on public works projects. Some enslaved people—especially well-trained, highly educated men—could expect manumission (sometime after they turned thirty, according to Augustus's *Lex Aelia Sentia*).[19] But many enslaved people were still enslaved when they died from sickness or injury, age, malnutrition, or bodily abuse. The opportunities for social advancement were quite limited, and even in manumission the status of slavery lingered. As in American history, enslavement in the Roman Empire privileged the enslaver at the expense of the slave.

There is one key distinction between slavery in the Roman Empire and the United States: Roman slavery was not racial. But while the Romans did not base enslavement on a constructed racial identity, they did associate particular ethnicities with enslavement. Cicero, for instance, declared both Jews and Syrians to be peoples "born for slavery" (*Prov. cons.* 10). Because these regions had been conquered by Rome, their people lacked the (manly) spirit of freedom.[20] Moreover, enslavers constructed enslaved people as lacking fundamental traits of humanity: the ability to reason, control one's impulses and desires, and exercise moral virtue.[21]

As these examples indicate, the Romans engaged in racialization, defined by Jeremy Williams as "a sociopolitical process that hierarchizes some humans as full humans, others as not quite human, and others still as non-human."[22] Bryson's guide to household management, for example, identifies someone who is a slave "by nature" as more like an animal than a human; such a

19. The *Lex Aelia Sentia* is recorded in Gaius, *Inst.* 1.18.
20. See also Tacitus on Britain in *Agr.* 21.
21. E.g., Bryson 56–60; Pliny, *Nat.* 33.27; Josephus, *Ant.* 3.18–20.
22. J. Williams 2025, 101–16 (quotation from p. 101), and also 2024, 24–28; cf. Isaac 2004, 170–212; Buell 2005, 2–3, 14–21; Hartman 2007, 5.

person requires external control from an enslaver to survive (57–57).[23] While the Romans were equally likely to enslave a Briton, a Judean, and an Ethiopian, the way the Romans racialized enslaved peoples as socially, culturally, and morally inferior bears comparison with White European and American constructions of African peoples as uncivilized, childish, prone to vice, and in need of White "civilization" to become more human.[24]

Slavery is a system of domination, oppression, and dehumanization, whether in the Roman Empire or the United States. Slavery is a living death, a conception reflected in Paul's captive slaves reeking of the grave (2 Cor. 2:14–16) and Callirhoe's lament for her child who would be born into slavery in Chariton's novel (*Call.* 2.9.6–7).[25] Both "living" and "death" matter here. Philosophers like Seneca insisted on the essential humanity of enslaved people (e.g., *Ep.* 47.10, 17). But a wide variety of sources also represent enslaved people as depersonalized tools whose lives mattered only insofar as they affected enslavers. So, for instance, in multiple letters Pliny the Younger claimed personal concern for the enslaved people he owned. He provided medical care for ill slaves and praised himself for allowing the fiction of property ownership by his slaves. But these elements of Pliny's interactions with enslaved people ultimately (and pertinently) benefited his own life and work. Along with these comments, he also wrote about his attempts to escape the noisy presence of the crowds of slaves in his home. Pliny treats the enslaved as persons to serve his own self-interest.[26]

How the enslaved people in Pliny's household reacted to Pliny's treatment, assessment, and disparagement of them is unknown and unknowable. They survive only as objects seen from Pliny's perspective. Yet they were human beings, with human desires, emotions, relationships, understanding, and personhood beyond Pliny's construction of their existence as an extension of himself. The study of slavery in the Roman world of the New Testament has historically centered and assumed the perspective of enslavers (sometimes sympathetically acknowledging enslavers' complaints concerning enslaved people, and sometimes emphasizing the oppressive nature of enslavement). Recent historians and interpreters also address the ways enslaved people

23. Translation from Swain 2013, 457. Cf. Aristotle, *Pol.* 1327b; Tacitus, *Agr.* 11.

24. This rhetoric is common in nineteenth-century speeches and writings: John C. Calhoun, "Slavery, a Positive Good," and Robert Knox, "Lecture on the Races of Men" (both excerpted in T. Wright 2020, 113–19, 140–41); see also Brownlow 1857, 14–16; Isaac 2004, 9–16.

25. See also Plato, *Gorg.* 483a–b; Diodorus Siculus 13.58.2; Publilius Syrus, *Sent.* 489; Seneca, *Ep.* 70.21, 77.18. The definition of slavery as a living death is indebted to the analysis of slavery as natal alienation in Patterson 1982, 1–12, and racialization as a process of making people "vulnerable to premature death" (J. Williams 2024, 27). See also Hartman 2007, 30–31.

26. See Pliny, *Ep.* 2.17, 3.14, 8.16, etc.; C. Martin 2005, 224; and Blake 2016, 95–96.

developed and asserted their own individualities, created communities and culture to resist the dehumanization of enslavement, survived the oppression of enslavement, and even (if rarely) thrived by manipulating their enslavers and the conditions of enslavement to their own advantage.[27]

Addressing slavery in the Americas, Vincent Brown challenges scholars of enslavement to seek out and heed both the strategies of domination employed by enslavers and also the perspectives of the enslaved. This balancing act holds the social death imposed by enslavers in tension with the resistance of enslaved people. These two sides of slavery are, Brown insists, intimately and inextricably related: "The struggles of slaves were not simply beset by the depredations of slavery but were shaped and directed by them. The activities of slaves could be more easily understood as having been compelled by the very conditions that slaves have been described as resisting."[28] With respect to the New Testament world, the limitations of the sources make this work more challenging.

As in the case of Pliny's letters, almost all the extant literary sources concerning Roman slavery are written by and for freeborn elites, the men who enslaved others. The involvement of enslaved people as researchers, scribes, writers, copyists, and readers complicates the question of authorship.[29] But despite the essential contributions of enslaved people to the creation of texts in antiquity, the sources assume and advance elite perspectives on enslavement. In this respect, it is important to recognize that literary representations of enslavement offer insight into how elite men constructed slavery and slaves. There are certainly reflections of lived experience in literary sources, but these sources often reveal more about enslavers' conceptions of enslavement and enslaved people than they do about the realities of enslaved people's daily lives.

The elite origins of representations of slavery means that basic concepts go unquestioned: that slavery is legally and morally justifiable; that enslavement is a beneficial system for both enslavers and enslaved people; that enslaved people belong entirely to their enslavers.[30] There are a few literary texts written by formerly enslaved people, including Phaedrus's *Fables*, Publilius Syrus's *Sententiae*, and Epictetus's *Discourses*. These works recognize the oppressive aspects of enslavement and the different ways enslaved people survived and

27. W. Johnson 2003, 115; J. Mason 2003, 9; C. Martin 2005, 223; V. Brown 2009, 1233–36; Vlassopoulos 2011, 123–28.

28. V. Brown 2009, 1246 (see also 1242–46).

29. See Blake 2012, 193–95; Powery 2022, 81–84; and Moss 2024, 12–13 (and throughout).

30. See esp. Bradley 1994, 6–8; 2008, 340–46; Joshel 2011, 214–15. Ramelli 2016, 3–5, 10–12, 52–53, and throughout, explores alternative perspectives among ascetic communities that recognized the injustice of slavery (e.g., Philo's Therapeutae, Gregory of Nyssa's monastic tradition, and some Stoic and Cynic philosophies).

resisted enslavement. However, these few texts developed within the constraints of the Roman system of slavery, and so they also tend to advance elite understandings and assumptions about enslavement.[31]

Taking account of the limitations of the sources, in this study I adopt what Chris de Wet has termed a doulological hermeneutic. De Wet defines doulology as "the discourse of slavery . . . that enunciative process in which slavery and mastery operate together as a concept 'to think/communicate with.'"[32] Informed by Brown's perspective on the interrelated elements of domination and resistance, I borrow from de Wet's doulological hermeneutic to attempt to analyze the public transcript of enslavers' perspectives on enslavement, to understand the parameters and limitations of slavery for enslaved people, and also to recover the hidden transcripts: the complex ways enslaved people may have survived, profited from, and resisted slavery.

The brutal domination of slavery is in no way balanced, ameliorated, or justified by the survival and resistance of enslaved people. I recognize that I am writing this book as a White American woman in the context of negative reactions to and retaliation against the 1619 Project, Black Lives Matter, Say Her Name, and diversity, equity, and inclusion programs. In response to social pressure and political policies, public schools and museums in the United States have shifted away from a focus on the horror of slavery in American history toward claims that slavery benefited enslaved people.[33] This interpretation of slavery is demonstrably untrue.[34] Enslaved people's ability to survive, create their own communities, use their situations to their advantage, or resist the racializing strategies of slavery is, as Brown and de Wet argue, always constrained by the domination of slavery. My attention to these possibilities acknowledges human ingenuity and the exercise of hope among the oppressed; I reject any suggestion that slavery was good for the enslaved people of the New Testament world (or any other slave society).

A word on the vocabulary of slavery in this respect: I primarily use the terms "enslaved people" and "enslaver" in order to keep the imposition and domination of slavery in view. I sometimes also use "slave," particularly when

31. Cf. Seal 2025, 198, arguing that slavery was an "unchangeable system" in the Roman Empire. Epictetus is an interesting figure in this respect. His *Discourses* reflect elite understandings of enslavement, but he used these understandings to redefine enslaved people as models of true freedom (e.g., 1.9.8, 3.26.1) and his elite audiences as "slaves" (1.4.14, 1.9.20, etc.). See further Wehus 2019, 234–38.

32. De Wet 2018, 8. See also Joshel and Petersen 2014, 6–15; Shaner 2018, xii–xvi; Beavis 2021, 6–8.

33. E.g., Joselow 2025; Kanno-Youngs 2025a; and 2025b.

34. Esp. Hartman 2007, 40, 130–32, 165; C. Smith 2020 and 2025; Wood 2022.

addressing the perspective of enslavers.[35] A doulological interpretation distinguishes "slaves" (seen from the enslavers' perspective) from "enslaved people" (reflecting the experience of those who were enslaved). This distinction can be exploited to question how a text's meaning or significance might change depending on the interpreter's position.[36]

To balance the biases of literary texts, the analysis of slavery in the Roman Empire necessarily incorporates a range of sources.[37] The literary and philosophical reflections of the elite indicate elite perspectives on enslavement, but approached with a hermeneutic of suspicion, the same sources can also suggest how enslaved people may have navigated slavery.[38] Personal letters, legal documents, and graffiti provide glimpses of the everyday experiences of enslaved people. Plays, novels, and satires suggest imaginable possibilities and popular perceptions of slavery. Interpretations of archaeological evidence of the potential artifacts and domestic spaces of enslavement further develop the reconstruction of the material, embodied experiences of slavery.[39] Inscriptions about enslaved people and on behalf of enslaved people add another layer. Funerary memorials use stereotypical language, but they nonetheless provide insight into how enslaved people situated themselves in the social systems of the first century.[40]

Contrary to the public transcripts of enslavers, enslaved people were human. They had the ability to reason, to govern themselves, and to exercise human capabilities and agency. They navigated enslavement in a variety of ways: by accepting and operating within enslavement; by manipulating their enslavers for personal gain; and by resisting and undermining their enslavers' efforts to oppress and subjugate them. It is not possible to recover fully the lives of enslaved people or their perceptions of their experiences and identities.

35. More broadly, the term "enslaved person" is preferred by scholars of slavery as a way to recognize the identity of the individuals involved, rather than reducing their identity to "slaves." See further Rinehart 2022; and, for the New Testament, Bonar and Cobb 2025, 8–10; and, on the complicated issue of translation, Powery 2025a, 32; 2025b, 4–7.

36. See also W. Johnson 2003, 112–19; and V. Brown 2009, 1236–39, 1243–46.

37. Glancy 2006, 3–7; Bell, Borbonus, and MacLean 2024, 11.

38. Cf. Joshel and Petersen 2014, 5–8; de Wet 2018, 6–7.

39. As demonstrated by Joshel and Petersen 2014, and in the more focused studies of, e.g., Severy-Hoven 2012; Baird 2015; and F. Green 2025.

40. Classical and New Testament scholars also sometimes draw analogies with slavery in the United States (see esp. McCoskey 1998, 37; Powery 2022, 73–74). The personal narratives of enslaved Americans offer a valuable point of comparison for reconstructing how enslaved people in the Roman Empire may have understood and navigated their own lives. I particularly appreciate the contribution of these studies to our understanding of the emotional toll, motivations, cultures, and range of means of resistance that enslaved people employ to survive. Since I lack the expertise to navigate and represent these sources well, in this book I primarily work within the sources of the Greco-Roman and biblical worlds.

Their understandings of slavery, strategies for survival, and daily experiences are masked by the words of enslavers.[41] But the (informed, thoughtful, careful, and imaginative) effort to reconstruct enslaved peoples' lives and self-understandings as well as we can is necessary to avoid accepting enslavers' assumptions or adopting enslavers' perspectives. To question the sources, to look for the purposes or motivations behind the practices of enslavement, and to seek the experiences of and responses to slavery by enslaved people allow us to remember, name, and honor those who experienced, benefited from, suffered, died, and survived Roman slavery.

Being Men in the New Testament World

"Be men" (ἀνέρες ἔστε): This rallying cry from Homer's *Iliad* reverberates around the ancient Mediterranean.[42] What "masculinity" meant in any particular time, space, or circumstance differed in details. Homer's heroes wept for their beloved companions, but centuries later Tacitus's Agricola displayed emotional control when his young son died.[43] Different arenas of masculinity overlapped and conflicted. While a soldier who saved a fellow soldier's life in battle was honored as a "father," the masculinity demonstrated by violence in war was inappropriate in a civic setting.[44] There were competing definitions of masculinity even in the same sociohistorical location, as is evident in the debate over the manliness of theatrical performance in Tacitus, *Ann.* 14.15–16. The centrality of authority over self and others, however, remained consistent. A manly man disciplined his body and desires; controlled his household as husband, father, and enslaver; and maintained social order as patron, military commander, and political leader.[45]

Masculinity was visible and audible in Roman cities.[46] Historiography, biography, and funeral speeches celebrated exemplars of masculinity. Inscriptions published manly deeds of benefaction and courage for passersby to see. In school, Roman boys were taught how to stand, walk, and speak like men. In dining rooms, theaters, baths, streets, forums, and temples, elite men performed masculinity in public view. The practice of masculinity was

41. C. Martin 2005, 222–23; Joshel 2011, 215; Joshel and Petersen 2014, 5–8.

42. Homer, *Il.* 5.529–30; 1 Sam. 4:9; Thucydides 5.9.9; Livy 9.40.4–6; Tacitus, *Agr.* 33.4.

43. Homer, *Il.* 19.4–6, and passim; Tacitus, *Agr.* 19.

44. Note Polybius 6.39.6–8, 10.38.1–2; Livy 1.19.1–2; Valerius Maximus 2.7.14, 5.2.4; Tacitus, *Hist.* 1.83–84.

45. See chap. 2, below; and C. Williams 1999, 145–48; Holmes 2012, 95–98; Asikainen 2018, 26–29; Robinson 2019, 50–51.

46. Cf. Boatwright 2011, 108–13.

essential to Roman identity, and acting like a man offered opportunities for social advancement.[47]

The vocabulary of masculinity is rare in the New Testament, surprisingly so given the centrality of masculinity in Greco-Roman and Second Temple Jewish texts.[48] Paul once exhorted the men and women followers of Jesus in Corinth to be men (ἀνδρίζομαι; 1 Cor. 16:13), signifying militaristic strength, courage, and endurance. Barnabas is called an ἀνὴρ ἀγαθός, a manly man, in Acts 11:24.[49] Virtue, ἀρετή, a concept that slips between masculinity and morality in Greco-Roman understanding, is slightly more common.[50] Despite the lack of technical vocabulary, however, the common conceptions of normative masculinity are apparent throughout the narratives and letters of the New Testament in men's display of power and authority, exhortations to self-control, militaristic metaphors and images, household regulations, and more.[51]

As the story of Jesus washing the feet of the disciples in John 13:1–17 exemplifies, there are also tensions, ambiguities, and disruptions to normative Greco-Roman masculinities in the New Testament.[52] It is unlikely that many participants in the communities of Jesus's followers represented in the New Testament had the political and socioeconomic status to enable them to attain the ideals of elite masculinity.[53] Moreover, men who castrate themselves for the kingdom of heaven (Matt. 19:12), Jesus's association with "tax collectors and sinners" (Luke 5:29–32), Paul's weak body and unimpressive speech (2 Cor. 10:10), and women's authority over the bodies of their husbands (1 Cor. 7:4) would, in Roman context, be perceived as un-masculine. Above all, the crucifixion of Jesus signified his slavish un-manliness.[54]

The range of masculinities and un-masculinities woven through New Testament books, often in the same contexts, presents a complicated picture. In

47. McDonnell 2006, 2–3.

48. Many common terms for masculinity, including ἀνδρεία, ἀνδρεῖος, and ἀνδραγαθέω, are not used in the New Testament.

49. As D'Angelo 2004, 286, points out, the term ἀνήρ (rather than the inclusive ἄνθρωπος) is more frequent in Luke-Acts than other books.

50. Phil. 4:8; 1 Pet. 2:9; 2 Pet. 1:3, 5.

51. See, e.g., D'Angelo 2002; Clines 2004; Liew 2004; Conway 2008; and for general introductions to masculinity studies and the New Testament, Moore 2004, 4–22; Conway 2008, 8–11; Wilson 2015, 14–18; and Robinson 2019, 20–40.

52. Cf. Levine 2019, 295–302, and (e.g.) Moxnes 2003 and 2016; Wilson 2015; Robinson 2019.

53. Cf. A. C. Miller 2014b, 79–81; Wilson 2017, 32, 37; Callahan 2022, 40, 51–52; Moss 2024, 57, 119.

54. My use of the hyphen in "un-masculine" and "un-manliness" is intentional, to provide a reminder of the ways masculinity and un-masculinity were constructed in conversation and contrast with each other.

this study, I focus on one particular concern: the intersection of masculinity with enslavement in Philippians 2:1–11; Mark 10:41–45 and Luke 22:24–27; and 1 Peter 2:18–25. Across the ancient Mediterranean worlds of the New Testament, masculinity was, at its core, concerned with authority over self and others. Enslavement—being owned by and under the legal, social, and moral authority of enslavers—encapsulated un-masculinity. The identification of Jesus, the twelve disciples, and all Jesus's followers with and as enslaved people establishes an alternative to normative masculine attitudes, behaviors, and rights.

In this study, I argue that the Christology and discipleship of enslavement are defined in the Gospels, Philippians, and 1 Peter by the voluntary rejection of competition for status and by self-humiliation (in terms of relative position and relationship to others) rather than self-worth. As "slaves," Jesus and his followers, including the figures of authority within the community, labor for and on behalf of others. They obey orders instead of giving them. If normative masculinities privilege the one (the elite man) at the expense of the many, the Christology and discipleship characterized by enslavement expect the one to give up privilege for the sake of the many.

This message is challenging in different ways. It challenges the potential and actual abuses of the practice of normative masculinity in Greco-Roman antiquity, evident in (for instance) Roman military occupation, social violence, economic inequalities, and the abuse of enslaved people in households, on agricultural estates, and in mills and mines. It is challenging to people who possess the status and authority that the discipleship of enslavement denies, as indicated by the long history of rewriting the texts to remove their bite (to "masculinize" them).

The discipleship of enslavement has also proven challenging for people who lack status and authority. The exhortation to be humble, to give up status for the sake of others, and to labor on behalf of others has most often been imposed on populations who already hold marginalized positions by reason of gender, poverty, or racialized identity. This history makes the New Testament texts that call for mutual enslavement into texts of terror for far too many readers.[55] As Emerson Powery concludes, interpreters of the New Testament "should not appropriate these *doulos* metaphors uncritically (if at all)."[56] There are other ways to express the messages of these texts without the problematic language, structures, and domination of enslavement.

55. H. Thurman 1996, 1–3; Powery and Sadler 2016, 123; Sechrest 2022, 5, 228–29; M. Smith 2023, 103–6.

56. Powery 2022, 85.

At the same time, recognizing the intersections of slavery and masculinity in the world of the New Testament offers a (partial) solution to the history of the abusive weaponization of the discipleship of enslavement. The relevant texts speak about and (I will argue) against the use of elite masculinity for personal benefit and advantage at the expense of the bodies and souls of people who were prevented from attaining masculine privilege. In this sense, the redefinition of masculinity around enslavement has liberative potential.[57] Another element in the solution comes in recognizing the terror and trauma of slavery, listening to readers who approach the biblical text with a variety of perspectives and experiences, and seeking readings directed toward justice.

Enslavement, Masculinity, and Justice

I begin classes on slavery in the New Testament with several warnings: First, the narratives, rhetoric, and artifacts of enslavement from the ancient Mediterranean world preserve a story of horrifying abuse. Enslavers defined enslaved people as human property, and they used enslaved people for their own benefit without significant or persistent regard for the humanity of the individual. To understand slavery from the perspective of the enslaved people who lived, suffered, survived, and died within this system, it is necessary to attend to the horror and abuse (and to question why enslavers committed and recorded such atrocities).

Second, the same horrifying abuse is present in the New Testament. Parables preserve a litany of violence and death (e.g., Mark 12:1–12). Narratives replicate enslavers' objectification and instrumentalization of enslaved people (e.g., Matt. 8:9). Moral exhortations advise enslaved people to obey their enslavers fully (e.g., 1 Tim. 6:1–2).

Third, the New Testament does not solve the problem of enslavement. The peoples whose stories are told in the New Testament and those who composed, read, and preserved the New Testament included enslaved people and enslavers. The system of slavery infiltrated and dominated their household relationships, religious practice, imperial economics, entertainment, markets, and graffiti. Despite this reality (or perhaps because of it), there is no call for the abolition of slavery or even a clear condemnation of slavery in the New Testament. Only a few texts recognize its injustices (e.g., 1 Pet. 2:18–21; Rev. 18:11–13). The use of New Testament texts and concepts to support slavery and other systems of oppression (as, for instance, in the United States) offers

57. See also H. Thurman 1996, 7–19; Stubbs 2007, 376–77; Glancy 2010, 145; Thompson 2015, 290; Powery and Sadler 2016, 1–3, 54–56; M. Smith 2022, 55–58.

a stark reminder that the Bible has often been, and continues to be, a "weapon of psychological, spiritual, and physical abasement."[58]

In the New Testament world, slavery and masculinity had to do with power. In both systems, elite interests were directed toward upholding the privilege of a few at the expense (and disempowerment) of many.[59] A hermeneutic informed by both doulological and masculinity studies allows the recognition and exploitation of the ambiguity of New Testament texts, particularly with respect to the different social positions and identities of interpreters. That is, the public transcripts of the ancient world provide a good sense of how elite men and (other) enslavers would interpret and use any particular text. But the primary participants in communities of Jesus's followers in the first century were non-elite men and women, including enslaved and freed people. They composed, read, and argued over the narratives and letters that now make up the New Testament.[60] The Gospels and letters formed only one part of a larger conversation in the first century. Imagining how different people in the audiences of these books might have understood, responded to, and used them opens space for creative interpretations that highlight what Love Lazarus Sechrest calls "liberative strands" and offers, in Howard Thurman's words, "a technique of survival for the oppressed."[61] Another entry point to this conversation is the recognition of the challenge that the Christology and discipleship of enslavement in the New Testament pose to normative masculinities.

Mary, Jesus, and Paul: Real or Metaphorical Slaves?

In Luke 1:38 and 48, Mary the mother of Jesus calls herself God's slave (δούλη). Paul represents Jesus as a humiliated, obedient, crucified slave (δοῦλος) in Philippians 2:7–8, a status echoed in Jesus's act of footwashing in John 13:1–17 and his identification as a server (using διακονέω) in Mark 10:45 and Luke 22:27. Paul also identifies himself with enslavement: δοῦλος of Christ (Phil. 1:1) and δουλόω to all (1 Cor. 9:19). These descriptions are most often interpreted as metaphor, but recently some scholars have questioned this conclusion. Three options for the interpretation of enslavement with reference to Mary, Jesus, and Paul will be explored here: first, the potential

58. Sechrest 2022, 5.

59. Cf. de Wet 2018, 8.

60. See Powery 2022, 71–74, 81–85; Moss 2024, 12–15, 85–92 (and throughout).

61. Sechrest 2022, 13–15; H. Thurman 1996, 18. See also Johnson-DeBaufre and Nasrallah 2011, 161–62, 174; Shaner 2018, xiii–xvi, xxiv; and Powery 2025a, 34–35, 38.

of their historical experience of enslavement; second, the biblical metaphor of slavery to God; and third, the specific background of the "servant" (and servants) in Isaiah.

Personal Experience with Enslavement

The pervasiveness of enslavement in first-century life explains its presence in the New Testament. But beyond the general presence of enslaved and freed people and enslavers in households, cities, rhetoric, law, and literature, the people who wrote, read, and preserved the books of the New Testament included enslaved and freed people. Emerson Powery and Candida Moss both suggest that enslaved scribes and readers influenced the content and interpretation of the Gospels and Paul's letters.[62] It has also been argued that Mary, Jesus, and Paul had personal experience with enslavement.

First, Paul: In his commentary on Philemon, Jerome reported a tradition according to which Paul's parents were exiled from Judea to Tarsus by the Romans.[63] While Jerome avoided the language of slavery, Roman conquests resulted in the enslavement and sale of captives across the empire. Presumably, then, Paul's parents were captured and sold as slaves (as is explicit in *Photii ad Amphilochium*, Quest. 116).[64] There are practical questions here concerning the potential that a married couple would remain together through captivity, enslavement, and manumission. Furthermore, if this tradition has any historicity, Paul himself must have been born after his parents were manumitted (since enslaved children were not freed with their parents).[65] A family history of enslavement could, however, explain the tradition of Paul's Roman citizenship, as citizenship was granted to enslaved people freed under particular circumstances.[66] Mary Ann Beavis also notes the possible slave origins of Paul's work as a tentmaker.[67] The positive perspective on labor in his letters in general reflects the social context of free and freed artisans.[68] The possibility that Paul's parents had been enslaved is not provable, but it is certainly plausible.

62. Powery 2022, 82–84; Moss 2024, 66–69, 85–37, and passim.

63. Jerome, *Comm. Phlm.* 23–24 (PL 26:762b–c).

64. Paul's parents are here identified as captives (συναλίσκομαι; PG 101:688c).

65. Fairchild 2025, 82, notes that Jerome preserves another tradition in which Paul was already born and accompanied his parents when they were taken out of Galilee (*Vir. ill.* 5). Fairchild's representation of Paul as a formerly enslaved man assumes the family was able to remain together, to be purchased together, and to be freed together (see pp. 9, 99, 110, and passim).

66. So Riesner 1998, 152–53.

67. Beavis 2021, 35. See also Fairchild 2025, 64.

68. De Vos 1999, 259.

Second, Mary and Jesus: The birth narrative in Luke 1 describes Mary as an enslaved woman (δούλη in vv. 38 and 48), and Jesus's father is glaringly absent from the early references to his parentage in Galatians 4:4–7 and Mark 6:3.[69] Paul presents Jesus himself as a slave in Philippians 2:7–8.[70] His ministry began around age thirty according to Luke 3:23, the age at which a person could be formally manumitted.[71] Jesus's parables incorporate the experiences of enslavement. His first public sermon in Luke's Gospel proclaims freedom for the enslaved (4:16–21).[72] On the basis of these traditions, Winsome Munro and Mitzi Smith have argued that Mary was an enslaved woman who was impregnated by her enslaver. Jesus was born and lived as a slave, either being freed (so Smith) or escaping (so Munro) to begin his ministry.[73]

The evidence adduced by Munro and Smith has been interpreted in different ways by other scholars, and I am not (yet) convinced by their arguments. However, as with Paul's parents, the possibility that Mary and Jesus were enslaved is plausible. As Candida Moss notes, Mary's lack of bodily autonomy in Luke 1, the questions concerning Jesus's paternity throughout the Gospels, and the comparison of Jesus with an enslaved person in Philippians 2:7–8 and John 13:1–20 could, and likely would, be understood as signs of their enslavement by audiences in the first century.[74] The use of the language, characteristics, and behaviors of slavery to depict Mary and Jesus is unexpected in the Roman context. The attention Munro, Smith, and Moss bring to the question of their legal status is important.

"There is nothing shameful about being born a slave."[75] Smith's reminder of the fundamental honor of all people, including enslaved people, offers a warning against adopting or assuming the perspective of enslavers, rather than centering the experiences of enslaved people, in New Testament interpretation. Slavery was a fact of life for countless people in the first century and throughout history—one that sometimes had to be accepted, often resisted, and always survived. If Mary, Jesus, and Paul experienced enslavement, then their stories offer solidarity with similarly marginalized and oppressed peoples. The possibility that their personal histories are histories of enslavement complicates the interpretation of their stories, especially with respect to the issue of power, and draws attention to potential messages of liberation and justice.[76]

69. Munro 1998, 548, 201–5, 262, 275; M. Smith 2022, 63.
70. Munro 1998, 174–75; M. Smith 2022, 57.
71. M. Smith 2022, 62.
72. Munro 1998, 321, 357–66; M. Smith 2022, 55, 62, 65.
73. Munro 1998, 397 (also suggesting Mary was a fugitive slave, 594); M. Smith 2022, 59–60.
74. Moss 2024, 94, 97–100.
75. M. Smith 2022, 58. See also Moss 2024, 105.
76. See M. Smith 2022, 61–62; Moss 2024, 99, 111–12.

Metaphors of Enslavement

Being a "slave of God" or, for Paul, a "slave of Christ" is often interpreted as a version of the Bible's metaphorical depiction of Israel and specific figures—including Moses, David, and the prophets—as God's slaves.[77] The identification of Israel as God's slaves develops from the exodus story. In the Torah, a consistent refrain claims God saved the people from oppressive enslavement in Egypt so that they could worship God alone, obey God, and enact justice (e.g., Deut. 5:6–7; 15:12–18; 24:17–22). Their worship and obedience identify the people of Israel as God's slaves.[78] Paul's use of slavery metaphors in Romans adapts this framework to explain salvation as freedom from slavery to sin to be God's obedient, justified, righteous slaves (e.g., 6:12–23).[79]

The biblical identification of kings and prophets as slaves reflects their identity as agents who spoke for and ruled on behalf of God.[80] In the Roman world, people enslaved in private households or for civic institutions ("public slaves") could also hold positions of authority on behalf of their enslavers, often to administer business or estates.[81] The imperial slaves who carried out the administrative work of the empire provide an instructive parallel. As representatives of the emperor, they exercised significant authority. They could take wealth and status with them into manumission. When the New Testament identification of Jesus or Paul as slaves is read within these contexts, "slave" becomes a title of leadership that recognizes the authority of Jesus and Paul as God's agents.[82] To be called "slave" is an honor, with no implications of socially imposed shame.

It is revealing that, among interpreters who emphasize the power and authority of Jesus or Paul as "slave," few regularly identify Mary as a figure of status, power, and authority. In such interpretations, gender intersects with power to disempower Mary. The intersections of gender and power extend to enslavement. Because slavery was gendered as un-masculine, Jesus and Paul are, like Mary, disempowered. Despite the identification of figures of authority as God's slaves, literal and metaphorical representations of slavery in the Bible also associate enslavement with social inferiority, violence, and

77. Combes 1998, 44–45, notes that Greek literature also identifies worshipers of a particular god as slaves, though not to the extent the metaphor is used in the Bible.

78. Deut. 32:36; 1 Kings 8:35–36; Ps. 22:31; 100:2; Isa. 56:6–7; Callender 1998, 77–80; Hezser 2005, 363–65.

79. Cf. Merz 2018, 97, 105.

80. Josh. 24:29; 1 Kings 3:7–9; 1 Chron. 17:7; Jer. 7:25; Hag. 2:23; Hezser 2005, 327–28.

81. Esp. highlighted by D. Martin 1990, 2–32.

82. D. Martin 1990, 51–55; Horsley 1998, 169; Merz 2018, 97, 100.

abasement.[83] That is, the metaphor of enslavement can be used in a positive sense to indicate devotion, obedience, or identification with God, but it also overlaps with the embodied experiences and rhetorical abasement of enslavement.[84] The same is true within Roman context, as elite disdain for freed slaves (especially wealthy or politically influential freed people) indicates. Even the few imperial and public slaves who operated as governmental agents carried the imposed dishonor and bodily limitations with them as both slaves and freed people (note that most imperial and public slaves worked as cooks, cleaners, hairdressers, nurses, or similar low-status occupations).[85]

Isaiah's Servant Songs

The essential dishonor of enslavement is reflected in another significant biblical influence on New Testament representations of Jesus, Paul, and other figures as slaves: Isaiah's "suffering servant." References to enslavement weave through Isaiah. Some relate to the expectation of enslavement as a consequence of wartime defeat (14:2–4; 19:23; 45:14). God's people are slaves in 41:8–9; 56:6; 63:17; and 65:8–9, 13–15. In the Servant Songs, the vocabulary of enslavement identifies a particular slave as God's agent, sent by God to carry out specific assignments (to bring justice to the nations, to regather the people of Israel, to bear people's sins).[86] The descriptions emphasize abjection. The "servant" engages in constant labor (42:4). His body is marked by physical disability (42:19) and deformity (52:14). He is an object of horror (49:7; 53:3) and abuse (50:6; 53:5).[87]

In a first-century context, these descriptions of the "servant" resemble enslavement. So, for instance, as many enslaved women in the Roman Empire were forced to bear children to be their enslavers' future property, Isaiah's slave was conceived to do God's work (49:5). The physical abuse and mockery

83. E.g., Gen. 16; Exod. 21:26–27; Judg. 19:19; 1 Sam. 17:32; 2 Sam. 9:6–8; 2 Chron. 28:10; Jer. 34:8–11. On enslavement in ancient Israel, see Callender 1998, 74–77; B. Wright 1998, 85–86; Ramelli 2016, 77–79.

84. De Wet 2018, 10–13, argues that the varied conceptions of slavery blur the lines between metaphor and legal status, so much so that early Christians would not have understood "slave of God" as metaphor rather than literal experience.

85. See Flexsenhar 2019, 13–18; Giannella 2024, 141–43, 162; Luciani 2024, 73–75; Joly 2024, 164–67. Garnsey 1996, 186, and A. Smith 2023, 182, critique D. Martin's conception of slavery as social advance for this reason.

86. The servant is עבד in the Hebrew text. The Greek translation (LXX) uses παῖς in Isa. 42:1; 49:6; 52:13; δοῦλος in 49:3, 5, 7; and δουλεύω in 53:11.

87. Cf. Hanson 1995, 45–46, 54 (on the representation of the servant as victim rather than victor); Brueggemann 1998, 142 (the servant as "a genuine outcast"); and Schipper 2011, 40–58 (highlighting the theme of disability in the Servant Songs).

represented in 50:6, with the slave turning his back to be beaten (instead of facing the enemy like a manly soldier) and having his beard yanked out, illustrates the un-masculinity of enslavement.[88] In addition to the general representation of the slave as despised and abhorred, the specific references to his remarkably (even bizarrely) unattractive appearance in 42:19–20; 52:14; and 53:2–3 bear comparison with the enslavement of people with disabilities or unusual bodies for entertainment among wealthy Romans.[89] With these associations as a backdrop, the innocence, vindication, and exaltation of Isaiah's slave disrupts common Roman perceptions of enslaved people (49:7; 50:7–9; 52:13; 53:12).

Isaiah's Servant Songs weave through the New Testament books in explicit quotations and more elusive allusions.[90] There is strong potential that they influenced New Testament depictions of Jesus, the twelve disciples, and Jesus's followers as enslaved, especially in the association of enslavement with humiliation, abuse, and horror. That is, the suffering of Isaiah's slave connects with the lived realities of enslavement in the first century. The vindication of Isaiah's slave in turn offers a means of interpreting the suffering of God's slaves as honorable and even praiseworthy.

The biblical imagery of slaves of God and, more particularly, Isaiah's suffering slave proved to be significant influences on New Testament texts. So did the rhetoric and realities of Roman slavery. The people who wrote, read, and discussed the books of the New Testament knew enslaved people; many (or all) of them likely were enslaved, freed, or enslavers. This study prioritizes the social contexts of the first century as determining factors for the interpretation of the representation of Jesus, Paul, the twelve disciples, and Jesus's followers in general as enslaved people.

Christ as Slave, Slaves of Christ: The Un-Manning of Enslavement

In John 13:1–17, Jesus removes his clothing, replacing it with a towel. He picks up a washbasin. He crouches at the disciples' feet, washing off dust, dung,

88. In the Roman Empire, scars on the back (as on enslaved people's bodies) represented un-masculinity, while scars on the chest (as on military men) signified manliness; see Valerius Maximus 3.2.24; Quintilian, *Inst.* 2.15.7–8; Josephus, *J.W.* 1.193; Plutarch, *Mor.* 1091e. The loss of a beard signifies un-manliness in 2 Sam. 10:4; Plutarch, *Ages.* 30.3; Artemidorus, *Onir.* 1.30; and enslaved men were forced to keep their faces beardless to remain sexually attractive to enslavers as a signifier of un-manliness (Seneca, *Ep.* 47.7, 95.24; Lucian, *Sat.* 24).

89. E.g., Quintilian, *Inst.* 2.5.11–12; Pliny, *Nat.* 7.75, 34.11; Plutarch, *Curios.* 520c–d; Garland 2010, 45–48; Gevaert and Laes 2013, 222–23.

90. There are explicit quotations or otherwise obvious references in Matt. 8:17; 12:18–21; Luke 4:18–19; 22:37; John 12:38; Acts 8:32–33; 13:47; Rom. 10:16; 15:21; 2 Cor. 6:2; 1 Pet. 2:22–25; Rev. 14:5. See further Beers 2013, 855–59; 2015, 81–82, 88–89, and passim.

and all the other detritus acquired on the streets of an ancient city. It is easy to imagine the skin hardened by walking, weeping blisters, the ripe aroma of sweat. In his clothing and equipment, his posture and relative position in the dining room, and the unpleasant labor itself, the scene depicts Jesus in the guise of an enslaved person. He embodies the opposite of the common cultural understanding of an honorable man, who would demonstrate his masculine status by reclining at the table as his bodily needs and desires are met by enslaved servers. And yet, in the New Testament, the un-masculinity of enslavement defines Christology, the exercise of authority, and discipleship.

Inhabiting the social humiliation, bodily vulnerability, and offensive labor of enslavement represents paradoxical glory and greatness in Philippians 2:1–11; Mark 10:41–45; Luke 22:24–27; and 1 Peter 2:18–25. For most people in the Roman Empire, elite masculinity was an unachievable ideal that oppressed and dominated those who could not (by reason of biological sex, legal status, age, or wealth) attain it. The un-masculinity of enslavement offers the opportunity for relationships beyond the competition for status and authority. It challenges those who sought to use the patterns and practices of normative masculinity to their own advantage to empty themselves of dominating authority, and it offers those who were denied social honor the chance to attain honor through the (imposed) practices of their daily lives. The intersections of masculinity and enslavement in the first-century contexts of the New Testament illuminate the paradoxical power of the metaphor of slavery.

1

1 Peter 2:18–25

Slavery and the Roman Empire

As free people, do not use your freedom to cover up evil—rather, as enslaved people owned by God, honor everyone, love the family of believers, fear God, honor the emperor.

—1 Peter 2:16–17

Another Spartan woman was sold as a slave. When the auctioneer asked what she knew, she said, "To be free." When the buyer commanded her to do something inappropriate for a free woman, she said, "You will regret begrudging yourself of this property," and she killed herself.

—Plutarch, *Mor.* 242d

First Peter is addressed to Christian communities across Asia Minor: Pontus, Galatia, Cappadocia, Asia, and Bithynia (1:1). Several of these regions featured in the imperial slave trade. Enslaved people in the Roman Empire were sometimes credited with Phrygian or Cappadocian ethnic heritage.[1] Major slave markets in Ephesus, Thyatira, Sardis, and other cities moved

1. E.g., *Life of Aesop* 1, 24; Persius, *Sat.* 6.75–78; Martial 10.76; Juvenal, *Sat.* 11.147–48.

enslaved peoples from the provinces into the rest of the empire.[2] An audience situated in these regions, described in 1 Peter 2:16 as both "free" and "enslaved people owned by God," could conceivably have witnessed lines of chained or roped people along roads leading to markets; the practices of slave traders (using cosmetics, force-feeding, delaying puberty, castration, and other methods to increase the sale price of their human merchandise); the markets themselves, with their displays of enslaved bodies and auctioneers' shouts; and the wealth of slave traders.[3]

Slavery was integral to daily life across the Roman Empire. Households and businesses relied on slave labor. Enslaved people and freed slaves ran the imperial administration. The people who composed, read and heard, interpreted, and preserved 1 Peter knew enslaved people, owned enslaved people, and were enslaved people. They would have understood the significance of enslavement for an individual. Enslaved people lacked human dignity and fundamental rights over their own persons. As property (κτῆμα in Plutarch's story of the Spartan woman), they were subject to their enslavers' authority, traditions, and desires. Enslaved people were human. Like the Spartan woman, they could and did resist the domination of enslavement. But their humanity always existed in tension with their identification as slaves—as tools for their enslavers to use and abuse.

The conjunction of freedom and enslavement in 1 Peter 2:16 seems contradictory in the context of Rome's slave society, but the conceptual association was not unknown. In Stoic philosophy, for instance, enslavement and freedom were defined as internal states, so someone who was enslaved to a human owner could be "free" by the exercise of reason and self-control. Likewise, a freeborn person could be enslaved by wealth, physical desires, or social demands (e.g., Seneca, *Ep*. 47.15–17, 65.20–22). But this particular definition was limited in scope. For Plutarch's enslaved Spartan to be free, she had to die (*Mor*. 242d). The embodied experience of enslavement, the focus of 1 Peter 2:18–21, makes the conjunction of "slave" and "free" in verse 16 an inherent contradiction.

In this respect, the identification of God as κύριος in 1 Peter 2:13 is multivalent. The term is part of the common translation of יהוה אלהים as κύριος ὁ θεός in the LXX. Importantly for 1 Peter, God, rather than the emperor, is "lord." Audiences encountering 1 Peter in the first century also knew κύριος

2. The slave trade in Asia Minor is commemorated in *IEph* 646 and 3025; *SEG* 36.587; *TAM* 5.2.932; etc. See further Bosworth 2002, 351–54; Koester 2008, 770–77; Scheidel 2011, 300–303; Nasrallah 2019, 48–54.

3. These practices are mentioned in Seneca, *Ep*. 80.9; Quintilian, *Inst*. 2.15.25; Pliny, *Nat*. 21.170, 24.35–36, 32.135; Martial 6.66, 9.5; Juvenal, *Sat*. 6.7373a–b.

as a term for enslavers in relation to the enslaved people they owned.[4] The vocabulary of 1 Peter distinguishes enslavement to God (δοῦλος and κύριος) from enslavement to human enslavers (οἰκέτης and δεσπότης).[5] Nonetheless, enslavement to God exhibits the common characteristics of Roman slavery: submission to authority (v. 13); attitudes and actions focused on the needs of others rather than self (v. 17); fear (vv. 17 and 18); and the obedience, violence, and injustice of household slavery (vv. 18–21).[6] As an example for enslaved people to follow, the identification of Jesus with Isaiah's suffering servant in 1 Peter 2:21–25 further defines slavery around abuse, bodily bruises, and crucifixion (i.e., the death of slaves). Enslavement to God carries the weight of the embodied experience of enslavement in the Roman Empire.

This chapter and the next explore 1 Peter 2:18–25 as a center for a survey of key elements in the rhetoric and embodiment of slavery in the Roman Empire. Establishing what enslavement meant, how enslavement functioned from the perspective of enslavers and the experiences of those they enslaved, and how these experiences intersected with the imagination of masculinity offers important context for understanding the use of enslavement to describe Jesus, the twelve disciples, and Jesus's followers throughout the New Testament. The context of enslavement in the first century is an essential element in developing a doulological interpretation of 1 Peter.

Considering Slavery in 1 Peter

In 1 Peter 2:18–25, enslaved followers of Jesus (οἰκέτης) are instructed to submit to their enslavers (their "masters," δεσπότης) in all fear, whether the enslavers are "good and reasonable" (ἀγαθός, ἐπιεικής) or "perverse" (σκολιός).[7] The state of enslavement is accompanied by unjust suffering (λύπαι πάσχων ἀδίκως). Enslaved people are told to follow the example set by Jesus, who also suffered despite his innocence. Jesus's body is depicted as an enslaved body marked by the scars or welts (μώλωψ) left by beatings. The imagery of 1 Peter 2:18–25 clearly acknowledges and arguably, given the

4. On the overlap of "lord" and "enslaver" in κύριος, see Roller 2001, 255–57; Powery 2022, 80–81; Alimi 2024, 3; Bonar and Cobb 2025, 23.

5. See further S. Smith 2016, 68–69, 74.

6. Contrast 1 Peter's vocabulary with Philo, *Sobr.* 55, where God is κύριος to the external senses but savior and benefactor (σωτήρ, εὐεργέτης) to the wise mind: "Wisdom is a friend to God, rather than slave (δοῦλος)."

7. Some interpreters read οἰκέτης in 1 Pet. 2:18–25 as a metaphor for Christian commitment (e.g., Jodoin 2009, 520–21; cf. J. Green 2007, 77–78). I assume the text refers to enslaved people, most likely in urban household settings (though οἰκέτης can also refer to people enslaved in other circumstances); see also Achtemeier 1996, 194.

vocabulary of injustice, condemns the violent oppression of enslavement in the first century.[8]

The authorial community and historical context of 1 Peter are debated.[9] With respect to the issue of slavery, detailing the precise context is somewhat less significant. The definitions, ideologies, and experiences of enslavement were broadly similar from ancient Greece to imperial Rome.[10] The association of 1 Peter with Asia Minor in the latter half of the first century offers a sufficient context for understanding its representation of enslavement. In this general background, hierarchies of authority ruled households, local society, Roman provinces, and the imperial administration.[11] An individual's relative status, power, and privilege determined their daily life, from education and occupation to familial and communal relationships to the quality of their food and clothing. The hierarchies of society are central to two intersecting themes in 1 Peter: the social dislocation of Jesus's followers and the suffering they endure.

Within the letter, the audience is depicted as former gentiles. As such, they used to live according to standard Greco-Roman cultural norms, including by worshiping other gods (see 2:9–10; 4:3–4).[12] Becoming God's people disrupted their former identity, making them outsiders in their own communities (expressed with the language of παρεπίδημος, παροικία, and πάροικος in 1:1, 17; 2:11).[13] In 1 Peter, their change in lifestyle is "good." Ἀγαθός and ἀγαθοποιέω express obedience to God, defined as avoiding evil, working toward peace,

8. Due to these factors, S. Smith 2016, 165, argues that 1 Peter is "the writing of the slave," meaning the authorial community consisted of "the underclass, not the overlord." Even more provocatively, Steetskamp 2020, 67, 107, 274, suggests that an educated enslaved person, probably a Jewish follower of Jesus captured during the First Revolt, composed the letter. Whether or not this particular proposal is accepted, Steetskamp and Smith's attention to the ways the letter might reflect the perspective of enslaved people is instructive.

9. One option accepts the letter's attribution to the apostle Peter, placing it in the mid 60s (so J. Green 2007, 10; Jobes 2022, 14–19; Reese 2022, 19). Other scholars identify the letter as pseudepigraphal, and date it to no earlier than the late first century (so Achtemeier 1996, 39–43, 49–50; Feldmeier 2008, 32–40; T. Williams and Horrell 2023a, 115, 162; see also Vouga 2013, 205–6).

10. See Hunt 2018, 2–3; Owens 2025, 149.

11. Cf. Briggs 2003, 176–77; Hellerman 2005, 6–7; Joshel 2010, 32–46; Bird 2011, 82–83; J. Williams 2024, 35, 64–65; Shaner 2025, 168, 170.

12. See J. Green 2007, 5; Vahrenhorst 2013, 74–75; T. Williams and Horrell 2023a, 209–15 (suggesting a mixed gentile and Jewish community). Jobes 2022, 23–24, however, argues for a Jewish audience.

13. The descriptors may reflect the legal and social status of the audience as foreign residents of Asia Minor (so, e.g., Jobes 2022, 24–26), but given the use of the terms to express Israel's identity in the Bible, they are more likely theological descriptors of the audience's changed identity through becoming followers of Jesus (see Horrell 2007, 126–28; S. Smith 2016, 20–22; T. Williams and Horrell 2023a, 273). Even if the descriptors are more theological than sociopolitical,

and enacting justice (or righteousness, δίκαιος) in 3:10–12.[14] But while doing good is God's will (2:15) and brings divine blessing (3:14), it also results in suffering: Jesus's followers are reviled and maligned by their former associates (2:11–12; 3:16–17).[15] Enslaved people and wives personify this tenuous position (2:18–3:7). For a Greco-Roman man, slaves and wives alike were outsiders in his household in the sense that they were not born into the enslaver's or husband's (legitimate) family.[16] In 1 Peter, slaves and wives face the threat of violence. They have something to fear (compare 2:18 with 3:2, 6).

The use of enslaved people and wives to represent the association of "doing good" with suffering suggests the particular problem in view is the destabilization of household and community hierarchies.[17] A variety of sources across antiquity name social destabilization as a concern for gentiles who adopt a Jewish or Christian identity.[18] Not participating in the imperial cult or household worship, leaving the household to gather with other followers of Jesus, and adopting non-normative values and behaviors could be seen as challenges to the authority of a husband or enslaver. To some extent, the good actions specified in 1 Peter counteract potential critiques by encouraging the audience to accept the structures of political authority (2:13–17). In recognition of the vulnerability of enslaved people and wives, they are encouraged to submit (ὑποτάσσω) to their enslavers and husbands—that is, they should, apparently, adhere to the social structures, values, and expectations of the men who exercised legal and social power.[19]

The submission of enslaved people and wives, however, remains superficial in 1 Peter. The comparison of wives with Sarah—who is sex trafficked

---

the overlap of religious and ethnic identity in antiquity gives the terms significance on multiple levels (see also Bird 2011, 61–66).

14. Reese 2022, 134–36.

15. See further Krull 1998, 484–85; Horrell 2007, 139–40; Joseph 2012, 28; Vahrenhorst 2013, 61–73.

16. See Parker 1998, 154–55; Labovitz 2010, 93–96; Golden 2011, 136.

17. Bauman-Martin 2004a, 66–67; Feldmeier 2008, 153–54. See more broadly T. Williams and Horrell 2023a, 241–49.

18. E.g., Tacitus, *Hist.* 5.4–5; Pliny, *Ep.* 10.96; Acts of Paul and Thecla; Tertullian, *Ux.* 2.4–8; Cassius Dio 67.14.2; Achtemeier 1996, 24–36; Feldmeier 2008, 2–10; El Mansy 2013, 157–67; Reeder 2015a, 521–22.

19. See Aageson 2004, 42–45; Moxnes 2014, 133; S. Smith 2016, 70–71; Reese 2022, 139. I use the terminology of "encourage" to recognize the syntactic questions around the use of the participles ὑποτασσόμενοι and ὑποτασσόμεναι in 1 Pet. 2:18 and 3:1. The participles have long been interpreted as imperatives (so most English translations; see T. Williams 2011, 64–77). The use of participles instead of the imperative form of the verbs may instead connect to preceding instructions ("submission" is the manner in which enslaved people and wives carry out the general expectation of submission to all creatures in 2:13, or of honor, love, and fear in v. 17; see Achtemeier 1996, 194).

by her husband into two royal harems (Gen. 12:10–20; 20:1–18)—illustrates the threat of bodily harm for wives who worship a different god than their husbands do (1 Pet. 3:1, 6).[20] Similarly, enslaved people will experience violence as they do good (ἀγαθοποιέω), regardless of their submission (2:19–20). The consistent association of good actions with suffering throughout the letter suggests the expected goodness does not match the standards of Greco-Roman society.[21] Even as enslaved people and wives accept their subordinate positions, they also upset household authority structures by worshiping God, not the household's gods, and by living according to the values of the followers of Jesus, not their household's traditions.[22]

The exhortation to submission and fear in 1 Peter 2:18–25 is horrifying. Contemporary interpreters have variously described this text as "dangerous for human well-being"; exploitative, objectifying, and abusive; "more troubling and more poignant" than similar instructions in other New Testament letters; and, simply, "disturbing."[23] Enslaved people are given no option other than obeying their enslavers, including enslavers who are perverse (v. 18). Even if they submit, even if their enslavers are good and reasonable, their lived experience is of injustice, and their obedience and their suffering as enslaved people are irrevocably tied to their identity as followers of Jesus. It is not difficult to find this text used in ways that further oppression. William C. Brownlow, a supporter of slavery in the United States, cited 1 Peter 2:18–19 (among other New Testament texts) as proof that "Christian masters" are required to care for and discipline their slaves like children, "and in the case of disobedience to *whip well*." According to Brownlow, even the "most abject condition of slavery" and "the absolute control of a slave" (by the enslaver) are biblically ordained.[24]

20. Cf. Cato, *Agr.* 143; Cicero, *Leg.* 2.19, *Off.* 1.55; Dionysius of Halicarnassus, *Ant. rom.* 2.25; Valerius Maximus 1.3.1; Livy 25.1.6–8, 39.18.3–6; Tacitus, *Ann.* 13.32; Plutarch, *Conj. praec.* 19; Reeder 2015a, 525–26.

21. So, e.g., the emperor is honored as a human authority, not worshiped (see Horrell 2007, 133–35; du Toit 2021, 414–24; both Horrell and du Toit are critiquing the proposal of Christian participation in the imperial cult made by Carter 2004, 17–18, 25–27). See also J. Green 2007, 1–4, 71–72; El Mansy 2013, 167–73; Reese 2022, 139, 142–43; T. Williams and Horrell 2023a, 277.

22. See esp. Achtemeier 1996, 195 (associating "fear" with obedience to God rather than enslavers); Bauman-Martin 2004a, 71–72 (arguing that "submission" in 1 Pet. 2:18–3:6 means accepting the punitive consequences of disobedience); Horrell 2007, 133–34; du Toit 2021, 425–26; Reese 2022, 152–53; T. Williams and Horrell 2023a, 249–51.

23. So (in order) Aageson 2004, 34; Bird 2011, 89–91; Glancy 2006, 148 (also noting the text's recognition of the injustice of enslavement); Jung 2022, 57.

24. Brownlow 1857, 17–18 (emphasis original). See also Edward Scott, speech given at the Roger Williams Freewill Baptist Church, Providence, RI, 1857 (full text in C. Ripley 1991, 366–68); S. Smith 2016, 163–64.

Brownlow's interpretation offers a reminder, if one is needed, that the representation of slavery in 1 Peter 2:18–25 is neither restorative nor life-giving. Readers today, especially readers in societies that (claim to) value freedom, equity, and justice, will want and expect more from the text. The use of a text like 1 Peter 2:18–20 by people in positions of power to reinforce systems of injustice also fails to recognize the importance of the marginalized, oppressed audience for interpretation.[25] The audience constructed in the letter are outsiders in their communities, just as enslaved people and wives were identified as outsiders in their households (perhaps explaining why they model Christian identity in 1 Peter).[26] Acceptance of social positions and submission to people who held higher social positions in the household and the broader community marked life in the Roman Empire. While enslaved people are given no option other than submission in 1 Peter, they also had very few legal or social options other than submission.[27] How might the descriptions and instructions concerning enslavement in 1 Peter sound in the context of a marginalized, oppressed community?

The injustices apparent in 1 Peter 2:18–25 sit at the intersection of enslavers' perspectives on slavery and the potential perspectives and probable experiences of enslaved people. The survey of slavery in the Roman Empire in this chapter addresses how enslavers defined, constructed, and managed the system of slavery to their advantage. I also seek to understand how enslaved people in the first century could have managed, used, and resisted enslavement for their own survival and even advantage.[28] I have no desire to hide the evil of slavery, the problematic nature of 1 Peter 2:18–25, or the oppressive ways the text has been used to uphold unjust systems. I do, however, want to explore options for a justice-oriented interpretation. The recognition of enslavers' perspectives and the experiences of the enslaved in a doulological interpretation opens possibilities in this respect. At the end of the chapter, I will return to the discussion of ethical interpretation to question the potential meanings of 1 Peter in the context of Roman slavery.

Defining "Slavery" in Rome

The references to freedom (ἐλεύθερος, ἐλευθερία) and enslavement (δοῦλος) in 1 Peter 2:16 and the address to people enslaved in households (οἰκέτης) in

25. Cf. H. Thurman 1996, 1–2; S. Smith 2016, 165; Whipple 2021, 15, 21; Callahan 2022, 40; Powery 2022, 73–74; Reese 2022, 153–54.

26. On 1 Pet. 2:18–3:7 as a central focus for the letter, see Bauman-Martin 2004b, 267–68; Steetskamp 2020, 29; Gäckle 2021, 274–75.

27. Cf. Steetskamp 2020, 44; Reese 2022, 152.

28. On the range of ways enslaved people might accept, benefit from, and resist enslavement, see W. Johnson 2003, 115–19; V. Brown 2009, 1245–46; Moss 2024, 5–6.

2:18–21 suggest these concepts are recognizable and culturally relevant for the authorial community and audience. At least some (and likely all) of the people who composed, read, and preserved 1 Peter had experiential knowledge of enslavement. The demands of obedience and the expectation of violence emphasize these aspects of the embodied experience of enslavement. First Peter 2:16 and 18–21 reflect shared understandings of the system of slavery across the Roman Empire.

The Roman Empire was a slave society.[29] This assessment draws on several intersecting concerns. First, the number and geographic spread of references to extensive slaveholding in urban households and agricultural estates is significant. Seneca claimed an attempt to differentiate enslaved people from free people by their clothing was abandoned because the enslaved people would realize they vastly outnumbered their enslavers (*Clem.* 1.24.1), a fear also expressed in Tacitus, *Ann.* 4.27.[30] Pliny referred to "legions" and "mobs" of enslaved people in urban households so that one slave was required to keep track of all the others (*Nat.* 33.26).[31] Precise numbers are impossible to determine, but researchers estimate at least 10 to 25 percent of the imperial population was enslaved. This number would be higher in major cities like Rome, Corinth, or Ephesus; the agricultural areas of Italy; and regions with a significant population of wealthy residents.[32]

"Numbers and nations of slaves" figure alongside vast villas, gold and silver, and fine art as evidence of excessive wealth in Tacitus, *Ann.* 3.53.[33] A second justification for naming the Roman Empire as a slave society is the foundational importance of slavery to the economy. Enslaved people are one of the trade goods listed in Revelation 18:11–13. The imperial government made money from the sale of wartime captives and taxes on slave markets.[34] Enslaved people like Titus Flavius Januarius, who worked in an imperial tax office, and Hierocles, a superintendent of public works in Rome, built and

29. So Bradley 1994, 12–16; 2011b, 244; C. Martin 2005, 227; Morley 2011, 285; Scheidel 2012, 89–90. Note, however, that Hunt 2018, 14, argues Rome's slave society was limited to Italy and that the provinces were not slave societies (based on the smaller percentages of the population who were enslaved, with consequently less reliance on slave labor for wealth or productivity).

30. Wealthy elites wore longer, more flowing garments made of finer fabrics than non-elite free and enslaved populations. Enslaved people and non-enslaved poor people wore shorter garments, often belted in at the waist, which facilitated labor (cf. Philo, *Contempl.* 51, 72; Suetonius, *Cal.* 26.2; Joshel 2010, 132–33; Olson 2014, 192–93; Cobb 2019, 95–97).

31. See also *ILS* 1514; Seneca, *Tranq.* 8.8; Pliny, *Nat.* 33.135; Apuleius, *Apol.* 93.4.

32. The demography of enslavement in the Roman Empire is addressed in Scheidel 1997, 158, and 2012, 90–92; Bradley 2011b, 251; Morley 2011, 267–68.

33. See also Pliny, *Nat.* 33.135–36; Martial 3.62.

34. W. Harris 1980, 117–18, 121–32; 1999, 74–75; Bradley 2004, 298–307; Scheidel 2012, 96–100; Roth 2025, 95, 98.

maintained the physical and administrative infrastructure of the empire (*ILS* 1552 and 1604).[35] In Italy, enslaved people farmed agricultural estates under the supervision of enslaved managers.[36] The production of household goods and the needs of daily life—from cooking and cleaning to childcare, managing household business interests, and embodying household status—depended on the labor of enslaved people.[37]

According to the freed person Publilius Syrus, for anyone raised to be an enslaver (*dominare*), to become a slave (*servire*) would be a horror (*Sent.* 250). Death was preferable to the shame of enslavement (489).[38] A third significant factor in the identification of Rome as a slave society is the racialized construction of enslaved people as less than human and as inferior in natural ability and virtue, and the consequent definition of enslavement as a state of disempowerment and humiliation.[39] This rhetoric was integral to social status, honor, and identity across the empire.[40] Elite freeborn men denied enslaved people the qualities of reason, self-control, and courage they claimed for themselves (see Seneca, *Tranq.* 8.7–9; and chap. 2, below). They compared enslaved people with, and treated them as, livestock—as living creatures who could not reason and so (at least by the enslavers' reckoning) needed freeborn people with the capability of reason to instruct, discipline, and control them.[41]

The racialization of slavery existed in tension with the responsibility enslavers gave to enslaved people to manage businesses and property, educate children, or run the imperial administration. The construction of enslaved people as lacking virtue and excelling in vice expresses elite concern to maintain social and political privilege at the expense of the enslaved people who made their privilege possible. Freeborn elite definitions of enslavement as disempowerment and humiliation offered a tool to maintain boundaries between the statuses of freedom and enslavement. Whether enslaved people accepted the fundamental humiliation of enslavement is largely unknowable,

35. See also Frontinus, *Aqueducts* 2.96; Josephus, *J.W.* 3.540 (noting that captive slaves from Galilee were sent to dig Nero's canal in the isthmus of Corinth); Morley 2011, 281–83; Hunt 2018, 12–13.

36. E.g., Varro, *Rust.* 1.17.4–7, 2.10.1; Columella, *Rust.* 1.8.1–2, 9.1.4; Pliny, *Nat.* 18.21; Florus, *Epit.* 2.7.19. See further Hunt 2018, 10–12.

37. Funerary memorials identify enslaved people as midwives, tailors, hairdressers, pedagogues, bakers, weavers, and more (e.g., *CIL* 6.6331, 6346, 8947, 9037, 9732). See Bodel 2011, esp. 312–18, 331–33; Edmondson 2011, 354–56.

38. So also Seneca, *Ep.* 77.14–15, 18; Josephus, *J.W.* 7.380–86.

39. On racialization, see the introduction, above; J. Williams 2024, 24–28; and 2025, 101.

40. Finley 1998, 164; Joshel and Murnaghan 1998, 2–3; Saller 1998, 90–91; Roller 2001, 223, 227; Owens 2025, 148–49. See also Vlassopoulos 2011, 117–20, on slavery as domination in classical Greece.

41. See, e.g., Seneca, *Ira* 3.34.1; Bryson 57; Artemidorus, *Onir.* 1.37, 4.56; and chap. 2, below.

though funerary inscriptions for enslaved and formerly enslaved people indicate enslaved people claimed social honor and moral virtue for themselves. For instance, an enslaved woman named Alimma was praised by her father, also enslaved in the same household, for her discipline and pious dutifulness (*CIL* 10.26).[42] The inscription uses standard language, but the emphasis on Alimma's honorable life disrupts the rhetorical association of slavery with the dishonorable absence of virtue. On the other hand, it is also easy to imagine that the widespread, consistent denigration of enslavement in rhetoric, philosophy, literature, and art affected the self-understanding and self-worth of enslaved individuals.

Enslavers associated enslaved people and "slavishness" with laziness, gluttony, cowardice, theft, deceit, overindulgence in emotion, and more.[43] While Alimma's memorial counters such assessments with its claim of virtue, a second, more subversive, avenue for resistance would be overtly enacting such vices by resting rather than working; consuming more food than the enslaver provided; completing tasks slowly or imperfectly; or choosing to deceive the enslaver. Plutarch described enslaved people as vile rascals who stole their enslavers' food (*Quaest. conv.* 678e–f; [*Lib. ed.*] 7–8), and Columella warned that people enslaved on agricultural estates might steal the harvest for their own use (*Rust.* 1.7.6–7). Horace represented an enslaved boy hiding under a staircase to escape the enslaver's attention (*Ep.* 2.2.14–15).[44] These complaints could be rewritten from the perspective of the enslaved people as means to survive malnourishment, exhausting work, and violent treatment.

Enslavers' complaints concerning enslaved people's behaviors or actions are stereotypical, masking the relationship of the complaints to the actual behavior of enslaved people along with the motivations of enslaved people for their (putative) behavior. Publilius Syrus commented that an enslaved person who did not desire to work was miserable and remained a "slave" anyway (*Sent.* 616). The despair evident in Publilius Syrus's statement suggests, for this former slave, the ultimate futility of resistance; continuous resistance is exhausting. It could also be the case that the enslaved person might find

42. Cf. also *CIL* 3.1854, and 6.5876, 6357, 9727. On the presentation of formerly enslaved people's virtue in funerary inscriptions, see further Borg 2012, 27–29; Ramsby 2012, 69–78; MacLean 2018, 35–43; Bell, Borbonus, and MacLean 2024, 3–11; Owens 2024, 218–38; Padilla Peralta 2024, 256–65.

43. Xenophon, *Oec.* 1.22; *Mem.* 2.1.15–16; Polybius 38.15.10; *IG* 12.7; Horace, *Ep.* 2.2; Pliny, *Nat.* 34.79; Plutarch, *Alex.* 52.3; *Cic.* 47.3; Appian, *Bell. civ.* 2.11.74. See further Finley 1998, 179; Bradley 2011a, 362–64, 373–75; Joshel and Petersen 2014, 7–8, and passim.

44. Greediness and food theft also feature in Horace, *Sat.* 1.3.80–83; Seneca, *Tranq.* 8.8; Pliny, *Nat.* 33.26–27; *Life of Aesop* 2–3. Truancy is noted in Juvenal, *Sat.* 8.172–82.

comfort and strength in resistance.[45] Phaedrus, for instance, identified fables as a means of resistance for enslaved people (*Fables* 3.prol.33–37). The enactment of behaviors that enslavers found undesirable resists slavery by disadvantaging the enslavers. These means of resistance to the psychological pressure of enslavement denied enslavers' claims over their persons.

From the perspective of elite enslavers, the association of enslavement with submission and obedience to household authority structures in 1 Peter 2:18–20 reflects their own constructions of enslaved people as incapable of self-control or reason. They need external authorities to control, direct, and discipline them. But while submission and obedience may echo enslavers' definitions of slavery, there is no justification for the domination of slavery in 1 Peter. In tension with enslavers' constructions of enslaved identity, the instructions are addressed directly to enslaved people, acknowledging them as individuals capable of independent action. Moreover, the description of some enslavers as perverse or unethical (σκολιός) and their association with unjust violence challenges enslavers' claims to moral superiority.[46] As "slaves of God" who are also free, moreover, the enslaved people in 1 Peter 2:18–20 are given the (Christian) task of ἀγαθοποιέω, demanding obedience to God above their enslavers. The representation of enslavers' perspectives in this text accompanies or perhaps masks its subversive construction of enslaved people as agents of God.[47]

Categorizing Enslavement

The Roman Empire primarily practiced chattel slavery in the first century. People entered the system of slavery by several means: birth to an enslaved mother;[48] capture in war;[49] the practice of infant exposure;[50] or (debatably)

45. See J. Mason 2003, 9; V. Brown 2009, 1232–33.

46. See Steetskamp 2020, 61, on the use of σκολιός to describe enslaved people (citing Theognis of Megara).

47. Reese 2022, 152–54. See also S. Smith 2016, 72–73; Steetskamp 2020, 65–66.

48. By Roman law, a child born to an enslaved woman was enslaved (*Dig.* 1.5.5). The father's status was inconsequential, and in fact many enslaved women were made pregnant by free men. See esp. Scheidel 1997, 167 (and passim), on birth as a major source of enslaved peoples in the Roman Empire (though Ramin and Veyne 1981, 481–82, suggest regional variance).

49. The enslavement of war captives was so common that slave traders traveled with the military. These populations included women and children (a practice that contributed to pathetic representations of defeat). See Cicero, *Att.* 89.7; Varro, *Rust.* 2.10.4; Livy 38.29.11; Josephus, *J.W.* 3.539–40, 6.384; Appian, *Hist. rom.* 3.6.1; Cassius Dio 54.31; and esp. Bradley 2004, 298–309.

50. Infant exposure occurred across the empire as impoverished families made difficult decisions to prioritize the survival of existing members of a household. As various Roman laws (and early Christian concerns over the practice) indicate, some of these infants were taken in

by selling one's self or children due to extreme poverty or for the purpose of professional training.[51] Enslaved people also came into the empire through trade with surrounding peoples.[52] Shops in Rome, regular markets in major cities, and seasonal fairs in rural areas offered human lives to purchasers. Enslaved people were displayed with placards describing their ethnic origins, professional qualifications, personality traits, and health; potential purchasers subjected their bodies to close examination (to the extent of stripping the person).[53]

In a satire addressing the disadvantages of adultery with the (free) wives of other men, Horace proclaimed his own preference for "easy" (*facilis*) sex with an enslaved woman or boy (*Sat.* 1.2.116–18). When he grabbed an enslaved woman to satisfy his sexual desire, he said, "I call her whatever name I want" (1.2.125–26). Horace's objectification of enslaved bodies has parallels in the records of the slave trade in the Middle Passage. Tracing glimpses of the archetypal enslaved woman through these records, Saidiya Hartman comments, "No one remembered her name or recorded the things she said, or observed that she refused to say anything at all."[54] Horace's proclamation, in other words, expresses the way enslavers deny slaves their individual personhood. Enslavement separated enslaved people from family connections, ethnic traditions, language, and even their own names, replacing their natal identity with "slavish" identity, values, and occupations.[55]

The processes of natal alienation and racialization as slaves would be experienced differently depending on how someone entered slavery.[56] A free

---

by wealthier households or slave traders to raise as slaves: Pliny, *Ep.* 10.66; *Dig.* 40.12.12.1; Tertullian, *Nat.* 1.16; Ramin and Veyne 1981, 475–76; W. Harris 1999, 74.

51. Roman perspectives on the humiliation of enslavement correspond with a general lack of discussions of the possibility of selling one's self or one's children; passing references are found in Diodorus Siculus 26.20; Tacitus, *Germ.* 24 (expressing surprise at German tribal customs); Dio Chrysostom 15.23; *Dig.* 1.5.5.1; and see further Ramin and Veyne 1981, 484–89; W. Harris 1999, 73; and (expressing caution at the historicity or commonality of the practice), Combes 1998, 27; Scheidel 2011, 300; Glancy 2006, 81–85. Self-sale for professional or social advance through work—as, e.g., a business manager for an enslaver—was uncommon, given the consequent loss of freedom, legal rights, and freeborn status (e.g., Seneca, *Ep.* 47.17; *Dig.* 28.3.6.5; P.Oxy. 46.3312; Ramin and Veyne 1981, 488, 493–96).

52. Diodorus Siculus 5.26.3; Strabo 5.1.8, 11.2.3, 14.5.2; Pliny, *Nat.* 6.172, 35.199; W. Harris 1999, 74–75; Koester 2008, 777–84.

53. See Cicero, *Planc.* 62; Horace, *Ep.* 2.2; Petronius, *Sat.* 29; Seneca, *Const.* 13.4; *Ep.* 80.9; Suetonius, *Aug.* 69; P.Oxy. 95; Aulus Gellius 4.2.1; Pausanias 10.32.15; Finley 1968, 172–73; Bosworth 2002, 351–56; Koester 2008, 770–71.

54. Hartman 2008, 1–2.

55. Finley 1968, 166; Patterson 1982, 5–6; Saller 1998, 86; Kamen 2012, 174–75; Chaniotis 2023, 190; Moss 2024, 23–24; Hartman 2007, 5, 85, 103.

56. See the discussion of racialization in the introduction. See also Moss 2024, 23–25; Padilla Peralta 2024, 248–49; J. Williams 2025, 101.

adult taken captive in war, for instance, would enter slavery with a personal history of freedom, life experience of familial and ethnic traditions, and (consequently) a developed personal identity. An example of one such person, Claudia Aster, a captive from Jerusalem, was able to maintain the memory of her origins until her death (*CIL* 10.1971). Entering enslavement as an older child or adult would imaginably be accompanied by a greater sense of loss (not to mention the trauma of war).[57] A person born into enslavement, on the other hand, would have had no experience of any other kind of life. An enslaved child was shaped and trained into slavery from a very young age. While freeborn children experienced education and play, enslaved children were forced into unskilled labor, apprenticeships, and bodily abuse.[58]

An individual's experience of enslavement also varied depending on the type of enslavement. All enslaved people ranked at the bottom of Rome's social hierarchy of wealth, power, gender, and identity. Within this overall social hierarchy, enslavement had its own hierarchy. The most prestige was held by the imperial *familia*, the people enslaved by the emperor, especially the few who administered the business of the government (note that most imperial slaves worked at more basic occupations—as hairdressers, nurses, cooks, etc.).[59] Musicus Scurranus, for instance, was in charge of the imperial treasury in Lyon. As Emperor Tiberius's slave, he exercised significant power. His position allowed him opportunities for personal gain; when he died, he was commemorated by a large group of his own enslaved people, including a treasurer, someone in charge of his wardrobe, a cook, a doctor, and more (*ILS* 1514).[60] Musicus Scurranus was enslaved, with all the disempowerment and social humiliation the state of slavery entailed.[61] His story exemplifies how an enslaved person could nonetheless use the system of slavery to their own advantage.

At the opposite end of the hierarchy, people enslaved on agricultural estates in Italy endured significant hardship, neglect, and violence.[62] Notably, the combination of a lack of oversight, the presence of large numbers of captives of war, and the harsh conditions these people endured boiled over into

57. See Horace, *Carm.* 3.3.67–68; Philo, *Spec.* 4.17; Seneca, *Ira* 3.29.1–2; Juvenal, *Sat.* 11.151–55; Josephus, *J.W.* 7.380–86; Lucian, *Merc.* 23. Chaniotis 2023, 193, quotes a funerary stele for an enslaved man who, though far distant from his place of birth, still longed for his homeland, and also a graffito from Delos representing the enslaved person's homeland.

58. On the experiences of enslaved children, see Laes 2008, 235–73. Laes notes that legally and economically (based on sales documents), enslaved children were expected to work from age five, but younger children are attested as workers in some sources (see esp. pp. 235–36, 241).

59. Morley 2011, 281–83; MacLean 2018, 104–29.

60. See also *ILS* 1519, 1763.

61. See further Flexsenhar 2019, 13–14.

62. Varro, *Rust.* 1.17.4–7; Pliny, *Nat.* 18.21; Florus, *Epit.* 2.7.19.

major slave revolts.[63] Some enslaved people lived and worked in still worse circumstances. Descriptions of enslaved people in mills and mines include body-breaking labor, severe physical abuse, and the absence of basic necessities like food, cleanliness, and rest.[64]

In between these extremes are people enslaved in urban households in close proximity to their enslavers, like the enslaved people (οἰκέτης) addressed in 1 Peter 2:18.[65] Some of these people would have been born into the same household as their (eventual) enslavers. Some may even have been the children or half-siblings of their enslavers, though they were unlikely to be recognized as such.[66] Most enslaved people referenced in the New Testament are household slaves (e.g., Luke 7:1–10; John 4:51–53; Col. 3:22–4:1), though—as in Jesus's parables—they may have been enslaved in rural villages, working at a mix of household and agricultural tasks (Matt. 13:24–30; Luke 15:25–27; 17:7–10).

Narratives and funerary inscriptions suggest that enslaved children born in their enslavers' households sometimes had a more affectionate relationship with their enslavers (at least until they grew up). One four-year-old named Aucta was commemorated by her enslaver as the "sweetest home-born slave" (*CIL* 6.12800).[67] Enslaved people in urban households would be more likely to receive the kind of education or training that would be of benefit if they eventually gained their freedom; educated, trained enslaved men were more likely to gain freedom before they died.[68]

Enslavers claimed to value the people they enslaved in their households, especially those born in their households, for their (perceived) loyalty and affection, celebrated in stories of exemplary self-sacrifice and demonstrations of "love."[69] However, the focus of such stories remains on the enslaver. Pliny the Younger's narrative of his uncle's presence at the eruption of Vesuvius includes enslaved people in his party, but their only significance in the story is to support his uncle's failing body; their perspective on the eruption, their enforced presence with Pliny the Elder, and their fate go unrecorded (*Ep.* 6.16.19). Enslavers feared household slaves on account of their physical

63. E.g., Livy 32.26, 39.29; Florus, *Epit.* 2.7.19; Tacitus, *Ann.* 4.27. Another major revolt was due to gladiators (Plutarch, *Crass.* 8–11). See Bradley 2011b, 247.

64. Diodorus Siculus 5.38; Plautus, *Men.* 966–83; Apuleius, *Metam.* 9.12.

65. On people enslaved in households, see esp. Bodel 2011, 312–16; Edmondson 2011, 340–54.

66. Pliny the Elder's surprise at the resemblance of enslaved people to freeborn Romans suggests the possibility of unrecognized genetic relationships (*Nat.* 7.53–54).

67. Translation in Hemelrijk 2021, 74. See also *CIL* 6.36525; Martial 6.28–29.

68. See Petronius, *Sat.* 29; Plutarch, *Crass.* 2.6; Suetonius, *Gramm.* 13, 23, 27; P.Oxy. 724; and on the education of enslaved people in a household, Laes 2008, 254–55.

69. Xenophon, *Oec.* 7.35–37; Valerius Maximus 6.8; Plutarch, *Mulier. virt.* 3; *ILS* 1583, 7479, 8532; Bradley 2008, 341–43.

proximity and the intimacy of their work.[70] Fear is consistently classified as a "slavish" emotion in antiquity. The fear of enslavers exposes the fragility of Roman slavery.[71]

In the end, the different categories of enslavement are all enslavement.[72] Whether a person was enslaved in an agricultural estate, a family household, or the imperial government, they were still subject to the oppression, humiliation, and subjugation that accompanied the identity of "slave." The fundamental dehumanization of enslavement far outweighs any differences there may have been between one experience of enslavement and another. Moreover, the necessary recognition of the dehumanizing nature of enslavement undermines the claim that, for some, enslavement was beneficial.[73] As the sale of enslaved individuals in markets indicates, legal and philosophical definitions categorized enslaved people as human property (Aristotle, *Pol.* 6–7; Dio Chrysostom 15.23–25): "The three sons of Herodion acknowledge that they have divided among themselves . . . the four enslaved bodies [δουλικὰ σώματα] that belong to them by inheritance from their father" (P.Mich. 5.323).[74] Enslavers numbered and distributed the "bodies" they owned in their wills; sales contracts described the "bodies" sold; and censuses included counts of enslaved "bodies."[75] The reduction of an enslaved person to a body shifts the balance from human to property.

Further emphasizing the property aspect of slavery, enslavers identified their slaves as tools to use to accomplish their own purposes. This understanding is clear in the description of enslaved people as ὄργανα ἔμψυχα (living tools) in Plutarch (*Crass.* 2.6). The convention of (re)naming enslaved people for the common tasks they performed; the characteristics enslavers valued (e.g., Onesimus, meaning "Useful"); or, ironically, qualities far from the experiences of slavery (e.g., Felix, meaning "Lucky") also expresses this objectification.[76] It is apparent in recommendations for assigning work to

70. Seneca, *Clem.* 24.1; Tacitus, *Hist.* 14.42–45; Pliny, *Ep.* 3.14.5. See esp. Parker 1998, 155–57.

71. Cf. Horace, *Ep.* 1.16.63–72; Publilius Syrus 363; Epictetus, *Diatr.* 3.26.1; Diogenes Laertius 6.2.75.

72. Arzt-Grabner 2010, 117; Hunt 2018, 18; Flexsenhar 2019, 13; Coleman 2025, 30.

73. Publilius Syrus's life story offers insight. He was enslaved as a result of war and was able eventually to gain his freedom (apparently because of his intellectual abilities). Despite his relative privilege as an enslaved man, however, he repeatedly described enslavement as misery or wretchedness (*miser*) and shame (*ignominiosus*; *Sent.* 250, 489, 616; see also 413, 569).

74. Modified translation from "P.Mich.inv. 1264; Recto," Advanced Papyrological Information System (APIS UM), https://quod.lib.umich.edu/a/apis/x-1347.

75. P.Oxy. 3.494; *Life of Aesop* 16, 19, 24; *SGDI* 1722.1–4; Glancy 2006, 10–11.

76. See Saller 1998, 85; C. Martin 2005, 228; Robertson 2008, 90–93 (on classical Athens); Chaniotis 2023, 190.

particular slaves based on physical attributes or intelligence (Columella, *Rust.* 9.1.4; Horace, *Ep.* 1.16.71–72) and in the ways enslaved people were instructed and trained for particular work according to the enslavers' needs (e.g., Plutarch, *Cat. Maj.* 21.1; P.Oxy. 1647).

As property or tools, enslaved people functioned as extensions of their enslavers. They were their owners' hands, feet, mouths, and breasts, employed to carry messages, run businesses, and nurse their enslavers' infants.[77] The example of the man who bought enslaved people specifically to memorize epic literature on his behalf indicates that enslaved people could also be their enslavers' memories (Seneca, *Ep.* 27.5–7).[78] The imperial government, urban households, and agricultural estates could run on enslaved labor because enslaved people were their enslavers' body doubles (in Jennifer Glancy's apt phrasing).[79] Artemidorus's explanation of a slave in the dream of an enslaver makes precisely this point: The slave is the enslaver's surrogate body, so what happens to the slave in the dream will happen to the enslaver in waking life (*Onir.* 4.30).

The definition of enslaved people as "living tools" (in Plutarch's phrase) exposes the dehumanization of slavery. From the perspective of enslavers, slaves existed for the owners' benefit. According to Plutarch's biography of Marcus Cato, he purchased young, healthy slaves in order to get as much work from them as he could, training them as if they were animals (*Cat. Maj.* 21.1). When they grew too old to work, he sold them (4.4; see Cato, *Agr.* 2.7). Plutarch objected to this practice of treating enslaved people as livestock, though Plutarch's own analogy of caring for slaves as for horses and dogs also dehumanizes enslaved people (*Cat. Maj.* 5.1–2). Plutarch's narrative exposes the inherent tension between recognizing enslaved individuals as human beings (with human capabilities, self-understanding, and relationality) and at the same time treating them as fungible property.

Enslavers did not grant enslaved people the freedom of an independent legal or social existence.[80] Consequently, an enslaved person did not have the legal right to marry and form their own familial unit (more on this in the next section). They could not legally own private property or make a legally binding will to distribute any property after their death. These rights belonged to their

77. Cf. Bryson 61, describing enslaved people as enslavers' limbs; Martial 14.220, describing an enslaved cook as the enslaver's taste buds; and Pliny, *Nat.* 21.7, where enslaved people participate in athletic competitions in their enslavers' place.

78. Cf. Cicero, *Mur.* 77; Pliny, *Nat.* 29.19. This aspect of enslaved people's work is also evident in their participation in researching, writing, and producing literary works for the nominal authors (their enslavers); see Blake 2012, 193–98; Moss 2024, 78–79.

79. Glancy 2006, 15–17. See also Joshel 2010, 41; Blake 2012, 197; 2016, 89–90.

80. See also Alimi 2024, 35–36.

enslaver. An enslaver might allow enslaved people to enter into informal familial relationships or to control personal property. However, enslavers could manipulate sexual or familial relationships for economic benefit, separate families at any time, or take the property of the enslaved for their own use.[81] Even if an enslaver had a reputation for generosity, the enslaved person was still entirely dependent on the enslaver's choices and desires.

The embodiment of enslavement had serious consequences for enslaved people, as evident in Seneca's use of an enslaved man to illustrate his own advanced age. On a visit to one of his properties, Seneca saw signs of deterioration in buildings, trees, and an elderly enslaved man. He described this man as decrepit, headed for death, and so old that he was almost a child again (having lost his teeth). The enslaved man then identified himself as Seneca's once-beloved *delicium* who, as a child, received treats from him (*Ep.* 12.3). The story demonstrates the difference between the enslaved, whose bodies represent a lifetime of hardship, and the freeborn elite, who (even in their own old age) benefit from a life of luxury and the care provided by the labor of enslaved people. The story also illuminates the relationships between enslavers and the enslaved people they owned. The enslaved man (at least, according to Seneca) remembered childhood treats with fondness, but Seneca's lack of recognition and derogatory dismissal display no reciprocal affection.[82]

In Seneca's story, the elderly enslaved man's body made visible the consequences of the conditions of enslavement: endless labor, minimal medical care, and restricted diet, clothing, and sleep.[83] In another letter, Seneca addressed the casual punitive abuse directed against enslaved servers in a dining room, who were hit with rods and lashes for sins like whispering or sneezing (*Ep.* 47.3). People enslaved in households lived with the threat and experience of violence on a daily basis. According to Plutarch, newly purchased slaves would urgently ask other enslaved people if the enslaver was kind or brutal (*Cohib. ira* 462a).[84] In addition to physical abuse, enslaved people faced what

81. See Xenophon, *Oec.* 9.5; Varro, *Rust.* 1.17.5, 2.10.6; Pliny, *Ep.* 8.16.1–3; P.Oxy. 3.494; Gaius, *Inst.* 1.51–52, 2.91; Wessels 2010, 152–53; Edmondson 2011, 347–50; Gardner 2011, 424–25; de Wet 2018, 3.

82. Note also Seneca's complaint concerning an enslaved woman who had lost her sight, calling her a drag on the household (*Ep.* 50.2).

83. Cf. Cato, *Agr.* 2.1–4; Phaedrus, *Fables*, Perotti's Appendix 20; Bryson 68; Juvenal, *Sat.* 14.59, 126–27; Suetonius, *Claud.* 25.2; Pliny, *Ep.* 8.24.5; Garland 2010, 22. Moss 2024, 28–31, addresses the physical and psychological consequences of ongoing labor, vigilance, and bodily control.

84. Violence is a consistent corollary to enslavement. See, e.g., Bryson 64–65, 72; Seneca, *Ira* 3.32.1; Josephus, *Ant.* 6.41; Martial 3.94, 14.69; Suetonius, *Aug.* 67; Plutarch, *Cat. Maj.* 21.3; *Mor.* 1091e; Artemidorus, *Onir.* 1.70, 1.76, 2.25.

we would today classify as sexual abuse.[85] Finally, enslavers always had the ultimate option of selling or executing an enslaved person.[86]

In [*Lib. ed.*] 8f–9a, pseudo-Plutarch argued that freeborn children should not be beaten like enslaved people because the children would experience physical and psychological consequences from the pain and outrageous dishonor. Notably, in this text there is no consideration for what enslaved people might experience. But living with the constant expectation and experience of abuse surely had serious consequences for enslaved people's bodies, minds, and spirits (cf. Juvenal, *Sat.* 14.20–22). As Publilius Syrus said, it was better to be dead than enslaved (*Sent.* 489).

In his commentary on the Torah, Philo discouraged "those who are called masters" (οἱ λεγόμενοι δεσπόται) from abusing the enslaved people they owned to the point that their bodies and souls were broken. His plea for decency had an economic edge. By refraining from excessive abuse, the enslavers would benefit from the labor of the enslaved people for longer, and the enslaved people would be more cheerful in their work (*Spec.* 2.90–91).[87] Philo's comments reflect fundamental assumptions concerning slavery across the Roman Empire: Enslaved people exist for the benefit of their enslavers, and enslavers have complete rights over their bodies and souls. Even decency on the part of enslavers is for the benefit of the enslavers, not the enslaved.[88]

This system of disadvantage is on display in 1 Peter 2:18–19. If the enslaved people represented here had "good" (ἀγαθός, ἐπιεικής) enslavers, they might have the ability to form familial relationships or exercise property rights over personal possessions. But even "good" enslavers claimed ownership over slaves, body and soul. As the description of enslavers as perverse (σκολιός) and the association of enslavement with injustice (ἀδίκως) confirms, Roman slavery was oppressive. Enslaved people's lack of independent legal or social identity had serious, significant consequences for their daily lives, their physical and mental health, and their recognizability as persons deserving of basic respect.

85. Since enslaved people lacked the right of consent, the use of their bodies for sex was not counted as assault by Greco-Roman definitions. See, e.g., Xenophon, *Oec.* 10.12; Horace, *Sat.* 1.2.116–19; Seneca the Elder, *Controv.* 1.2.9–10; Martial 1.58; Artemidorus, *Onir.* 1.78; and chaps. 2 and 5, below.

86. E.g., Diodorus Siculus 15.7.1; Seneca, *Clem.* 1.18.2; Pliny, *Nat.* 9.77; Artemidorus, *Onir.* 1.50, 2.68.

87. Cf. Aristotle, [*Oec.*] 1.1334c; Xenophon, *Oec.* 7.35–37; Columella, *Rust.* 1.8.9. See also Pliny, *Ep.* 5.19.3–7, 8.1, on providing medical care for enslaved people so they can continue their work. Rhee 2022, 212–13, points to the evidence of hospitals for enslaved people in first-century Rome to preserve the health of the enslaved workforce.

88. Cf. Aristotle, [*Oec.*] 1.334c; Xenophon, *Oec.* 7.35–37; Columella, *Rust.* 1.8.9; Finley 1998, 142–43; Wessels 2010, 149–53, 158; Joshel 2011, 224–29; Blake 2012, 95–96.

The Relationships of Enslavement

The enslaved people pictured in 1 Peter 2:18–20 belong to the community of Jesus's followers. The enslaved people in the audience of 1 Peter were individuals with their own life experiences. Some of them may have been enslaved in the same households. It is likely that, as reflected in other New Testament epistles, some were enslaved to other followers of Jesus. The absence of any instructions to enslavers is occasionally taken as an indication that there were no enslavers in the community. But the descriptor ἀγαθός, applied to enslavers in verse 18, is otherwise associated with the followers of Jesus in the letter, and the (free and freed) wives and husbands in 3:1–7 would, in the first-century context, likely be enslavers.[89] Whatever their personal circumstances, these enslaved people were embedded in communities—communities with their enslavers, communities with other enslaved people, and communities beyond their households with other followers of Jesus.

The possibilities for relationships between enslavers and the enslaved people they owned excluded enslaved people on agricultural estates or in mines, who had little contact with enslavers. This would also be true of many people in vast urban households, where, Pliny said, enslavers would not necessarily know or recognize every person in the "legions of slaves." Pliny further separated enslaved people as a "mob of outsiders" (*turba externa*; *Nat.* 33.26), marking their disconnection from the (male) enslaver's family line. This boundary persisted even for the enslaved people who were genetically related to their enslavers as their (generally unrecognized) children or siblings. While power imbalances were a feature of personal relationships across Roman society, the particular power imbalances of slavery complicated relationships between enslaved people and their enslavers.

Nonetheless, some enslaved people had close, intimate relationships with their enslavers (including sexual relationships, to be addressed in chaps. 2 and 5). Enslaved people bathed, groomed, and dressed the bodies of their enslavers. They assisted enslavers with basic bodily needs (e.g., urination and vomiting). They cared for enslavers in sickness and old age.[90] Enslaved women nursed their enslavers' infants, and enslaved people participated in raising and educating their enslavers' children.[91] As is evident in the story of Seneca and the elderly slave discussed above, there are numerous accounts of

89. See further Krentz 1998, 283; Moxnes 2008, 180–81; 2014, 130; S. Smith 2016, 72; T. Williams and Horrell 2023a, 231–32.

90. Examples of body care are in Diodorus Siculus 13.19–20; Josephus, *Ant.* 13.314; Pliny, *Ep.* 3.16.8, 8.18.9; Epictetus, *Diatr.* 3.26.21–22; *CIL* 6.8958, 6.9732; and there are satirical representations of body care in Petronius, *Sat.* 27.5–6; Martial 3.82.15–17, 14.119.

91. E.g., *BGU* 4.1058; *CIL* 6.4352, 6331, 9758; Bakke 2005, 36–37.

enslavers treating (some) enslaved children as objects of affection. Funerary inscriptions represent these relationships as loving and enduring for both the enslaver and enslaved.[92]

Familial relationships between enslavers and enslaved people sometimes shaped the enslaved person's experience of slavery. Vitalis, whose enslaver was also acknowledged as his father, worked as a business manager for his enslaver.[93] Other familial relationships were established by manumission, patronage, and adoption, as in the case of Marcus Aurelius Zosimus, who identified his former enslaver as a second father to his own freeborn children.[94] Cicero's brother was very excited when Cicero manumitted Tiro, an enslaved man who had, as a result of close work with Cicero, become a friend (*Fam.* 44).[95]

How sincere were these relationships? The beloved freeborn children raised by beloved enslaved people were also their enslavers. So, regardless of any friendship with Tiro, Cicero and his family members continued to treat and address Tiro with the language, imagery, and assumptions of enslavement (e.g., *Fam.* 219.1, 351.1).[96] Cicero also warned that close relationships with enslaved nurses and pedagogues should not continue into an enslaver's adult life (*Amic.* 74; see also Martial 11.39). For their part, enslaved people might truly respect and care for their enslavers, but the imbalances in the power dynamics of their relationships (imbalances which, as evidenced by Tiro's story, persisted into "freedom") problematize expressions of affection. Notably, enslavers often expressed fear that enslaved people disdained or hated their enslavers.[97]

The enigmatic story of Acte indicates how enslaved people might deploy intimate access to their enslavers for their own advantage. According to a curse written by her former enslaver and husband, Acte ran off with another man, "stealing" two others enslaved in the household (possibly her own family members) and abandoning her enslaver/husband to a sad old age.[98] His curse threatens Acte with "permanent branding" (*stigmata aeterna*), strangling, and

92. Enslaved (or formerly enslaved) people honor the freeborn children they raised in *CIL* 6.25808, 6.18032. Enslavers honor their nurses and pedagogues in *CIL* 6.16450, 6.2210, 8.1506, 10.6432 (see also Pliny, *Ep.* 6.3). Cf. Bakke 2005, 41.

93. *CIL* 3.14206.21. On this inscription, see Bond 2022, 175–76, who notes that the inscription places responsibility for any financial shenanigans on Vitalis.

94. *CIL* 14.2290; cf. *AE* 1992.959.

95. Tiro was well educated and worked as Cicero's scribe; in the collections of Cicero's correspondence (probably compiled by Tiro), there are additional letters between Tiro and Cicero. See also Bell and Ramsby 2012, 7.

96. See Joshel 2010, 12; McCoskey 2024, 67–73.

97. See, e.g., Seneca, *Tranq.* 8.9; Pliny, *Nat.* 33.27; Tacitus, *Ann.* 14.43–44; Plutarch, *Cic.* 47.3.

98. Women like Acte who were freed for the purpose of marriage had limited rights (see chap. 5, below). The husband/enslaver's curse represents enslavers' perspectives on the danger

burning (*CIL* 6.20905). Acte's perspective is unrecoverable, but the enslaver/husband's curse illustrates the impossibility of honest, equal relationships amidst the inequalities, injustices, and violence of enslavement.[99] Even if an enslaved person was part of the enslaver's *familia*, they did not have the legal or social rights of a freeborn family member, and they would not be treated as a freeborn family member.

As the enslaved people who fled with Acte indicate, the people who were enslaved in the same household or agricultural estate created their own community.[100] One funerary inscription records the friendship between two enslaved people and their care for each other in life and death: "To Italia, dressmaker of Cocceia Phyllis. She lived 20 years. Acastus, her fellow slave, put this up because she was poor" (*CIL* 6.9980).[101] Of course, as in any human community, enslaved people also sometimes disliked, derided, and mistreated one another.[102] Communities of enslaved people extended beyond the immediate boundaries of a household through relationships with enslaved people in other households, as well as through relationships with enslaved and non-enslaved people in religious, professional, or funerary associations.[103]

The religious practices of enslaved people were varied. In Roman households, the maintenance of ancestral worship was considered to be significant to the family's prosperity and survival. Enslaved people participated (willingly or not) in regular worship of the enslavers' ancestral gods and in various festivals.[104] Such worship would have been a significant concern for enslaved

of "illicit" sex for enslaved people (that is, sexual intercourse beyond the enslaver's choice; see Perry 2015, 56–69).

99. Grubbs 2002, 230–36; Baird 2015, 168–70; and esp. Huemoller 2020, 123–26, 137.

100. Pliny, *Ep.* 8.16.3, comments on the existence of a "homeland" within the household among the community of natally alienated slaves. Household-based associations (*collegia*) were formal organizations for the enslaved and freed people owned by the same family; see Joshel 2010, 144. My discussion here attends instead to the ways enslaved people shaped their own relational identities.

101. Translation from Lefkowitz and Fant 2005, 223. See also *CIL* 6.6326, 6.7671, 6.38513, 6.22355a; *CEL* 1.3 (in Bathrellou and Vlassopoulos 2022, 190). Ramsby 2012, 71–73, notes the creation of a community of formerly enslaved freed people in Trimalchio's home in Petronius. See also V. Brown 2009, 1232–33; Bond 2022, 173–74; Huemoller 2024, 119–20.

102. E.g., Varro, *Rust.* 1.17.4; Tacitus, *Agr.* 31.2; *Life of Aesop* 2–3, 9–11, 16–18; and the curse tablets: *AE* 2008.792; and 2010.108.

103. Relationships beyond households are not necessarily (or at least not obviously) part of the written record, but the presence of enslaved people in public spaces and in organizations naturally allows for friendships (and more). See Columella, *Rust.* 1.8.1–2; *CIL* 6.2209, 4012, 30982; 14.2112; *SEG* 40.1044. For a hypothetical construction of enslaved people's use of household and urban spaces for companionship, see Joshel and Petersen 2014, 82–84, 100–115.

104. Note the lararium located in the kitchen in the House of Sutoria Primigenia in Pompeii and the inclusion of enslaved people in a lararium painting in the House of Obellius Firmus. See also Cicero, *Leg.* 2.27; Dionysius of Halicarnassus, *Ant. rom.* 4.14.3–4; Plutarch,

Jews and Christians.[105] It is likely that enslaved people's participation was compulsory. Petronius, *Sat.* 53.3, suggests an enslaved person might refuse to participate, but in this scene, cursing the enslaver's *genius* (his guardian spirit) ends in the enslaved person's crucifixion.

Enslaved people also participated in worship outside their enslavers' households, as various inscriptions indicate.[106] In temples and shrines, enslaved people, freed people, and freeborn people worshiped together.[107] Enslaved people were owned by and worked for temples and synagogues.[108] For Niall McKeown, the lack of complaints from enslavers concerning enslaved people's participation in cultic worship suggests it was not generally viewed as subversive or problematic. Participation in "foreign" worship—often classified as "superstition," Jewish worship included—was not necessarily regarded favorably (as may be evident in the comments on enslaved women participants in early Christian communities in Pliny, *Ep.* 10.96.8).[109] But if McKeown is correct, the enslaved people who participated in the communities of Jesus's followers, gathering regularly for worship and shared meals—people such as those 1 Peter addresses—were not doing anything particularly unusual. Such contexts offered opportunities for relationships beyond the household.

Sometimes the relationships of enslaved people were familial, with committed partners and children. Since enslaved people could not enter legally recognized marriages, marital partnerships were normally described as *contubernium* (e.g., *CIL* 6.7297). Such families existed by the enslavers' tolerance and could easily be broken (for instance, by the sale or manumission of one individual, as in P.Oxy. 3.494).[110] The normative experiences of family life—living, working, and eating together; sexual fidelity; parental care for and authority over children; independent property ownership—were not possible

Quaest. conv. 693f–94a; Lucian, *Sat.* 13; Macrobius, *Sat.* 1.24.22–23; Clarke 2003, 76–78; Edmondson 2011, 345; North 2012, 71; Zelnick-Abramovitz 2012, 96–100.

105. Hezser 2005, 34–36, 50–51; 2011, 440–41; and Bühner 2023, 200–206, discuss whether Jewish slaves would have difficulty in practicing their own traditions or if they could maintain their own identities in non-Jewish households. See also Bauman-Martin 2004b, 267.

106. *CIL* 1^2.2685, 6.74.

107. Cf. Ascough 2003, 51–55; Neutel 2012, 135–38; North 2012, 69–74. McKeown 2012, 287–91, notes that enslaved people were a minor presence in the *collegia*, which maintained a social hierarchy (so enslaved people would hold the lowest status in the group).

108. E.g., *CIL* 6.2209; *CIRB* 74 (quoted in Bain); Bain 2014, 161–62.

109. McKeown 2012, 280. On the disfavor toward Judaism, early Christianity, and other non-Greco-Roman cultic systems, see, e.g., Cato, *Agr.* 5.3; Cicero, *Leg.* 2.25–26; Valerius Maximus 1.3.3, 6.3.7; Tacitus, *Ann.* 2.85; Pliny, *Ep.* 10.96.

110. Chaniotis 2023, 197–98, also cites a third-century CE sarcophagus from Aphrodisias with an inscription to an enslaved man and his enslaved son, each belonging to different enslavers.

for enslaved people.[111] It is notable in this respect that the household instructions in 1 Peter separate enslaved people from wives and husbands (in Eph. 5:21–6:9 and Col. 3:18–4:1, enslaved people are also separated from parents and children). Enslaved "wives" must submit to and fear their enslavers, not their husbands, and enslaved "husbands" cannot live wisely with their wives (1 Pet. 3:1–7)—at least, not from the perspective of the enslavers. But, notably, a graffito from Pompeii ascribed love and marital harmony to enslaved partners (*CIL* 4.2457). Enslaved people claimed familial relationships for themselves despite the contingencies of enslavement.[112]

While enslaved people created their own communities, enslavers also attempted to control the relationships enslaved people managed to create. To return to Plutarch's life of Marcus Cato, Cato's enslaved people could enter someone else's home only under orders by Cato or his wife (*Cat. Maj.* 21.1). Enslaved men were allowed access to enslaved women's bodies for sex only if they paid a fee (21.2).[113] Plutarch further accused Cato of starting disagreements between the enslaved people in his household, apparently from a concern that good relationships would allow the enslaved people to conspire with one another against his authority (21.4). Cato's control over and manipulation of the people enslaved in his household offer a reminder that enslavers prioritized their own profit over the humanity of their enslaved property. Considering these limitations, the frequent references to familial connections between enslaved people and the persistence of familial relationships beyond slavery among freed people indicate their significance for enslaved people across the Roman Empire. Such relationships allowed the enslaved to develop their own existence, to claim their own degree of human experience, independent of their enslavers.

Freedom in and from Slavery

In 1 Peter 2:16, the audience of the letter is identified as both "slaves of God" and "free." As free enslaved people (ἐλεύθερος and δοῦλος), they should use

111. As exemplified by the fictional story of a freed slave purchasing the enslaved woman who was his "wife" in slavery to protect her from sexual use by her enslaver (Petronius, *Sat.* 57.6; cf. Valerius Maximus 7.3.7). See also Joshel 2010, 150–51; Edmondson 2011, 347–50; Huemoller 2024, 122–29.

112. Note the references to enslaved people as spouses, children, and siblings in *AE* 1981.442; *CIL* 6.15585, 6.37783, 8.24734, 10.26; *ILS* 1583, 1763, 5231; *SEG* 40.1044. See further Chaniotis 2023, 197–99.

113. Cf. Xenophon, *Oec.* 9.5; *IG* 12.7, for a complaint from an enslaver concerning, among other perceived wrongs, a man of uncertain status who seduced the enslaver's property (an enslaved woman) against the enslaver's will.

their freedom for good, not evil. But in verses 18–20, some of these free enslaved people are also enslaved to human enslavers, laboring in their enslavers' households (οἰκέτης under a δεσπότης). There is a contradiction between their status as "free slaves" of God and as human property under the ownership of an enslaver. The contradiction raises an important question: What could freedom mean for enslaved people?

Slavery and freedom provided a common collocation of metaphors for philosophers, rhetoricians, and other writers because the system of slavery was ubiquitous; the figure of an enslaved person was carefully constructed; and, as Sandra Joshel argues, "slave" was an eminently useful concept—just as an enslaved person was an eminently useful tool for the benefit of their enslavers.[114] Publilius Syrus, a freed person, applied the hierarchies of slavery to describe social inequalities (*Sent.* 61, 641), responsibility (264, 538), and moral virtue: A wise person rules their own emotions and desires, but a fool is enslaved by them (40, 50, 51). Publilius Syrus internalized slavery as the state of being controlled by emotional impulses, physical needs, luxuries, and vice. Freedom, by contrast, is evident in the exercise of self-control over such matters.[115] Consequently, an enslaver might in fact be a slave by virtue of their lack of self-control, and an enslaved person might truly be free.[116] The internalization of freedom and enslavement allows the enslaved people of 1 Peter 2:18–20 to be, at the same time, the "free slaves" of verse 16.[117]

The internalization of freedom and slavery in Greco-Roman philosophy offers insight into the ways these concepts could be used to reinterpret the social statuses of free and enslaved. However, in practice the association of self-control with education, wealth, and privilege (not to mention masculinity, the topic of the next chapter) limited even this philosophical "freedom" to the elite.[118] This limitation is evident in Seneca's declaration that all life was slavery of a sort; the "enslavers" he listed include public office, wealth, and social status (*Tranq.* 10.3). Seneca explicitly denied that the internalization of freedom and slavery offered any challenge to the system of slavery (*Ep.* 47.17–19). Rather, the elevation of the mind, signifying reason as the exercise of freedom, over the body, signifying enslavement to emotion and desire,

114. Joshel 2011, 240.

115. See also Xenophon, *Oec.* 1.17–23; Philo, *Leg.* 3.202; Epictetus, *Diatr.* 3.22.45–49.

116. This use of slavery and freedom is particularly evident among Stoic philosophers, e.g., Seneca, *Ep.* 47.15–17, 77.14–15, 85.27; Dio Chrysostom 15.29–32; Epictetus, *Diatr.* 3.22.45–49, 3.26.23–24.

117. See esp. Sommer 2021, 481–90.

118. Roller 2001, 272–85; Bradley 2011b, 259; Sommer 2021, 475, and passim; Alimi 2024, 39–44; Joly 2024, 170–73. Wehus 2019, 237–38, notes that Epictetus is a rare exception; in his *Discourses*, he turned the rhetoric of enslavement against the elite.

reinforced the hierarchies of enslavement.[119] In this respect, the definition of freedom as slavery to God in 1 Peter 2:16 doubly enslaved the household slaves in verses 18–20.[120]

There is a significant difference between the philosophical metaphors and slavery and freedom as discussed in 1 Peter. The philosophers spoke about and to elite audiences. Enslaved people might eavesdrop as scribes, readers, or servers at dinners where philosophical essays were read for entertainment. However, enslaved people were an incidental, rather than intended, audience. In 1 Peter, enslaved people were addressed directly as part of the community, as "free slaves." The inclusion of people who experienced institutional enslavement overlays the metaphors of freedom and slavery in 2:16 with the ways enslaved people understood and claimed the status of freedom: rebellion, escape, manumission, and death.

A few major rebellions involving armies of enslaved people (and requiring the Roman army to suppress) are scattered through Roman history.[121] But rebellion mostly happened on a small scale. Enslavers' complaints suggest individuals resisted enslavement through acts of disobedience, refusal to work, negligence, and sometimes murder.[122] Escape offered another accessible, flexible option for enslaved people. Epictetus, himself a freed person, describes enslaved people fleeing with very limited resources, doing all they could to travel far away (*Diatr.* 3.26.1)—fast enough, presumably, to avoid the dangers of recapture. The number of laws concerning runaway slaves, the advertisements for the capture of runaway slaves, and the punishments for recaptured slaves suggest that flight was not uncommon.[123] Equally, the fear of severe punishment (including branding, beatings, and crucifixion), the hope of legal manumission, and relationships with friends and family may have prevented many enslaved people from claiming their freedom through escape.

Manumission was possible for enslaved people in urban households or the imperial government: "Serve [δουλεύω] me faithfully and devotedly so that you may gain your freedom from me" (*Life of Aesop* 64[124]). New Testament scholars sometimes cite Cicero, *Phil.* 8.32, to argue that enslaved captives of

119. So Finley 1998, 188–89; Fitzgerald 2010, 157–59; Joshel 2011, 234. See further Bradley 2008, 340–43, on Seneca's conception of enslavement.

120. Cf. Schüssler Fiorenza 2009, 127.

121. Diodorus Siculus 36.1–10; Livy 32.26; Tacitus, *Ann.* 4.27; Appian, *Bell. civ.* 1.14.116–20.

122. E.g., Xenophon, *Mem.* 2.1.15–16; Aristotle, *Rhet.* 2.3.5; Polybius 38.15.10; Tacitus, *Ann.* 14.42–45; Pliny, *Ep.* 3.14; Juvenal, *Sat.* 11.190–92; *Life of Aesop* 38–41; Artemidorus, *Onir.* 2.11; Bradley 1994, 115–17; Joshel 2010, 153–59.

123. See Pliny, *Nat.* 28.13; Plutarch, *Conj. praec.* 41; P.Oxy. 3616, 3617; Bruns 159.3 (available in Wiedemann 2005, 192); *UPZ* 1.121; *Dig.* 11.4.1; Bradley 1994, 117–21; 2011a, 367–73.

124. Translation from Karla 2024, 113. See also P.Oxy. 494.

war could expect freedom after six years of slavery, but "six years" is more likely a rhetorical device reflecting the time since a recent event (Caesar crossing the Rubicon).[125] Cassius Dio recorded a minimum twenty-year enslavement of captives under Augustus (53.25.4), and Dio Chrysostom recognized that some captives were enslaved for the remainder of their lives (15.14–15). A funerary inscription from first-century Egypt relays that a woman named Valeria who was enslaved as a captive of war at age four only escaped when her brother found her and purchased her (and her daughters) thirty-eight years later (*SEG* 39.1711). Manumission was possible, but it was a limited privilege.[126]

Some enslavers chose to manumit a certain number of enslaved people upon the enslaver's own death (a process with legal restrictions, since the enslaved "bodies" represented inheritable household wealth).[127] An enslaver could also free an enslaved person in recognition of that person's character or skills, or to honor familial relationships.[128] Enslavers (usually men, but sometimes women) also freed enslaved people for the purpose of marriage (in the case of enslaved women) or adoption (usually enslaved boys).[129] It was also possible (though difficult) for enslaved people to purchase their own lives, and for formerly enslaved people to purchase the lives of their family members or friends.[130]

Manumission brought a measure of freedom. Enslaved people formally manumitted by Roman citizens received social status (marked by adding their former enslavers' familial *nomen* to their own name) and, sometimes, citizenship (Gaius, *Inst.* 1.13–22, details the different possibilities).[131] Enslavers' complaints about the power or wealth of freed people suggests that at least some people, most likely those who had been enslaved in the imperial government or wealthy households, gained positions of political and social power (though Juvenal, *Sat.* 7.199–202, claimed this situation was less common

125. Harris 1980, 133; Koops 2020, 64.

126. See Bradley 2011b, 255–56; Morley 2011, 281; Flexsenhar 2019, 14–15; Koops 2020, 39. Bonar 2025, 66–73, helpfully surveys the possibilities of manumission.

127. Pliny, *Ep.* 4.10; Gaius, *Inst.* 1.42–43; P.Oxy. 3.494; *BGU* 326; Diogenes Laertius 5.4.72–74.

128. Cicero, *Fam.* 44; P.Oxy. 722; Pliny, *Ep.* 7.16.4, 7.32; Suetonius, *Gramm.* 13, 27; Gaius, *Inst.* 1.19.

129. For male enslavers marrying enslaved women, see *CIL* 5.1071, 6.2170, 6.23848. Inscriptions identifying women enslavers freeing and marrying male slaves include *CIL* 6.14014, 6.20673, and 12.682a (Nasrallah 2019, 58, notes that a free woman who took an enslaved man as a marital partner could be enslaved, since her relationship with an enslaved person infects her with slavishness). Manumission for the purpose of adoption is apparent in *ILS* 7479; *GDI* 1803, 1806; *FD* 3.3.333. See Huemoller 2024, 122–32.

130. See Dionysius of Halicarnassus, *Ant. rom.* 4.24.4; *GDI* 1708 (from Delphi); Petronius, *Sat.* 57.6; *CIL* 11.5400; *Dig.* 40.4.1; Koops 2020, 51, 54–58; and Bonar 2025, 71 (noting the extreme rarity of this possibility).

131. See Bradley 2011b, 254–57; Bell, Borbonus, and MacLean 2024, 4–7.

than a white crow).[132] Manumission also brought the standard privileges of free status: the right to marry, the right of recognition as parents for children born in freedom, the right to own property, and the ability to claim moral virtue.[133] However, women who were freed for the purpose of marriage had fewer legal rights than freeborn wives.[134]

While manumission clearly privileged freed people in multiple ways, it also benefited enslavers. In any type of manumission, the enslaved person's life cost money; enslavers received financial remuneration for the loss of their "property."[135] Moreover, people who had been freed were required to continue to work for their former enslavers a certain number of days each year, to pay debts to (or ransoms for) their former enslavers, and to respect and honor their former enslavers (*obsequium*).[136] In some categories of manumission, upon the freed person's death their property was inherited by their enslaver, not their own children.[137] The Greek practices of manumission in Delphi from about 200 BCE to 100 CE are striking in this respect. Enslaved women who were "freed" were required to continue living with and working for their enslavers, bearing children for their enslavers (to replace their own enslaved bodies), and honoring their enslavers, under threat of punishment and re-enslavement (*FD* 3.6.36, 3.3.333, and passim).[138] In such cases, manumission was a means of further enslavement (Artemidorus, *Onir.* 2.31).

As the quotation above from *Life of Aesop* indicates, the simple hope of manumission benefited enslavers by motivating hard work and submissive attitudes among enslaved people.[139] Many enslaved people would have been physically worn out by the time their freedom was legally granted—over age thirty, according to Augustus's *Lex Aelia Sentia* (Gaius, *Inst.* 1.18), and likely older for women, around the age of menopause. In other words, freedom came when enslaved people were no longer as valuable to their enslavers as workers

132. Polybius 38.15.10; Pliny, *Nat.* 18.41, 33.134–35, 33.145, 35.200–201; Martial 10.76. See further Roller 2001, 264–67; MacLean 2018, 2–3; Joly 2024, 179–81.

133. See Bell and Ramsby 2012, 2–7; Borg 2012, 27–29; and esp. MacLean 2018, 15–18, and passim, on the culture developed by freed slaves in Rome.

134. Huemoller 2020, 129–34; Bonar 2025, 70. Manumission for the purpose of marriage is further discussed in chap. 5, below.

135. Roth 2010, 102–6, 115–16, explores the enslaved person's responsibility to reimburse their enslaver for the cost of their own life.

136. *CIL* 6.11027, 6.13732, 6.22355a; *ILS* 8283; *Dig.* 37.14.1, 38.1; Wessels 2010, 157–58; Scheidel 2012, 101–2; MacLean 2018, 37–40, 53–54; Bell, Borbonus, and MacLean 2024, 4.

137. Roth 2010, 107–11, 117–18; Bonar 2025, 69.

138. See Tucker 1982; Nasrallah 2019, 68–71; Bonar 2025, 70–71; and chap. 5, below. Similar expectations are attested in Egypt in P.Oxy 494.

139. Also Aristotle, [*Oec.*] 1344b.19; Wessels 2010, 155–57; Bonar 2025, 71–73.

or as sources of new enslaved bodies.[140] It is also important to note that the status of slavery lingered into freedom.[141] A freed person was defined as a "freed slave" (*libertus*), not "freeborn" (*ingenuus*). They could be punished, re-enslaved, or executed as punishment for perceived wrongdoing.[142]

Freedom brought a degree of personal honor, the possibility of control over one's own body, and some legal rights to familial relationships and property ownership. These are significant advantages for freed people. But all the conditions of enslavement were not redressed by manumission. Freed people remained natally alienated, without the ability to reclaim their ancestry or even their father's name.[143] Plutarch denies freed slaves the emotional range of the freeborn: A freeborn man whose body is unmarred by enslavement experiences a pure joy that a freed slave whose body is scarred from beatings cannot attain (*Mor.* 1091e). The identity imposed by enslavement lingered into freedom. The state of being a freed slave was not entirely honorable or free.

"Hilara, slave of Hermia. 14 years old" (*CIL* 6.6395).[144] As this funerary inscription attests, perhaps the most common path to freedom for enslaved people was death. There is little indication that people enslaved in the mines, public works, or agricultural estates ever had the opportunity for manumission. Even in urban households, many enslaved people died in the status of slavery, as in the case of Hilara. Hilara may have had a natural death as a result of disease, injury, malnutrition, or the physical consequences of labor. Enslaved people also died from old age.[145] Enslaved people were killed by their enslavers, either deliberately by execution for perceived wrongdoing or accidentally as a consequence of physical abuse.[146] Some enslaved people took their own lives, a choice reflecting their despair or, as in Plutarch's story of the Spartan woman quoted at the beginning of the chapter, a protest against the system of enslavement.[147]

140. Cf. Wessels 2010, 156; Koops 2020, 41–43, 69.

141. See esp. MacLean 2018, 2–3, 37–41; Giannella 2024, 142 (noting that freedom is "insecure and unprotected" for formerly enslaved people); Joly 2024, 164–73.

142. Cicero, *Att.* 7.2.8; Valerius Maximus 2.6.6–7; Suetonius, *Aug.* 67; *Claud.* 25.1; Giannella 2024, 141–62.

143. Joshel 2010, 42–43, notes that enslaved and freed people were classified as illegitimate (a social stigma in Roman society).

144. Translation from Lefkowitz and Fant 2005, 224.

145. See also *ILS* 1583, 1604, 5231, and 7771; Phaedrus, *Fables*, Perotti's Appendix 20. Suetonius, *Claud.* 25.2, notes cases of enslavers abandoning sick or elderly enslaved people to die (apparently to save the expense of caring for them).

146. Cicero, *Clu.* 187; Seneca, *Ep.* 70.19–27; Pliny, *Nat.* 9.77; *AE* 1971.88; *Dig.* 48.8.11.

147. E.g., Seneca, *Ep.* 70.20–26, 77.14–15; Apuleius, *Metam.* 8.31; Bradley 2011a, 378; Lenski 2016, 292.

Despite the freedom proclaimed in 1 Peter 2:16, the enslaved people in verses 18–20 are not offered any hope of manumission. Instead, they are exhorted to follow the model of Jesus, who was executed by crucifixion (known to the Romans as the death of slaves; vv. 21–25).[148] The association of enslavement with unjust suffering allies the enslaved people exhorted by 1 Peter 2:18–20 with other enslaved people who regularly faced violence, even to the point of death, across the empire. Their freedom comes through death—the death of Jesus, and perhaps also their own.

Empowering Enslaved People in 1 Peter 2:18–25?

In 1 Peter 2:18–25, the instructions to enslaved people correspond with the perspective of enslavers: The enslaved people are to obey, fear, and endure violence. The instructions directly benefit enslavers by shaping their "slaves" into obedient, fearful, silent tools. Though the enslaved people are also "free" (v. 16), their freedom is masked by enslavement not only to human enslavers but to God, a theological oppression added to the social and legal injustice of their lives. Read against the public transcripts of the Roman Empire, the representation of enslavement in 1 Peter is dire. The historic use of this text to support the power of enslavers, or other figures of authority in various social hierarchies, at the expense of the safety and well-being of the people under their authority demonstrates its danger for enslaved people and other marginalized peoples.[149]

As addressed in the introduction, this very common approach to interpreting a text like 1 Peter 2:18–25 is useful: It demands that readers pay attention to the structures of injustice revealed by the text and the potential for using the text to perpetuate injustice. The interpretation of a problematic text requires care, lest the interpretation further the oppression. But a potential disadvantage of this interpretive approach is its lack of attention to the various creative, life-affirming ways enslaved people, and other marginalized populations, may have used 1 Peter 2:18–25 for their own survival, self-worth, and thriving.[150] A doulological approach demands attention to both the public transcripts of enslavers and the hidden transcripts that allowed enslaved people to navigate their daily lives, resist the oppressive dehumanization imposed by their enslavers, and claim freedom for themselves.

148. For crucifixion as the death of slaves, see Cicero, *Verr.* 2.6.14, 2.66.169; Livy 22.33.2; Juvenal, *Sat.* 6.219–21; and chap. 3, below.

149. Cf. Bird 2011, 91.

150. See also S. Smith 2016, 70–71, 165; Steetskamp 2020, esp. 50, 65–66; Jung 2022, 57–59.

With respect to a text like 1 Peter 2:18–25, the explanation Phaedrus gives for his own interest, as a formerly enslaved man, in fables is illuminating. Fables allow enslaved persons to hide their own opinions in plain sight, using imaginative stories to protect themselves from violent punishment that might come in response to their critiques or complaints concerning their enslavers.[151] Enslaved people were participants in early Christian communities, and as scribes and readers, they were involved in composing the letters and narratives that eventually became the New Testament. As Candida Moss argues, then, the perspectives of enslaved people may also be hiding in plain sight in the New Testament.[152] At the least, doulological interpretation can suggest ways enslaved people might have used texts for their own survival; at the most, these potential meanings were intentionally incorporated by means of attention to enslaved characters, ambiguous imagery, and tensions that raise questions about and critiques of the oppressive practices of enslavement.

Through this chapter, I have suggested a few ways to decenter enslavers' perspectives in 1 Peter 2:18–25. First, it is important to recognize that the letter was written, read, and preserved by minoritized, marginalized communities that included enslaved people. The absence of any reference to enslavers within the audience constructed in 1 Peter emphasizes the marginalization of the community.[153] These communities existed within an unjust system that deprivileged anyone who lacked wealth, political power, or Roman identity. They had very little opportunity to change their personal circumstances (e.g., for enslaved people to attain free status). The association of enslavement with violence and injustice is clearly descriptive, rather than prescriptive. What if the association of enslavement with submission and fear is also descriptive?

The fear in 1 Peter 2:18 may reflect the fear of God in the previous verse.[154] However, fear and submission were fundamental attributes of the Roman system of slavery (see further in chap. 2). An audience in the first century would at least also, if not only, identify the fear of verse 18 with enslavement.[155] If the verse is read as an assessment of enslaved people's position—they are people

151. Phaedrus, *Fables* 3.prol.33–37; J. Strong 2021, 111, 259–67. For examples of this strategy in the fables, see esp. 1.15, 3.19, and Perotti's Appendix 12 and 17 (other fables encourage living within the system of slavery for survival, as in Perotti's Appendix 20). See also Stewart 2008, 72–93, on the character of the trickster slave in Plautus's plays and *Life of Aesop*.

152. Moss 2024, 3–6, and passim.

153. Cf. Reese 2022, 153–54. Steetskamp 2020, 243–44, suggests there can be no instruction to enslavers in 1 Peter because the "new reality" of the community precludes enslavement; see also S. Smith 2016, 72–73.

154. So, e.g., Steetskamp 2020, 192; Jobes 2022, 190; Reese 2022, 153.

155. So T. Williams and Horrell 2023a, 791–92. Steetskamp 2020, 32, identifies the fear of God as a slave perspective for the entire community to adopt.

forced by their circumstances to obey enslavers, with reason to be afraid in their very vulnerable position in the enslavers' households—then the text as a whole, in its recognition of the injustice of the system, offers enslaved people tactics for survival; for reinterpreting their oppression as divine grace; and for establishing their own identity as "free slaves."[156]

Second, the recognition and recommendation of standard household authority structures in 1 Peter 2:18–21 is undermined by the exhortation for enslaved people to enact "good." As noted at the beginning of this chapter, doing good in 1 Peter aligns with obedience to God (the divine enslaver), rather than with adherence to Greco-Roman social expectations. In other words, for enslaved people to do good, adopting values and practices distinct from local culture (note 2:11–12; 4:3–4), they would need to disobey their enslavers.[157] The unjust violence endured by enslaved people, then, corresponds with insubordination. The instructions to enslaved people challenge the enslavers' presumption that enslaved people exist for their benefit. Enslaved people, not enslavers, determine what is good.

Third, enslaved people were thoroughly invested in the work of writing a letter like 1 Peter, reading it in community gatherings, and preserving it and passing it on to other communities. These were tasks performed by enslaved people in the first century.[158] When this letter was read at an early Christian gathering, enslaved people and enslavers together heard themselves described as "slaves of God" who are also free. The descriptor would have different significance for people who were legally free and people who were legally enslaved, and enslavers (as evidenced in antebellum America) could use it to preserve and advance their power.[159] But the use of the descriptor before the specific address to people enslaved in households establishes the shared identity of the community members as free enslaved people belonging to God.[160] However unlikely such a possibility would be, it is not utterly impossible to imagine enslaved people (and freed people) using this letter to challenge the injustice of enslavement, as indeed contemporary readers can.[161]

156. See esp. Bauman-Martin 2004a, 73–74. Similar interpretations are explored in Schertz 2004, 434; Moxnes 2014, 139–40; S. Smith 2016, 72–74; Steetskamp 2020, 62, 190–99; Sommer 2021, 491–92; and Ruiz 2023, 21–23.

157. Bauman-Martin 2004b, 267–71, particularly insists that "submission" cannot mean obedience in 1 Pet. 2:18–21. (A contrasting perspective on submission as judicious conformity to social norms is represented by, e.g., Horrell 2007, 133–34; T. Williams and Horrell 2023a, 851–52.)

158. Blake 2012, 193–95; Powery 2022, 82–84; Moss 2024, 12–13, 42–49, and passim.

159. Cf. Moss 2024, 205–7.

160. The description of the audience constructed in 1 Peter as exiles and foreigners (e.g., 1:1; 2:11) also characterizes them with the natal alienation experienced by enslaved people.

161. See esp. McKeown 2012, 293–95; Steetskamp 2020, 240–41; Jung 2022, 58.

Fourth, if the community was familiar with traditional Greco-Roman instructions for household management, they would have been surprised to hear enslaved people addressed first, before (freeborn and freed) wives and husbands. This reversal of the hierarchical ordering of household relationships in, for instance, Ephesians 5:21–6:9 and Colossians 3:18–4:1 gives priority to enslaved people. Moreover, the enslaved people are compared with Jesus, whose story is one of a beaten, crucified slave and also one of life and healing (ζάω and ἰάομαι, 1 Pet. 2:24). The text clearly identifies the suffering of enslaved people as the same injustice suffered by Jesus (ἀδίκως in v. 19, in contrast with God's justice in v. 23).[162] The direct connection between enslaved people and Jesus makes enslaved people exemplars of Jesus for the broader community (note the similar content of the instructions to enslaved people, the model of Jesus, and the commands given to the entire community in 3:8–22).[163] Within the communities that composed, read, and preserved 1 Peter, enslavers would hear enslaved people identified as the primary models of discipleship. The enslaved, not their enslavers, most easily and naturally followed the model set by Jesus.[164] If enslavers wanted to follow Jesus's model, they would have to live like the enslaved people in their communities.

These potential avenues for redefining and resisting enslavement in 1 Peter 2:18–25 do not erase or redress the fundamental evil of enslavement.[165] The vocabulary and the comparison of enslaved people with Jesus in the precise issue of unjust suffering represents slavery as an oppressive, violent, dehumanizing reality. However, the letter does not call for the system to be abolished, nor even for enslaved people to seek to change their status. The recognition of injustice stands in tension with the response to injustice offered in the text, a response that encourages the oppressed to continue to be oppressed and even (by their submission and fear) to participate in their own oppression. A doulological interpretation threads between recognizing the oppression represented by a text like 1 Peter 2:18–25 and recognizing potential opportunities in the work of interpretation for marginalized, oppressed peoples to survive and resist, even if thriving was unimaginable.

This chapter has focused on reconstructing Roman enslavers' perspectives on enslavement and on bringing the experiences of people who were enslaved in the Roman Empire to light. The next chapter addresses the intersections of

162. Moxnes 2014, 138; Joseph 2012, 123; Jung 2022, 58.

163. So also, e.g., Krull 1998, 490–91; Bauman-Martin 2004b, 265; Schertz 2004, 434; Moxnes 2014, 138; Steetskamp 2020, 183.

164. Jobes 2022, 188, 191; T. Williams and Horrell 2023a, 232.

165. As emphasized by Moxnes 2008, 179–80; 2014, 134–35, 138, and passim; Sommer 2021, 484–91. See also Bird 2011, 30, on women in 1 Peter.

gender and enslavement. Within ancient Mediterranean cultures, "gender" meant masculinity. Whatever their biologically or socially constructed sex, people were judged on a spectrum of masculinity. Enslaved people in many ways represented the absence of masculinity. This raises important questions for the gendering of communities of "slaves of God," for the gendering of enslaved people, and the gendering of Jesus, who is compared with an enslaved person in 1 Peter 2:21–25.

2

Masculinity and the Un-Gendering of Enslavement

> Christ suffered for you, leaving you an example so that you can follow in his footsteps. . . . When he was insulted, he didn't respond with insults, and when he suffered, he did not threaten in return. . . . By the welts [on his body], you are healed.
>
> —1 Peter 2:21, 23, 24

> Neither the manly [*fortis*] nor freeborn [*ingenuus*] can endure insult. . . . For the wise, to be despised is more oppressive than a beating is for a fool.
>
> —Publilius Syrus, *Sent.* 114, 118

The example of Jesus stands between the exhortations to enslaved people in 1 Peter 2:18–21 and to wives in 3:1–6. The description in 2:22–25 emphasizes Jesus's innocence, nonretaliation, and suffering. That the suffering is physical is clarified by "in his body" (ἐν τῷ σώματι αὐτου; v. 24): Jesus experienced beatings that marked his body, and he died by crucifixion.[1]

1. The reference to crucifixion in 1 Pet. 2:24 is veiled. Rather than the direct vocabulary of crucifixion or cross, the text refers to Jesus's body being on a tree. This may be connected with Deut. 21:22–23. "Tree" is also a euphemism for "cross" in Cicero, *Rab. Perd.* 4.13; Philo, *Somn.* 2.213; Acts 5:30; 10:39; 13:29. See further T. Williams and Horrell 2023a, 837–38.

These elements of 1 Peter's description incorporate quotations from Isaiah 53:3, 5–6, and 9, making this text one of the most explicit connections of Isaiah's Servant Songs with the person of Jesus in the New Testament. The integration of Isaiah 52:13–53:12 into 1 Peter 2:22–25 develops Jesus's innocence and interprets Jesus's suffering and death as redemptive in nature.[2] For the enslaved people who follow Jesus's example, suffering consequently signifies divine grace (χάρις in vv. 19–20).[3]

As suggested in the introduction, audiences in the first century would see Roman slavery in the descriptions of Isaiah's servant and Jesus. In 1 Peter 2:23–24, Jesus's nonretaliation aligns with the inability of enslaved people to defend themselves. Welts and scars were visible signs of enslavement, and crucifixion was the death of slaves. Jesus is not directly named as an enslaved person in 1 Peter 2:22–25, but the descriptors associate Jesus with the status and experience of enslavement. That Jesus's enslavement is implied is supported by the explicit connection with the enslaved people addressed in verses 18 through 21.

In 1 Peter 2:20–21, Jesus is an example or pattern (ὑπογραμμός) for enslaved people to follow.[4] Like Jesus, they suffer abuse and injustice. And also like Jesus, they should be innocent of wrongdoing and endure abuse without retaliation. "Likewise" (ὁμοίως) in 3:1 incorporates wives into this community of unjust suffering. As noted in chapter 1, enslaved people and wives shared the status of outsiders in a Roman man's household. In 1 Peter, they are connected by submission to household hierarchies of authority and by their fear (2:18; 3:1–2, 5–6).[5] As the hinge between the exhortations to enslaved people and wives, the representation of Jesus is both slavish and womanish.

The association of Jesus with enslaved people and wives draws attention to the un-masculine characteristics in the depiction of Jesus in 1 Peter 2:20–25. Across the Roman Empire, masculinity was expressed by the exercise of authority. A manly man had authority over his own person, evident in his self-control and the ability to protect his bodily boundaries and avenge violations. He also had authority over other people, including the legal and moral right to transgress their bodily boundaries. Publilius Syrus's maxims illustrate this basic definition of masculinity. Insults and abuse are unendurable for manly, freeborn men, and it is oppressive for a wise person (presumably a man) to be despised, more so than for a fool to be beaten (*Sent.* 114, 118). By these

2. See Achtemeier 1996, 200–204; J. Green 2007, 85–87; Gäckle 2021, 279–80; Jobes 2022, 193–94; Williams and Horrell 2023a, 823–27, 832–37, 844–46.

3. So Gäckle 2021, 283.

4. See T. Williams and Horrell 2023a, 819–21.

5. Briggs 2003, 174–75.

standards, Jesus ranks as a fool. His failure to respond to abuse and insults in 1 Peter 2:23 is not the response of a manly, freeborn man but (by implication) an un-manly slave. The example set by Jesus represents the opposite of authority over one's self or others.

Jesus's un-manly behavior is the model for enslaved people and wives, two populations who were (in Roman understanding) naturally un-masculine by virtue of their legal status and anatomy.[6] But, as the parallel between 1 Peter 2:21–25 and 3:8–18 indicates, Jesus's un-manly behavior is also the model for all the "slaves of God," the entire community of Jesus's followers, including husbands in 3:7 and authority figures in the community in 5:1–5. In effect, 1 Peter 2:18–3:6 sets up un-masculinity as the model for Christian identity, with enslaved people and wives as the most Jesus-like in the community and, as a consequence, the most visible examples of Jesus-likeness in the midst of the community.

This chapter develops the standard Roman definitions of masculinity and the significance of these definitions for the (un)gendering of enslavement as a context for interpreting the New Testament. Slavery was a significant tool for thinking in the Greco-Roman world. With respect to gender, elite perspectives on slavery contributed to the construction of elite masculinity. The conception of gender in the Roman Empire provides one lens for interpreting the New Testament representations of Jesus as an enslaved person, and exhortations to Jesus's followers to model themselves on enslaved people.

Masculinity and the Roman Empire

For the Romans, as for many other ancient Mediterranean cultures, gender was broadly defined as a single-sex system. Masculinity represented the ideal for humanity, with individuals categorized along a spectrum from greater masculinity to lesser (i.e., more feminine or effeminate).[7] Women, that is, were evaluated as more or less masculine along with men. Seneca encouraged his mother to demonstrate masculinity by emotional control, and Plutarch's virtuous (or "manly," ἀρετή) women exhibit courage, the willingness to die rather than be defeated, and good military tactics.[8] In general, however, wealthy, powerful, aristocratic Roman men were assumed to be the most capable of attaining normative masculinity.[9]

6. Cf. Vander Stichele and Penner 2009, 69–70.

7. E.g., Gleason 1995, 58–59; McDonnell 2006, 2; Boatwright 2011, 108–10; Myers 2017, 21; Cobb 2025, 121.

8. Seneca, *Helv.* 16.3–7; *Marc.* 3.1–2, 16.1–4; Plutarch, *Mulier. virt.* 244b–d, 245a–b, 245d–e, and passim.

9. P. Brown 1988, 9–11; Vander Stichele and Penner 2009, 68.

Gender is complicated, and shifting political, cultural, and social situations shaped distinctive definitions of masculinity across time, space, and cultural contexts.[10] The discussion in this chapter surveys the standard components most consistently associated with masculinity in Greco-Roman conceptions, with reference as well to comparative constructions in biblical and Second Temple sources. Tacitus's portrait of Germanicus, the adopted son of Tiberius and father of Gaius Caligula, provides a useful focus for exploring first-century elite Roman masculinity (*virtus*; *Ann.* 2.72–73).

First, Tacitus noted Germanicus's physical form (cf. also Livy 28.35.6–7 on Scipio). Anatomical attributes, including musculature, body shape, genitalia, and hirsuteness, were fundamental to masculinity.[11] Biological women were evaluated as more or less masculine, but they could never attain full masculinity (unless, as in various legends, they experienced a sex change).[12] Likewise, men whose genitals were modified by injury or castration were not clearly identifiable as men (a concern also present in biblical and Second Temple rhetoric).[13] Along with anatomical features, masculinity was evidenced by physical strength and endurance (see esp. Livy 5.6.4–8).[14] Manly men maintained an erect posture, walked in a determined fashion with a long stride, and carefully controlled their body's movements and physiological responses like sneezing (a clear sign of a failure of masculinity!).[15]

Anatomical and bodily attributes were associated with sexual intercourse and reproduction. Manliness required being the active participant (the penetrator) in intercourse. To be penetrated, by contrast, marked a person as

10. Cf. Dench 1998, 121–23; McDonnell 2006, 167–72.

11. Polemon, *Phys.* 18a, 25a–26a (Hoyland 2007, 377, 393–95); Artemidorus, *Onir.* 1.30, 45; Vander Stichele and Penner 2009, 64–67; Olson 2014, 186–93.

12. Diodorus Siculus 32.10–11; Pliny, *Nat.* 7.36. Garland 2010, 1, notes that when the male body is perceived to be the ideal (as in Aristotle, *Gen. an.* 4.767b), then the female body displays deformity.

13. In the story of a man who amputated his own penis, Valerius Maximus concluded the person could no longer be judged either male or female (7.7.6). See also Herodotus 8.105–6; Diodorus Siculus 32.12; Suetonius, *Nero* 28.1; Polemon, *Phys.* 19a (Hoyland 2007, 379); Connolly 1998, 144; and "Enslaved Men and Genital Modification," below in this chapter. For this concern in biblical and Second Temple sources, see Lev. 21:18–20; Deut. 23:1; Philo, *Spec.* 3.41; Josephus, *Ant.* 4.290–91.

14. See also Valerius Maximus 8.13, ext. 1; Livy 10.28.3–4, 38.17.4–7; Appian, *Hist. rom.* 4.7–8; Adamantius, *Phys.* B44; Wilcox 2006, 79–80.

15. These concerns are particularly emphasized in the physiognomists in the second and third centuries CE, but they are also evident in earlier sources. See Aristotle, *Pol.* 1.1254b; Bryson 143–44; Quintilian, *Inst.* 11.3.159; Polemon, *Phys.* 18a, 41b–42a (Hoyland 2007, 377, 439–41); Adamantius, *Phys.* B16, B40; Anonymous Latinus, *Phys.* 5, 11, 62, 76, 90; Philostratus, *Vit. soph.* 623; Diogenes Laertius 7.5.173; Gleason 1995, 60–61; Corbeill 1997, 121–22; Connolly 1998, 134–35.

un-manly, whether the person was biologically categorized as male or female.[16] Sexual virility, especially as evidenced by begetting many children, demonstrated masculinity for Romans and Jews.[17] Germanicus had nine children. Valerius Maximus similarly idealized Masinissa of Numidia, father of fifty children (the youngest born when Masinissa was in his eighties) as an exemplar of manliness. Even the land he ruled was fertile (8.13, ext. 1). As an extension of procreation, manliness corresponded with the exercise of authority over a household. A manly man was a productive *pater familias* in terms of procreation, household functionality, and the increase of familial wealth.[18]

Second, Tacitus noted Germanicus's age, around thirty, in between the extremes of youthful impetuosity and the declining strength of the elderly.[19] Self-discipline was central to masculinity. A manly man controlled his own emotions and bodily needs.[20] Self-control included avoiding overindulgence in sex.[21] In the Second Temple period, Jewish writers identify bodily and emotional control in the face of serious physical violence as a sign of manliness among male and female martyrs.[22] Boys and young men were generally considered to lack the maturity needed for well-developed, masculine discipline.[23] Elite Roman education consequently prioritized training boys to recognize and perform masculinity.[24] The un-manliness of childhood sometimes returned in old age as someone who had attained masculinity

16. E.g., Seneca, *Ep.* 122.7; Juvenal, *Sat.* 10.304. See also Philo, *Spec.* 3.37–39. Sexual penetration as a core element in Greco-Roman masculinity is explored in Walters 1997, 30–32; C. Williams 1999, 18, and passim; Holmes 2012, 79–98; Burke 2013, 74–75; Hallett 2015b, 410–11.

17. See Onasander 1.12; Philo, *Spec.* 3.39; Josephus, *Ant.* 4.290; Suetonius, *Aug.* 34.1–2; Plutarch, *Pyrrh.* 28.3; Cassius Dio 56.2–4; b. Yebam. 36a; C. Williams 1999, 37–43; Huber 2008, 9–10, 13–15.

18. Cf. Cornelius Nepos, *Att.* 13–14, 17; Seneca, *Ben.* 4.27; *Clem.* 1.14–16; *Ep.* 64.7; Plutarch, *Cat. Maj.* 20.1–2; [*Lib. ed.*] 7e; McDonnell 2006, 178–89. See also Josephus, *Ag. Ap.* 2.201; b. Yebam. 62b.

19. See also Livy 3.12.3–8; Onasander 1.9; Tacitus, *Ann.* 13.6; Cassius Dio 50.17.

20. E.g., Cicero, *Tusc.* 2.47–50, 48; Seneca, *Ep.* 63.1, 13; *Marc.* 13–14; Tacitus, *Agr.* 29; Plutarch, *Cat. Maj.* 1.3–4, 4.1–3; [*Lib. ed.*] 7e–f; *Rect. rat. aud.* 37c–e; Dench 1998, 121–23; Valentine 2017, 150, 158; Hylen 2022, 165, 170. Josephus borrowed this conception of masculinity for his biblical narratives (*Ant.* 3.18–20); see also Satlow 1996, 22, 27; Valentine 2017, 188.

21. Polybius 8.9.1–12, 36.15.4–5; Livy 39.16.1; Tacitus, *Ann.* 14.15; *Hist.* 1.22; Cassius Dio 50.27; P. Brown 1988, 19–24; Harper 2013, 53–60.

22. E.g., 2 Macc. 6:27–28; 4 Macc. 6:16–35; 13:1–12; 16:12–24; Moore and Anderson 1998, 252–58.

23. See Polybius 5.29.2–3; Sallust, *Bell. Cat.* 3.3; Petronius, *Sat.* 57.8; Appian, *Bell. civ.* 2.11.74.

24. Bryson 105–6, 115, 150–51; Quintilian, *Inst.* 1.2.6–8; Seneca, *Ira* 2.21.1–6; Juvenal, *Sat.* 14.70–74; Plutarch, *Cat. Maj.* 20.4–6; [*Lib. ed.*] 5a–c; Cassius Dio 52.26; Diogenes Laertius 2.8.72; Gleason 1995, 70–71, 159; Connolly 1998, 133–37; McDonnell 2006, 181–84.

lost their physical and mental strength, reverting to childish greed, indulgence, and cowardice.[25] Men like Cato and Masinissa were celebrated for their unusual ability to maintain their manly strength and discipline through their long lives.[26]

Third, Germanicus was part of the imperial family. He ascended the social hierarchy, the *cursus honorum*, through various political and military positions. Ancestral heritage, social position, and political authority all contributed to masculine status.[27] Rhetorical skill demonstrated masculine reason, virtue, and control over voice and body.[28] Wealth allowed a man to act as a patron, receiving public recognition for using his resources on behalf of the community as well as the honor and respect expected from personal clients.[29] Tacitus particularly celebrated Germanicus's military prowess. The vocabulary of masculinity overlaps with wartime courage (e.g., ἀνδρεία, ἀνὴρ ἀγαθός, *virtus*).[30] The battlefield provided space for demonstrating masculinity from ancient Israel and Greece to Rome.[31] Manly men displayed physical strength by enduring battle; self-control in withstanding the terrors of fighting; the willingness to die rather than surrender; and a careful mix of courage and audacity, disciplined obedience, and strategy in waging war.[32]

Germanicus's external displays of power in the household, society, political appointments, and the military offered evidence of his moral virtue, a fourth key component of Roman masculinity.[33] Sallust praised the Roman past as a golden age of manly virtues: civic harmony, piety, loyalty, justice, and wartime courage (*Bell. Cat.* 9.1–5).[34] Moral virtue overlapped with the ability to reason. For Polybius, the logical, reasonable actions of the Roman Senate in response to a military threat displayed manliness (ἀνδρωδῶς; 3.118.7–9). Tacitus praised Agricola's virtuous self-control in both political and private

25. So Seneca, *Const.* 12.2; Pliny, *Nat.* 28.56; Tacitus, *Ann.* 1.34–35; *Hist.* 4.24.

26. Cicero, *Sen.* 3–4, 7, and passim; Valerius Maximus 8.13, ext. 1; Plutarch, *Cat. Maj.* 4.3.

27. Polybius 4.8.1–4, 38.12.9; Diodorus Siculus 15.88.3–4; Tacitus, *Ann.* 1.75; Pliny, *Nat.* 7.139–40; Cassius Dio 50.24; *ILS* 1259; Boatwright 2011, 109–11.

28. E.g., Onasander 1.13; Quintilian, *Inst.* 2.20.4–10; Tacitus, *Ann.* 13.2, 15.48; *Dial.* 31; Polemon, *Phys.* 43a–b (Hoyland 2007, 443–45).

29. Cf. Hylen 2022, 164–69.

30. Lendon 2007, 509; Reeder 2019, 32–35.

31. 1 Sam. 4:9; 17:8–10; Homer, *Il.* 8.174, 15.734; Thucydides 5.9.9; Livy 9.40.4–6; Tacitus, *Agr.* 33.4.

32. E.g., Polybius 3.108.5, 10.3.5–7, 11.2.9–11; Sallust, *Bell. Cat.* 7.4–6; Caesar, *Bell. gall.* 3.19.3, 7.80.5; Valerius Maximus 2.7.15e, 3.1.1, 3.2.7; Livy 3.67.11, 4.32.2; McDonnell 2006, 195–204; Reeder 2019, 35–40.

33. Roller 2001, 22–26; McDonnell 2006, 107–10, 293–300, 385–88; Wilcox 2006, 76.

34. See also Sallust, *Bell. Jug.* 3.1; Tacitus, *Ann.* 11.23.

life. He was prudent, just, and moderate in ruling; restrained in his emotions; and modest in his self-presentation.[35]

Vitellius's soldiers "lost their energy [*labor*] and their valour [*virtus*] as they became accustomed to pleasure" (Tacitus, *Hist.* 2.62 [LCL]): The bodily strength, moral discipline, and self-control of a manly man were under constant threat from the lures of vice and comfort.[36] One recognized threat to manly fortitude was overreliance on the labor of enslaved people.[37] Epictetus argued that possessions (including living possessions) enslaved their owner. Consequently, a slave is the only true philosopher, free from the fetters of social relationships, possessions, desires, or emotions (3.22.45–49, 3.22.100–106).[38] Epictetus, formerly enslaved himself, here redefines natal alienation as a philosophical virtue.

It is difficult to escape enslavers like social relationships, possessions, desires, and emotions, but (as discussed in chap. 1) the internalization of freedom and enslavement allowed elite men to claim freedom even as they continued to depend on and benefit from their possession of enslaved people. Various stories also externalize this manly freedom. Military commanders in particular limited the possibility for indulgence in physical comforts. Scipio purged sex laborers (prostitutes), merchants, and comfortable bedding from a military camp, and Vespasian decommissioned an officer who smelled of perfume.[39] Masculinity was a lifelong practice requiring constant vigilance.[40]

Tacitus's Germanicus represents elite Roman masculinity, limited to the privileged few: Roman men from aristocratic households, with the benefits of education, political and social position, and wealth. Elite Romans guarded masculinity from non-elite populations by, for instance, critiquing ostentatious displays of wealth or contrasting the citizenship granted to freed people with the gift of citizenship to free people for deeds of *virtus*.[41] But while

35. Onasander 1.2–8; Tacitus, *Agr.* 8.3, 9.3–5, 29.1–2. See also Sallust, *Bell. Cat.* 53.1, 54.6, on Cato.

36. Dionysius of Halicarnassus, *Ant. rom.* 14.8; Sallust, *Bell. Cat.* 11.5–6; Caesar, *Bell. gall.* 1.1, 2.15; Valerius Maximus 4.2 pref.; 9.1, ext. 1–2; Livy 23.45.2–4; Tacitus, *Ann.* 15.48; *Hist.* 3.2; Olson 2014, 186–87.

37. Bryson 150–51; Seneca, *Tranq.* 8.8; Epictetus, *Diatr.* 3.26.21–26; Dio Chrysostom 10.10.

38. See also Horace, *Sat.* 2.7.46–88.

39. Sallust, *Bell. Cat.* 11.5–6; Valerius Maximus 2.7.1–2; Livy 9.40.4–6; Suetonius, *Vesp.* 8.3; Appian, *Hist. rom.* 6.14.84–85; Phang 2008, 92–96.

40. Holmes 2012, 77–79.

41. For critiques of wealth, see Petronius, *Sat.* 28.1–30.4, 53.1–9; Seneca, *Tranq.* 8.6–7 (cf. Sallust, *Bell. Cat.* 12.1). Distinctions between the citizenship given to freed people and the citizenship granted on the basis of deeds of *virtus* are evident in Dionysius of Halicarnassus, *Ant. rom.* 4.24; Pliny, *Nat.* 35.200–201; Tacitus, *Ann.* 3.40, 13.54 (see also Martial 10.76). Cf. Joly 2024, 180–83.

access was restricted, elite masculinity was also widely promulgated through such mediums as rhetoric, historiography and biography, funerary speeches and gravestones, and monuments and statues.[42] Non-elites and non-Romans mimicked elite Roman conceptions of masculinity. In funerary memorials for non-elite men, for example, the depiction of the deceased man reclining to dine (symbolic of elite status), surrounded by family members and enslaved servers, ascribed masculinity to him, and inscriptions celebrated family lineage, property, and patronage.[43] To counter Roman characterizations of the Jews as dishonorably "effeminate," Josephus associated Jewish masculinity with disciplined obedience to torah and applied elite Roman definitions of masculinity to biblical characters and the rebel fighters of the First Revolt.[44]

Non-elite Romans and non-Romans also developed their own definitions of masculinity beyond elite constructions. The celebration of labor by freed people and other non-elites provides a key arena of alternative masculinity. With the exception of agriculture (a traditional occupation for wealthy Roman men), elite Romans expressed significant disdain for physical labor, material production, and occupations that existed for the purpose of making money.[45] Against elite disdain, freed people and other non-elite populations celebrated labor and professional attainment in funerary memorials.[46] As Dominic Machado points out, the tomb of Eurysaces, a freed person, in Rome is a massive monument not to the manliness of victory in war but to the power of the bakery.[47]

How does 1 Peter fit within this context? The vocabulary of masculinity—including terms like ἀνδρεία, ἀνδρίζομαι, and ἀνδραγαθία—does not appear in 1 Peter. While ἀγαθός is somewhat common, it is not used in the collocation ἀνὴρ ἀγαθός. The one instance of ἀρετή describes God (2:9), and the three uses of ἀνήρ refer to husbands (3:1–7). But beyond vocabulary, the

42. E.g., Polybius 6.53.2–3; Diodorus Siculus 31.15.1; Josephus, *J.W.* 1.200; Tacitus, *Agr.* 1.1; and the reliefs of the Ara Pacis, imperial statues displaying the emperor as a muscled warrior, the imagery of coins, etc. (see, e.g., Ferris 2000, 36–38; McDonnell 2006, 149–52).

43. E.g., *CIL* 6.4012, 11.5400; *SEG* 40.1044; and the reclining diners discussed in Roller 2006, 22–34.

44. E.g., Josephus, *Ag. Ap.* 2.234–35, 272; *Ant.* 3.49, 4.143, 4.153, 6.160, 12.284; *J.W.* 1.271, 3.268, 6.42, 6.80. See Reeder 2015b, 71–76, 83–84.

45. Elite perspectives on labor as un-manly are evident in, e.g., Plato, *Resp.* 2.371c; *Theaet.* 175e; Aristotle, *Pol.* 8.1337b; Cicero, *Off.* 1.151; Horace, *Ep.* 1.16.63–72; Plutarch, *Art.* 11.5; *Per.* 2.1.

46. *AE* 2001.1785; *CIL* 1^2.1210, 9.1721, 11.5400; Petronius, *Sat.* 29.3–6; Epictetus, *Diatr.* 3.26.7, 23–24; and the examples of funerary, domestic, and business art in Clarke 2003, 95–128. See further Borg 2012, 27–29, 34–40; Ramsby 2012, 71–76; MacLean 2018, 16–17 (and 12–15 on the freed subculture alternative to the elite *cursus honorum*); Bond 2022, 164–65.

47. See Machado 2023, 321.

letter's emphasis on avoiding vice and fostering virtue intersects with Roman masculinity. In 4:1–3, the audience is challenged to avoid human passions or lusts (ἐπιθυμία), represented by activities including drunkenness, wild parties, and idolatry—behaviors that exhibit a lack of self-control (ἀσέλγεια). With the exception of idolatry, these are the sorts of vices that elite Romans also identified as dangerous to masculinity.[48] Ἀσέλγεια in particular represents un-manliness and womanish weakness in Polybius 10.26.3–8; Dio Chrysostom 4.104–5; and Lucian, *Merc. cond.* 25. The exhortation to discipline and sobriety (σωφρονέω, νήφω) in 1 Peter 4:7 is, in this context, an exhortation to masculine virtue.[49]

The letter assumes men's authority in the household (1 Pet. 3:1–7). Enslaved people, wives, and the young should accept the authority of those who hold power over them (2:18; 3:1; 5:5). It is notable, however, that 1 Peter focuses attention on enslaved people and wives, the subordinate members of the household, as model imitators of Jesus.[50] Moreover, the power of people with authority in the household or Christian community is tempered in 3:7 and 5:1–3.[51] While a judicious use of authority is not un-masculine, the limitations on power are important to note, especially in light of the exhortations to humility in 5:5–6 (ταπεινόω, ταπεινός, and ταπεινοφροσύνη). Humility (or, better, humiliation) was not a masculine virtue. It was associated with women and enslaved people.[52] The tempering of husbands' and elders' authority and the un-masculine expectation of humility open space to question 1 Peter's construction of masculinity.

Gendered Binaries

In 1 Peter, the exhortation to manly self-control addresses the entire audience: men and women; adults and children; and free, freed, and enslaved people. At the same time, wives are described as "weaker" than their husbands (ἀσθενής in 3:7). If masculinity is the standard for human gender, all people, regardless of their biological sex, are evaluated by its norms. But not all people can attain elite Roman masculinity. Non- or less-masculine categories, including women,

48. See, e.g., Xenophon, *Oec.* 1.22; Aristotle, *Eth. eud.* 3.1231a; Diodorus Siculus 16.87.1–2; Plutarch, *Ant.* 9.3; *Oth.* 9.4; Appian, *Bell. civ.* 1.113.

49. Cf., e.g., σωφρονέω in Aristotle, *Pol.* 7.1334a (and νήφω in 5.1314b); Plutarch, *Cat. Maj.* 16.5; *Virt. mor.* 449b.

50. Cf. Krentz 1998, 279, 282; Bauman-Martin 2004b, 265, 271–72.

51. Cf. El Mansy 2013, 167–69. It is unclear if the elders in 1 Pet. 5:1–3 include women. On the definition of κατακυριεύω, see chap. 4, below.

52. See Isocrates, *Paneg.* 152; Diodorus Siculus 5.29.3; Plutarch, *Cat. Min.* 32.1; [*Lib. ed.*] 1b–c; Epictetus, *Diatr.* 2.16.18, 3.24.54–58; and chap. 3, below.

children, non-Romans, and enslaved people, were constructed as un-masculine in order to develop the definitions of masculinity (a process that can be seen as part of the racializing dehumanization of marginalized populations in Roman society).[53] These constructions in turn were incorporated into critiques of political or military enemies in order to discredit them.[54] The contrasts between manly men and these "un-manly" populations emphasized power and authority over self and others as the central concerns of masculinity.

Elite women were exhorted to and honored for masculine virtues, including self-control over desires and emotions, wartime courage, and familial loyalty.[55] But as in 1 Peter 3:1–7, men generally held positions of authority in the household and society around the ancient Mediterranean world, and women were subject to male rule.[56] The definition of wives as "weaker vessels" (ὡς ἀσθενεστέρῳ σκεύει) in 1 Peter 3:7 reflects their legal and social disempowerment. Elite men constructed women as deficient in the necessary bodily strength and mental discipline to control their desires for luxury, their emotions, and their morality.[57] Defining masculinity around the degree of power a person has over their own legal identity, rights, and the lives of other people limited how "masculine" even an elite Roman woman could be.

Consequently, the categories of male and female became useful representations of power: "If they were men (ἀνήρ) [and started a war], they would not lack allies; but if they were womanish (ἀνδρόγυνος), they would not lack lords [to rule over them]" (Polybius 38.12.9). The indulgences of rich food, fine clothing, and luxurious furnishings made a man "womanishly" soft (Caesar, *Bell. gall.* 1.1; Livy 23.18). Weeping and rejoicing alike turned manly men into women (Livy 3.68.8, 25.37.10).[58] Women's vices, especially unrestrained

53. Cf. Joshel and Murnaghan 1998, 3, 11–14; Parker 1998, 170; Burke 2013, 68–69; A. Smith 2023, 176.

54. E.g., Polybius 12.24.5; Cicero, *Pis.* 25; Livy 38.17.4–7; Tacitus, *Ann.* 6.46, 14.15–16; Dench 1998, 122–23.

55. Bryson 91; Valerius Maximus 3.2.2, 4.3.3, 5.4.6; Seneca, *Marc.* 1.1; Tacitus, *Ann.* 15.63; *Hist.* 1.3; McInerney 2003, 320–35; McDonnell 2006, 161–65; Wilcox 2006, 73–74; and chap. 5, below.

56. This structure is reflected across Greco-Roman and Jewish antiquity: Aristotle, *Pol.* 1259a37, 1260a9; Livy 34.2.1–2; Philo, *Decal.* 165–67; Plutarch, *Conj. praec.* 6, 11, 18, 22, 33, and passim. Women did, of course, have their own power in households (with advantageous family connections, essential contributions to household life, and the responsibility of raising and educating children), and society (for elite women, from their use of personal wealth on behalf of the community and their participation in civic and cultic organizations; and for non-elite women, from their businesses and labor).

57. So Bryson 92; Valerius Maximus 9.1.3, 9.12.2; Livy 3.48.8, 34.2.13, 34.7.7; Josephus, *Ant.* 3.5; Tacitus, *Ann.* 3.33. On 1 Pet. 3:7, see Reese 2022, 184–85; Williams and Horrell 2023b, 64–65.

58. The gendering of emotion varied significantly through antiquity. Homer's heroes could enact extreme emotion without threatening their masculinity, but in imperial Rome the centrality

sexuality and the usurpation of (men's) power, threatened men's ability to enact manliness (Tacitus, *Hist.* 1.22, 1.48; *Ann.* 2.55). In historiography and rhetoric, women and "womanishness" are used to construct masculinity, critique "un-masculine" men, and preserve elite male privilege.

The identification of the audience of 1 Peter as children and infants (τέκνον in 1:14; ἀρτιγέννητον βρέφος in 2:2) fits within the letter's theme of new identity for the people of God. Like children, they are learning and developing a new pattern by imitating God as father.[59] The metaphor is used positively in 1 Peter, but in general to be like a child was to be un-masculine. Children were incomplete adults in Roman understanding, defective in their inability to reason or control their emotions.[60] Childishness (like womanishness) indicated a lack of self-control (Polybius 11.14.7). Children's inexperience and cowardice provided a descriptor for soldiers easily tricked or frightened by an enemy's stratagems, or unprepared for the physical labor and violence of war.[61] Childishness equated to foolish thoughtlessness, which was inappropriate for mature masculinity.[62]

The common collocation "women and children" aligns these populations over and against men. Women and freeborn children in a household had some authority, including over the enslaved people they owned. However, husbands and fathers held the ultimate authority over the (free) women and children of their households, and they had the manly responsibility of protecting their women and children from enemies. Masculine reason and discipline contrasted with the (constructed) illogical, inexperienced, fearful, emotional weakness of women and children.[63] In terms of social structure, legal regulations, and rhetorical constructions, women and children provided a useful distinction to masculinity in the Roman world (and beyond).

The primary contrasts between masculinity and femininity and masculinity and childishness bleed over into two additional contrasts: Roman manliness versus "barbarian" (un)manliness, and elite masculinity versus enslavement. Since masculinity was core to Roman self-understanding, Roman authors define non-Roman peoples as lacking in masculinity.[64] There were exceptions

of self-control defined public displays of emotion as "womanish." See van Wees 1998, 11–18; Wilcox 2006, 74–75; Lateiner 2009, 105–8.

59. Cf. the education of children by example in Quintilian, *Inst.* 1.2.8; Juvenal, *Sat.* 14.1–74; Plutarch, *Cat. Maj.* 20.5; and husbands educating much younger wives by their example in Plutarch, *Conj. praec.* 47.

60. Diodorus Siculus 36.2a; Philo, *Leg.* 3.210; Seneca, *Const.* 12.2; *Helv.* 5.5; Plutarch, *Dion* 55.4; Bakke 2005, 16–19.

61. Homer, *Il.* 2.337–38; Polybius 5.29.2–3, 5.75.1–5, 16.2.6; Livy 7.17.3–5; Josephus, *J.W.* 2.346. See also Seneca, *Ep.* 24.18.

62. Polybius 4.17.1–3, 12.3.2; Pliny, *Nat.* 37.41.

63. So Homer, *Il.* 7.235–36; Caesar, *Bell. gall.* 7.17; Seneca, *Ira* 20.3.

64. Cf. McDonnell 2006, 3; Lendon 2007, 509.

to the general rule. The Spartans (men and women) were exemplars of manliness throughout antiquity, as were Caesar's Gallic tribes—especially those farther from the corrupting influences of civilized luxury.[65] In other cases, non-Romans were defined with the stereotypical characteristics of un-masculine womanishness and childishness (e.g., Livy 38.17; Appian, *Hist. rom.* 4.7–8).[66] Roman authors repeatedly derided peoples from the eastern Mediterranean as "effeminate" in their easy, luxurious lifestyles.[67]

Appian associated the "effeminacy" and cowardice of non-Roman peoples with their defeat and subjugation by Rome (*Hist. rom.*, pref. 32–33). Tacitus claimed that the conquest and subsequent colonization of the British tribes pacified them into slavery (*Agr.* 21). Josephus made a similar assessment of the Jews when he claimed that Pompey's victory represented their national enslavement (*J.W.* 2.356, 6.42). So for Cicero, the Jews and Syrians were peoples "born to be slaves" (*nationibus natis servituti*; *Prov. cons.* 5.10)—that is, born to be ruled by Rome. In these examples, "barbarian" identity overlaps with enslavement to emphasize the un-masculine character of the peoples in focus.

The most consistent, fundamental attribute of masculinity was the exercise of authority over one's own person and over other people. Enslavement was defined by the absence of control over self or others. Enslaved people were the property of their enslavers, who included men, women, and children. To be under the power of people who had limited power themselves, who might be (by reasons of gender and age) less powerful than their slaves if their slaves were free, increases the powerlessness of enslaved adults. They were constructed as "bodies" to carry out these enslavers' desires. As a consequence of their lack of external control, enslaved people were defined as "womanish" and "childish" in their (attributed) lack of internal discipline. Enslaved people enabled elite Roman masculinity by embodying its opposite. Slavery was un-masculinity.

Slavery as Un-Masculinity

The representation of enslaved people in 1 Peter 2:18–25 centers on submission, fear, and especially suffering. The enslaved person is an object of violence, whether it is (by the logic of slavery) "deserved" or not. Jesus, the model provided

65. Caesar, *Bell. gall.* 2.15, 4.1–2; Valerius Maximus 3.2, ext. 3; Josephus, *Ag. Ap.* 2.130–31; Plutarch, *Mor.* 238b–c, 240e–f.

66. Further emphasizing the failure of masculinity among "barbarian" men, the women enact manly leadership, courage, and (wartime) violence in, e.g., Polybius 5.78.1–2, 15.30.9–10; Livy 38.23.8–9; Tacitus, *Agr.* 16, 38; *Germ.* 7–8, 18; Reeder 2019, 56–57.

67. Valerius Maximus 2.6.1; 9.1, ext. 6–7; Livy 10.28.3–4, 38.17.17–18; Appian, *Hist. rom.*, pref. 9; Hall 1993, 111–26.

for enslaved people, accepts similar violence without complaint or retribution. The enslaved people are compared with wandering sheep, in need of the guidance of a shepherd. These factors denote the un-manliness of enslavement.

"Is an enslaved person human?" ("Ita servus homo est?") This question surfaces in Juvenal's frankly brutal satire concerning (free) women's relentlessly immoral attitudes and actions (*Sat.* 6.222).[68] In this particular scene, the question is asked by a woman enslaver who has decided to crucify an enslaved person. Her husband provides a voice of reason: There must be a solid case, with evidence, to justify execution. In response, the wife's question denies the status or rights of a human being to the slave. Juvenal's rhetoric represents the wife's question as ridiculous. Comparably, Seneca reminds his elite audience that enslaved people breathe the same air, feel the same sunlight, and live and die just as their enslavers do (*Ep.* 47.1, 10). Juvenal's audience should identify with the husband's reasonable, thoughtful, manly justice. The wife's question nonetheless resonates with the embodied experience of enslavement in the ancient Mediterranean. As I argued in chapter 1, the identification of enslaved people as human property often emphasized the property element over the humanity in order to enable enslavers' control. The un-gendering of enslaved people is one element in their dehumanization.[69]

The dehumanization (or racialization) of enslaved people is most clear in the consistent comparison with animals. In Artemidorus's *Onirocritica*, dreaming of being or becoming an animal—a horse, donkey, dog, ox—means the dreamer will be enslaved (1.20, 1.37, 2.11, 3.18). Obstinate livestock and lazy slaves are irritants in a (wealthy) man's life (Seneca, *Ira* 3.34.1). Enslaved people took over the animal imagery for their own purposes.[70] In Phaedrus's *Fables*, a donkey voicing the perspective of an enslaved person challenges the enslaver's privilege (1.15). The donkey imagery also appears in a graffito from the Paedagogium, possibly a school for enslaved people in the imperial government. The image of a donkey harnessed to a millstone is captioned, "Work, little ass, as I have worked, and it will advance you."[71] Here, the (enslaved) graffiti artist rewrites the dehumanizing comparison made by enslavers to create a community among the oppressed, with proverbial wisdom pointing toward potential advantages for each (the donkey and human laborer).[72]

68. The satire allies "women" and "slaves" as a contrast to reasonable, disciplined masculinity. See further Joshel and Murnaghan 1998, 3–6.

69. Cf. Cobb 2025, 121.

70. Bradley 2000, 120; Joshel and Petersen 2014, 143–46.

71. Translation from Joshel and Petersen 2014, 143.

72. This interpretation is indebted to the concept of kinship between humans and animals in Berkowitz 2023, 636–39. Joshel and Petersen 2014, 143–44, alternatively suggest the graffito

From the enslavers' perspective, comparison with animals reduces the enslaved person to their labor and its value to the enslaver.[73] In addition to commodification, the animalization of enslaved people by enslavers facilitated brutality. Enslaved people were chained to their work like oxen on agricultural estates or like dogs in urban doorways.[74] They were abused like animals, as the horrifying analogy between the enslaved people and donkeys in a grain mill in Apuleius, *Metam.* 9.11–15, illustrates.[75]

Free people were also compared with animals, often with gendered characteristics. Manly men are variously strong like lions, authoritative like bulls, and free like eagles, for instance.[76] Enslaved people, however, are fearful mice (Artemidorus, *Onir.* 3.28).[77] Xenophon recommends training enslaved people for their work as animals are trained, with close attention from the trainer (the enslaver) and rewards of food and praise (*Oec.* 12.18–20, 13.6–9).[78] The implied denial of human intelligence to enslaved people in Xenophon is explicit in Bryson's comparison of enslaved people with livestock; both livestock and slaves need a reasonable, disciplined "master" to control and manage them (57). Plutarch contrasts honorable, fierce men with slavish, passive sheep (*Sept. sap. conv.* 147d). Sheep represent weakness, an absence of discipline, and mindless stupidity.[79] Note that the sheep of 1 Peter 2:25 need a shepherd to control their impulse to wander. These specific comparisons deny enslaved people the masculine attributes of courage, self-control, and reason (cf. Cicero, *Off.* 1.50). The dehumanizing animalization of enslaved people is also an un-gendering.

The spectrum of masculinity in Roman understanding is a spectrum of freedom: freedom over one's self (legally and morally) and freedom in society (to command, form relationships, control property, etc.). Valerius Maximus explicitly juxtaposed *virtus* with captivity, pointing to the manliness (*virtus*)

---

is ironic; a donkey tied to a millstone only advances in circles, and enslaved laborers likewise see no advantage to their work.

73. Cf. Aristotle, *Pol.* 1.1252b, 1254b; Cato, *Agr.* 2.7, 10.

74. Cato, *Agr.* 56; Columella, *Rust.* 9.1.4; Pliny, *Nat.* 18.21.

75. Bradley 2000, 112–16.

76. Dio Chrysostom 2.69–71; Artemidorus, *Onir.* 4.56; Polemon, *Phys.* 26a (Hoyland 2007, 395).

77. Robertson 2008, 91–92, notes the use of animal-based names to distinguish free citizens from enslaved people in classical Athens: Free citizens' names came from lions and horses (associated with wealth and privilege), while enslaved people's names came from oxen (used for labor), monkeys (signifying an un-manly appearance), and mice and mosquitoes (unwanted pests).

78. Cf. Plutarch, *Cat. Maj.* 21.1.

79. Epictetus, *Diatr.* 2.9.4–5, 2.10.3, 3.23.4–5; Dio Chrysostom 49.2; Plutarch, *Mor.* 992d; Apuleius, *Metam.* 8.16; Polemon, *Phys.* 5a (Hoyland 2007, 341–43).

of a military commander who took his own life upon capture to avoid enslavement (3.2.7, 3.2.12). By contrast, the soldiers who surrendered to enslaved people during a slave revolt were thereby emasculated. Valerius Maximus interpreted their punishment as a way to make them "pray like men for the death they had feared like women" (2.7.9 [LCL]).[80] If freedom belongs to masculinity, enslaved people lack both.

The un-gendering of enslavement was expressed in a variety of ways. One of the most basic is the categorization of adult men who were enslaved as "boys" (e.g., παῖς or *puer*) rather than "men" (ἀνήρ or *vir*).[81] Second, as already noted, elite Roman men constructed enslaved people as irrational and incapable of self-discipline. Like free children and women, enslaved people are characterized by emotional outbursts, immoral behaviors, and cowardice.[82] Third, these factors contributed to the representation of enslaved people in visual and literary imagery. In paintings and sculpture, enslaved people are childishly small in comparison with free adults. The artistic convention focused attention on the free people, but notably, the small stature of the slaves was interpreted by the second- and third-century physiognomists as feminine.[83]

The implication of feminization in art is explicit in literary depictions of enslaved men as servers at dinner parties. In such scenes, the men are dressed, shaved, and made up as women.[84] The visible feminization makes enslaved men and boys into wonders or prodigies, the opposite of the marvel of a woman growing a penis (see Diodorus Siculus 32.10–12). The un-gendering evident here is also present in depictions of enslaved people's postures: crouching, hunching, and bending over. Even if their posture was necessitated by or resulted from strenuous labor, it was interpreted as un-masculine weakness.[85]

80. See also Plato, *Resp.* 4.431c–d; Philo, *Spec.* 4.14–16; Florus, *Epit.* 2.7.19; Diogenes Laertius 1.10.113.

81. Walters 1997, 31; Glancy 2006, 24–25; C. Martin 2005, 228; McDonnell 2006, 159.

82. E.g., Horace, *Sat.* 1.3.80–83; Columella, *Rust.* 1.8.1–2; Quintilian, *Inst.* 1.2.5; Livy 26.2.11; Seneca, *Tranq.* 8.8; Pliny, *Nat.* 33.26–27, 34.79; Plutarch, [*Lib. ed.*] 5b and 5d; *Quaest. conv.* 678e–f; Pliny, *Ep.* 3.14; Demand 1998, 70–72; Parker 1998, 154–56; Valentine 2017, 170–73.

83. For examples of visual images depicting enslaved people, see, e.g., the frescoes of Pompeii: the House of the Chaste Lovers, the House of the Triclinium, and the House of Sutoria Primogenia. See also Polemon, *Phys.* 25b (Hoyland 2007, 395); Adamantius, *Phys.* B2; Bain 2014, 141–42; Joshel and Petersen 2014, 45–46.

84. Petronius, *Sat.* 126.1–2; Seneca, *Ep.* 47.7; Corbeill 1997, 118–21; Olson 2014, 187–93; chap. 4, below.

85. Plautus, *Cas.* 124–25, associates stooping with the effects of labor (and see F. Green 2025, 46–47, on the bent posture required by the low furnishings in kitchens in Pompeii). Hunched posture is associated with slavery in Horace, *Ep.* 1.16.63–64; *Sat.* 2.7.60–61; Seneca, *Ep.* 47.5, 65.16, 21; Plutarch, *Alc.* 4.3; Lucian, *Somn.* 13. Slouching and hunching over are identified as signs of womanishness, cowardice, and immorality in Polemon, *Phys.* 18a, 42a (Hoyland 2007, 377, 441); Adamantius, *Phys.* B16, B40; Anonymous Latinus, *Phys.* 55, 62; Connolly 1998, 134.

Additional examples of the embodied un-masculinity of enslavement come in the fad for purchasing, displaying, and mocking imperfect bodies in the Roman Empire.[86] As in Tacitus's verbal portrait of Germanicus, the ideal male body was strong, upright, whole, and beautiful. The association of enslaved people with bent posture and bodily imperfections un-manned them.

Fourth, the normative social and relational experiences of biological sex and age did not entirely apply to enslaved people (as was also often the case for free people who were impoverished). All enslaved people—men, women, and children—performed the same sorts of labor (with a few notable exceptions, such as nursing infants).[87] Enslaved people who had children were not given the legal authority to parent them.[88] All enslaved people, including adult men, faced physical violence. The relative sameness of social, relational, and bodily experiences across enslavement removes the significance of biological sex, procreation, and bodily integrity as core elements in definitions of gender.

A fifth signifier of the un-gendering of enslavement was the violation of bodily integrity. Given the significance of protecting the body from violation and avenging violation for elite masculinity, bodily violation was particularly problematic for adult men who were enslaved. Three specific concerns demonstrate the un-masculinity of bodily violation: first, enslaved men as objects of violence; second, enslaved men as objects of sexual penetration; and third, the genital modification of enslaved men.

Enslaved Men as Objects of Violence

Philo contrasted athletes with enslaved people with respect to physical violence. Athletes were beaten in training or competitions, but their engagement in violence was active and persistent. According to Philo, the athlete thus symbolized a man whose power of reason controlled his bodily responses to violence and pain. The athlete is comparable to Spartan men, famous in legend for the ways they beat their own bodies to train themselves to endure pain (Plutarch, *Mor.* 238d). An elite man who controlled his bodily and emotive responses to physical violence thereby demonstrated his masculinity.[89] Philo did not ascribe manly endurance to the enslaved person who

86. Bodily imperfections included unusually small or large height, spinal curvature, missing or abnormal arms or legs, and mental differences. See Petronius, *Sat.* 28.4; Quintilian, *Inst.* 2.5.11–12; Pliny, *Nat.* 7.75, 34.11–12; Martial 6.39.15–17, 7.38, 12.93; Tacitus, *Ann.* 15.34; Plutarch, *Curios.* 520c–d; Garland 2010, 32–35, 45–49.

87. So also Hezser 2005, 84; Bain 2014, 139, 151–55. Cobb 2025, 121–23, notes the distinctive occupations of enslaved men and women as well as the similarities.

88. Cf. Shaner 2025, 172.

89. Cicero, *Tusc.* 2.52; Quintilian, *Inst.* 11.1.40; Epictetus, *Diatr.* 2.2.13, 4.1.127.

could, in his perspective, only submit to being beaten. He compared the enslaved person to a sheepskin, which—as an inanimate object—is passively trimmed (in contrast to a living person who somehow actively participates in a haircut).[90] The enslaved person for Philo represented a person without the "free" and "powerful" ability to utilize reason in order to withstand suffering (*Leg.* 3.201–2).

Philo's analogy is revealing. The enslaved person is dehumanized (even de-animated) in the comparison with a sheepskin. Their (imagined) passivity separates them from the manly endurance of the athlete. More specifically, masculinity required an active response to verbal insult or physical attack. As in the quotation from Publilius Syrus at the beginning of this chapter, the ability to protect one's own body from abuse and avenge injury were fundamental privileges and responsibilities of freeborn masculinity.[91] Enslaved people faced casual and punitive violence as a fact of life. To be beaten with a lash was to be treated as a slave; enslavers constructed enslaved bodies as legitimate objects of violence.[92]

The ascription of manliness to elite men who endured violence with equanimity facilitates the same ascription to enslaved people.[93] Perhaps this possibility is the reason Philo presented the enslaved person as a passive sheepskin, removing any opportunity for slaves to actively endure pain or control their bodily and emotional reactions to abuse. Philo's enslaved person is un-manly by virtue of their passive experience of violence and their fundamental inability to protect or avenge dishonor and abuse (see also Plato, *Gorg.* 483a–b)—that is, with respect to the experience of violence, the enslaved person is un-manly because they are enslaved, not free.

The violence experienced by enslaved people left bodily reminders: broken bones; welts and bruises from whips, canes, and fists; scars left by beatings,

90. The Greek word Philo uses here is κῴδιον, which refers to a sheepskin used as bedding, clothing, or for other purposes. Note that the LCL translation expands the term to represent a sheep, but the word does not seem to be used in this way elsewhere.

91. Publilius Syrus, *Sent.* 114. See also Aristotle, *Eth. eud.* 3.1231b; Plautus, *Bacch.* 438–43; Diodorus Siculus 14.65.4; Seneca, *Clem.* 1.7.3; Plutarch, *Alc.* 8.1–2; Walters 1997, 30, 37–39; Burke 2013, 69; Perry 2015, 64–65.

92. So Demosthenes 21.180; Plautus, *Asin.* 627–28; *Merc.* 414–16; Cicero, *Verr.* 2.139–40; Valerius Maximus 1.7.4, 6.1.9; Martial 7.86.11. Examples of the everyday violence faced by enslaved people can be found in, e.g., Plautus, *Asin.* 627–28; *Merc.* 414–16; Phaedrus, *Fables*, Perotti's Appendix 12.1–4, 17.9–16; Valerius Maximus 1.7.4, 6.1.9; Pliny, *Nat.* 5.77; Martial 3.94, 7.86.11; Plutarch, *Cat. Maj.* 21.3; Artemidorus, *Onir.* 1.70, 76; Saller 1998, 90; Glancy 2006, 12–14; Lenski 2016, 275–80 (noting that physical actions directed against enslaved people would not be classified as violence by enslavers); J. Williams 2024, 76–77 (on the intersections of punishment with hierarchies of status).

93. Cf. Moss 2024, 31.

chains, and manacles.[94] Scars were not necessarily un-masculine; soldiers' manly courage was made visible by the scars on their chests.[95] But these scars were manly by virtue of the context of war and soldiers' courage, endurance, and victory. The unavoidable reality of experiencing beatings denied a similar manliness to enslaved people.[96] Plutarch, for instance, contrasted (manly) freedom with the scars and welts left by a whip on an enslaved person's body (*Mor.* 1091e).[97] An elite man viewing an enslaved person's body saw un-masculinity in the evidence of physical violence.

Enslaved Men and Sexual Penetration

"Unchastity (*impudicitia*) is a crime for the freeborn, a forced necessity for slaves, and a duty for freed people" (Seneca the Elder, *Controv.* 4, pref. 10). While Seneca scorned the "duty" of sexual intercourse as a standing joke, the fundamental differentiation of freeborn people and enslaved people in terms of their access to sexual morality is quite serious. The privilege of sexual morality belonged to the freeborn. Because enslaved people were property, their bodies (male and female, adult and child) were available to their (primarily male[98]) enslavers to use for their own pleasure, or to be forced into sex labor (prostitution) for their enslavers' financial gain.[99]

By contemporary standards, what happened to enslaved people can be categorized as rape and sexual assault. Conceptions of rape in the ancient Mediterranean do not map precisely onto modern definitions. In particular, the contemporary emphasis on consent is not part of legal or moral definitions

94. E.g., Aristophanes, *Pax* 743–47; Columella, *Rust.* 1, pref. 10, 9.14; Valerius Maximus 6.8.7; Seneca, *Ira* 3.32.1; Pliny, *Nat.* 18.21; Martial 3.94; Juvenal, *Sat.* 7.15, 14.15–22; Lucian, *Prometh.* 10; Artemidorus, *Onir.* 1.70, 1.76, 2.25; Lenski 2016, 283.

95. Valerius Maximus 3.2.24, 7.7.1; Josephus, *J.W.* 1.193, 197.

96. Walters 1997, 40.

97. Cf. also the contrast of a soldier's wartime scars (on the chest) and the scars of debt slavery (on the back) in Livy 2.23.4, 7. In Plutarch, *Ages.* 30.3, cowardly soldiers are punished by legal restrictions on the activities of masculinity (marriage, public office); poor clothing; a half-shaved beard; and public beatings.

98. Male enslavers' use of enslaved people for sex is widely attested: Horace, *Sat.* 1.2.116–19; Suetonius, *Tib.* 42–44; Josephus, *J.W.* 7.382, 385; Dio Chrysostom 4.102; Artemidorus, *Onir.* 1.78; P.Oxy. 42.3070; C. Williams 1999, 30–32; Marchal 2011, 751–58; Perry 2015, 56–57; and on Jewish sources, Labovitz 2010, 98. There are a few references to women enslavers using enslaved men for sex (e.g., Petronius, *Sat.* 126.5–6, 10; Pliny, *Nat.* 34.11–12; Martial 6.39; *Life of Aesop* 32).

99. See Flemming 1999, 40–56; Glancy 2006, 21–24, 50–57; Hezser 2005, 179–83; Baird 2015, 163–64, 169–70; Valentine 2017, 23–37; Levin-Richardson 2021, 189–202. On the specific issue of the use of enslaved children for sex, see esp. McKeown 2007, 58–61; Richlin 2015, 352–53, and passim. Cobb 2025, 131, uses "sex labor" to indicate the non-voluntary nature of enslaved sex work.

of assault in the first century. Among other terms, ὕβρις and βία in Greek and *stuprum* and *contumelium* in Latin can represent sexual violation.[100] The identification of a sex act as a violation (rather than as seduction or adultery) depends on the evidence of violence and, significantly, the bodily inviolability of the individual (in Latin, *pudicitia*), as well as the rights of the person who has authority over an individual (a father or husband, for instance).[101] Inviolability was a privilege limited to the freeborn.[102] Enslaved people lacked bodily inviolability, and thus they lacked the ability to consent to or refuse sex demanded by their enslavers.[103] Consequently, under Roman law and cultural assumptions, an enslaved person could not be raped. Or perhaps it is more accurate to say that an enslaved person was not rape-able. Only if their bodies were being used beyond their enslavers' desires would what happened to them be counted as assault, but the victim in such a case was the enslaver, not the enslaved.[104] Sex in antiquity, as J. A. Baird argues, is a way to maintain social hierarchies.[105]

Several stories illustrate the association of sexual chastity with freeborn status. First, a freeborn girl named Verginia was claimed as a slave by a man who wanted to have sex with her. Rather than allow her to be enslaved (and her body to be used for sex), her father killed her to protect her freeborn chastity (Livy 3.48.4–5). Second, Plutarch encouraged a new bride to accept her husband's use of enslaved people's bodies for sex. The husband shows respect for his wife's chastity by indulging his own desires in this way (*Conj. praec.* 16). No such respect is given to the enslaved people in the scenario. Third, Valerius Maximus's examples of chastity include the story of a young freeborn man who was forced into debt slavery. He was beaten "like a slave" by his enslaver when he refused the enslaver's sexual advances. The Senate imprisoned the enslaver as punishment for threatening the chastity of a freeborn Roman (6.1.9 [LCL]). By implication, if the young man had been enslaved from birth or because he had been taken captive, his enslaver would have had the right to use (and abuse) his body.[106]

100. See Reeder 2017, 366, on the vocabulary of sexual violence in antiquity.

101. Rabinowitz 2011, 7 (noting that no women had the power of consent in antiquity, as the rights to their bodies were held by the male authorities over them); Robson 2013, 102–5; E. Harris 2015, 298–304 (finding more evidence for women's consent in antiquity than is often assumed); Reeder 2017, 365–67.

102. See C. Williams 1999, 96–99; Robson 2015, 316–17; Yamada 2008, 39–41.

103. See, e.g., Xenophon, *Oec.* 10.12; Seneca the Elder, *Controv.* 1.2.1–12; Livy 39.9.5; Valerius Maximus 6.1.6; Walters 1997, 36–37; Burke 2013, 78–80; Reeder 2017, 367–68; Perry 2021, 255–56; A. Strong 2021, 174–79.

104. Perry 2015, 56–70; 2021, 257–58.

105. Baird 2015, 169–70. See also Walters 1997, 39–40; Briggs 2003, 181.

106. Cf. Walters 1997, 33–35; Joshel and Murnaghan 1998, 18; Burke 2013, 113.

The "necessity" of sex for enslaved people had gendered implications.[107] As noted above, the signifiers of masculinity included acting as the penetrator in sex. For an enslaved man to be penetrated by an enslaver consequently signified un-masculinity. Seneca vividly portrayed this connection by picturing a mature male slave dressed in women's clothing, with his face kept as hairless and smooth as a young boy's, used for his enslaver's sexual pleasure (*Ep.* 47.7).[108] The message is also evident in the careful distinctions drawn between freeborn and enslaved boys. Plutarch explained that freeborn Roman boys wore a *bulla* (a large pendant necklace) as either a reminder of militarized masculinity, or to mark off their bodies as impenetrable (*Quaest. rom.* 287f–288b). For a free adult man to use a freeborn boy's body or a young man's body for sex was punishable by imprisonment (Valerius Maximus 6.1.7, 10–11); for a free adult man to use an enslaved boy's body or an enslaved man's body for sex was standard practice.[109]

The ability to use the bodies of others, so long as the people in question were not under the ownership or protection of another freeborn man, was a privilege of freeborn masculinity. Enslaved men did not have this privilege. The right to enter into a familial relationship or even simply to engage in voluntary sexual intercourse was ultimately controlled by the enslaver.[110] The distinction between freeborn and enslaved men's ability to exercise sexual desire is clear in Valerius Maximus's stories of enslavers executing enslaved men for having sex with (or, in one case, kissing) the freeborn daughters of the enslavers (6.1.3–4).

These stories also demonstrate the masculine responsibility of guarding the sexual chastity of wives and children. Enslaved men were not able to protect their own bodies from penetration, nor could they protect or police the bodies of their partners or children (who were not legally recognized as their partners or children in any case). The absence of this privilege for enslaved men is most obvious in stories of freed men claiming it for themselves. One formerly enslaved man who had been forced to work as a sex laborer in his youth later executed his (freeborn) daughter for sexual immorality (Valerius Maximus 6.1.6). A very different story in Petronius, *Sat.* 57.6, depicts a formerly enslaved

107. This discussion centers masculinity. The issue of sexual morality and enslaved women is addressed in chap. 5, below.

108. See also Martial 4.42.14, 10.98; Anonymous Latinus, *Phys.* 115.

109. E.g., Cicero, *Phil.* 2.45; Petronius, *Sat.* 74.8, 75.11; Martial 1.58, 4.42, 6.39.12–14, 9.59.1–6; Apuleius, *Metam.* 8.26; Burke 2013, 80–84; Harper 2013, 25–29; Richlin 2015, 355–58; A. Strong 2021, 180–84.

110. See, e.g., Xenophon, *Oec.* 9.5; *BGU* 4.1058 (limiting a wet nurse's sexual availability); Varro, *Rust.* 1.17.5; Plutarch, *Cat. Maj.* 21.2; Perry 2021, 259–61; Porter 2021, 90–97 (on classical Greece).

man purchasing and freeing his enslaved partner to protect her from other men. This story recognizes both the necessity of sex for enslaved people, even for those in a committed partnership (*contubernium*), and the privilege of free masculinity to protect women and children from assault. In both stories, the formerly enslaved men can act as they do because they are free; if they had still been enslaved, they would not have been able to protect (or avenge) themselves, their wives, or their children from violation.

In a series of interpretations of dreams concerning enslavers, enslaved people, and sex in Artemidorus, *Onir*. 1.78, the image of male enslavers using enslaved people for sex signifies the enslaver's enjoyment of his possession. For the enslaver to dream of being penetrated by an enslaved man, however, signifies disaster for the enslaver. Likewise, for an enslaved man to dream of his enslaver caressing his penis means the enslaved person will be beaten. The shifting interpretations reflect the gendering of the actors in the scenes. Elite masculinity corresponded with the privilege of protecting one's own body from transgression, protecting the bodies of people under one's authority, and making use of others' bodies for one's own pleasure. The un-gendering of enslaved people, male and female, denied them these privileges. In particular, enslaved men could not use others' bodies without restriction, nor protect their own bodies or the bodies of their partners or children from penetration. For enslaved men, these factors signified their lack of masculinity.

Enslaved Men and Genital Modification

The most obvious, visible consequences of the un-gendering of enslaved men were castration and cross-dressing. Seneca identified dressing in women's clothing or attempting to look like a young boy as unnatural for a free, adult man—as unnatural as a free, adult man allowing himself to be penetrated by another man (*Ep*. 122.7–8). However, what was considered unnatural for free men was not uncommonly forced upon enslaved men.

As the stories of assault on freeborn boys and the consistent accounts of enslaved boys and young men being used for sex by their male enslavers indicate, boys and young men were objects of sexual attraction for adult men. Slave traders capitalized on this attraction with depilation and drugs to delay puberty (Pliny, *Nat*. 21.170, 32.135) and by castration.[111] Castration resulted in different anatomical (and sexual) outcomes for the victim depending on whether the operation occurred before or after puberty. The operations were not medically necessary, of course, but instead reflected the desirability to

111. Note that the forced castration of enslaved boys and men was reportedly prohibited by Domitian (Suetonius, *Dom*. 7.2).

potential enslavers of either childish enslaved men with undeveloped genitals and secondary sexual attributes or infertile enslaved men with well-developed genitals.[112]

Martial pictured an enslaved boy mourning his lost masculinity (*virilitas*) following his castration (9.5). No matter when the surgery occurred, castration was the ultimate un-gendering for a man.[113] It marked the complete absence of bodily autonomy for the enslaved person, as the surgery was the decision of the slave trader or enslaver. It embodied the commodification of the enslaved person, as castration increased his economic value for the slave trader and sexual value for potential enslavers. And it removed a fundamental element of the enslaved person's potential claim of masculinity. To be a mature man required functional genitalia, capable of procreation. Castration made someone who should have the manly qualities of aggression, strength, and hirsuteness into someone gentle and hairless, into no man at all.[114]

Bodily violability, penetrability, and modifiability distinguished enslaved boys and men from freeborn masculinity. Plato claimed the very ability to define ἀρετη, a term used to indicate both virtue and manliness, is itself masculine. A "slavish" person would not be able to explain what masculinity was (*Leg.* 12.965d). Freeborn elites characterized enslavement with actions and behaviors signifying un-masculinity: timidity (the lack of manly daring) in Publilius Syrus, *Sent.* 414; obsequiousness in Tacitus, *Ann.* 6.32; the inability to endure hardship in Josephus, *Ant.* 3.18–20; cowardice in Plutarch, *Mor.* 241b.[115] Servility—the moral quality of being enslaved—disqualified a man from military service, the ultimate venue for practicing and demonstrating masculinity (Valerius Maximus 7.6.1a).[116] In the world of the New Testament, enslavement un-manned its victims.

Manly Slaves?

Polybius's narrative of Prusias II of Bithynia illustrates the contrast between masculinity and enslavement. According to Polybius, when Prusias first

112. Seneca the Elder, *Controv.* 10.4.17; Martial 2.48; Juvenal, *Sat.* 6.369–73; Burke 2013, 98–99, 108–12.

113. Cf. Quintilian, *Inst.* 5.12.17–18; Suetonius, *Nero* 28.1; Dio Chrysostom 77/78.36–37; Polemon, *Phys.* 19a; Anderson and Moore 2004, 88–89; Burke 2013, 107–10, 119–20.

114. See esp. Plautus, *Asin.* 237; Juvenal, *Sat.* 6.366–67; Apuleius, *Metam.* 7.23.

115. See also Owens 2025, 155–57.

116. Cf. Cicero, *Verr.* 2.5.7; Pliny, *Ep.* 10.29, 10.30; Appian, *Bell. civ.* 2.11.74. The involvement of enslaved people in the military may be more complicated than these sources indicate. The Roman military traveled with enslaved people. According to Josephus, they were trained to fight (*J.W.* 3.69).

welcomed Roman officials to Bithynia, he dressed up as an enslaved person being manumitted. He called himself a *libertus* and promised to ingratiate himself to the Romans, imitating them in everything (the sort of behavior exhibited by "slavish" conquered peoples in Tacitus, *Agr.* 21). Polybius further accused Prusias of debasing himself when he visited Rome by bowing to the ground and calling the senators gods. He ultimately characterized Prusias as un-manly, womanish, and slavishly obsequious (ἀνανδρία, γυναικισμός, and κολακεία; 30.18.1–7).[117] Prusias's self-presentation as an enslaved person who had been freed by his enslaver and his dishonorable actions were, for Polybius, an un-gendering.

As evident in Polybius's account of Prusias or Philo's contrast between the manliness of athletes and the un-manliness of enslaved people, the various philosophical and rhetorical metaphors based in slavery and freedom introduced in chapter 1 often had a gendered edge. So, for instance, the distinction between internalized enslavement and freedom in Dio Chrysostom 15.29–30 rests on the demonstration of the manly virtue of ἀρετή.[118] Consequently, philosophers identified enslaved people who exhibited the qualities of masculinity as free men in their souls, and free men who exhibited "slavish" qualities as enslaved un-men in their souls.[119] But these metaphors rely on elite constructions of masculinity and enslavement. While accusations of un-manly slavishness were often lodged against wealthy elites (especially against political opponents), elite recognition of masculinity among enslaved people was rare.[120]

In Plutarch, [*Lib. ed.*] 5a–c, a lack of education corresponded with slavishness (ἀνδραποδώδης), which is defined here as engaging in a variety of immoral or socially unacceptable behaviors, keeping company with non-elite peoples, and being controlled by vice rather than controlling one's self.[121] The process of maturing into masculinity internalized the control over bodily desires and

117. Polybius further described Prusias as dishonorably womanish and cowardly in acts of war; unattractive; lacking in the bodily strength to endure hardship; and unable to exercise self-control. He was feminine in his body and soul (32.15.7–9, 36.15.1–6). See also Diodorus Siculus 31.15.1–3; Appian, *Hist. rom.* 12.2.4–5. Both Livy 45.44.3–18 and Valerius Maximus 5.1.1e provide more positive assessments of Prusias.

118. See also Seneca, *Ep.* 47.15–17; Roller 2001, 272–75.

119. See, e.g., Xenophon, *Oec.* 1.17–23; Horace, *Ep.* 1.16.63–68; Philo, *Leg.* 2.70; *Opif.* 158; Seneca, *Ep.* 77.14–15; Epictetus, *Diatr.* 3.26.21–26.

120. Among other examples, note Diodorus Siculus 14.65.4 (disparaging enemies as less manly than a slave); Tacitus, *Ann.* 6.32 (Vitellius's *virtus* turns to slavishness in the city of Rome); and Cassius Dio 50.5, 27 (Antony, enslaved by Cleopatra, loses his manliness).

121. The association of education with mature masculinity and a lack of education with enslavement is also found in Plato, *Theaet.* 175d; Xenophon, *Mem.* 4.2.22–23; Diogenes Laertius 2.8.72.

emotions formerly managed by (enslaved) pedagogues and tutors (the irony of enslavers' reliance on enslaved people to teach freeborn boys how to be masculine demands recognition of the constructed nature of masculinity).[122] Plutarch contrasted mature masculinity with irrationality, ignobility, and involuntary action (*Rect. rat. aud.* 37d–e)—all descriptors associated with enslavement. As these examples illustrate, the un-gendering of enslavement rested on the overlapping concerns of the dehumanizing construction of enslaved peoples by their enslavers; the rhetorical construction of elite masculinity; and the usefulness of slavery-based descriptors and metaphors for categorizing, comparing, and condemning.

The un-masculinity of enslavement is consistent and persistent in Greco-Roman antiquity. Nonetheless, a number of historiographic and moral narratives demonstrate the possibility of masculinity from an elite perspective. During the wars with Carthage, enslaved men who volunteered for the military in exchange for their eventual freedom were trained by their freeborn elite commander into an army of men who fought with courage and won victories for Rome. Livy contrasted this group with an army of freeborn Roman men who destroyed their masculinity with slavish vices (26.2.10–11). Valerius Maximus praised a number of enslaved men for displays of extreme loyalty to their enslavers, to the point of courageously enduring torture and execution (6.8.1, 3, 5). Plutarch characterized Spartacus, leader of a major slave revolt, as a true ἀνήρ: wise, thoughtful, and with noble ancestry (*Crass.* 8.2–3). He was an honorable enemy for the Roman military.

In these stories, the "manliness" ascribed to enslaved people ultimately benefits their enslavers, either directly (by protecting enslavers) or indirectly (by marking enslaved people as honorable enemies for elite men). The stories, in other words, identify enslaved people with masculinity in order to advance and protect elite enslavers and their masculinity. In Livy's narrative of the battle in which the enslaved soldiers earned their freedom, the commander separated the enslaved soldiers according to their demonstrations of manliness and cowardice. The cowards received freedom, but they were also punished for their un-manly behavior by retaining the signifiers of enslavement (specifically, standing to dine; 25.12–13).[123] The reminder of enslaved cowardice counters the potential destabilization of elite masculinity in the manly bravery of enslaved people.

122. Quintilian, *Inst.* 1.2.5, and Plutarch, [*Lib. ed.*] 5b, both encouraged care in selecting pedagogues and tutors for this reason. See further Connolly 1998, 137–41; Moss 2024, 39–40.

123. The story points toward the ambiguity of soldiers' masculinity. Soldiers were exemplars of both manliness (in displays of wartime courage) and un-manliness (due to the hierarchies of authority in the military). See Reeder 2019, 37–40.

The stories of enslaved Spartans contribute to elite masculinity in a slightly different way. In the various versions of the story presented at the beginning of chapter 1, a Spartan is captured in war and sold into slavery.[124] Upon being commanded to perform an offensive or dishonorable task, the enslaved Spartan instead takes their own life. Seneca (in *Ep.* 77.14–15) and Plutarch ([*Apoth. Lac.*] 234c; *Mor.* 242d) used this story to illustrate true freedom as control over one's own life, rather than being under the control of another person or concern (such as wealth or business). This control is internal, of course; as in other examples of metaphors of slavery and freedom, neither Seneca nor Plutarch advocated for discarding external wealth or position.[125]

For Seneca and for Philo (in *Prob.* 114), the story of the enslaved Spartan also demonstrates that death is better than enslavement.[126] Even if an enslaved person enacts masculinity, the humiliation of enslavement lingers (cf. Publilius Syrus, *Sent.* 489). That several of the traditions of enslaved masculinity center on dramatic deaths is also significant. Elite men can demonstrate masculinity in a variety of venues throughout their lives, but for an enslaved person to be recognized for masculinity by elite men, they must be tortured, take their own life, or risk their life on behalf of their enslaver.[127] In the stories of the enslaved Spartans, their identity as people who were born free and their legendary Spartan manliness (ascribed to both men and women) outweigh the problematic un-gendering of their enslavement.

There are only a few traditions in which enslaved people are granted a measure of masculinity. More often, enslaved people are categorized with women and children as irrational creatures who are prey to their desires and emotions and are therefore in need of the control of rational, masculine men (so Plato, *Resp.* 4.431c–d). For Seneca, the inferiority of enslaved people meant their only opportunity of attaining internal masculinity depended on the instruction provided by their enslavers (*Ep.* 47.11–12, 15–16). In practice, internalized masculinity required external status. To be identified as "free" and "manly" was the privilege of wealth, education, and aristocratic social standing. The

124. In one version, the Spartan is a boy; in another, a man; and in another, a woman.

125. Note the play on the concept of property in Plutarch's story of the Spartan woman in *Mor.* 242d. See further Roller 2001, 276–79; Joshel 2011, 232–34.

126. This message is also evident in a series of stories in Seneca, *Ep.* 70.19–27, of enslaved gladiators who die by suicide. The gender identity of gladiators was complicated by the combination of the un-masculinity of enslavement with the extreme masculinity of bodily strength, courage, and ability as fighters. Seneca's letter maintains the tension between the two, suggesting the gladiators ultimately proved their masculinity by killing themselves to escape the dishonor of enslavement.

127. Cf. McDonnell 2006, 160; Bradley 2008, 342–43. The problem is defined by a story in Cicero: An enslaved shepherd who killed a wild boar that threatened his flock was himself killed for using a (manly) weapon prohibited to (un-manly) slaves (*Verr.* 2.5.7).

definition of enslavement as a contrast to masculinity was useful to elite men precisely because of its intersection with the constructed realities of enslavement. In this sense, the enslaved people served their enslavers as symbols of enslavement, which in turn reinforced the system of enslavement.[128]

The realities beyond the rhetoric are more complicated to recover. As noted through this discussion and in chapter 1, many aspects of the rhetorical construction of enslavement and "slavishness" by elite enslavers are contradicted by the way enslavers used enslaved people. The ascribed lack of reason or self-control, for instance, is belied by the responsibility given to enslaved people to run businesses, manage households and estates, or administer the government. The involvement of enslaved pedagogues in teaching masculinity to elite boys demands recognition of the ability of enslaved people to understand, model, and inhabit masculinity.

Seneca, Plutarch, Valerius Maximus, and others spoke to and for elite audiences. Nonetheless, enslaved people joined their conversations about masculinity and slavery in their work as scribes, readers, educators, or servers at a dinner. The presence of enslaved people in philosophical depictions of masculinity (or un-masculinity) suggests the ability of enslaved people to judge their enslavers.[129] After all, enslaved people lived and worked under the constant surveillance of their enslavers.[130] This observation also means that enslavers were under constant surveillance by enslaved people. Enslaved people witnessed their enslavers' behavior, their posture, their emotional displays, their bodily control, and more, both in public and in private. Their omnipresence gave them a privileged position with respect to judging their enslavers' masculinity.

A story in Aulus Gellius 1.26.3–9 illustrates this potential. As an enslaved man in Plutarch's household is being beaten, the enslaved man argues that Plutarch is displaying an un-manly lack of control (using Plutarch's own words, e.g., in *Cohib. ira* 459d–e, against him). Unfortunately for the enslaved man, Plutarch remains in full control of his emotions as he calmly, non-wrathfully has the enslaved man beaten. Although the enslaved man's argument fails to disrupt the dominating practices of masculinity and enslavement, the story suggests that it was imaginable for enslaved people to turn their enslavers' philosophical discourses against them. Their adoption of philosophical perspectives to resist the un-gendering of enslavement, identifying themselves as "free" in contrast to their enslavers' enslavement to wealth, social position, or vice, is also imaginable.

128. Joshel 2011, 233–34.

129. E.g., Phaedrus, *Fables* 3.19; Petronius, *Sat.* 57.4–11; Seneca, *Ep.* 47.4, 6–8; Plutarch, *Cohib. ira* 461b–c, 462a; Juvenal, *Sat.* 14.59–67; Epictetus, *Diatr.* 3.26.21–26.

130. See esp. C. Martin 2005, 223, 236–39; Moss 2024, 28–29.

Other sources indicate enslaved people claimed elements of elite masculinity for themselves. Funerary memorials that name familial connections give enslaved and freed men the manly roles of father and husband, and freed men's involvement in public benefaction associates them with the masculinity of wealth and social position.[131] Enslaved and freed people also expanded the boundaries of elite masculinity by commemorating their labor in funerary inscriptions.[132] Rose MacLean notes that, in the first century, elite Romans adopted the virtues of modesty, industry, and deference celebrated by freed people.[133] In this case, enslaved and formerly enslaved self-constructions influenced elite masculinity.

"Jucundus, slave of Taurus, a litter-bearer, was a real man [*vir*] as long as he lived. Throughout his life he watched out for himself and for the others. Callista and Philologus, fellow slaves, set this up" (*CIL* 6.6308).[134] The lives and experiences of the three enslaved people named in this inscription are otherwise unknown. What Callista and Philologus may have meant by describing Jucundus as "a real man" is likewise unknown, though the reference to his protection of himself and others is suggestive. At a minimum, the inscription offers a memorial to enslaved people's recognition of the significance of masculinity in Rome and the ways they might take over masculinity for themselves, despite the exclusionary constructions of the elite.

Returning to a discussion begun in chapter 1, the contradictory concepts of freedom and enslavement as identifiers for the community in 1 Peter 2:16 make sense within this context. The concept of freedom gives Jesus's followers the capability of attaining masculine-coded moral virtue, reason, and self-control. Enslaved people are included in the community of "free slaves" and therefore also ascribed the characteristics of masculinity. These factors stand in tension with the un-gendering of slavish submission, fear, and abuse in verses 18 through 21. The intersections of 1 Peter's representation of Christian identity, enslaved people, and Jesus with Greco-Roman constructions of masculinity are complex.

Slavery, Masculinity, and 1 Peter

The implications of un-masculinity are strong in the concepts of submission, fear, and violence in 1 Peter 2:18–25. But at the same time, this text is explicitly

131. E.g., *CIL* 10.26, 11.137, 11.5400, 14.2469; *ILS* 8341; note also Petronius, *Sat.* 57.6; and Valerius Maximus 6.1.6 (discussed above).

132. See under "Masculinity and the Roman Empire," above.

133. MacLean 2018, 55–61.

134. Translation from Knapp 2011, 142. See also *TAM* 2.466, in which eight enslaved people recognize a fellow slave as a manly man (ἀνὴρ ἀγαθός, ὁ ἀγαθός, and προφανής ἀνήρ).

directed toward enslaved people as moral agents with the capability of enacting what is good by the standards of the community of Jesus's followers. Elite masculinity was not the only masculinity on offer in the Roman Empire. Non-elite peoples and non-Romans sometimes (likely often) accepted elite perspectives, but they also developed and celebrated their own definitions of masculinity. The pairing of manliness with care for self and others in the funerary memorial to Jucundus is suggestive in this respect. It is possible to see both adherence to elite norms and an alternative to elite masculinity in 1 Peter 2:18–25.

Un-Masculine Slaves in 1 Peter

In 1 Peter 2:18–25, after the household slaves are compared with Jesus, they are compared with wives (see "likewise," ὁμοίως, in 3:1). Both enslaved people and wives are instructed to submit to the authority over them. The concern of fear is present for both. While it is not as explicit in the case of wives, violence is an issue for them too.[135] The power of the resulting comparison between enslaved people and wives comes from the intersections of gender, status, and power in the Roman world. Like the (free) wives described as "weaker pots" in 3:7, the enslaved women and men in 1 Peter are un-masculine. The concern of gender is particularly evident in the exhortation to submit and fear, the comparison of enslaved people with sheep, and the response to violence.

First, in elite constructions of masculinity, submission and fear are categorized as "slavish." As is apparent in 1 Peter 2:13; 3:1; and 5:5, submission occurs within hierarchies of authority. Socially inferior peoples, including free women, freeborn children, and enslaved people, must be subject to the free men who are their social superiors (Dionysius of Halicarnassus, *Ant. rom.* 1.5.2). In Greco-Roman texts, political subjugation is sometimes gendered. It is manly to rule; by contrast, it is un-masculine to be subject to another's rule.[136] The distinction is particularly evident in stories of war. Honorable masculinity requires a refusal to be subject to the victor even in defeat (suicide is preferable).[137] Epictetus explicitly connected the state of being in subjection to the power of another with un-manly failures in self-discipline and reason; submission is enslavement (*Diatr.* 1.4.19, 3.24.71).

The connection of submission with un-masculine "slavishness" colors the reference to fear in 1 Peter 2:18. Fear is a common concept in 1 Peter. Just before the address to enslaved people, the entire community was exhorted to fear God

135. Reeder 2015a, 527–30.

136. Polybius 6.7.1–9; Diodorus Siculus 12.50.1, 16.1.4. This distinction is also apparent in texts concerning husbands and wives (1 Cor. 14:34; Plutarch, *Conj. praec.* 33).

137. Polybius 31.18.15; Diodorus Siculus 13.22.1–2, 15.8.2–3.

(v. 17). In this sense, the fear ascribed to enslaved people offers a model for the community (cf. also 3:2, 16). Outside 1 Peter, however, fear is a frequent companion to slavery (e.g., Rom. 8:15; Eph. 6:5; Col. 3:22).[138] In several cases, the danger of violence for enslaved people elicits fear.[139] Unsurprisingly, given that the definition of masculinity revolves around demonstrations of courage and control over one's own emotions, fear is coded as un-masculine. Pliny (*Ep.* 8.24.6) dissociated fear from elite masculinity, and Epictetus derided fear among freeborn elites with the (for a free man, unsettling) image of an enslaved person fearlessly escaping slavery (*Diatr.* 3.26.1).[140] Together, the submission and fear of enslaved people in 1 Peter 2:18 represent un-manliness.

Second, the animalization of the enslaved people as sheep in verse 25 corresponds with the dehumanization of enslavement. The metaphor is biblical. Israel as a whole are sheep under the care of a shepherd, sometimes identified with God and sometimes with kings or other authorities (a metaphor found also in Greco-Roman texts).[141] The references to Isaiah's Servant Songs through this section of 1 Peter identify the wandering sheep with Isaiah 53:6 in particular.[142] As such, the entire audience, not just people who were enslaved in households, may be included in the "you" in 1 Peter 2:25.[143] Given the focus on people enslaved in households in verses 18–20 and the attention to violence through the entire section, however, enslaved people at least have priority in verse 25. And for an audience in the Greco-Roman world, the association of sheep with enslaved people would bring the animalization of enslaved people into focus.

Unlike donkeys or oxen—two common comparisons emphasizing the labor of enslaved people—sheep are commodities raised for wool, milk, and meat. In this sense, the metaphor reduces enslaved people to their most basic definition: household possessions to be used up for the benefit of (and to enrich) the owners. The specific image of the sheep wandering off in the Bible represents straying from God's torah (Ps. 119:176; Isa. 53:6) and wartime defeat (Jer. 50:6). Comparable imagery in Greco-Roman texts associates sheep with a herd mentality, a tendency to ignorant thoughtlessness, and weakness.[144] Sheep,

138. See also Plato, *Resp.* 9.578d–579d; Horace, *Ep.* 16.65–66; Diogenes Laertius 6.2.75.

139. Plautus, *Men.* 977; Josephus, *Ant.* 6.41; Plutarch, *Cohib. ira* 459d–e.

140. Seneca, *Ep.* 85.27, 95.37; Dio Chrysostom 1.12–13; Epictetus, *Diatr.* 2.16.18–22. On the other hand, Onasander 14.1 encourages fear as a way to inspire manliness.

141. For Israel (under the shepherding of God, king, or other leaders), see Ps. 74:1; 77:21; 80:1; 100:3; Jer. 23:1–3; Mic. 7:14. For Greco-Roman metaphors of people as sheep under the care of a king as shepherd, see Epictetus, *Diatr.* 3.22.35; Dio Chrysostom 1.17–20; Plutarch, *Cat. Maj.* 8.2; Artemidorus, *Onir.* 2.12.

142. See Achtemeier 1996, 200–204; Jodoin 2009, 524–28; T. Williams and Horrell 2023a, 846.

143. So Jodoin 2009, 520–21; T. Williams and Horrell 2023a, 852–53.

144. E.g., Epictetus, *Diatr.* 3.23.4–5; Seneca, *Vit. beat.* 1.3; Plutarch, *Cat. Maj.* 8.2; *Mor.* 992d; Dio Chrysostom 49.2. A fable attributed to Phaedrus is comparable (Perotti's Appendix, fable 26).

in other words, signify the opposite of strong, fierce, reasonable, disciplined masculinity.[145] They need a shepherd to herd and protect them—pastoral imagery that echoes the social hierarchy of enslavers' authority over enslaved people: the (constructed) need for the external control of a rational caretaker (a man, in the first century) to keep the enslaved people in check.[146]

Third, the issue of violence remains central throughout 1 Peter 2:18–25. The text assumes that enslaved people will experience violence from their enslavers. The violence is primarily represented from the point of view of the enslaved people as suffering. But the text also assumes the enslavers' perspective that enslaved people should be beaten whether they "deserve" punishment or not (note v. 20). An enslaved person has either committed an infraction worthy of punishment or, as a slave constructed as lacking in self-control and reason, needs the discipline inflicted by the enslaver. Their bodies are vulnerable and penetrable.[147] The violence imposed on enslaved people is connected to the un-gendering of enslavement.

Each of these elements is open to reinterpretation, however. As noted in chapter 1, doing good in 1 Peter requires adherence to the standards of the community of Jesus's followers, not the standards of Greco-Roman society. Enslaved people's submission is, consequently, not the subordination to household rule imposed on enslaved people. Read in connection with 1 Peter 2:17, moreover, the fear of enslaved people is directed toward God more than toward their enslavers.[148] The violence they face is not due to their (constructed) need for manly oversight and control, nor is it punishment for wrongdoing. They face violence precisely because they do good, because they are participants in the community of Jesus's followers.

Embracing Un-Masculinity

As Spartans, soldiers, and athletes demonstrate, to be the object of violence is not in itself un-masculine.[149] However, the response to violence modeled by Jesus in 1 Peter 2:21–24 is not entirely manly. As discussed above, masculinity requires a response to violence in defense of bodily integrity and social

145. See esp. Epictetus, *Diatr.* 2.9.4–5, 2.10.3, 4.5.21; Plutarch, *Sept. sap. conv.* 147d; Anonymous Latinus, *Phys.* 78, 115.

146. Cf. Dio Chrysostom 1.17–19.

147. See further C. Martin 2005, 235. Bauman-Martin 2004a, 70–75, explores the potential for sexual abuse of enslaved women in this text. Enslaved men were also vulnerable to assault, of course.

148. See J. Green 2007, 79; Feldmeier 2008, 170; Gäckle 2021, 275–76.

149. In addition, many gladiators were enslaved, further blurring the lines between masculine courage, endurance, and enslavement (see E. Thurman 2004, 143–44; Lenski 2016, 290; Moss 2024, 31).

honor. In 1 Peter's version of the passion story (told through the lens of Isa. 52:13–53:12), Jesus does not enact retribution or threaten his attackers. Instead, his body exhibits the welts that signify his lack of manliness. The acceptance of violence, or even submission to violence, is not unknown for a free man. Plutarch's Hipponicus, an honorably masculine man, refused retribution against a man who punched him on a dare (*Alc.* 8.1–2).[150] By comparison, Jesus's nonresistance could be interpreted as manly. However, manliness is more commonly associated with countering violent acts. Plutarch's story emphasizes how surprising the lack of retribution was (see also Valerius Maximus 5.1, ext. 2b). Insofar as they are exhorted to follow Jesus's un-masculine model, the enslaved people who submit to their enslavers, fear, and suffer violence are participating in their own un-manning.

An enslaved pedagogue is mocked for complaining about a freeborn boy's violence against him in Plautus, *Bacch.* 438–48, and Bryson's household code condemns yelling, crying, and begging in response to physical abuse as "slavish" (152). In 1 Peter 2:20, enslaved people are encouraged to endure suffering. Endurance (ὑποφέρω, ὑπομένω) is a masculine trait, associated with fortitude in battle.[151] The manly endurance of suffering in turn calls attention to the representation of some of the enslavers as crooked or perverse (σκολιός), a judgment that aligns with the slavish un-masculinity of vice rather than the manliness of virtue in Plato, *Theaet.* 173a. Un-manly vice is also present in the identification of the enslaved people's suffering as unjust. While all slavery is injustice, this particular description marks the enslavers' violence as a failure of reason and self-control.[152] These aspects of the characterization of enslavers in 1 Peter 2:18–21 place the enslaved people in the role of judging enslavers' masculinity and, the text suggests, finding it lacking.

The dehumanization and un-gendering of enslaved people are obvious in 1 Peter 2:18–25. Enslaved people are like the wives in 3:1–6, fearing and obeying the authority of their enslavers. They are compared with witless sheep and subject to violence that they (like Jesus) cannot avoid or avenge. But their manly endurance and the implicit questioning of the enslavers' own manliness creates a gendered tension, opening space for the enslaved people to resist their enslavers' attempts to dehumanize them through the

150. See also Cicero, *Tusc.* 2.52; Plutarch, *Mor.* 239d; Epictetus, *Diatr.* 4.1.127.

151. Polybius 3.54.6; Diodorus Siculus 15.55.4–5. But also note that there is a difference between enduring battle and enduring suffering imposed by others as a social inferior (see Punt 2022, 118).

152. Seneca, *Ira* 3.24.2–3, 3.32.1–3; Plutarch, *Cohib. ira* 459b–e, 463a–b; [*Lib. ed.*] 7e. See also Plato, *Leg.* 6.777d–f. Often, however, any disapproval for acts of violence was tied to best practices for getting the most labor from an enslaved person: Xenophon, *Oec.* 3.4; Varro, *Rust.* 1.17.5; Philo, *Spec.* 2.90–91; Plutarch, *Cohib. ira* 459c–d.

violence of enslavement by claiming and enacting their own version of (un-) manly honor. In this respect, the model of nonretaliation set by Jesus offers a different version of masculinity, one that would be decidedly un-masculine by elite standards, for the enslaved people (and, as evident in 3:7 and 5:1–3, the whole community) to adopt.

The Un-Masculinity of Enslavement in the New Testament

Gender, power, and status were interlocking concerns in the cultures of the ancient Mediterranean. In the Roman Empire, masculinity was the measure of humanity. The demonstration of mature masculinity depended on elite status, wealth, and political power. A manly man had authority over his own person and property. In addition, a manly man exercised authority over other people in his own household and beyond. If the qualification for humanity was a measure of masculinity, and masculinity was defined by control over one's self and others, then an enslaved person, whether male or female, is un-gendered. The Roman construction of enslavement as the state of being under the ownership of an enslaver and lacking in the fundamental attributes of morality, maturity, and discipline marked out enslaved people as the embodiment of the opposite of honorable masculinity.

Enslavement was rhetorically constructed as the opposite of (elite, freeborn) masculinity. The un-gendering of enslavement defined masculinity around—and in essence limited masculinity to—elite status, privilege, and honor. Masculinity was not available to all people. The un-gendering of enslavement supported the domination of enslaved people by their enslavers. If enslaved people are identified as un-masculine, as incapable of attaining the ideals of reason, self-control, and moral virtue, then enslaved people need their freeborn, elite enslavers to exercise these attributes on their behalf. As a system, enslavement relies on and continually reinforces imbalanced power relations to disempower some to the benefit or advantage of others. The un-gendering of enslavement was a means of control and power.

In some ways, the representation of enslavement in 1 Peter 2:18–25 accepts elite constructions of enslaved people as un-masculine. But there are also challenges to elite masculinity in the attribution of goodness to enslaved people, their endurance of unjust violence, and the exhortation to follow Jesus's model of nonretaliation. These elements challenge the definition of masculinity among enslavers to shape a variant un-masculinity for the community of Jesus's followers. Like Jesus himself, they are called to embrace the un-manliness of enduring unjust violence and refusing to respond with more violence.

Jesus is a third party in the comparison of enslaved people and wives in 1 Peter 2:18–3:6. The comparison is, therefore, instructive for the gendering of Jesus in this text. The representation of Jesus as someone who suffers unjustly has parallels in Roman constructions of masculinity (particularly in those that incorporate Stoic endurance). Jesus is the shepherd who controls the sheep in 2:25 (cf. 5:4). However, Jesus also experiences the common components of enslavement when his bodily boundaries are violated (represented by the bruising on his body), and he does not defend himself against or avenge the abuse. The reminder of Jesus's crucifixion in 2:24 further destabilizes the attempt to claim masculinity for Jesus as a patient sufferer. Crucifixion, the death associated with slavery, humiliates its victims (see chap. 3, below). Jesus, who is compared with enslaved people and wives, is un-manned by this reminder of crucifixion, which in turn reinforces the un-manning of his failure to protect his own bodily boundaries or respond to the violation of his body.

Jesus is identified with enslaved people in 1 Peter 2:18–25. While 1 Peter does not explicitly name Jesus himself as "slave," this comparison is clear in Philippians 2:5–11: Christ Jesus "emptied himself, taking the form of a slave." Paul's representation of Jesus's enslavement emphasizes dishonor and abuse. Jesus humiliates himself. He becomes obedient until he dies. He is crucified—the most abject, dehumanizing, horrifying, and "slavish" death possible in the Roman Empire. And this is the model for Jesus's followers to adopt; they too should "empty themselves," humiliate themselves, and sacrifice themselves for one another. In the next chapter, the representation of Jesus as "slave" and its centrality to Paul's formulation of Christian identity will be analyzed through the dual lenses of slavery and masculinity.

3

Imitating Christ the Slave

Masculinity and Christian Identity in Paul

> [Christ Jesus] emptied himself, taking the form of a slave, becoming in human likeness. And once he was found in human appearance, he humiliated himself by becoming obedient to the point of execution—execution by crucifixion.
>
> —Philippians 2:7–8

> When Odysseus was shipwrecked and cast ashore, did his necessity humiliate his spirit, or break it? . . . [He trusted] in his own strength, that is, his judgements about the things which are under our control, and those which are not under our control. For these are the only things that make people free, that make people unhampered, that lift up the neck of those who have become humiliated, that make them look with level eyes into the faces of the rich, and the faces of tyrants.
>
> —Epictetus, *Diatr.* 3.26.33–35 (LCL, slightly modified)

For a relatively short letter, Philippians has attracted significant attention from interpreters, especially the Christ hymn in 2:5–11. This section of the letter, possibly a pre-Pauline creed or hymn, begins by ascribing the "form of God" to Jesus and ends with God exalting Jesus. The representation of Jesus as a humiliated, obedient, crucified slave centers the hymn. The descriptors that run through verses 7 and 8 define Jesus's slavery as abject, oppressive, and—as I argue in this chapter—un-masculine.

The contrast between Paul's representation of Jesus's willing humiliation and Epictetus's celebration of Odysseus's refusal to be humiliated clarifies the concern of gender. Epictetus's discourse addresses the manly courage of enduring physical deprivation with equanimity. This courage is modeled by what is an unexpected example of escaped slaves and elderly beggars in *Diatr.* 3.26.1–7. As a former slave himself, Epictetus used the experiences and rhetoric of enslavement in different ways than philosophers who had not been enslaved.[1] To be a manly man (ἀνὴρ ἀγαθός in 3.26.27) requires Stoic self-control, the mindset demonstrated by Odysseus. Paul's own example in Philippians 4:11–13 is comparable with this kind of masculinity; unlike Odysseus, though, Paul relies on external power for his self-control.

The representation of Jesus in Philippians 2:7–8 could also be counted as masculine by Epictetus's definition. Jesus's enslavement is voluntary, and (at least in the Christ hymn) he is not defined by the fear or worry derided as un-manly by Epictetus. For Epictetus, the fear of death is the greatest evil. It un-mans a person (*Diatr.* 3.26.39). That Jesus obeys until death signifies his manliness, then. But with respect to humiliation, Jesus and Odysseus are far apart. Odysseus's self-control overcomes the humiliation that enslaves humanity. Jesus embodies himself as a slave and humiliates himself by obeying like a slave. In this context, Jesus's execution by crucifixion further un-mans him, even if he does not demonstrate the un-manly fear of death.

The specific descriptors applied to Jesus in Philippians 2:7–8 are coded as slavish and consequently, as established in the previous chapter, un-masculine by standard Roman constructions of masculinity. Moreover, Paul exhorts the Philippians to adopt the mindset demonstrated by Jesus's un-manly humiliation, obedience, and crucifixion (note vv. 1–5), adding the "fear and trembling" missing from verses 7–8 in verse 12. With respect to masculinity, then, the text is somewhat muddled. Jesus's resolve and willingness to die signify masculinity, but his humiliation, Paul's own reliance on an external source of strength, and the community's fear as they adopt Jesus's mindset of humiliation construct a different model of masculinity for Jesus and his followers.

The representation of Jesus the slave as a model for the Philippian community presents particular ethical concerns for interpretation. Philippians as a whole has often been described as a gentle, kind, loving letter of friendship, one that reveals a caring relationship between Paul and the followers of Jesus in Philippi. There are some problems, primarily disunity and suffering

1. See esp. Wehus 2019, 230–31, 234–36.

as a consequence of imprisonment (for Paul) or persecution (for the people in Philippi). But the letter is essentially positive, with a strong emphasis on mutuality, encouragement, and joy.[2]

This positive portrayal of the letter contextualizes the identification of Paul and Timothy as "slaves of Christ"; the representation of Jesus as a humiliated (most often translated as "humble"), crucified slave; and the exhortations for the Philippian community to adopt these models (1:1; 2:1–11; 2:19–22). For many interpreters, the imagery of enslavement reflects both biblical "slaves of God" as authority figures and the virtue of humility.[3] Joseph Hellerman identifies Paul's use of enslavement as a challenge to Greco-Roman systems of status and authority.[4] Following a similar thread, Davorin Peterlin sees the Christ hymn as a challenge to anyone who would abuse their own status and authority over others.[5] Carolyn Osiek also suggests Paul's imagery of Christ as a humiliated slave offers exaltation to the oppressed.[6]

An alternative interpretation, however, has argued that Philippians is a letter of authority. So, for instance, Cynthia Kittredge sees the central point of the letter as the establishment of Paul's (sole) authority in the community, particularly over the two troublesome women, Euodia and Syntyche (4:2–3). In Philippians, Paul demands the obedience of the community to his authority.[7] Joseph Marchal develops this approach in significant ways. His survey of the rhetoric of friendship in Roman antiquity demonstrates its hierarchical, elitist, and exploitative nature.[8] In Philippians, he argues, friendship accompanies a variety of other rhetorics of domination, including militarization and unity (which, for Marchal, indicates oppressive conformity).[9] Like Kittredge, Marchal identifies obedience to Paul as the authority for the community as the primary purpose of the letter.[10]

The focus on issues of power and authority in Philippians corresponds with a more critical approach to the language of enslavement. For Sheila Briggs, Paul's use of slavery to develop theological concepts is deeply problematic given the domination and violence of the resulting concepts.[11] Colleen

2. E.g., Fee 1995, 6–7; Fitzgerald 2007, 293–96; Reumann 2008, 283; Keown 2012, 305–7. Marchal 2006b, 77–82, reviews the scholarship on Philippians as a letter of friendship.

3. So R. Martin 1976, 60; Witherington 1994, 30–31; Fee 1995, 188.

4. Hellerman 2005, 118.

5. Peterlin 1995, 67.

6. Osiek 2000, 67. Osiek also sees power at work in the representation of Jesus as slave (p. 34).

7. Kittredge 1998, 91–92, 99–100, 105–9. Kittredge sees this message as in tension with the themes of friendship and affection in the letter (pp. 63–65, 98).

8. Marchal 2006a, 35–48; 2006b, 82–95.

9. Marchal 2006a, 50–64, 97–98; 2006b, 95–99.

10. Marchal 2006a, 121–23; 2007, 250–52.

11. Briggs 2000, 117–18.

Conway, interpreting Philippians 2:5–11 as a divine apotheosis, suggests the representation of Jesus here establishes his authority as ruler.[12] Rose MacLean argues that Paul's slave language is intended to keep others under control; to identify himself as "slave" legitimates Paul's authority.[13] Likewise, Marchal identifies the Christ hymn as exploitative, violent imperialist rhetoric that, in the context of Philippians, demands the community's obedience to Paul.[14]

Is the representation of Jesus as a humiliated, crucified slave in Philippians 2:5–11 an expression of solidarity with the oppressed? Does the exhortation for the community to follow Jesus's model, setting aside self-interest for one another's sake (2:1–4), challenge Roman social hierarchies with mutuality and communal care? Or do these texts further the oppression already experienced by so many in the Roman world, forcing those who were subordinated by social, legal, or economic status or gender to be even more subordinated as members of Paul's community? These questions are not just of academic interest. How Philippians 2:1–11 is interpreted and used within communities of faith matters to the lives of the people in those communities.

Enslavement was a system of dehumanization, abuse, and injustice. These factors carry over into New Testament texts, including Philippians. As Briggs notes, the particular representation of Jesus as "slave" in the Christ hymn emphasizes abasement and violence. When the imagery of enslavement is tied to demands for obedience and experiences of suffering, the work of interpretation needs to proceed with caution. The vocabulary and imagery of enslavement in Philippians, as in other New Testament texts, is deeply troubling. The problem is increased given the use of such texts through history to support hierarchies of authority and subjugate particular members of communities of faith, often the people who are already vulnerable to abuse, oppression, and exploitation.[15]

Philippians incorporates named and unnamed individuals with different experiences of enslavement: Paul and Timothy, Christ's "slaves" (Phil. 1:1); the anonymous enslaved or freed scribes who collaborated with Paul and Timothy in writing, reading, and interpreting the letter; Epaphroditus, Clement, Euodia, and Syntyche, possibly each enslaved or freed;[16] the enslaved people in the

12. Conway 2008, 80. See also Tsang 2005, 72.

13. MacLean 2018, 63–69.

14. Marchal 2006a, 134–37; 2007, 248–54. Marchal 2015, 168–72, also interprets the references to Epaphroditus in Phil. 2:25–30 and Euodia and Syntyche in 4:2–3 as indicative of the exploitation of enslaved people (including the sexual exploitation of Epaphroditus by Paul, a point countered by Wire 2015, 178–79; Charles 2020, 79).

15. Cf. Marchal 2007, 253–54; Stubbs 2007, 366; Tamez 2017, 72–73.

16. So Ascough 2003, 124–28; Marchal 2015, 144–45; Nasrallah 2019, 125–26.

imperial household (4:22);[17] and all the enslaved, freed, and free followers of Jesus in Philippi. Their different experiences of enslavement would encourage different interpretations of and responses to the letter. As Elsa Tamez notes, some people did not need to be told to empty themselves, humiliate themselves, or sacrifice their own lives and interests for others. The enslaved people and (many) non-enslaved women in the community already lived this reality. It is wealthy elites, men and women enslavers who had positions of privilege in society, who would have to change their lives in response to Paul's exhortations.[18]

In this chapter, I argue that the intersection of enslavement with the concerns of masculinity shapes the imagery of Philippians in this particular direction. As the contrast with Epictetus's free, unhumiliated Odysseus indicates, the imagery of enslavement, humiliation, and crucifixion un-mans Jesus. The vocabulary of the exhortation for the followers of Jesus to adopt his mindset in Philippians 2:1–5 likewise emphasizes characteristics associated with un-manliness, including the absence of self-determination or ambition, humiliation, and a focus on the needs of others. The development of enslavement in verses 7 and 8 matters for the interpretation of Paul and Timothy as "slaves." Enslavement as a metaphor and reality of Christian identity redefines masculinity for the Philippian community.

Philippians in Philippi: Citizenship, Status, and Gender

Paul, Timothy, and their scribe(s) wrote their letter to the Philippians while Paul was imprisoned, most likely in either Ephesus around 50 CE or Rome in the early 60s.[19] The descriptions of Paul's situation equally emphasize the ongoing success of the proclamation of the gospel and his suffering, to the point that death would be better for him (Phil. 1:12–26). Suffering is a major theme of the letter. Epaphroditus, a member of the Philippian community who was sent to Paul as an apostle and cultic minister (ἀπόστολος and λειτουργός), nearly died in the course of his work (2:25–30). The Philippian community had also experienced suffering and opposition (1:29–30).

In part, the suffering may reflect conflicts between the followers of Jesus and their larger social communities, similar to the situation of 1 Peter (discussed in chap. 1, above).[20] The representation of Paul's experience of imprisonment

17. See Flexsenhar 2019, 28, 35–36.

18. Tamez 2017, 66–73. See also Reumann 2008, 314–15; Park 2024, 465.

19. Osiek 2000, 29–30, and Reumann 2008, 7, place the letter in Ephesus. Peterlin 1995, 15, and Holloway 2017, 22–23, opt for Rome. Another suggestion from Hawthorne 1983, xli–xliv, places the letter during Paul's imprisonment in Caesarea Maritima around 60 CE.

20. E.g., Osiek 2000, 50; Cousar 2009, 15.

also refers to competition between different preachers of the gospel (Phil. 1:15–17), and he warns against individuals he identifies as enemies of Christ's cross (3:18–19). The letter's strong emphasis on unity suggests to many interpreters that either the Philippian community is internally divided or the community has diverged from Paul's own teaching. As mentioned above, some interpreters argue that the specific reference to Euodia and Syntyche in Philippians 4:2–3 associates them with the problem of disunity.[21]

There are many suggestions concerning the precise nature of the suffering and opposition in the historical community of Jesus's followers in Philippi. Given the interest of this study in enslavement and masculinity, the description of the "enemies of the cross of Christ" offers a helpful focus.[22] In the Christ hymn, the cross represents the absolute obedience and humiliation of Jesus as "slave" (2:8). Paul exhorted the Philippian community to adopt Jesus's mindset, the way of thinking, φρονέω, that ended in crucifixion (v. 5). To be enemies of the cross, then, would be to have the opposite way of thinking: not humiliation, but self-promotion; not attentiveness to others, but attentiveness to one's own concerns (note vv. 3–4). Their mindset, φρονέω, is directed toward "earthly things," human desires and glory (3:19). They are not citizens of heaven (v. 20).

The issue of citizenship and the characterization of the "enemies of Christ's cross" in Philippians reflect the paired concerns of identity and status in ancient Philippi. The city was a Roman colony with a mixed population of Roman citizens, including descendants of the military veterans who were settled in the region in the late first century BCE as well as local Thracians, Greeks, and Macedonians. A major trade road, the Via Egnatia, passed through the city.[23] Some people in the city would have been quite wealthy, though many likely lived at a subsistence level.[24]

Philippi was strongly Romanized in the first century, indicated by the presence of the imperial cult, the use of Latin in inscriptions, and its architectural style.[25] Additional elements of Romanization included local pride in the political status of the city as a colony and the competition for social status. These intersecting concerns are illustrated by the many inscriptions

21. On the issue of disunity, see esp. Peterlin 1995, 9, 37–39, and passim; Osiek 2000, 30–31, 48. De Vos 1999, 262–81, ties the issue of disunity to persecution (different members of the community advocate different responses); Oakes 2001, 77–96, connects the disunity with the economic disenfranchisement of the community. Note, however, that Reumann 2008, 283, is more cautious; the theme of unity does not necessarily indicate a significant problem with disunity.

22. See esp. D. Williams 2002, 28–38, 225, 235; and also Kraftchick 2008, 258–59.

23. Bond 2022, 164–69.

24. Nasrallah 2019, 105–22, surveys the history, economy, and Romanization of Philippi.

25. De Vos 1999, 236–49; Oakes 2001, 3–18, 34–37; Rizakis 2022, 39, 42; Sève 2022, 18–26.

decorating the public spaces and cemeteries of Philippi: "Publius Cornelius Asper Atiarius Montanus, honored with equestrian status, also with the decorations of a decurion and of the duumviri, priest, flamen of the divine Claudius in Philippi, 23 years old, lies buried here."[26] The concern with status evident in this inscription intersects with standard constructions of masculinity surveyed in chapter 2, above. Inscriptions like the one for Publius Cornelius celebrate honorees' status—and, therefore, masculinity—with details of family lineage; political, cultic, and military appointments; civic honors; and financial contributions to the city, temples, or voluntary associations.[27] The city's inscriptions also include elite women, represented as office holders and benefactors (but with more limited information concerning their ancestry).[28] In addition, inscriptions commemorate people with little social status. Some of these inscriptions imitate elite values, but they also include the references to occupation and business found in non-elite inscriptions across the empire.[29]

The people addressed in Philippians were likely among the poorer residents of the city (cf. 2 Cor. 8:1–2).[30] This population included the free, freed, and enslaved poor who worked as artisans, in small businesses, or in household-based labor. As noted above, the personal names in Philippians are attested as names of enslaved people.[31] Though the individuals mentioned do not appear in Philippians, the story of Paul in Philippi in Acts 16 is also populated by non-elites: Lydia,[32] a nameless enslaved woman, and a jailer (a role sometimes filled by a public slave). Lydia and, in Philippians 4:2–3, Euodia and Syntyche commemorate the presence of women in the community. The descriptors applied to Euodia and Syntyche—Paul's "fellow combatants" (συναθλέω) and "colleagues" (συνεργός) who deserve the support of the community—indicate their importance as leaders.[33] That two of the four (or five, if σύζυγος is a

26. 001/L027, translation from Hellerman 2005, 98. On the city's inscriptions, see esp. de Vos 1999, 245–46; Oakes 2001, 74–75; Hellerman 2005, 46, 89–101, and passim; and Reumann 2008, 325, 330.

27. Hellerman 2005 includes many quotations of the inscriptions from Philippi. See also the helpful chart of common elements in Philippian funerary memorials separated by ethnic identity in Oakes 2022, 257.

28. The inscriptions honoring women quoted in Hellerman 2005, 83, include the women's names, their father's names, and a single title (002/L028 and 226/L344). By contrast, the inscriptions honoring men include their fathers' names, their tribal affiliation, their social status, multiple titles, and sometimes other honors (e.g., 202/L313, 058/L047, 213/L347, quoted in Hellerman 2005, 78–79, 89–96).

29. Hellerman 2005, 100–107; Bond 2022, 163–64, 173–77.

30. So Oakes 2001, 89–96; Nasrallah 2019, 124–28; Quigley and Nasrallah 2022, 227.

31. De Vos 1999, 252–57; Ascough 2003, 118, 124–28; Nasrallah 2019, 125–28.

32. On Lydia's ethnic identity and characterization as a non-elite merchant, see esp. Gruca-Macaulay 2016, 118–44.

33. Cf. Ascough 2003, 126–27, 134; Tamez 2017, 4.

personal name) of the Philippian community named in this letter are women is unusual. Along with the likely low status of the community members, the focus on the women diverges somewhat from the concern with competition for masculine status in Philippi.

The social and political context of Roman Philippi establishes elite Roman masculinity as a concern for the residents of the city. The question of masculinity is present in the letter in the representation of Christ as a crucified slave, the significance of Euodia and Syntyche as leaders, and Paul's self-presentation. Although the vocabulary of masculinity is not used in Philippians (or in most of Paul's letters), there are several reflections of standard Roman constructions of masculinity.[34] Paul's unflappability in the face of need, as noted above, gives him the qualities of Stoic masculinity (Phil. 4:10–13). Members of the community are called to be exemplars of virtue (2:14–15; 4:8). Athletic and military metaphors associate Paul, Epaphroditus, and the Philippian community, including the women (explicitly in the case of Euodia and Syntyche), with these arenas of masculinity (e.g., 1:30; 2:25; 4:2–3).[35] Paul calls himself Timothy's father (2:22), identifying him with a primary element of masculinity.

As in 1 Peter, however, these examples of standard masculinity are disrupted by alternative constructions. Paul's fatherhood is the only reference to household life, and this significant arena of masculinity is therefore largely missing from the letter. Furthermore, Paul's fatherhood is undermined by the fact that he and Timothy work together as enslaved people (Phil. 1:1; 2:22). Enslaved people were often related, and they commemorated their relationships in funerary inscriptions. But, as discussed in chapters 1 and 2, enslaved fathers were not recognized as fathers, nor were they granted normative masculine authority or responsibility over their children. Because Paul identifies himself as a "slave," his fatherhood cannot be counted as manly by Roman standards. The manliness of enduring physical deprivation and suffering is likewise obscured by Paul's reliance on Christ.[36] Paul's imprisonment; the representation

34. See also Clines 2004, 182–90 (on Paul's self-presentation as a manly man); Knust 2004, 168–72 (on gender stereotypes across Paul's letters); Conway 2008, 68–73; Charles 2020, 79. The imperative ἀνδρίζεσθε in 1 Cor. 16:13 is a rare example of the vocabulary of masculinity in Paul's letters. In context, it possibly carries the significance of "manly" courage. As 1 Cor. addresses men and women, the command to "act like a man" also addresses women (cf. Westfall 2016, 51).

35. Contra Clines 2004, 184–85 (his dismissal of women as soldiers is contradicted by Hallett 2015a; Mayor 2016). See further Westfall 2016, 46–49, 185–86. Westfall highlights the significance of Paul's use of masculine-coded metaphors for the entire Christian community, including women, and equally his use of feminine-coded metaphors for the entire community, including himself as leader and other men in their positions of authority as husbands (e.g., pp. 52–53, 57–59).

36. Cf. D. Martin 1997, 209–11.

of Jesus, Paul, and Timothy as enslaved; and the potential that the community in Philippi included a significant number of enslaved or formerly enslaved people further complicate the question of masculinity in the letter.

Paul and Timothy, Slaves of Christ

The first words of the letter name Paul and Timothy as "slaves" of Christ. The language of slavery describes Paul and his colleagues in the work of preaching, teaching, and directing Christian communities in, for instance, 1 Corinthians 9:19; 2 Corinthians 4:5; and Galatians 1:10.[37] It is possible to interpret these references in relation to the model of Jesus in Philippians 2:5–11, therefore defining leadership as willing self-enslavement on behalf of the participants in the Christian community.[38] But these references are sometimes accompanied by declarations of authority and power, as in the combination of "slave" and "apostle" in Romans 1:1 (note also Gal. 1:1, 10–12).

As discussed in the introduction, some interpreters identify Paul's language of slavery and references to labor with a family history of enslavement.[39] In this case, the association of slavery with power in Paul's letters offers an example of the ways enslaved and freed people resisted the disenfranchisement of enslavement. Other interpreters define Paul's enslavement through the biblical description of prophets as God's slaves, making "slave" into a title of honor and authority for Paul.[40] Enslaved people were granted the authority to conduct business and arrange legal affairs on behalf of their enslavers in Roman society.[41] Paul's slavery metaphors have also been compared with Stoic philosophy, suggesting spiritual realities are in view rather than legal status. Against these various backgrounds, Paul exploits slave language to develop his own claim to authority.[42]

37. In addition, Paul often uses the non-elite language of work or labor to describe himself and his colleagues (e.g., κοπιάω, ἐργάζομαι, and συνεργός in Rom. 16:3, 6, 9, 12, 21; 1 Cor. 3:9; 4:12; 16:10, 16; Phil. 2:16; 1 Thess. 2:9; Seesengood 2019, 141–44). See also Acts 16:17; 20:18–19; Col. 4:12; 2 Tim. 2:24.

38. Cf. Ramelli 2016, 105, 109–10.

39. See de Vos 1999, 259; Beavis 2021, 45; Fairchild 2025, 64, 80–83.

40. E.g., R. Martin 1976, 60; Hawthorne 1983, 3–4; Tsang 2005, 68, 72; Cousar 2009, 24; Merz 2018, 97, 100.

41. Cf. D. Martin 1990, 54–55; Merz 2018, 97–98. This suggestion forms part of Martin's argument that slavery in Paul's letters reflects the social mobility of enslaved people in Roman society (pp. 51–84). As should be evident from the previous chapter and this one, however, the opportunities for social advancement were very limited. Martin's argument works only for a very small subset of enslaved people (well-educated and trained men enslaved in wealthy, elite households); cf. Garnsey 1996, 186.

42. MacLean 2018, 62.

These various options lead to quite distinctive interpretations of Paul's language of enslavement. In Philippians specifically, the concept of enslavement is defined by the representation of Jesus as a humiliated, obedient, crucified slave and by the context of Paul's imprisonment.[43] The honor or authority attached to prophets as God's (enslaved) agents or the enslaved people operating on their enslavers' behalf does not match the insistence on the abasement of enslavement in Philippians. Likewise, within a Stoic framework, the person who is truly free is master over (him)self—his body, his emotions, his desires; Paul's self-identification as slave in Philippians 1:1 is not this.[44] As Matthew Roller says, freeborn Romans would not willingly identify themselves as "slave."[45] The non-enslaved people in the Philippian community may have been disconcerted by the identification of Paul and Timothy as enslaved, but so may the enslaved and freed people who also lived within the realities of Roman social norms.

Whether it is primarily metaphorical or preserves a personal history of enslavement, the language of enslavement in Philippians 1:1 and 2:22 overlaps with embodied experience.[46] As residents in the Roman Empire, Paul and Timothy would necessarily be aware of the common perceptions, constructions, and experiences of enslavement. They saw enslaved people all around them, from those who were (relatively) privileged to those who were required to complete difficult and demeaning tasks. They were unavoidably familiar with the various kinds of abuse that enslaved people faced and the lack of adequate care. These concerns were also common knowledge for the people in the Philippian community, some or many of whom were enslaved or freed. Moreover, Paul and Timothy were Jews. From Pompey's conquest of Jerusalem into the second century CE, Jewish captives from Judea and Galilee were enslaved across the empire.[47] In *Prov. cons.* 5.10, Cicero derided the Jews as a "slavish" people, a descriptor that had only dishonorable connotations. If Jerome's account that Paul's parents were enslaved as wartime captives has any echo of historical experience, Paul may have grown up with family stories of the experience of Jewish slavery in Roman households.[48]

43. Cf. Combes 1998, 68–69, 92; Hellerman 2005, 118–20; Westfall 2016, 250–52; Schwaller 2017, 47–48; de Wet 2018, 20.

44. So also Garnsey 1996, 18; Combes 1998, 89.

45. Roller 2001, 223, 227 (see also Ascough 2003, 123, on Philippians).

46. De Wet 2018, 10–13, and Kartzow 2018, 8–11, 22–26, address the movement between reality and metaphor in early Christian slavery language. See also Glancy 2023, 157–58.

47. E.g., Philo, *Legat.* 155; Josephus, *J.W.* 3.132–34, 3.539–40, 6.416–20, 7.208, and passim; Tacitus, *Ann.* 2.85. Cf. Wilson 2017, 37; Bühner 2023, 200–202; Park 2024, 446; Seal 2025, 210, 213.

48. Jerome, *Comm. Phlm.* 23–24; see also the introduction, above. It is at least imaginable that Timothy, son of a gentile father and Jewish mother, may have had a family history of

Given the context of the first-century slave society of the Roman Empire and Paul and Timothy's Jewish identity, the language of slavery in Philippians may not be as much a manipulative power play as an association with the enslaved and formerly enslaved people in the community. Notably in this regard, Paul introduced himself as "slave" in letters to the communities in Corinth, Galatia, Philippi, and Rome. The populations of enslaved and freed people in Rome and Corinth were disproportionately high, and apart from Paul and Timothy, the personal names in Philippians are all also attested as names for enslaved people. Paul's identification as "slave" in these specific contexts could represent an act of resistance to the dehumanizing, humiliating realities of enslavement, a way to reclaim the humiliating un-masculinity of "slavishness" as something worthwhile.[49]

The intersections of enslavement and masculinity add nuance to the analysis of Paul as "slave." The concern of gender is most obvious in Galatians and the two letters to the Corinthians. Women are almost entirely absent from Galatians, which is concerned to a significant extent with the exclusively male issue of circumcision (see esp. 5:2–12).[50] The analogy of a child's education under an enslaved pedagogue and the references to inheritance and adoption in Galatians 3:23–4:11 and 4:21–5:1 would, for a first-century audience, primarily represent the experience of men.[51] The letter begins with a declaration of Paul's authority over the community as a divinely commissioned apostle (Gal. 1:1). There is no vocabulary of masculinity here, but the declaration would certainly resonate with masculinity for a first-century audience in the Mediterranean world.

Paul's authority in the first verses and the analogy of freedom later in the letter are disrupted by enslavement.[52] First, Paul counters his personal

---

enslavement (as enslaved women might be freed for the purpose of marriage with their enslaver), though I am unaware of any traditions that suggest this.

49. See Tamez 2017, 38.

50. Paul does not pass on personal greetings in Galatians. He refers to Sarah and Hagar in an allegory of freedom and slavery, and there are two references to childbirth (Jesus is born of an unnamed woman, and Paul himself gives birth to the Galatians). Of course, Gal. 3:28 is Paul's infamous declaration of unity in Christ for "male and female." But circumcision (problematic for Jewish masculinity in the Greco-Roman world; see Wilson 2015, 197; Stroup 2017, 57–60), the use of "brother" language, and the masculine imagery of the letter make Galatians seem more masculine than Paul's other letters. See further Gaventa 2007, 63–64, 70–75; Punt 2013, 162–64; and, on the similar wet-nurse imagery in 1 Cor. 3:1–2, Robinson 2019, 129–30.

51. Girls could have pedagogues, and enslaved women worked as pedagogues. Women also inherited under Roman law. But the language of pedagogues, inheritance, and adoption primarily reflects men's experience in the first century, as the consistent references to sons (υἱός) in Galatians suggest.

52. See also Barrier 2008, 358–61; Burgett 2022, 2–9, and passim; and Fairchild 2025, 117–34, on the vocabulary and imagery of slavery in Galatians.

authority with his identification as a "slave of Christ" (Gal. 1:10). This enslavement, according to Paul's assessment, brings him no social honor or status. In fact, his own body is marked by Christ's στίγμα, a term referring to the brands and tattoos imprinted on enslaved people (especially as punishment for what the enslaver perceived as wrongdoing; 6:17).[53] Second, after proclaiming the freedom of the Galatian audience, Paul exhorts them to enslave themselves to one another as an enactment of love (5:13). The challenge of mutual enslavement defines freedom as a status centered on care for others—a status that, in the first century, conflicted with core elements of elite masculinity.[54]

The letters to the Corinthian churches develop Paul's masculine image. He compares himself with an athlete. Like a good Stoic, he enslaves his body (1 Cor. 9:24–27).[55] The violent imagery of paternal discipline in 1 Corinthians 4:15–21 and warfare against opponents in 2 Corinthians 10:3–6 reflect standard demonstrations of masculinity.[56] At the same time, Paul also characterizes himself as weak, cowardly, foolish, and incapable of persuasive public speech (1 Cor. 2:1–5), descriptors that indicate slavishness rather than manliness.[57] He speaks publicly of crucifixion, a topic considered ludicrously shameful for audiences in the Roman Empire (1 Cor. 1:18–25).[58] Paul presents himself as a captive on display in a triumphal parade, reeking of death (2 Cor. 2:14–16).[59] In contrast to the manliness of victory, this image of shameful defeat signifies un-masculinity in the Roman world.[60] The description also reflects the Roman understanding of slavery as a living death (cf. Seneca, *Ep.* 77.18). Like any enslaved person, Paul's body is marked by the wounds of beatings (2 Cor. 4:7–11). The litany of abuse endured by Paul in 2 Corinthians

53. E.g., Aristophanes, *Frogs* 1510–14; Cicero, *Off.* 2.25; Philo, *Spec.* 1.58; Juvenal, *Sat.* 14.23–24; Plutarch, *Cohib. ira* 463b; Dio Chrysostom 14.19, 15.11; Athenaeus, *Deipn.* 13.612c; Grubbs 2002, 236; Barrier 2008, 353–54; Fairchild 2025, 133–34.

54. The metaphor of freedom and enslavement in Gal. 5:13 could be compared with the Stoic understanding of "enslavement" of bodily desire to the mind (so MacLean 2018, 62). Self-control features strongly in the list of vices and virtues in 5:16–26. But importantly, Paul's metaphor calls not for enslaving one's own body to serve the mind, but rather for enslaving one's self to others in the community.

55. See further Garnsey 1996, 77; Fitzgerald 2010, 166–68.

56. Robinson 2019, 133–34, however, argues that 1 Corinthians represents Paul as a failed father.

57. Larson 2004, 89–90; Robinson 2019, 118–21; Seal 2025, 213.

58. Robinson 2019, 120; Seal 2025, 212–13. Robinson in particular explores Paul's "misperformance" of elite masculinity in 1 Corinthians as a way to limit the potential abuses and oppressions associated with masculinity (see pp. 1–4, and passim); he also points out that Paul encourages un-masculinity for his audience (e.g., pp. 192–93).

59. N. Elliott 2004, 76–77.

60. Cf. Livy 40.39.9; Josephus, *J.W.* 7.118, 121–57; Appian, *Hist. rom.* 6.15.98; Reeder 2019, 147–49.

11:22–28, particularly in the context of his self-humiliation, anxiety, and weakness (vv. 7, 28–30), catalogues his un-masculinity.[61]

In the midst of this gendered ambiguity, Paul repeatedly identifies himself and his colleagues as enslaved people. Their authority comes not from themselves but from their divine enslaver (who was himself crucified like an enslaved person).[62] Paul and his colleagues are Christ's ὑπηρέτης and οἰκονόμος (1 Cor. 4:1). Paul describes himself as both free and enslaved to all. As Ruben Bühner argues, the imagery of enslavement in 1 Corinthians 9:19–22 is shaped by the way enslaved people were forced to modify their own identity and behavior for their enslavers' households; adaptability is a mark of enslavement.[63] In 2 Corinthians 4:5, Paul again declares his enslavement to Christ. The opposition of "lord/enslaver" (κύριος) and "slave" (δοῦλος) in this text emphasizes Paul's lack of status.[64] This instance of enslavement explains the failure of Paul's message among audiences in the Roman world (4:3–4); a slave is not an authoritative presence or a compelling, convincing speaker.[65] In 1 and 2 Corinthians, Paul's bodily display, shameful speech, and enslaved identity complicate the masculinity of authority, patriarchy, and violence.

The identification of Paul and Timothy as "slaves of Christ Jesus" in Philippians 1:1 echoes Galatians and 1 and 2 Corinthians. In connection with Paul himself, the descriptor is filled out by his experience of being chained (Phil. 1:7). Chains (δεσμός) represent imprisonment, but enslaved people were also chained for transport to slave markets and for particular labor.[66] Prisons were arenas of suffering (1:17), with the sorts of food deprivation, beatings, and abuse also experienced by enslaved people. The custom of restraining enslaved people in underground prisons (*ergastula*) evidences direct overlap between imprisonment and slavery.[67] Paul's imprisonment aligns with enslavement. Moreover, Paul's body is an instrument to display Christ (1:13–14), similar to the use of enslaved bodies as surrogates for their enslavers. Paul also expresses a desire for death as an escape from suffering (1:20–24). Slavery

61. So Larson 2004, 94, and esp. Punt 2022, 118–23. Both Larson and Punt argue that Paul's exhibition of weakness redefines weakness (and thus un-manliness) as power, but as Larson points out, it is not a foolproof strategy (p. 96).

62. Seal 2025, 212–13, highlights the incongruity of enslavement to a crucified enslaver.

63. Bühner 2023, 207–8, particularly addresses the concerns of enslaved Jews in non-Jewish households.

64. Cf. Westfall 2016, 252.

65. Cf. Plutarch, *Galb.* 11.1–2; [*Lib. ed.*] 5a–c.

66. See Herodotus 3.129.3; Xenophon, *Mem.* 2.1.16; Columella, *Rust.* 1.pref.10, 9.1.4; Chariton, *Call.* 4.2.5; Juvenal, *Sat.* 7.15, 14.23–24; Plutarch, *Cohib. ira* 463b; Florus, *Epit.* 2.7.19; the tombstone of Aulus Caprilius Timotheus (*SEG* 36.587); and the relief of chained slaves from Izmir at the Ashmolean Museum (accession number ANMichaelis.137).

67. Lenski 2016, 278–79; see also Moss 2024, 70–72; and J. Williams 2024, 87–89.

was understood to be a living death.[68] If Paul's introduction as "slave" at the beginning of the letter is a conversation partner with his contrast of life and death, his desire for death also fits within the realm of slavery.[69]

In Philippians 1:20–26 Paul describes his embodied life as labor for Christ and the church. This conception of life resonated with the experience of enslaved people, who labored on behalf of others (and for whom death meant freedom), and freed people who valued labor as a sign of social honor (among the freed community, if not for elites). By contrast, Paul described Epaphroditus, who may have been enslaved or freed by status, with the more masculine descriptors of brother, coworker, fellow soldier, apostle, and cultic minister. His willingness to die for Christ makes him worthy of honor (2:25, 29–30). The contrast between the description of Epaphroditus and the slavery and imprisonment of Paul points toward Paul's un-masculinity.

The association of Paul's enslavement with dishonor, humiliation, and violence, with labor, and with living death blurs the lines between metaphor and reality. Paul's descriptions of his experience in Philippians aligned him with people who existed at the bottom of the hierarchy of humanity, including the men and women who lived beyond the boundaries of normative masculinity. The conceptualization of enslavement for Paul and Timothy carries through in the Christology of Jesus as slave in Philippians 2:5–11.

Philippians 2:5–11: Preliminary Concerns

The representation of Jesus as humiliated slave and exalted lord in Philippians 2:5–11 has attracted intense interpretive attention.[70] The unique style, vocabulary, and theological concepts (for instance, the use of κενόω, δοῦλος, and χαρίζομαι in reference to Christ) suggest the text may be a pre-Pauline composition, possibly even a hymn or creedal statement familiar to the Philippian community.[71] If this is the case, then Philippians 2:5–11 offers a glimpse of very early Christian understandings of Jesus. But since the hymn survives only in Philippians, the letter itself is the primary context for interpretation.

68. The option of suicide as a way to preserve freeborn honor despite enslavement is a consistent thread in first- and second-century sources (Publilius Syrus, *Sent.* 489; Seneca, *Ep.* 70.19–27, 77.14–15; Josephus, *J.W.* 7.380–86; Plutarch, *Mor.* 242d). See the introduction, above.

69. Cf. Combes 1998, 87–88.

70. Reviewing the scholarship on Phil. 2:5–11 would take a book in itself. Helpful surveys can be found in D. Williams 2002, 60–71; Marchal 2007, 246–49; Reumann 2008, 333–39; and Keown 2017, 351–79.

71. Perhaps the majority of scholars identify the text as pre-Pauline (though Hellerman 2005, 129, and Holloway 2017, 115, suggest it was composed by Paul). See Reumann 2008, 365; Cousar 2009, 52–53.

The question of origins relates to the potential backgrounds of the imagery in Philippians 2:5–11. The various suggestions for the source of the imagery draw attention to different focal points. One common option compares Philippians 2:5–11 with Greco-Roman apotheosis traditions in which exceptional humans become gods. The Philippian community would likely be quite familiar with such traditions. This potential background identifies the exaltation of Jesus as the primary point of the hymn.[72] A second option focuses on the concept of becoming human in Philippians 2:7. Drawing on conceptual similarities with Genesis 1:26–27, this option suggests Jesus is a new Adam. A connection with Adam draws attention to Jesus's refusal to seek his own self-interest and his obedience to God.[73] A third option straddles the dichotomy of divinity and humanity. The allusion to Isaiah 45:23 in Philippians 2:10–11 encourages a connection with Isaiah's Servant Songs (as in 1 Pet. 2:22–25; and esp. Isa. 52:13–53:12), making Jesus the slave who suffers as a human but is exalted as God.[74] Although the connections are more thematic than lexical, the frequency of references to Isaiah's Servant Songs in the New Testament and their use in the depiction of Jesus in 1 Peter 2:21–25 make this background a strong possibility.

Another possible background situates the Christ hymn in the context of the Philippian community. Peter Oakes notes the parallels between the description of Jesus in Philippians 2:5–11 and the Roman emperor: worldwide dominion; the title "lord" (note also "savior" in 3:20); and the implications of divinity.[75] In addition, emperors were ethical paradigms for their subjects to follow, as Jesus is in Philippians 2:5–11.[76] In Philippi, the imperial cult was spatially and rhetorically central to the city, and participation offered a means of advancing social status through engaging with imperial identity and authority.[77] The Philippian community would hear Philippians 2:5–11 as a claim of Christ's superiority to the emperor. This connection suggests that adherence to Christ offered an alternative avenue toward social status.

72. So Kittredge 1998, 77–81. See also Marchal 2006a, 134, emphasizing the message of divinity and ruling power.

73. Argued particularly by Dunn 1998, 282–88; Gorman 2009, 16; Hunsinger 2020, 55.

74. Potential parallels include exaltation from Isa. 52:13 in Phil. 2:9–11; "to death" in Isa. 53:8, 12 in "until death" in Phil. 2:8; humiliation from Isa. 53:8 in Phil. 2:8; and pouring out the soul in Isa. 52:13 in the kenosis of Phil. 2:7. See Hansen 2009, 150–55; Ware 2021, 256–57, 265–66; Hunsinger 2022, 51.

75. Oakes 2001, 138–57, 160–71. See also Heen 2004, 137–53; Reumann 2008, 368–70.

76. Oakes 2001, 158–59, 173, particularly highlights the expectation that the emperor would sacrifice his own self-interest for the sake of the state.

77. See Hellerman 2005, 68, 81–83 (including translations of relevant inscriptions from first- and second-century Philippi); Moessner 2009, 131–32; Shaner 2017, 359–60.

The Philippian community would also recognize the irony of the comparison of Christ with the emperor. Crucifixion was a public display of Rome's power over its subjects (see further below), and yet crucifixion is the axis on which the Christ hymn turns. Within the context of imperial standards, Jesus's superiority is indelibly shaped by inferiority. As Philippians 2:1–4 indicates, any attempt to use adherence to Christ to advance through the Roman social hierarchy is empty-glory (κενοδοξία).[78] Joseph Hellerman consequently identifies Philippians 2:6–11 as a *cursus pudorum* rather than *honorum*.[79]

The comparison of Jesus with the emperor conflicts with his humiliating, obedient enslavement. Another significant background for Philippians 2:5–11 is the Roman system of slavery.[80] The presence of enslaved and freed people and enslavers in the Philippian community provides living illustrations of the descriptions of Jesus as "slave." For this community, the representation of Jesus is "decidedly negative and socially shameful."[81] Part of the shame comes from the un-masculinity of enslavement.

Jesus the Slave: Christology, Slavery, and (Un-)Masculinity

The hymn begins and ends by equating Jesus with God (Phil. 2:6, 9–11). Initially, Jesus is in the form (μορφή) of God and equal (ἴσος) with God, paired concepts that suggest a shared appearance, character, or glory (for μορφή), and comparative equivalence (for ἴσος).[82] For an audience in Philippi, both terms would resonate with the conception and visual representation of the imperial cult.[83] But Jesus's identity and status is not initially reason for glorification or worship. Rather, Paul says, Jesus did not "cling to" (NLT), "grasp" (NAB, ESV), or "exploit" (NRSV, CEB) his equality with God. As these various translations of ἁρπαγμός indicate, the significance of this unique term is debated.[84] The lexical group includes theft, acts of injustice by people in positions of power, and the violence of capture in war or attack by wild animals.[85] The violent overtones suggest that, in Philippians 2:6, Jesus did not

78. Cf. Oakes 2001, 159–60; Reumann 2008, 368–69; Tamez 2017, 74.

79. Hellerman 2005, 129. See also Moessner 2009, 142.

80. See esp. Hawthorne 1983, 86–87; Hellerman 2005, 136–42; Reumann 2008, 368–70.

81. Hellerman 2005, 138.

82. For μορφή, see Isa. 44:13 LXX; Wis. 18:1; Tob. 1:13; Mark 16:12; 4 Macc. 15:4. For ἴσος, see Deut. 13:7 LXX; Isa. 51:23 LXX; Matt. 20:12; John 5:18. See further Fee 1995, 207–8; Hellerman 2005, 131–33; Shaner 2017, 361 (emphasizing the bodily dimension).

83. See Heen 2004, 137–39; Gorman 2009, 18–19; Shaner 2017, 360–61.

84. Shaner 2017, 347–50.

85. Ἅρπαγμα, ἁρπαγή, and ἁρπάζω describe robbery in Lev. 5:23 LXX; Isa. 61:8 LXX; and Matt. 12:29; injustice in Isa. 3:14; 10:2 LXX; and Ezek. 22:25, 27 LXX (cf. Matt. 23:25 // Luke

exploit or abuse his equivalence with God, or, following Katherine Shaner, did not use his divine identity to abuse and oppress others (as the Roman emperors did).[86]

The rejection of exploitation fits with other themes of Philippians: Paul's prioritization of the interests of the community over his own interests (1:21–25), and the call for the members of the community to set aside their own desires to seek the interests of others (2:1–4). Instead of abusing his privileged position, Jesus "emptied himself" (ἑαυτὸν ἐκένωσεν) by assuming the "form of a slave" (μορφὴ δούλου) and "human likeness" (ὁμοίωμα ἀνθρώπων). Jesus replaced the "form of God" and its associated status, power, and privileges with the altogether human identity of an enslaved person.[87] Shaner insightfully compares Philippians 2:6–8 with the imperial imagery from Aphrodisias, which depicts manly, heroic emperors overpowering defeated peoples represented as women. By contrast, the implications of the imperial cult in Philippians 2:6 are reversed in verses 7 and 8. Instead of the powerful emperor, Jesus embodies the status and identity of a subjugated, enslaved woman.[88]

Not exploiting his own position and taking on the form of a slave together mark Jesus's enslavement as voluntary. Furthermore, as Cynthia Kittredge notes, no enslaver is named in this text (Jesus is not enslaved to someone or something).[89] These fundamental differences from the normative experience of slavery in the Roman Empire raise questions concerning the reality or legitimacy of Jesus's enslavement.[90] But, as noted in chapter 1, people did (albeit rarely) enter slavery by choice, either to seek opportunities for social

11:39); wartime plunder in Deut. 28:31 LXX; Jdt. 2:11; and Bar. 4:26; and animal attacks in Job 29:17 LXX; Amos 3:4 LXX; and John 10:12. The word group does not always include violence (e.g., 2 Cor. 12:2, 4; 1 Thess. 4:17), but it usually does (Shaner 2017, 347–48).

86. Shaner 2017, 346, 358. Heen 2004, 138, 149, also connects the term with the imperial cult: Jesus did not "grab" for divine honors. See further Hooker 2003, 112–13; Hellerman 2005, 133–34; Keown 2012, 312.

87. Cf. O'Brien 1991, 216–17; Witherington 1994, 66–67; D. Williams 2002, 132; Hooker 2003, 113. Alternatively, Jesus's kenosis has been understood as a self-sacrificial "pouring out" rather than a giving up of specific attributes or characteristics (so Fee 1995, 210; Hellerman 2005, 135). Moessner 2009, 135, 139, associates κενόω with status and public recognition, arguing Jesus "'deprives himself' of any genuine status recognition by others" (cf. Gorman 2009, 21).

88. Shaner 2017, 361. See also de Wet 2018, 41–42, on the embodiment of Jesus as slave.

89. Kittredge 1998, 79–80. In Rom. 6:16–20 and 8:15, all humanity is enslaved to sin and death. Given the conceptual links between Phil. 2:6–8 and Romans (esp. the connection of slavery, obedience, and death in Rom. 5:10–21; 6:3–10), it is likely this is the context of Jesus's enslavement (see Osiek 2000, 61–62; Gupta 2010, 6–11). This suggestion narrows the broad concept of enslavement to "demonic forces" made by, e.g., Käsemann 1968, 67, 86; Cousar 2009, 55. Alternatively, the connection of enslavement with obedience suggests God is the enslaver (Holloway 2017, 124).

90. Marchal 2007, 248–49.

or professional development (Petronius, *Sat.* 57.4–6; *Dig.* 28.3.6.5) or, more commonly, to survive extreme poverty (Diodorus Siculus 26.20.2; Seneca, *Ben.* 4.13.3). In this context, Jesus's voluntary enslavement is at least understandable, even if it is unlike most enslaved people's experience of involuntary enslavement.

The rarity of references to self-sale indicates the shame associated with enslavement. Both Diodorus Siculus and Petronius criticized such a choice as dishonorable (cf. *Dig.* 48.19.14), and Dio Chrysostom warned that those who sell themselves enter into horrifying experiences (15.23).[91] The voluntary enslavement Paul describes in Philippians 2:7 would have been unsettling and strange for the Philippian audience to contemplate. Rather than choosing the dishonor of enslavement, enslaved people sought the honor and dignity of freedom. Paul's story of Jesus's self-enslavement challenges the Roman emphasis on social status as a significant factor in human worth (and, given the importance of social status for elite constructions of masculinity, especially for free men).[92]

This challenge is apparent in the equivalency between being enslaved and being human in Philippians 2:7. This equivalency is reinforced by the phrase σχήματι . . . ὡς ἄνθρωπος. While the term σχῆμα ("appearance") is rare in the Bible, both Josephus and Philo associate it with humiliation and enslavement.[93] Josephus depicted Aristobulus adopting a slavish and humiliating appearance when he sought Roman support for his rule. According to Josephus, Aristobulus himself was uncomfortable with his behavior (μὴ φέρων δουλεύειν ταῖς χρείαις ταπεινότερον τοῦ σχήματος; *J.W.* 1.132).[94] A similar association of σχῆμα with slavery is made in Philo's description of the Therapeutai. Because they considered enslavement to be contrary to the essential freedom of humanity, they replaced the work of enslaved people with voluntary mutual service by freeborn Therapeutai (esp. young men; *Contempl.* 70–71). But even as the freeborn did the kinds of tasks an enslaved person would do, they did not adopt a "slavish appearance" (δουλοπρεπὲς σχῆμα; 72). In both stories,

91. Note also the representation of freeborn men who "sell" themselves as (free) attendants to wealthy men in Lucian, *Merc. cond.* 23–24. Although the people in question are not enslaving themselves, Lucian's disdain suggests their self-sale for financial gain is a shameful humiliation.

92. Cf. Hellerman 2005, 135; Keown 2012, 312; Park 2024, 463–64.

93. For the connection of σχῆμα with enslavement, see Josephus, *Ant.* 2.41–42, 3.282; Philo, *Spec.* 2.82. The term is associated with humiliation in Josephus, *Ant.* 13.415; Philo, *Migr.* 147, *Spec.* 2.106.

94. This story of Aristobulus contrasts with Herod the Great's appearance before the Sanhedrin, with his power and privilege on display (rather than presenting himself with a humiliating σχῆμα; Josephus, *Ant.* 14.171–74). Cf. also Philo, *Migr.* 147, which warns against adopting an excessively humiliated manner (τὸ ταπεινοῦ καὶ ἀφανοῦς μεταποιεῖσθαι σχήματος εὐεπίβατον).

adopting the manner or identity of an enslaved person is dishonorable, comparable with the story of Prusias in chapter 2. The work of slavery may not always be shameful, but by elite standards, the status of slavery is.

For some interpreters, Jesus's slavery in Philippians 2:5–11 is a metaphor of honor, as the figure of ultimate authority positions himself as "slave" to those under his authority.[95] But the literary and rhetorical context of Philippians 2:5–11 coincides with the social context of Rome's racializing, demoralizing, and violent system of enslavement to define Jesus's slavery around humiliation, obedience, and crucifixion. Furthering the disruption of the expectations of masculine domination in the imperial cult, these three aspects of enslavement reinforce the dishonor of Jesus's status as a subjugated slave. They also characterize Jesus as un-masculine.

Humiliation (Ταπεινόω) in Philippians 2:8

According to most English translations of ἐταπείνωσεν ἑαυτὸν in Philippians 2:8, Jesus "humbled himself" (so CEB, ESV, KJV, NIV, NRSVue, etc.). A few verses earlier, Paul contrasted a related noun, ταπεινοφροσύνη, with selfishness and vanity (v. 3). In this sense, humility is a virtue (cf. Eph. 4:2; Col. 3:12). Philo particularly drew on this meaning, explaining the disciplined, reasonable "humiliation" of self-interest as a means of developing masculine virtue.[96] The translation of ταπεινόω in Philippians 2:8 with the concept of humility makes the Christ hymn an example of a consistent biblical motif: God raises up those who are humble, and God lowers those who exalt themselves.[97]

The ταπειν- lexical group has a broad range of meaning. In the Bible, ταπεινόω, ταπεινός, ταπείνωσις, and related terms often express acts of violence and abuse (including rape);[98] military defeat and political oppression;[99] and the consequences of sin (including divine punishment).[100] In these contexts,

95. Cf. Oakes 2001, 158–59.

96. Philo's discussion of two variations of "humiliation" in *Post.* 46–48 is particularly illuminating. Sometimes, humiliation indicates weakness (ἀσθένεια), which destroys reason, self-control, and virtue, but sometimes humility indicates virtuous strength. See also *Det.* 13, 16, 32–34; *Fug.* 207; *Leg.* 3.18–19, 3.84.

97. E.g., 2 Sam. 22:28; Ps. 18:28 (17:28 LXX); Prov. 18:12; 29:23; Sir. 3:18; 7:11. This motif is also present in the New Testament: e.g., Matt. 18:4; 23:12; Luke 14:11; 18:14; James 1:10; 4:10; 1 Pet. 5:5–6. This interpretation of ταπεινόω is followed by, e.g., R. Martin 1976, 89; Hawthorne 1983, 69–70; and Klassen 1998, 99–100.

98. So, e.g., in LXX Gen. 31:50; 34:2; Deut. 22:24, 29; Judg. 19:24; 20:5; 2 Sam. 13:12, and passim; Lam. 5:11.

99. As in LXX Judg. 4:23; 12:2; 1 Sam. 7:13; 2 Sam. 7:10; Ps. 54:20 (55:20); Isa. 51:23; and also in 2 Macc. 8:35.

100. E.g., LXX Lev. 16:29; 1 Kings 8:35; 2 Chron. 28:19; Ezra 8:21; Isa. 2:9–12; 3:17; 5:15; Lam. 1:8; 2:5; 3:32–34; Hos. 5:5.

the terms carry the negative connotations of subjugation, abasement, or humiliation rather than humility. The word group is also associated with enslavement.[101] With reference to enslaved women specifically, the ταπειν- word group describes the abuses of slavery (Gen. 16:9, 11; Deut. 21:14).

"Humility" is rarely an admirable characteristic outside the Bible and the few instances in Philo. Even Josephus, with his significant biblical heritage, only infrequently expresses positive assessments of individuals with the ταπειν- word group.[102] Sometimes the lexical group carries a relatively neutral meaning of non-elite socioeconomic status.[103] The connotations are more frequently negative, describing undesirable attributes, behaviors, or status.[104] The primary uses of the ταπειν- word group indicate abuse, oppression, and enslavement. In particular, the various terms signify humiliation imposed by an external system, nation, or individual. For instance, the ταπειν- word group portrays defeat in war.[105] Relatedly, it expresses political defeat or oppression.[106] Sometimes, the "humiliation" of low social status corresponds with dishonorable labor and enslavement.[107] An enslaved man is an example of a status-less person, ταπεινός, in Plutarch, *Publ.* 4–5. The word group also sometimes describes "slavish" characteristics or attributes ascribed to enslaved people by the elite.[108]

The characteristics associated with the ταπειν- lexical group consistently portray un-manliness in the Greco-Roman world.[109] Josephus defined warfare as a space for manliness, ἀνδραγαθία, in opposition to the humiliation of defeat and submission (*J.W.* 1.376).[110] Soldiers who ran away from battle were humiliated by the removal of masculine privileges of political office, marriage, physical appearance, and the right to protect one's own body from

101. E.g., LXX Gen. 15:13; Exod. 1:12; Lev. 25:39; Deut. 26:6. Enslavement to God is also described with ταπειν- vocabulary in Luke 1:48 and Acts 20:19.

102. Josephus does use the ταπειν- word group positively in *Ant.* 6.263, 10.11. See also Plato, *Leg.* 4.716a; Xenophon, *Lac.* 8.2; Plutarch, *Ant.* 73.3, *Cat. Min.* 12.4–5 (though Cato's "lowliness" in self-presentation results in poor treatment by others).

103. Aristotle, *Eth. nic.* 1124b; Philo, *Post.* 109; Josephus, *Ant.* 6.200; Plutarch, *Per.* 24.4; *Sull.* 3.4.

104. Aristotle, *Pol.* 5.1315b; *Rhet.* 2.13.5; Philo, *Migr.* 147; Josephus, *Ant.* 18.147; Plutarch, *Cat. Min.* 32.1; *Dem.* 21.2; [*Lib. ed.*] 1b–c; Feldmeier 2013, 251–52.

105. E.g., Thucydides 2.61.3; Isocrates, *Paneg.* 95; Polybius 3.85.7; Josephus, *Ant.* 6.179; *J.W.* 6.395; Plutarch, *Ages.* 29.4, 30.3; *Cim.* 12.1.

106. Polybius 14.1.3; Diodorus Siculus 2.45.2; Dionysius of Halicarnassus, *Ant. rom.* 6.45.3; Plutarch, *Sol.* 22.2.

107. Dionysius of Halicarnassus, *Ant. rom.* 6.45.3; Plutarch, *Art.* 11.5; *Per.* 2.1.

108. Aristotle, *Rhet.* 2.13.5; Polybius 14.1.13; Plutarch, *Art.* 11.5; Epictetus, *Diatr.* 2.16–18.

109. Apart from Philo (see above), I am aware of one text in which the ταπειν- word group portrays manliness: Xenophon, *Ages.* 11.11, 14.

110. See also Isocrates, *Archid.* 89; *Paneg.* 95; Diodorus Siculus 5.29.3; Philo, *Leg.* 1.68.

abuse (Plutarch, *Ages*. 29.4, 30.3).[111] The un-manliness of the ταπειν- word group extends beyond the battlefield. According to Aristotle, a "slavish" man lacks the drive to respond to and overcome humiliation (*Eth. eud.* 3.1231b). Humiliation is "womanish" (θῆλυς) according to Euripides, *Heracl.* 1412–13. Plutarch derided "weak" (ἀσθένεια), "effeminate" (μαλακία) men who humiliated their wives in order to claim authority over them (*Conj. praec.* 8).[112] Despite the potential for humility to develop manly discipline and reason, Philo contrasted honorable, manly freedom with the mindset and behavior of a slavish, humiliated person (*Prob.* 24). Likewise, for Epictetus it is slavishly un-manly to be ταπεινός or ταπεινοφροσύνη (*Diatr.* 3.24.56–61).

In biblical and Greco-Roman contexts, the association of ταπεινόω with enslavement in Philippians 2:7–8 makes the meaning of "humiliation" probable. Given the process by which Jesus humbles or humiliates himself—through obedience to the point of execution by crucifixion—the issue of humiliation takes priority over the use of the term to indicate virtuous humility.[113] And despite Philo's definition of humiliation as the manly exercise of reason, for a reader in the first century, the connection of Jesus's act of ταπεινόω with slavery and execution would naturally draw out the term's connotations of subjugation, violence, and un-masculinity.

Obedience (Ὑπήκοος) in Philippians 2:8

Most often, ὑπήκοος refers to the relationship of people as subjects to their ruler, sometimes with the specific connotation of military subjugation. Rulers command, and subjects obey (note Philo, *Legat.* 69).[114] In the Bible, the concept of obedience to a superior party is expanded to include obedience to God and, in the New Testament, to Jesus.[115] In Philippians 2:8, Jesus is positioned as the subject who obeys, rather than the ruler who is obeyed.

As these uses indicate, obedience occurs within relationships of imbalanced or unequal status. Philo highlighted the imbalance in *Decal.* 165–67: "Subjects"

111. See also Thucydides 2.61.3; Xenophon, *Hell.* 6.4.16.

112. Note also Diodorus Siculus 2.45.2, where the "manliness" of the Amazonian women is paired with the humiliating enslavement of their men, and Josephus, *Ant.* 11.54–55, where strong women humiliate weak men (a concubine and king, in this particular instance).

113. So also Hellerman 2005, 143; Reumann 2008, 370. Cf. Osiek 2000, 54; Hansen 2009, 154; Feldmeier 2013, 253–55.

114. The general meaning of being subject to a ruler is in, e.g., Plato, *Leg.* 3.701b; 1 Macc. 10:38; Josephus, *Ant.* 8.215; Appian, *Bell. civ.* 1.3.21; and Plutarch, *Fab.* 4.2. Subjugation in war is found in Deut. 20:11; Polybius 2.1.7; Plutarch, *Alcib.* 21.1; and Josephus, *Ant.* 7.104. See further Kittredge 1998, 42–51.

115. Ὑπήκοος in Acts 7:38; ὑπακούω in LXX Gen. 22:18; Lev. 26:14; and Isa. 65:12; ὑπακοή (to Jesus) in 2 Cor. 10:5–6; 1 Pet. 1:2, 14, 22. See also Philo, *Opif.* 72; Josephus, *Ant.* 1.21, 233.

are aligned with children and enslaved people as the inferior parties under the authority of rulers, parents, and enslavers (see also *Spec.* 2.226–27). The vocabulary of obedience is used of wives, children, and enslaved people in relation to the men who hold authority over them in the Bible and beyond.[116] The inclusion of these categories brings the concept of obedience into conversation with gender.

While the obedience of subjects to a ruler is not generally gendered as un-masculine, it can be. Josephus made this connection concerning the Jewish people, conquered by and long obedient (ὑπακούω) to Rome, so much so that they have become slavish and lack the manliness to free themselves from their subjection (*J.W.* 2.355–57).[117] Manliness is demonstrated by the refusal to obey shameful, humiliating commands, as in the case of Plutarch's Spartan captive who obeyed only until (μέχρι) commanded to perform a dishonorable task. He killed himself rather than empty a chamber pot (Plutarch, *Mor.* 234c).[118] The gendered connotations of obedience in these texts also appear in the metaphorical rule of the mind or reason over the body and its physical and emotional desires. Philo positioned the mind as masculine and the body as feminine, with the feminine, of course, being subject to the rule of the masculine.[119]

As with Jesus's assumption of enslavement, his obedience represents an act of will. But given the concerns of status embedded in the lexical range of ὑπήκοος (and related terms), it is also possible to read Jesus's obedience in Philippians 2:7–8 as representative of the condition of enslavement and, consequently, a further indication of his un-masculinity.[120] Enslavers did not grant enslaved people the freedom to choose whether to obey. The enslaved Spartan's refusal to obey a command to perform a dishonorable (un-manly) task demonstrates his reclamation of masculinity. This example contrasts sharply with Jesus, who obeyed as far as (μέχρι) death. Crucifixion, the means of death, was a much more public demonstration of shameful un-manliness than emptying a chamber pot would be.

116. Wives (with ὑπήκοος, ὑπακούω): Josephus, *Ag. Ap.* 2.201; Plutarch, *Cat. Maj.* 20.1. Children (with ὑπήκοος, ὑπακούω): Deut. 21:18–20; Prov. 4:3; 13:1; Eph. 6:1; Col. 3:20; Plato, *Resp.* 5.463d; Philo, *Ebr.* 84; Plutarch, *Mor.* 237d. Enslaved people (with ὑπακοή, ὑπακούω): Rom. 6:16; Eph. 6:5; Col. 3:22; Philo, *Ebr.* 198; *Prob.* 35–36; *Spec.* 2.80; Plutarch, [*Apoth. Lac.*] 234c; Kittredge 1998, 79.

117. This description is inverted in Josephus, *Ant.* 7.390, where the manliness of King David is in part demonstrated by his subjects' obedience.

118. By contrast, Josephus represented Antony as "enslaved" to Cleopatra, though he does refuse to obey particularly unjust commands (*Ant.* 15.93; *J.W.* 7.302).

119. Philo, *Migr.* 8; *Opif.* 165; *Spec.* 1.200. See also Plato, *Resp.* 3.389d–3, 4.441e.

120. The gendering of obedience generally goes unnoticed, but its association with enslavement is addressed by, e.g., Hellerman 2005, 143. Reumann 2008, 372, however, argues that Jesus's obedience would be seen as virtuous citizenship in Roman Philippi.

Death by the Cross in Philippians 2:8

For a first-century audience, crucifixion was synonymous with abject suffering and humiliation (note, e.g., Cicero, *Verr.* 2.3.7, 2.6.14, 2.66.169). As a spectacle to punish, warn, and entertain, imperial officials utilized crucifixion to signify Rome's power to terrorize, deform, and display the bodies of enslaved women and men and rebellious foreigners.[121] So, for instance, the stories of the slave revolt associated with Spartacus end with the crucifixions of six thousand enslaved people along the main road from Capua to Rome (Appian, *Bell. civ.* 1.120.559). Josephus's account of the siege of Jerusalem in 70 CE includes the crucifixion of captive men and women in unusual poses for the amusement of the Roman soldiers, and the terrorizing of onlookers from the city (*J.W.* 5.451). The act of crucifixion made visible Rome's ability to deny their victims' personhood.

Crucifixion was commonly associated with slavery.[122] Because of this association and the horror of crucifixion as a form of execution, Cicero claimed Roman citizens should not be crucified (*Verr.* 2.65.168, 2.66.170). He identified crucifixion as a cruel punishment unworthy of manly men (*vir fortiori*; *Rab. Perd.* 10–11). As developed in chapter 2, manliness was demonstrated by bodily control, posture, physical strength, and the ability to protect one's own body from abuse. Crucifixion destroyed these aspects of masculinity.

The process of crucifixion began with a parade of violence, which might include public beating, burning, and torture.[123] The crucifixion itself was a spectacle of bodily horror and physical agony (see esp. Seneca, *Ep.* 101.14). In addition to the physical effects, victims of crucifixion lost their cognitive faculties (Seneca the Elder, *Controv.* 7.7.18). Passersby participated in the process by mocking victims (as in the story of Jesus in Mark 15:29–32). The victims of crucifixion were traditionally denied the honor of burial. Their memorial was instead the graphic description of rot in various sources: bodies melting, dripping, and decaying; eaten by vultures; and defiled by witches.[124]

121. Philo, *Flacc.* 83–84; Josephus, *J.W.* 5.289, 7.302; Pseudo-Quintilian, *Lesser Declamations* 274.13; Hengel 1977, 46; J. Williams 2024, 77–79.

122. E.g., *AE* 1971.88; Seneca the Elder, *Controv.* 7.6; Petronius, *Sat.* 126.9; Livy 22.33.2; Valerius Maximus 2.7.9; Juvenal, *Sat.* 6.219; Tacitus, *Hist.* 4.3; Appian, *Bell. civ.* 4.81.343. The association of slavery with crucifixion also appears in literary fiction: Xenophon of Ephesus, *Anthia* 4.2.1; Chariton, *Call.* 4.2.6–7; Petronius, *Sat.* 53.3. See further Hengel 1977, 52–59; Cook 2014, 358–59. Perhaps the second most common association of crucifixion was with war: e.g., Diodorus Siculus 15.53.4, 17.46.4, 26.23.1; Josephus, *Ant.* 12.256, 17.295, *J.W.* 2.306.

123. See, e.g., Cicero, *Verr.* 2.6.14, 2.63.163; *AE* 1971.88; Philo, *Flacc.* 72; Josephus, *J.W.* 3.321, 5.449; Cook 2014, 374–85, 423–29; Wilson 2015, 201–4.

124. Lucan, *Civil War* 6.545–49; Seneca the Elder, *Controv.* 8.4; Valerius Maximus 6.9, ext. 5; Juvenal, *Sat.* 14.77–80; Pliny, *Nat.* 36.107–8. Some victims were buried (see Cook 2014, 387).

As a public display of broken minds and beaten bodies, of people suffering an agonizing death and the shameful mockery that accompanied it, and of decaying corpses, crucifixion humiliated and emasculated its victims.

Within masculinity studies, the portrayal of Jesus's death in Philippians 2:8 is sometimes interpreted as an example of a noble, voluntary, and (consequently) manly death.[125] While the emasculation of crucifixion is rarely interrupted or interrogated in antiquity, there are a few texts in which a free man's endurance of crucifixion signified masculinity. First, Seneca utilizes the gory, horrifying imagery of crucifixion to deride Maecenas's desire to preserve his life no matter what the circumstances. According to Seneca, instead of manly endurance and the willingness to die, Maecenas, in his dishonorable, weak effeminacy, sought survival (*effeminati turpitudo*; *Ep*. 101.10–14). This particular example is inverted in the story of Theodorus of Cyrene. When threatened with crucifixion, he replied that he could rot on the ground or above it all the same. His equanimity and disdain for death made him an exemplar of masculinity (*virtus*) for Valerius Maximus (6.2, ext. 3).[126] Jesus in Philippians 2:8 obeys until death; his willingness to die would, in company with Theodorus (and in contrast to Maecenas), signify masculinity.

The second example is the story of Regulus. Regulus was a Roman captured by the Carthaginians. Sent as an emissary to Rome by the Carthaginians, he refused to encourage his people to surrender and therefore, in some versions of his story, he was crucified by the Carthaginians as punishment. Seneca honored his faithfulness, endurance, and manliness (*virtus*) in suffering for what was right (*Prov*. 3.9–10; *Ep*. 98.12).[127] Josephus similarly honored a soldier captured in Jotapata who refused to reveal the city's secrets even though he was tortured and crucified (*J.W*. 3.321). To be crucified for a "manly" act of resisting the enemy or to endure crucifixion in a "manly" manner overcomes its humiliating emasculation. According to Hebrews 12:1–2, Jesus's endurance of the shame and pain of crucifixion allies him with men like Regulus and Josephus's captives.[128]

125. Conway 2008, 67–73, notes the apparent conflict between the emasculation of crucifixion and Paul's adherence to hegemonic masculinity. She argues that the voluntary nature of Jesus's death for the benefit of others makes even crucifixion manly. However, Sheckler and Leith 2010, 77–78, identify crucifixion as "a primary signifier of passivity and emasculation" in the Roman Empire.

126. See also Cicero, *Tusc*. 1.102; Plutarch, *Mor*. 499d.

127. On Regulus, see also Florus, *Epit*. 1.18.2.25; Hengel 1977, 64–66.

128. Note also the representation of crucifixion as glory in John 12:23–24 and 13:31–32. See further Scaer 2005, 42–53, and passim, on the use of noble death traditions in the New Testament (specifically, Luke's passion story). A number of interpreters have challenged the interpretation of Jesus's death in the Gospels as "noble": J. Ripley 2015, 230–33; Wilson 2015, 209–35; Moore 2021, 84–86.

But the association of masculinity with crucifixion is quite limited and fleetingly rare. Neither Maecenas nor Theodorus is actually crucified; rather, crucifixion provides a rhetorical device in these traditions. Seneca's visceral descriptions of the suffering of a human body in the act of crucifixion underscores the un-manliness of its victims, unless they have the elite self-control and reason needed to maintain a Stoic disdain for death (*Ep.* 101.11–14). Here, too, the example of Jesus in Philippians 2:6–8 falls short. Jesus does not endure crucifixion because he disdains death. He is crucified because he is an obedient, humiliated slave. The descriptors in the Christ hymn distinguish Jesus from the manliness of Regulus and Josephus's captive soldier.

Cicero declared crucifixion to be so dishonorable that speaking or even thinking of crucifixion had no place around freeborn Romans (*Rab. Perd.* 16). The narrative of Jesus's crucifixion in Mark 15:15–39 draws attention to its dishonorable nature with scenes of public beatings and mockery. Though Paul does not include narratival details, he elsewhere identified the crucifixion of Jesus as a foolish message (1 Cor. 1:18) and an offense (Gal. 5:11). Similarly, in Hebrews 12:1–2, it is a shame. The collocation of humiliation, obedience, and crucifixion in Philippians 2:6–8 displays Jesus's low status in a horrifying spectacle that is, in Roman context, also a display of un-manliness.[129]

In the Christ hymn, then, Jesus is an enslaved un-man.[130] Perhaps the best support for this conclusion comes from early Christian interpreters who, Chris de Wet and Tyler Schwaller argue, rewrote Philippians 2:6–8 to demonstrate Jesus's manliness.[131] So, for instance, Clement of Alexandria declared Jesus to be in control of or above human passions and desires. His enslavement, consequently, was only external, not internal; Clement omitted the humiliation, obedience, and crucifixion that define Jesus's enslavement in Philippians 2:7–8 (*Paed.* 1.2.4, 3.1.2). Jesus's manly self-control provides a point of contrast to women who decorate their bodies with elaborate clothing, hairstyles, and makeup and are condemned as sex laborers (prostitutes) by Clement (3.2.4–5). Men who similarly concern themselves with their physical appearance womanize themselves (γυναικίζω; 3.3.15). That Jesus instead dressed himself as an enslaved person proves his manliness. Clement's attempt to redefine Jesus's enslavement in terms of masculinity suggests Philippians 2:6–8 was problematic in this respect. In the context of Greco-Roman antiquity, the Christ hymn un-manned Jesus.

129. Commentators often emphasize the dishonor of crucifixion in Phil. 2:8; so Fee 1995, 217, 229–30; Osiek 2000, 63; Oakes 2001, 159–60; Hellerman 2005, 144–47; Hanson 2009, 157.

130. See also Shaner 2017, 361; Schwaller 2021, 43.

131. De Wet 2018, 47–64; Schwaller 2017, 107–13; 2021, 44–49.

Exalting the Slave: Philippians 2:9–11

"Death by crucifixion" (Phil. 2:8) concludes the first section of the Christ hymn and begins the second half, which concerns exaltation. God gives Jesus a name above all others, so that all creatures in the heavens, on earth, and under the earth kneel and confess Jesus to be κύριος, "lord" or "enslaver." The exaltation of a "lord" to divine status echoes the imperial cult, with Jesus taking the place of (and surpassing) the emperor.[132] The specific imagery in Philippians 2:9–11 is influenced by Isaiah 45:23, which identifies God as the object of worship and confession. The end of the hymn, then, returns to its initial message: Jesus is once again equated with God. For many interpreters, the exaltation that frames Jesus's humiliating enslavement is the point of Philippians 2:5–11.[133]

The shift from abasement to exaltation is a common biblical motif (as noted above in the discussion of the ταπειν- lexical group). This general theme finds specific representation in Isaiah's Servant Songs. In Isaiah 49:6–7, God's "slave" (עבד, παῖς LXX) disregards his own life. He is perceived by the nations to be despicable and repulsive. Nonetheless, the rulers of the nations, his enslavers, will bow to him. Likewise, in 52:13–53:12 (LXX) God's slave will be lifted up (ὑψόω) and glorified (δοξάζω), even though his appearance is repellent and he embodies divine punishment. Unlike 1 Peter 2:22–25, Paul's Christ hymn does not explicitly use the vocabulary of Isaiah's Servant Songs, but there are clear parallels with the narrative represented in Philippians 2:5–11.[134] The exaltation of the humiliated slave whose tortured, deformed body is displayed in public view reflects the shifting representation of the servant in Isaiah.

What would an audience in Roman Philippi, situated within the status structures of Rome's slave society, hear in Philippians 2:9–11? One possibility is the experience of manumission. In the second section of the hymn, Jesus receives a new name, a common element in formal manumission. For instance, an enslaved woman named Aphrodisia added Flavia, the familial name of her former enslavers (the Flavian imperial household), upon her manumission (*ILS* 1519). Freed people joined Rome's social hierarchy by forming families, seeking acclamation as patrons, and often becoming enslavers themselves. The praise accorded to Jesus as "lord/enslaver" in Philippians 2:11 would

132. Cf. Oakes 2001, 149–50, 160–63, 170–71; Heen 2004, 149.

133. E.g., Kittredge 1998, 80; Oakes 2001, 159–60 (arguing that Jesus's self-effacement proves his right to rule); Marchal 2006a, 134–37, 165; Feldmeier 2013, 255–57; Shaner 2017, 362–63 (arguing that the disruption of imperial domination in vv. 6–8 is a momentary blip).

134. The hymn in Philippians does not use the Greek vocabulary of Isaiah in the LXX, but see Ware 2021, 256, on the possible parallels with the Hebrew text.

be imaginable for a freed person. If God is taken to be the enslaver in verses 7 and 8, the fact that the exaltation of Jesus glorifies God also makes sense. Manumission offered a way for enslavers to gain honor for themselves (Dionysius of Halicarnassus, *Ant. rom.* 4.24), and freed people remained legally and socially attached to their former enslavers' households so that their social position would affect their enslavers (see chap. 1, above).[135]

The connections are incomplete, of course. There is no vocabulary of manumission in Philippians 2:9–11. The hymn clearly says that Jesus died as a slave (death was the most common way enslaved people "escaped" slavery). But the parallels between Philippians 2:9–11 and Roman practices of manumission intersect with the problem of status anxiety in Roman society.[136] The many honorific inscriptions in Philippi express individuals' attempts to gain status through social recognition. Likewise, people who had a measure of status feared its loss. As noted in chapter 1, free elites expressed concern over the wealth and public honor associated with freed people, seeing in the social advance of the formerly enslaved a danger to their own freeborn privilege. For anyone in the Philippian community who possessed or aspired to a degree of social status, the exaltation of a humiliated slave may have been a source of discomfort or anxious concern. The alliance between exaltation and disempowerment, embodied by a humiliated, un-manned slave, diverges from imperial social values.

Crucifixion acts as the hinge between humiliation and exaltation. Prioritizing the exaltation at the beginning and end of the Christ hymn interprets the middle as a display of divine glory and power. But it is also possible—and, given the literary construction of Philippians 2:6–11, preferable—to prioritize crucifixion, the lowest point of the humiliation, as the means of interpreting exaltation. Equality with God and exaltation to the highest place do not cancel out the emasculating humiliation, obedience, and crucifixion of slavery in Philippians 2:7–8. Jesus is recognized by God and exalted as an un-manned slave.[137] So Michael Gorman argues that the beginning of the hymn should be understood as signifying both "although" Jesus was in the form of God and "because" Jesus was in the form of God: The narrative of descent in verses 7 and 8 demonstrates who Jesus (and therefore God) is. The "form of God" is made visible in the "form of a slave."[138]

135. In this respect, Hellerman 2005, 107–8, notes the inclusion of enslavers' names on funerary inscriptions for freed people in Philippi (though, as he says, this was a common practice across the Roman Empire).

136. See Roller 2001, 264–72.

137. Cf. Heen 2004, 151; Hellerman 2005, 131; Moessner 2009, 141–42; Holloway 2017, 124.

138. Gorman 2009, 24–28, 32. See also Stubbs 2007, 371, 374.

The representation of Jesus as an enslaved person reflects the real oppression, injustice, and suffering of enslavement in the Roman Empire, and this embodied experience of enslavement centers the hymn. The vast expanse of rhetorical space between exaltation and humiliation draws attention to the abasement of enslavement. The sorts of humiliation imposed by Roman slavery, the necessary obedience to enslavers' varied commands, and the constant threat of violence were a lived reality for some, or possibly many, participants in the Philippian church. Enslaved and freed people could have seen their own experience in the depiction of Jesus's humiliation, obedience, and emasculation. The hymn's celebration of a humiliated slave may have offered them hope that they, too, could be recognized and honored for the simple fact of their existence.

The imagery of humiliation, obedience, and enslavement is also recognizably oppressive for enslaved and freed people. The cross was a particular fear and horror for the enslaved (and formerly enslaved).[139] In this sense, the hymn is a text of terror rather than celebration. The imagery may also have horrified free people in the audience, particularly those who held or aspired to elite status, though for very different reasons. The Christ hymn redefines the core elements in the (constructed) oppression of slavery as the attitudes and behaviors that bring honor. Instead of aspiring to the emperor's model of manly authority, dignity, and patronage, Paul uses the hymn to challenge the Philippian community to adopt Jesus's model of un-manly obedience, to reject the honor of social status, and to take up the practices that decentered self-interest in order to serve the interests of others.

Imitating Jesus the Slave

In Philippians, Paul's militaristic and athletic metaphors encourage manly endurance for women and men (1:27; 4:3). His equanimity in a variety of situations demonstrate his own (Stoic-esque) masculinity, and he encourages the community toward manly virtue (ἀρετή; 4:8–13). These representations of normative masculinity correspond with the Romanized context of the community in Philippi. As the evidence of the inscriptions found in the city indicates, people from various backgrounds sought social honor and status.[140] Gender distinctions in the standard information given in inscriptions

139. E.g., Horace, *Ep.* 1.16.48; Seneca the Elder, *Controv.* 3.9; Valerius Maximus 8.4.2; Petronius, *Sat.* 126.9 (and note the crucifixion of freed slaves in Josephus, *Ant.* 18.79; Suetonius, *Cal.* 12.3). Note, however, that crucifixion was also the subject of black humor in the Roman Empire (see Harley-McGowan 2020, 134–35).

140. Cf. Hellerman 2005, 100–107; Bond 2022, 163–64.

particularly implicate men in the competition for honor and status.[141] Normative constructions of masculinity depended on ancestry, political or social position, and wealth (including the use of wealth for patronage; see chap. 2, above). Consequently, Philippian men published their family trees, political and cultic appointments, and acts of patronage to demonstrate their masculinity.

In contrast to inscriptions of honor, the Christ hymn in Philippians 2:6–11 displays Jesus's humiliating, un-manned enslavement. The Christology of slavery is jarring in a social context centered on status and power. For a free man with divine identity to give up authority over his own person, his own body, would be perceived as dishonoring and dehumanizing. The representation of Jesus in Philippians 2:6–11 deliberately depicts this undesirable state as a model for the church to adopt.[142] The Christ hymn is integrated into the ethical exhortation in verses 1–5 and 12–15 by a common vocabulary: φρονέω (vv. 2, 5); κενόω and κενοδοξία (vv. 3, 7); ταπεινόω and ταπεινοφροσύνη (vv. 3, 8); ὑπήκοος and ὑπακούω (vv. 8, 12). The introduction to the hymn in verse 5 clarifies that Jesus's mindset or attitude, his way of thinking and living (φρονέω), is the pattern for the community to follow.[143] The challenges of this Christology for understandings of what it means to be human, which for the Roman Empire was what it means to be masculine, are broad.[144]

Throughout Philippians, Paul, Timothy, and Epaphroditus demonstrate the working out of Jesus's model.[145] Paul and Timothy are "slaves" (1:1) who set aside their own needs, desires, or advantages for the sake of others (1:21–26; 2:19–21). Paul's autobiography in 3:4–11 follows the trajectory of giving up privileges or advantages to identify with a suffering, crucified Jesus in the hope of sharing Jesus's resurrection. Epaphroditus's near-death experience (μέχρι θανάτου) in his work on behalf of the community brings him honor (2:29–30). Paul's and Epaphroditus's examples also demonstrate what the

141. Hellerman 2005 does not thoroughly address masculinity as an element of social honor, but see pp. 165–66.

142. On Phil. 2:5–11 as an ethical exhortation, see, e.g., Osiek 2000, 68–69; Keown 2012, 310; Cuvillier 2014, 379.

143. Among other interpreters, Cousar 2009, 55–57, protests that this interpretation is "naïve idealism." While I agree that Paul's ethics are idealistic, the exhortations of Phil. 2:1–5 are not unique among his letters (cf. Rom. 12:1–21; Gal. 5:13–14). I do also take Cousar's point that Phil. 2:5–11 tells the story of Christ's victory over the powers that oppress humanity and his consequent remaking of the cosmos (Cousar 2009, 57–58, influenced by Käsemann 1968); I would argue that the letter's encouragement to be citizens of Jesus's heavenly reign has implications for how the community should live in Philippi too (see also Stubbs 2007, 366–70; Gorman 2009, 36–37).

144. See esp. de Vos 1999, 284–86; Oakes 2001, 204–6; Reumann 2008, 314–15, 326–28; Tamez 2017, 66–67.

145. So Peterlin 1995, 66–67; Oakes 2001, 103–4; H. Williams 2012, 350–53; Cuvillier 2014, 382–83; Park 2024, 468.

divine exaltation of 2:9–11 might mean for Jesus's followers. They are not given names above every name, but they do share elements of Christ's exaltation (note 2:15; 3:20–21).[146]

The ethical exhortation begins in Philippians 1:27–30. Paul and the Philippian community suffer and struggle together (vv. 29–30). As they withstand opposition, community members should live in a way that is worthy of the gospel. In particular, they should be united with one another and with Paul (having "one spirit" and "one mind," v. 27). Unity remains in focus in Philippians 2:1–4, defined here around a shared identity and purpose (v. 2) and demonstrated by the other-centered attitude and behavior of community members (vv. 3–4).[147]

While the emphasis on unity in Philippians is sometimes taken to represent Paul's insistence on his own (sole) authority and the suppression of alternative perspectives, it can also be interpreted as the solidarity of a marginalized community in response to opposition from the majority (cf. Diodorus Siculus 17.69.6). In Philippians 2:1, the community's unity encourages mutual comfort in the midst of suffering (παράκλησις, παραμύθιον, and κοινωνία).[148] Reflecting the emphasis on joy in the letter, Paul's own joy is filled by the community's unity in thought, love, and identity (the rare σύμψυχος).[149]

The specific characteristics that illustrate unity in Philippians 2:1–4 reflect the pattern set by Christ: giving up one's own status and self-interest, adopting humiliation in place of glory, and redefining masculinity around enslavement. The vocabulary of slavery does not appear in verses 1–4, though the return to the exhortations to the community in verse 12 encourages the slavery-coded concepts of obedience and fear. Nonetheless, the essence of enslavement runs through the encouragement to set aside self-centered desires to care for the needs of others. These qualities are characteristic of enslaved people whose enslavers did not grant them the legal or moral independence to pursue personal ambition, vanity, or pride. Of course, some enslaved people were able to advance their own interests. Others reclaimed community with one another, supporting one another and befriending one another in defiance

146. Cf. Oakes 2001, 201–3.

147. On unity in Phil. 1:27–2:4, see Peterlin 1995, 52; de Vos 1999, 277–78; Marchal 2006a, 91–98 (identifying the message of unification as a hierarchical demand for obedience); Stubbs 2007, 370; Park 2024, 460.

148. See παράκλησις in LXX Isa. 57:18; and Jer. 38:9 (31:9); and in 2 Cor. 1:3–7; παραμυθία in 1 Thess. 5:14; and in Greco-Roman literature: Diodorus Siculus 17.69.6; Dionysius of Halicarnassus, *Ant. rom.* 2.3.3, 8.41.3; Plutarch, *Amat.* 22; and see κοινωνία in Phil. 3:10.

149. Χαρά and χαίρω weave through Philippians: 1:4, 18, 25; 2:17–18, 28–29; 3:1; 4:1, 4, 10. Bloomquist 2007, 274–81, notes the subversive significance of joy in a letter written from prison and concerned with suffering.

of their enslavers' control (as in the funerary inscription for Jucundus, quoted in chap. 2, above).[150] In this sense, the enslaved and freed people in the Philippian community join Paul, Timothy, and Epaphroditus as living examples of the model established by Jesus.

The qualities Paul encourages the church to adopt in Philippians 2:1–4 and 12–15 are not all inherently gendered, but as with the characterization of Jesus in verses 7–8, several terms carry gendered significance. Vanity (κενοδοξία) in verse 3 is problematic for ideal masculinity according to 4 Maccabees 8:19 and Polybius 3.81.9 and 3.105.9. Any implication of manliness in the prohibition of vanity, however, is countered by the potential danger to masculinity posed by the compassion (σπλάγχνον) and pity (οἰκτιρμός) of Philippians 2:1.[151] As already discussed above with respect to ταπεινόω and ὑπήκοος, the humility or humiliation (ταπεινοφροσύνη) in verse 3 and obedience (ὑπακούω) in verse 12 are associated with un-manliness.[152] Finally, the collocation "fear and trembling" (φόβος καὶ τρόμος) in verse 12 is characteristic of women (Isa. 19:16) and, in conjunction with obedience, slaves (Eph. 6:5). In 1 Corinthians 2:3, fear and trembling signify weakness (ἀσθένεια), a distinctly un-manly quality.[153] As is the case for the pattern set by Jesus, the exhortations given to the community correspond with un-manliness.

In Philippians 2:1–11, to adopt Christ's mindset means to set aside personal interests and desires for the sake of others. Within Greco-Roman society, patronage and benefaction provided ways to meet the needs of other people. The system was geared toward advancing the status and honor of the patron.[154] The exhortation to regard others' interests or needs instead of one's own in verse 4 contrasts with standard practices of patronage.[155] Humiliation requires abandoning the endemic aspirations of social status, choosing the lowest position rather than chasing the highest. In Jesus's example, obedience extends even to the point of death by crucifixion. The function of crucifixion as a public display of disempowerment, therefore, replaces honorific inscriptions

150. See also *CIL* 6.4012, 38513; *TAM* 2.466; and a letter from an enslaved person to his enslaved friends (*CEL* 1.3).

151. Note σπλάγχνον in Sir. 30:7; 4 Macc. 15:23; and οἰκτιρμός in 4 Macc. 6:24 (cf. οἰκτείρω in Josephus, *Ant.* 14.481).

152. For the formerly enslaved philosopher Epictetus, ταπεινοφροσύνη reflects both a lack of status and a dependency on others; it is characteristic of a slave (δοῦλος), in contrast to the freedom, power, and strength of masculinity (ἀνὴρ ἀγαθός; *Diatr.* 3.24.56–61).

153. Fear is generally associated with women, children, and enslaved people in contrast to manly men (see chaps. 2–3).

154. This purpose is apparent in Philippi's inscriptions (e.g., 213/L347; Hellerman 2005, 89, 92–100, 105–6). See also Hoyer 2018, 28–30; and chap. 4, below.

155. Cf. Witherington 1994, 64; Oakes 2001, 181, 186; Reumann 2008, 329. Engberg-Pedersen 2003, 199–203, connects this ethic with Stoic views on the individual as part of a community.

as a demonstration of identity, status, and masculinity. The crucified, abased, un-manned Jesus redefines masculinity for the Philippian community.

Adopting the mindset of Jesus in Philippians 2:6–8 would be natural for those who already lived at the bottom of Rome's social hierarchy: enslaved women and men; freed people; free laborers; and, to a more limited extent (in relation to the male authorities over them in households and society), elite women. In contrast to the "enemies of the cross" in 3:18–19, adopting Christ's mindset as a way of life requires those with status, authority, or privilege—in Roman society, elite men (and to a limited extent, their wives)—to set aside their own interests to identify with and as enslaved people in their humiliation, suffering, and un-masculinity.

Interpreting Christ the Slave

The Christ hymn in Philippians 2:5–11 defines Jesus's life around the voluntary loss of status, privilege, and freedom. In becoming human, Jesus becomes a humiliated, crucified slave and dies a dehumanizing, shameful death. Reading the progression of loss in verses 6–8 within Rome's intersectional definitions of masculinity, Jesus is un-manned. The hymn ends with exaltation. But while exaltation restores the sense of equality with God introduced in verse 6, the logical connection between the two halves of the hymn suggests that Jesus is exalted precisely as the humiliated, obedient victim of crucifixion.

How this imagery would be understood within the Philippian community might vary depending on social location, wealth, and status. For enslaved members of the community, the Christology and discipleship of slavery may have offered a reinterpretation of the oppression of their daily lives or, alternatively, reinforced it—if Christ obeyed to the point of death, so should they. For a freed person or someone of low social status, the exhortation to humiliation may have offered reassurance of their worth even if they could not gain status, or it may have shamed them for desiring status. For an elite man, the rhetoric of humiliating, obedient enslavement and the redefinition of exaltation around crucifixion would have been significantly challenging.

With respect to these speculative responses, Tyler Schwaller draws a helpful comparison between Paul's Christ hymn and the Palatine graffito of Alexamenos and the crucified god. Dating to the late second or early third century, the graffito was found on the wall of a building used by enslaved and freed people in the imperial household.[156] In other words, the graffito was most likely created by an enslaved person, about an enslaved person. It offers an

156. See Harley-McGowan 2020, 108, 113.

intriguing glimpse of how the story of Jesus's crucifixion may have been understood by enslaved people.

The graffito's text, "Alexamenos worships his god," identifies the players in the scene. Alexamenos, wearing a short garment (possibly the standard outfit for an enslaved person[157]), stands before a person being crucified. The figure on the cross wears the same very short garment, but instead of a human head, the figure has the head of a donkey. There are several possible interpretations of this example of animalization. Felicity Harley-McGowan points to parallels among humorous and satirical depictions of gods and (elite) men.[158] Enslaved people were also animalized, as discussed in chapter 2, above. They were often symbolized by hardworking, abused donkeys; the graffito of a donkey at work in a mill in the same building preserves an example of this symbolism from an enslaved person.[159] The crossover between the two symbolic fields in the graffito identifies the figure on the cross as both enslaved and Alexamenos's god.

The standard interpretation of the Alexamenos graffito identifies it as a mockery of Christians: Alexamenos worships a real ass.[160] From the perspective of the Roman elite, the representation of Jesus as a humiliated, crucified slave is foolish, shameful, and horrifying—to be avoided at all costs (cf. 1 Cor. 1:18–25). Harley-McGowan and Schwaller both wonder if a more positive interpretation of the image is possible. For Harley-McGowan, the image represents widespread awareness of early Christian claims that crucifixion symbolized Christ's power (as Paul insists in 1 Cor. 1:18).[161] Schwaller highlights the creation of the graffito by enslaved people, suggesting the image indicates enslaved people's identification with Jesus precisely as an enslaved, crucified un-man—whether the artist intended to mock Alexamenos or not. "The parody may be the point: a crucified god makes a mockery of what counts for masculine mastery, suffering in solidarity with the enslaved, and this becomes the basis for hope and devotion."[162] Alexamenos worships a god who chose to become a slave like him.

In this respect, it is notable that Paul, the figure of authority who writes to the Philippian community to encourage them to obey him (Phil. 2:12), is portrayed in the letter as a suffering prisoner and laboring slave. Epaphroditus, possibly an enslaved or freed man, is by contrast a brother, coworker, soldier, apostle, and cultic official—designations that fit within normative

157. Suggested by Harley-McGowan 2020, 137; see also Olson 2014, 192–93; Schwaller 2021, 53.

158. Harley-McGowan 2020, 126–34.

159. See Joshel and Petersen 2014, 143–45; Schwaller 2021, 56–58.

160. Cf. Harley-McGowan 2020, 132.

161. Harley-McGowan 2020, 106–7.

162. Schwaller 2021, 59.

masculinity (2:25). These different representations indicate that the discipleship of enslavement could work out in distinctive patterns. If there were, in fact, some or many enslaved and freed people in the Philippian community, they may have interpreted the representation of Jesus as a humiliated, crucified, un-manned slave as an affirmation of their own worth.[163] If Jesus is like them, then they—in their (involuntary) attentiveness to the needs of others, in their humiliated status, and even in their un-masculinization—are like Jesus. By virtue of their enslavement, the enslaved people in the community already follow the pattern of Jesus's enslavement.

Roman society was saturated with the desire to use every advantage to increase one's status, wealth, and social honor. The ethical exhortation that surrounds the representation of Jesus as slave offers a different option: to set aside self-interest and the search for status in order to meet the needs of others in the community. These exhortations decenter and upset the centrality of domination and masculinity as the forces that govern politics, wealth, and social power. By the standard constructions of Roman society, enslaved people were worthless. But in Philippians 2:1–11, they become exemplars of Christian identity.

As addressed at the beginning of the chapter, there is serious potential for abuse if Paul's exhortations are imposed on people who lack authority or power (enslaved people, women, racialized populations) by those who treat a position of social or economic power as something to be seized (ἁρπαγμός) and exploited for their own gain. There is a long history of texts like Philippians 2:1–11 being used to advance the power or authority of a few at the expense of those who lack power or authority. Interpreters must be cognizant of, and work to avoid, such abuse and seek readings that advance communal equality and justice.[164]

Practically, the exhortation to adopt Jesus's mindset as a humiliated, unmanned slave is most difficult for the elite men at the top of the hierarchies of Roman society. That the Christ hymn initially situates Jesus in a position of honor, in the form of and equal with God, before narrating his voluntary enslavement challenges the elite in particular ways. Consequently, Elise Tamez insists that the exhortations in Philippians 2:1–11 must be directed toward the people who possess status, power, or masculine privilege.[165] In the Synoptic Gospels, the challenge to follow Jesus's model of willing enslavement is aimed at precisely this population: men in privileged positions (the twelve disciples), just as they sought to advance their own status and power. The next chapter explores the implications of un-masculinity in the challenge to become like enslaved people in Mark 10:41–45 and Luke 22:24–27.

163. So Park 2024, 465. See also Peterlin 1995, 67.
164. See esp. Stubbs 2007, 365–66, 376.
165. Tamez 2017, 72–74. See also Peterlin 1995, 67; Osiek 2000, 54.

4

Slave of All

Masculinity and Authority in the Dining Room

The greatest among you must become like the youngest, and the leader like a server. For who is greatest, the one who reclines to dine or the one who serves? The one who reclines, right? But I am among you as a server.

—Luke 22:26–27

That is why I smile at those who think it degrading for a man to dine with his slave. But why should they think it degrading? It is only because purse-proud etiquette surrounds a master [*dominus*] at his dinner with a mob of standing slaves. . . . The poor slaves may not move their lips, even to speak. The slightest murmur is repressed by the rod; even a chance sound—a cough, a sneeze, or a hiccup—is visited with the lash. There is a grievous penalty for the slightest breach of silence. All night long they must stand about, hungry and silent.

—Seneca, *Ep*. 47.2–3 (LCL, modified)

As the exploration of John 13:1–20 in the introduction showed, the dining room in a Roman home functioned as a stage for the performance of masculinity. Diners reclined around the space in order of social status, so a man's location in the dining room made his relative greatness visible. His behavior demonstrated his degree of masculine control over bodily movements, speech, appetites, and desires. Philosophical debate or readings of historical narratives taught masculine ideals. Equally, the wild excesses possible at a dinner party full of freely flowing wine, rich foods, sexualized entertainment, and beautiful enslaved bodies available for the taking offered opportunity for indulging in the rights and privileges of masculine power.

The answer to Jesus's question, "Who is greatest, the one who reclines to dine or the one who serves?" (Luke 22:27), is clear. The man who reclines has the leisure to enjoy a long, relaxed meal; cooks, waiters, and cleaners to prepare, serve, and clear the food; and guests to make the meal enjoyable and profitable. In terms of social, political, and financial significance, the men who recline at a meal are the "great" of the world. Their bodily position separates them from those who, by elite standards, count for nothing: the enslaved servers who stand, bend, and crouch as they carry out the various tasks necessary for a dinner.

In Seneca's portrayal of common dining practices in *Ep.* 47.2–3, the posture and position of the enslaved people signify their subjugation—they stand around the room, rather than reclining like men. "Purse-proud" hosts demonstrated their wealth and good taste in expensive furnishings, tableware, and gastronomic delicacies. In this description, enslaved bodies become part of the furnishings of the dining room, living representations of the enslaver's economic status. The enslaver expects these bodies, like tables and couches and plates, to be inanimate—standing still, not eating or speaking or making any voluntary or involuntary noise—under threat of violence should they break the fiction.

Seneca's description is deliberately hyperbolic.[1] It functions to critique the imagined host of the dinner for overindulgence, signifying his failure of masculine self-control (especially for a Stoic like Seneca; *Ep.* 47.2). As his initial question—why some should consider it "degrading for a man to dine with his slave"—suggests, the contrast of the supposed exalted status of the host with the un-manned enslaved servers contributes to Seneca's exhortation to elite men to civilize (some) enslaved men into a semblance of masculinity (47.15–16).[2] In Seneca's letter and in Jesus's question to the disciples in Luke

1. As Bradley 2008, 338, argues, the hyperbole reflects known practices of dining represented across a variety of sources (see further below in this chapter).

2. Seneca's letter has been cited as evidence of his (more) ethical perspective on enslavement: Enslaved people are human, capable of internal freedom, and they should be recognized as such by being invited to dine with free elites. The letter also, however, reveals his sense of elite superiority. The inclusion of enslaved people at a free man's dinner table is intended to masculinize them through the enslaver's (patronizing) education, indicating that they have little chance of developing internal freedom or masculinity on their own. See further Bradley 2008, 336–46.

22:26–27, the elite men who recline around a dining room and the servers who stand and move through the space embody, respectively, masculinity and its opposite, enslavement.

In this chapter, I develop the intersections of masculinity and enslavement in the dining room as context for interpreting the representation of Jesus as a "server" and the challenge to the twelve disciples to become like servers in Luke's Gospel. The pericope is a version of the story found in Mark 10:41–45, so the chapter begins with a study of the key concerns of slavery, service, and leadership in this text. The stories in Mark and Luke both bear comparison with Philippians 2:1–11.[3] Unlike in Philippians, the explicit vocabulary of enslavement (δοῦλος) is applied only to the disciples in Mark, and it is entirely absent from Luke, perhaps reflecting historic discomfort with the identification of Jesus as "slave." But, as the comparison with Seneca's dinner scene indicates, in the context of the dining room, those who serve (διακονέω) are enslaved. As in Philippians, then, Jesus is portrayed in Mark and Luke as an enslaved person, and his followers are encouraged to adopt his example.

In contrast to Philippians' broad exhortation to enslavement for all followers of Jesus, the exhortation is targeted in Mark 10:41–45 and Luke 22:24–27. Jesus's audience in both stories is the twelve (male) disciples as they argue over their relative status. The disciples' argument concerns the core elements of masculinity: the exercise of authority over self and others. I argued in chapter 3 that the people who would find the message of Philippians 2:1–11 most challenging were the elite men (and, to a certain extent, elite women) who held positions of power or privilege. The connection of Jesus's enslavement with the exercise of power among his followers in Mark and Luke directly addresses the centrality of power in normative constructions of masculinity.

Mark and Luke were written by and for followers of Jesus in the Roman Empire. As is the case for Philippians and 1 Peter, the authorial community of each Gospel included free, freed, and enslaved people. The lived experiences and rhetoric of enslavement, consequently, were familiar to the people who wrote, read, and preserved these books.[4] Mark was likely written in the late 60s or early 70s and Luke in the later 70s or the 80s.[5] This was a complicated

3. The parallels are noted by, e.g., Hawthorne 1983, 87; Marcus 2009, 757.

4. Moss 2024, 66–68, suggests Papias's comments on the origins of Mark's Gospel identified Mark as an enslaved scribe. A. C. Miller also connects Luke with a lower-status community; see 2014a, 421; 2014b, 79.

5. On the dating and location of Mark, see Marcus 2000, 35–36, 39; Boring 2006, 14–19; and Yarbro Collins 2007, 8, 14, 101 (arguing for the eastern Mediterranean); Winn 2014, 326–29, and Tan 2016, 4–6 (arguing for Rome). For Luke's Gospel, see esp. Tiede 1980, 66–68; Fitzmyer 1981, 54, 57; Edwards 2015, 11–12.

time period for masculinity in the Roman Empire.[6] Nero's influence led to the incorporation of decadent luxury and entertainment into elite portrayals of masculinity. The civil wars during the Year of the Four Emperors demonstrated the dangers of uncontrolled masculine violence. The Flavians in turn signaled their own adherence to a traditional conception of Roman masculinity. The First Jewish Revolt and its commemoration by the Flavian emperors provide a particularly important context for the constructions of masculinity in Mark and Luke. The rhetoric of defeat included accusations of Jewish emasculation—made visible by the Judea Capta coins (which depicted defeated Judea as a woman seated at the feet of a victorious Roman warrior), the triumph in Rome, and the bodies of enslaved Jews across the empire.[7] The gendering of Jesus and the twelve disciples in Mark and Luke responds to this broad context in different ways.

The chapter begins with an analysis of Mark 10:41–45 in relation to the development of masculinity in Mark's Gospel. Two questions are particularly important. First, does the pericope reflect Greco-Roman philosophical traditions in which good rulers act as servants of their people? Second, does the διακον- lexical group indicate high-status positions of authority or humiliating slavery? These questions are significant for understanding the pericope's representation of masculinity, leadership, and the identity of Jesus's followers.

The same questions also matter for Luke's version of the story, the focus for the rest of the chapter. The contextualization of the scene in the narrative space of a dining room during the celebration of Passover clarifies and complicates the concern with masculinity and enslavement. The scene is one of a series of parables and stories in this Gospel that feature enslaved people, questions of status and authority, and meals. As the culmination of the series, the conversation between Jesus and the disciples in Luke 22:24–27 redefines normative masculinity within the community of Jesus's followers around the un-manliness of enslaved servers. The conceptual association of the challenge of enslavement with the masculine business of exercising authority offers an important contribution to the intersections of masculinity and slavery in the New Testament.

Mark 10:41–45: "Slave of All"

Three "passion predictions" structure Mark 8:27–10:52. In each, Jesus's announcement of his betrayal, suffering, execution, and resurrection is met by

6. See Alston 1998, 215; Tuck 2005, 241; and 2016, 109–25.
7. See Reeder 2015b, 65–67.

challenges from the twelve disciples.[8] Following the first announcement, Peter rebukes Jesus. Jesus in turn warns his followers (including, but not limited to, the twelve disciples) that they must deny themselves, pick up a cross, and follow him (8:31–34). The reference to crucifixion foreshadows Jesus's death in Mark 15. As demonstrated in chapter 3, crucifixion enacted Roman power over enslaved people and non-Romans. The command to pick up a cross and follow Jesus is shaded with un-masculinity.[9]

In the second passion prediction, the disciples' failure to understand what Jesus has told them is demonstrated by their ensuing debate about their relative greatness (9:30–37). Jesus's response to their debate has two components. First, he tells the twelve disciples that to be first, they must be last (ἔσχατος) of all and servant (or agent, διάκονος) of all. Second, he uses a young child to illustrate his point, placing the child in the center of the group and hugging the child. Affectionate embraces are more commonly associated with mothers (and, notably, can endanger boys' potential masculinity).[10] Children, as noted in chapter 2, were gendered as un-masculine in their immaturity, emotionality, dependency, and powerlessness.[11] For the disciples to welcome or receive the little child as Jesus demonstrates in the scene would be for them to give up their search for social status in favor of association with the statusless (see also the exhortation in 10:15 to become like children in order to enter God's kingdom).[12]

The third passion prediction is the most intense of the three in its challenge to the standard conceptualization of masculinity around power, authority, and status. Jesus's announcement of his coming death is graphically represented with mockery and violence in Mark 10:32–34. Indicating their continued misunderstanding, James and John immediately approach Jesus

8. On the literary pattern of the passion predictions, challenges from the disciples, and increasingly pointed responses from Jesus, see Kaminouchi 2003, 56–57; and Santos 2003, 5–6, 146.

9. See Asikainen 2018, 159–60; and also Boring 2006, 244–45, and Yarbro Collins 2007, 408, on the shock (and historical reality) of the imagery.

10. Embracing or hugging (ἐναγκαλίζομαι in Mark 9:36; 10:16) a child is consistently associated with women, particularly in the context of the worship of Cybele: Diodorus Siculus 3.58.3; Plutarch, *Cam.* 5.2; Callistratus 14. On the danger of parents' affectionate care for children, see Quintilian, *Inst.* 1.2.6–8; Seneca, *Prov.* 2.5. Gundry 2008, 150, 154–58, discusses the significance of Jesus hugging children in Mark.

11. While aspects of Jewish perspectives on children were more positive than those represented in Roman texts, children were nonetheless figured as irrational and un-masculine, in need of instruction and discipline to mature into adulthood. See Reinhartz 1993, 73–77 (on Philo); Barclay 1997, 69–72.

12. So also Asikainen 2018, 95. Asikainen further argues that Mark interweaves the passion predictions with contrasting perspectives on masculinity (with the disciples adopting a "self-assertive" model and Jesus correcting them with a "self-controlled" model; pp. 76, 79–80, 158–59).

to request positions of authority in his kingdom (to be at his right and left hands; vv. 35–40). The remaining disciples are angry with James and John, likely (given Jesus's response) because they also wanted positions of authority (v. 41). Addressing this desire, Jesus warns the disciples against following the patterns of leadership practiced by the gentiles. Instead, to be great and first, they must become servants or agents (διάκονος) and slaves (δοῦλος) of all, following the pattern of Jesus himself (vv. 42–45).

The context of this message in Jesus's announcement of his own death; the themes of authority, status, and hierarchy; and the demand for enslavement together identify masculinity as a relevant concern for Mark 10:41–45. Whether the scene develops or challenges normative masculinity is debated. Three concerns offer important background to the analysis of the text: the depictions of masculinity in Mark's Gospel as a whole; the representation of rulers as servants or slaves of their people in Greco-Roman philosophy and rhetoric; and the range of meaning of the διακον- word group.

Masculinity and Mark's Gospel

In the first half of Mark's Gospel, Jesus is characterized as a man of power who heals, subdues demons, and speaks with authority (e.g., 1:21–34; 2:10–11; 4:35–41).[13] Jesus (symbolically) defeats a legion of enemy troops, expelling them from the land (5:1–20).[14] Public recognition affirms his authority (3:7–8; 4:1; 5:21–23). These aspects of the narrative point toward Jesus's essential manliness by the standard cultural measures of Second Temple Judaism and imperial Rome. But even as it is established, Jesus's masculinity is interrupted by his lack of a wife, children, or ancestral lineage (note 6:1–3), his dismissal of kinship obligations (3:31–35), his association with people of questionable social status (2:13–17), and public accusations of insanity (3:21).[15]

The ambiguity of Jesus's masculinity in Mark's portrayal becomes more emphatic after Jesus is recognized as the Messiah in 8:27–30. The explicit acclamation of his authority disappears from the narrative.[16] Jesus fails to con-

13. See Liew 1999, 13–14; and 2004, 98–105; Conway 2008, 91–92; Mayordomo 2013, 371–72; Carter 2015, 142–43.

14. Esp. Carter 2015, 143–49.

15. See Mayordomo 2013, 368–69. Moss 2024, 94, 98, particularly emphasizes Jesus's fatherlessness in Mark as problematic for his status (suggesting he could have been identified as illegitimate or enslaved in the context of Rome's slave system). See further Moxnes 2003, 67–69, 96–97, on social dislocation as un-masculinity in the Gospels (but for a counter perspective, Liew 2004, 103–4).

16. Jesus's authority (ἐξουσία) is mentioned five times before Mark 8 (1:22, 27; 2:10; 3:15; 6:7), but after chapter 8 it is only questioned once (11:27–33). See, however, Liew 1999, 18–19, 26, on Jesus's implicit authority to command the disciples and his power in the passion narrative.

trol his own bodily needs and emotions (11:12–17). His emotional upheaval and (womanish) weakness, ἀσθενής, in the Gethsemane scene is particularly notable (14:32–42).[17] The public mockery and abuse associated with Jesus's trials and execution further complicate the development of Jesus's gender (14:65; 15:15–32). He is portrayed as the victim of Roman power rather than the conqueror.[18] The empty tomb vindicates Jesus's announcements of his resurrection, but Jesus himself does not reappear in the story. The ending of the Gospel in women's silence and fear extends the ambiguity of Jesus's masculinity (16:8).[19]

The masculinity of the twelve disciples, the most significant characters in the Gospel after Jesus, is equally ambiguous.[20] Jesus empowers them to heal, exorcise, and announce his kingdom (3:13–19; 6:7–13). Like Jesus (and following the practices of enslavement), they are also separated from the context of honorably patriarchal households (1:16–20; 10:28–31).[21] They also question, resist, and fear Jesus (4:35–41; 5:31; 9:32; 10:13–16). "They were utterly confused, for they did not understand about the bread. Their hearts were hardened" (6:51–52): The disciples' understanding of Jesus's teachings is consistently problematic in Mark (4:10–13; 8:14–21, 31–33). The failure of the twelve disciples culminates in their betrayal, abandonment, and denial of Jesus (14:43–52, 66–72) and in their absence from Jesus's crucifixion, death, and burial (15:21–47).[22] The twelve disciples are not as "manly" as the women who remain faithful to the end of Jesus's life, though at the very end of the story, the women also fail.[23]

Though their own embodiment of masculine norms is unstable, throughout the narrative the twelve disciples act as spokespeople for standard hegemonic masculinity. Peter's response to Jesus in Mark 8:31–33 is representative. Like

17. E. Thurman 2007, 198–201; Conway 2008, 100–101; Asikainen 2018, 142–45, 149–50, 161–62.

18. So Mayordomo 2013, 373–75; Asikainen 2018, 167–77; W. Moore 2021, 84–86. E. Thurman 2007, 205–20, compares Mark 14–16 with the story of Habrocomes in Xenophon's *An Ephesian Tale*. His analysis highlights the fundamental ambiguities in Mark's representation of Jesus's resolve, silence, subordination, abuse, and endurance, concluding that this portrayal of Jesus "destabilizes" Roman imperial masculinity (pp. 226–29; also 2004, 143–44). This approach to analyzing masculinity in the passion narratives offers a fruitful alternative to the more common comparisons with "noble death" traditions (e.g., Liew 2004, 106–11, on Mark; Scaer 2005, 90–116, on Luke's Gospel).

19. Cf. Conway 2008, 104.

20. See also Asikainen 2018, 76–77.

21. The convergence of discipleship with enslavement in the loss of kin and home is addressed by Levine 2019, 301; Moss 2024, 227.

22. Cf. Liew 2004, 115–17.

23. On the female disciples as superior to the male disciples in Mark, see Kinuwaka 2001, 174; Carey 2023, 61–64 (arguing that the women do not fail in Mark 16).

other Jews of the first century, Peter most likely expected a militaristic messiah to defeat the Romans. Consequently, he challenged Jesus's proclamation of his own victimization. The disciples' disagreements over their relative status in 9:33–34, James and John's request for positions of authority in 10:35–37, and the remaining ten disciples' anger with them in 10:41 similarly indicate their adherence to the norms of masculine power. They expect and seek the exalted status of leading men, not the statuslessness of children.

Servant Kings?

The ambiguity of masculinity in Mark's narrative is reflected in Jesus's conversation with James, John, and the other disciples. While Jesus deflects James and John's request, he does not reject the idea of ruling entirely (note 10:40). Likewise in verses 43–44, the alternative path to greatness and primacy does not abolish the concepts of greatness or primacy.[24] In this respect, a number of interpreters argue that the service and enslavement of Jesus and the twelve disciples reflect the definition of rulers as "servant kings" in Greco-Roman philosophy. The intersections of masculinity and enslavement in discourses concerned with rule, however, complicate this context for the interpretation of Mark 10:41–45.

Primarily addressing Paul's use of slavery metaphors, Dale Martin suggests that the description of leaders in the early Christian communities as slaves indicated their honor, status, and power. To be Christ's slave is to exercise Christ's authority with the reward of increased status, authority, and power; "slave" is simply a title for leaders in the early Christian community.[25] David Seeley identifies the apparent critique of oppression in Mark 10:42 as a common element of Greco-Roman philosophies of ideal rulers who serve their people. He suggests the humility or "lowness" evident in Mark 10:43–45 was influenced by Cynic philosophy.[26] Colleen Conway integrates Seeley's work into her analysis of Jesus's masculinity in Mark, concluding that the Greco-Roman construction of kingship and political power around "service" to the subjects of the kingdom defines the servility of 10:43–45 as an honorable expression of manly rule.[27]

Martin, Seeley, and Conway refer to a variety of Greco-Roman sources in support of their approach.[28] Many of the texts are broadly concerned with

24. So Liew 1999, 18, 26; Conway 2008, 100; Myles 2010, 73–75 (on Mark 9:33–37).

25. D. Martin 1990, 54–55.

26. Seeley 1993, 235–45. See also E. Thurman 2004, 155 (noting that Epictetus's Cynics are feminized, so the parallel does not masculinize Mark's disciples); Winn 2014, 341–44.

27. Conway 2008, 99–100.

28. See also G. Theissen 2002, 240–41; Winn 2014, 330–39; and Bermejo-Rubio 2018, 62–63, highlighting the connection of self-sacrifice with ideal kingship.

a good ruler's beneficence to his subjects ("his" specifically, reflecting the assumption that the good ruler is male). As noted in chapter 2, the ability to provide beneficence is a mark of elite masculine status. In philosophical discussions of good leadership, beneficence expresses kindness and generosity. It is not, however, associated with service or enslavement.[29] This connection is made in the Bible. Kings (and other leaders) are God's "servants" or "slaves" (עבד, translated with δοῦλος in the LXX).[30] In 1 Kings 12:7 and Ezekiel 34:23, the identification of the king as "slave" is associated with care for the king's subjects.[31]

There are a few Greco-Roman texts that define a ruler's behavior with the vocabulary of slavery. Publilius Syrus (who was himself a freed person) associated service (*utilis*) to one's country with slavery (*mancipium*; *Sent.* 519). Suetonius praised Tiberius's refusal to accept excessive honors, flattery, or obsequiousness from the senators. Instead, Tiberius referred to himself as "enslaved" (*servio*) to the senators (his *dominus*) and citizens (*Tib.* 28).[32] Cassius Dio's account of two consuls who secured their positions by "serving" (θεραπεύω) and showing deference to the population more explicitly connects leadership with service, though only to explain why Cato (who did not show deference to others) was not elected consul. Slavery also weaves through Plutarch's description of Alexander's uncontrolled grief over the death of Cleitus in *Alex.* 52.3–4. One advisor accuses Alexander of enslavement (ἀνδράποδον) to his sorrow; he should be acting as ruler (ἄρχω, κρατέω) instead of slave (δουλεύω). But while Plutarch subtly critiqued this perspective by connecting it with Alexander's self-interest and pride, he did not identify enslavement as a positive model for the exercise of power.

Three more significant developments of leadership as service or slavery come from Plato, Seneca, and Dio Chrysostom. First, Plato, *Leg.* 6.762e–763b, suggests that someone who has never "slaved" (δουλεύω) cannot be a good master (δεσπότης). Rulers should be self-sufficient (that is, not dependent on the work of enslaved peoples) and proficient in the manly activities of fighting and hunting. Here, the "slavery" of leadership aligns with honorable

29. E.g., Plato, *Resp.* 5.463b (contrasting ideal philosopher-rulers with rulers in other nations who treat their subjects as slaves), 7.540b; Xenophon, *Mem.* 3.2.1–4; Plutarch, *Galb.* 11.1–2; *Publ.* 4–5; Dio Chrysostom 1.34–35.

30. E.g., 1 Sam. 23:10–11; 2 Sam. 3:18; 1 Kings 3:6–9; 1 Macc. 4:30.

31. See also Bermejo-Rubio 2018, 61. Wischmeyer 1999, 35–38, also finds parallel texts in early Judaism (including the association of service and sacrifice in Jos. Asen. 13.12, 20.2–3; T. Job 11–12, 15.1–4; Philo, *Legat.* 51).

32. While I make no claims to have read every Greco-Roman text connecting leadership with service, it is striking that this is the clearest example that I have found in which a ruler is identified with the explicit vocabulary of slavery in a positive sense.

masculinity. However, Plato limited honorable slavery (κάλως δουλεῦσαι) to respect for the laws and the gods and deference to elders and others who deserve honor. It is not a general state of enslavement to the populations over whom the rulers rule.

Second, Seneca identified various factors, including wealth, the ownership of enslaved people, and public office, as potential enslavers that limit a (free) man's time, attention, and resources (e.g., *Tranq*. 8.6–9, 10.3).[33] Similarly, he compared the limitations on an emperor's speech and desire for punitive vengeance with enslavement (*servitus*). This slavery is an ironic consequence of the immense power wielded by the emperor (*Clem*. 1.8.1–5).[34] It does not indicate service to his subjects. As Matthew Thiessen has shown, Seneca imagined the emperor as the head in charge of the body (the people; *Clem*. 1.3.5).[35] The emperor's enslavement indicates the benevolent nature of his rule (1.1.2–4); he is (or rather, should be) limited from doing whatever he desires to the people over whom he rules.[36]

In a discussion of the role of philosophy as a guide for life in *Ep*. 90, Seneca addressed people in positions of power over the weak who are subject to their rule. The qualities of their authority include strength, power, and victory over others, each of which is coded masculine. He cited the philosopher Posidonius's praise for the distant past when political leaders exhibited wisdom and virtue, self-control, courage, and kindness. Importantly for this discussion, these ancient exemplars also provided for and protected their subjects. For such leaders, ruling was a service (*officium*) in contrast to overpowering or subduing the people under their control (90.4–5 [LCL]). But while Seneca identified good leadership with care for the population, *officium* does not indicate service (with connotations of slavery) as much as duty, obligation, or favor—concepts that again appropriately reflect elite values.[37] For Seneca, as Matthew Roller argues, harsh or oppressive rulers

33. These "enslavers" intersect with Seneca's internalized freedom: A truly free man remains steady through changing circumstances and fortunes. Roller 2001, 276, notes that Seneca also identified suicide as a manly escape from the enslavement of business or wealth (*Ep*. 77.306, 14–15). He further argues that this move allows Seneca to maintain elite privilege against the threats of tyrannical emperors and wealthy, powerful freed men (pp. 108–22, 272–73).

34. The "glorious slavery" of a king who is gentle rather than violent to his subjects in Aelian, *Var. hist*. 2.20, is comparable.

35. M. Thiessen 2016, 457–61 (citing a number of parallel concepts in other authors).

36. The emperor in question was Nero, who was rather famously unbenevolent. Roller 2001, 285, notes that the internalized freedom of self-control, especially over anger, excludes emperors who indulge their emotions in acts of violence.

37. Note that *officium* is distinct from *ministerium* and *ministro*, the terms commonly used to translate the διακον- lexical group.

enslave the population, but good rulers are fathers of their people rather than their slaves.[38]

Third, Dio Chrysostom's discourses on kingship define good rulers as those who work for, love, and care for their subjects (e.g., 1.12–21). Good kings are like bulls who direct and protect their herds and yet also accept the authority of those who are superior (the herder for the bull, while for the king, the superior party is the gods; 2.69–72). Dio Chrysostom praised the king's labor for his people as good and honorable, a distinctive virtue that opposes him to those who are "effeminate," μαλακός, or pleasure-seeking, φιλήδονος. Dio Chrysostom exhorted rulers to be manly, ἀνδρεία; self-controlled, ἐγκράτεια; and wise, φρόνησις (3.55.50–58). While Dio Chrysostom emphasized the king's care for his subjects, he also maintained the superiority of the king to his subjects. The latter are consistently identified as weaker and in need of the king's care to survive. Although Dio Chrysostom said a good king prefers not to be called "master," δεσπότης, even by his own slaves (1.22–23), he did not identify the king as the slave of his people. He is their superior in every way.

In *Septem sapientium convivium* (*Dinner of Seven Wise Men*), Plutarch incorporated slavery into a discussion of good practices of ruling. As with Seneca, however, it is the subjects of the ruler who are the "slaves." Plutarch argued that anyone who prefers ruling over slaves (ἀνδράποδον) to ruling over men (ἀνήρ) lacks honor. Such a person is like a farmer who harvests weeds instead of crops; they would be better off ruling livestock than people. Glory comes from ruling the good (ἀγαθός), so long as rulers are greater than their subjects (*Sept. sap. conv.* 147d).[39] Plutarch's separation of slavery from ruling, and his association of ruling with being better and greater than one's subjects, offers a counterpoint to the argument that a good ruler should be a slave to his people.

Greco-Roman traditions certainly expect a good ruler to care for his subjects. Benefaction is tied to the ruler's power, authority, and (socially recognized) greatness, concepts that are integral to standard constructions of elite masculinity. As might be expected given the un-masculinity of enslavement, the vocabulary of enslavement is very rarely applied to rulers. When it is, it is buttressed by reminders of masculinity (as evident in Seneca and Dio Chrysostom). More frequently, enslavement stands in sharp distinction to honorable

38. Roller 2001, 217–45. Roller specifically argues that for a freeborn Roman to be identified as "slave" would be degrading (p. 227). See also Marcus 2009, 748–49, 755; and the discussion of metaphors of enslavement in chap. 2, above.

39. Cf. Aristotle, *Pol.* 5.1315b, on the honorable ruler's ability to shape his subjects into honorable (instead of humiliated, ταπεινόω) people.

rulership.[40] The development of the qualities of ideal rulers in Greco-Roman discourse offers a helpful context for Mark 10:42–45, but this background does not entirely answer the question of masculinity raised by the definition of greatness or leadership as enslavement.[41]

The Διακον- Word Group (Διακονέω, Διάκονος, and Διακονία)

In Mark 10:43 and 45, διάκονος and διακονέω are usually translated with "servant" and "serve." But as my addition of "agent" as a possible translation of διάκονος has signaled, the range of meaning for the διακον- lexical group includes a variety of situation-specific tasks, such as being royal companions (Polybius 15.25.20), preparing food (Luke 12:37), carrying out imperial orders (Josephus, *Ant.* 18.265), being used for sex (Dio Chrysostom 4.102), and preaching the gospel (2 Cor. 3:7–9). The multivalency of the lexical group raises questions concerning the use of the terms in Mark 10:43 and 45.

In their extensive research on the meaning of the διακον- word group, John Collins and Anni Hentschel prioritize the uses of the terms for the fulfillment of a task on behalf of someone else. While the person who commands the task is generally the superior in a hierarchical relationship with the person who is commanded, the one who enacts the task can themselves hold a high social or political status. Moreover, the person carrying out the task operates with significant authority on behalf of the person who commands it.[42] Collins and Hentschel consequently interpret the διακον- word group in the New Testament as the work of ministry, particularly the tasks of preaching and teaching.[43] The referents in these texts are not humble servants. Rather, they are tasked by God with the work of the divine household.[44]

In Mark 10:43 and 45, then, neither διάκονος nor διακονέω necessarily indicates a special (or specially "Christian") attitude or behavior. While Collins and Hentschel do not address the potential intersections with masculinity, the recognition of the status of the person carrying out the task ameliorates any un-masculinity inherent in obeying another person's commands.[45] With respect to Jesus in particular, both Collins and Hentschel identify Jesus's

40. In addition to the sources discussed here, see Polybius 30.18.1–7; Diodorus Siculus 12.50.1, 16.1.4; Philo, *Decal.* 165–167; Tacitus, *Ann.* 6.32; Plutarch, *Tim.* 13–15.

41. So also Asikainen 2018, 94–95. Wischmeyer 1999, 38–39, also distinguishes Mark 10:41–45 from Greco-Roman traditions on the basis of thematic differences.

42. Collins 1990, 73–176; 2012, 295–96; Hentschel 2007, 86–87, 433.

43. E.g., Acts 6:4; 20:24; Rom. 12:7; 15:25; 16:1–2; 1 Cor. 3:5; 12:5; Philem. 13; Heb. 6:10; Collins 1990, 196–97, 206–13; Hentschel 2007, 92–95, and (on Phoebe specifically) 168–72.

44. E.g., Hentschel 2007, 181–82, 434–38.

45. Cf. Hentschel 2007, 285; Smit 2018, 296 (arguing for the masculinity of the διακον- word group from a slightly different angle).

διακονέω as an honorable official act carried out under divine authority.[46] Hentschel applies this model to the disciples as well, though Collins suggests the disciples' paired identity of διάκονος and δοῦλος in Mark 10:43 introduces a sense of humility or lowliness.[47]

Collins and Hentschel provide ample evidence to support the broad use of the διακον- word group with reference to honorable, high-status people and tasks. This provides an important context for διάκονος and διακονέω in Mark 10:43 and 45. But the range of meaning of the διακον- word group also includes dishonorable, low-status tasks and people. This significance is particularly evident when the διακον- word group is paired with the vocabulary of slavery, as it is in Mark 10:43.[48] At times, the διακον- word group seems to act as a synonym for enslavement and the work of slavery.[49] These tasks include everyday labor, the basic activities necessary for the enslaver's household to survive and thrive, carried out under the command of enslavers.[50]

Notably, when freeborn people carry out similar tasks, their work is judged honorable and praiseworthy. Among Philo's Therapeutai, the διακονικός of young freeborn men is even ascribed masculinity (*Contempl.* 70–75).[51] Other uses of the διακον- word group, however, contrast people of high social status with those who lacked status. Plato claimed that a truly free man lacks the knowledge or skill for "slavish services" (δουλικὰ διακονήματα), further defined as putting away bedding, cooking, or obsequious speech. These are the tasks and behaviors (διακονέω) of enslaved people (*Theaet.* 175e). Epictetus identified those who "serve" (διακονέω) as inferior to those who receive the benefit of their work, just as a horse is inferior to the rider or an official or attendant (ὑπηρέτης) is inferior to the king (*Diatr.* 2.23.16, 3.7.28). Dio Chrysostom similarly linked the services (διακονέω) of enslaved people (οἰκέτης) to their inferiority to their freeborn enslavers (children, in this instance; 10.13).[52]

46. Collins 1990, 251; 2012, 307; 2014, 80, 85; and Hentschel 2007, 277–79. See also Smit 2018, 298–303.

47. Collins 1990, 247–48; Hentschel 2007, 277–79, 284, 288 (she also suggests that the representation of the disciples is not entirely honorable by the standards of antiquity).

48. Collins 1990 consistently dissociates the διακον- word group from menial labor, slavish character, or people of low status (e.g., pp. 80, 87–88, 97), though he does also note that sometimes the διακον- word group is synonymous with slavery (p. 151). Hentschel 2007 rejects any menial or slavish significance. In her analysis, the terms refer only to the task, not to the social status of the one who carries out the task (e.g., 85–86, 276, 433).

49. So Aristophanes, *Av.* 70–78; Aristotle, *Pol.* 2.1261b; Diodorus Siculus 5.26.3, 5.40.3; Epictetus, *Diatr.* 2.23.7; Plutarch, *Comp. Lyc. Num.* 2.4; Appian, *Hist. rom.* 12.13.90; and Pausanias 1.27.7.

50. E.g., Aristotle, *Pol.* 1.1255b, 2.1263a; Diodorus Siculus 11.57.6; Strabo 11.3.6; *Life of Aesop* 24.

51. See also Plato, *Leg.* 1.633c, 6.763a; Plutarch, *Mulier. virt.* 249d; Dio Chrysostom 10.10.

52. In this text, Dio Chrysostom argued that children should not be raised to depend on the labor of enslaved people so that they will grow up to be manly, strong, and honorable

The inferiority of enslaved "service" in these texts intersects with the un-masculinity of enslavement. In some cases, the διακον- word group expresses the oppressive abasement of slavery. This includes enslavers' sexual use of enslaved bodies. Xenophon identified a female slave as an appropriate διάκονος for her owner's sexual desires (*Oec.* 10.12).[53] Physical violence is also represented. Philo recommended that enslavers limit their abuse of slaves (δοῦλος) because, he said, if the bodies and minds of the enslaved were broken by their owners, the owners would not benefit from their work. Decent treatment corresponds with longer years of service (διακονία; *Spec.* 2.90–91). For Appian, even after manumission, a formerly enslaved person continues to serve (διακονέω) their former enslaver. They cannot escape the work of slavery (*Hist. rom.* 12.13.90).[54]

So, the διακον- word group consistently indicates tasks carried out under the authority of a social superior. When the agent of such tasks is freeborn, the work can be honorable—and, consequently, the tasks do not in themselves detract from the commissioned agent's masculinity. But the word group also indicates enslaved people and enslaved labor, with the associated connotations of dishonor and shame, the violability of the body, and inferiority. Διάκονος and διακονέω in Jesus's challenge to the disciples and his description of himself in Mark 10:43, 45, occur in conjunction with enslavement (δοῦλος in v. 44). Together with the contrast with standard practices of ruling in verse 42, the paradoxical glory of suffering in verses 35–40, and the un-masculinity of Jesus's passion prediction in verses 32–34, the association of διάκονος and διακονέω with enslavement complicates the masculinity of Jesus and the twelve disciples.

Masculinity and Slavery in Mark 10:41–45

The masculinity of Jesus and the twelve disciples in Mark's Gospel is ambiguous. There are indications of normative masculinity in Jesus's authority (shared with the disciples) and also indications of un-masculinity in the abandonment of households; in association with people who were considered dishonorable; and above all, in suffering, mockery, and crucifixion. Within a conversation about greatness and ruling power, the reflections of Greco-Roman discourse concerning ideals for leadership and the potential honor

(instead of lazy). The services of enslaved people, in other words, are detrimental for freeborn masculinity.

53. See also Josephus, *Ant.* 10.242, 12.187–88; and (of enslaved men and women) Dio Chrysostom 4.102.

54. See also Josephus, *Ant.* 18.192–94.

of acting as a διάκονος for a person of superior status situate Mark 10:41–45 within the boundaries of normative masculinity in the Roman Empire. But the inclusion of the language of enslavement in verse 44 unsettles this conclusion. Given the construction of enslavement as un-masculinity, might Mark 10:41–45 redefine masculinity for the disciples?

The question of masculinity in this text begins with the final (and most graphic) of the three passion predictions. In Mark 10:32–34, Jesus announces his betrayal, condemnation to death, and the bodily consequences of condemnation: He will be mocked, spat on, whipped, and executed.[55] These details depict emasculation. In military contexts (a primary arena for displays of masculinity), mockery indicates the humiliating abuse of the defeated, whose masculinity has proven insufficient.[56] Spitting on a man enacted public shaming for dishonorable behavior (e.g., the refusal to fulfill patriarchal duties in Deut. 25:9).[57] Being beaten (μαστιγόω) is both a regular experience of enslavement and a means of public humiliation for people accused of wrongdoing.[58] Physical abuse of condemned criminals was a normal aspect of public punishment and execution in antiquity, and such abuse was also used to increase the humiliation of military or political defeat.[59] The brief reference to "rising again" at the end of the statement does little to ameliorate the violence and humiliation of the statement as a whole.

A condemned person's reaction to the abuse—showing fortitude and endurance, refusing to be humiliated, turning the humiliation back on its enactors, or choosing to take their own life rather than endure the humiliation—could bring acclaim.[60] Eleazer's willingness to die for the torah expresses his

55. Mark's narrative of Jesus's execution incorporates these elements (note 14:65; 15:19–20, 31). See also Watts 1997, 265–69; Marcus 2009, 742, 745–46; and Shively 2021, 170, on the parallels with Isaiah's suffering servant (esp. Isa. 50:6; 53:12). Note that the parallel passage in Matt. 20:18–19 omits ἐμπτύω and shifts the syntax from active verbs with Jesus as the object to less personal infinitives; Matthew also replaces "kill" with "crucify."

56. Ἐμπαίζω in 1 Macc. 9:26; Herodotus 4.134.2. Note that the term is also used for sexual abuse in LXX Gen. 39:14; Judg. 19:25; and (with ταπεινόω) Judg. 20:5. With respect to Mark 14–15, E. Thurman 2004, 152, notes the irony of the mockery that also acts to confirm Jesus's identity.

57. Cf. Num. 12:14; Philo, *Leg.* 2.66; T. Zeb. 3.7; Diogenes Laertius 6.32. Note, however, that spitting on a defeated enemy is itself shameful in Plutarch, *Mor.* 189a; Cassius Dio 47.8.4.

58. Cf. μαστιγόω in Exod. 5:14 LXX; Deut. 25:1–3 LXX; Tob. 3:9; Philo, *Flacc.* 75, 77. Examples of the flogging of enslaved people can be found in, e.g., Plautus, *Asin.* 627–28, *Merc.* 414–16; Valerius Maximus 1.7.4, 6.1.9; Martial 7.86.11. Cicero, *Verr.* 2.163, declared flogging to be dishonorable for a Roman man. See further Saller 1998, 90.

59. See Philo, *Legat.* 368; Plutarch, *Ag. Cleom.* 30.1; *Dion* 35.4–5; *Mor.* 239d; Athenaeus, *Deipn.* 14.616c; E. Thurman 2004, 149.

60. In the story of Saul's death in battle in 1 Sam. 31:4 LXX, Saul chooses the manly option of suicide to avoid the mockery (ἐμπαίζω) of his victorious enemies. See also 2 Macc. 6:30;

"manliness" (ἀνδρείως, γενναίως, and ἀρετή; 2 Macc. 6:18–31). His example is followed by the mother and her seven sons who likewise endure torture while encouraging one another to manliness (γενναίως; 7:1–41).[61] In these stories, masculinity is evident in the protagonists' voluntary action, verbal response to the torturers, and disregard for pain. By contrast, Jesus is the passive object of the actions taken against him in Mark 10:33–34, and there are no proclamations of endurance, fortitude, courage, or other signifiers of masculinity (in this text, or in the passion story).[62] Rather, the list of abuses enacted on Jesus's body compares him with un-masculine Vitellius—stripped, mocked, and beaten as he was dragged through the streets of Rome for all to see (Suetonius, *Vit.* 17.1–2).[63] The third passion prediction un-mans Jesus.

The implications of gender in the third prediction flow into the ensuing conversation between Jesus, James, and John. The brothers, identified as "sons of Zebedee" (a reference that recalls their introduction in Mark 1:19–20), request to sit by Jesus's side when he reigns in "glory" (10:37).[64] In other words, they seek positions of status, power, and authority. For the third time in this section of Mark, the disciples have failed to understand the significance of Jesus's passion prediction. The rest of the twelve disciples are outraged with the brothers (10:41). Jesus's response suggests that their anger is attributable to their desire for the power and status James and John sought.[65] Given the association of social, political, and economic status with manliness in the Greco-Roman world, the disciples' desired "greatness" includes hegemonic masculinity.[66]

Jesus initially deflects James and John's request by warning that their request intersects with his own fate. The positions at his right and left next

---

Quintilian, *Inst.* 11.1.40; Valerius Maximus 9.12.5; Seneca, *Ep.* 70.25–27; *Helv.* 13.7–8; Plutarch, *Phoc.* 36.2; Epictetus, *Diatr.* 4.1.127.

61. The themes of masculinity portrayed through the endurance of torture are emphasized in 4 Macc. (note, e.g., 1:1–12). See further Moore and Anderson 1998, 252–58; E. Thurman 2007, 185–88; Asikainen 2018, 157–58.

62. See also E. Thurman 2007, 201. As discussed above, the portrayal of Jesus's prayer in Gethsemane, arrest, trials, and crucifixion in Mark 14–15 indicate his un-manliness (see Conway 2008, 100–103).

63. On Vitellius, see also Tacitus, *Hist.* 3.66, 84–85. Plutarch accused Perseus of un-manly cowardice for refusing to take his own life rather than experience the humiliation of being a spectacle in Aemilius's triumph (*Aem.* 34.3–4). Finally, note also the intersection of sexual impotence with being beaten, spat on, and otherwise abused in Petronius, *Sat.* 132.2–5.

64. Kaminouchi 2003, 93–94, notes that the reminder of their paternal household affirms their potential masculine status. See in general his thoughtful analysis of the conversation on pp. 93–115.

65. Kaminouchi 2003, 116; Boring 2006, 299, 301. Goodrich 2018, 169–70, notes that James and John's request makes sense in the context of first-century Jewish eschatological expectation.

66. Cf. E. Thurman 2004, 153–54; Myles 2010, 73.

appear in Mark 15:27 at the crucifixion, filled by unnamed rebels.[67] If James and John seek authority in Jesus's "glory," they will have to share his cup and his baptism (apparent references to his suffering and death; cf. Mark 14:36). Jesus also tells them that he lacks the power to grant their request (10:40), further complicating his own masculinity. Finally, addressing the entire group of twelve disciples, Jesus says that, unlike among the gentiles, among his disciples, greatness is defined by becoming a διάκονος within the community (represented with a second person plural pronoun), and being first requires becoming δοῦλος to all (πᾶς; 10:42–44).

The references to political rule in Mark 10:42 have several possible connotations. First, the rulers are described rather ambiguously as "those who think they rule" or, alternatively, "those who are considered rulers" (οἱ δοκοῦντες ἄρχειν τῶν ἐθνῶν). The phrasing in the first option discredits the rulers' claim to authority.[68] Second, the verbs used to express political rule may indicate oppressive domination: The rulers "lord it over" their subjects (NRSV, ESV, NIV), and the great are "tyrants" (NRSV).[69] These interpretations take the prepositional compound κατα in κατεξουσιάζω and κατακυριεύω as an intensifier. While κατεξουσιάζω is quite rare, κατακυριεύω can connote injustice or oppression.[70] This sense generally comes from the larger context (e.g., Acts 19:16). Κατακυριεύω often simply indicates the exercise of power (e.g., Gen. 1:28 LXX; Dan. 11:39 LXX; Sir. 17:4), and it is associated with justice in Psalms 72:7 (71:8 LXX) and 110:2 (109:2 LXX). The significance of the two verbs in Mark 10:42 is unclear, but there is nothing in the context to indicate that oppressive rule is necessarily in view.[71] Jesus's message may prohibit the disciples from oppressing others or ruling unjustly (the more likely option), or it may prohibit them from ruling or exercising authority at all.[72]

The replacement of κατακυριεύω and κατεξουσιάζω with διάκονος ("servant" or "one who takes orders") and δοῦλος ("enslaved person") gives some support to the second option. As Collins and Hentschel have demonstrated,

67. See Kaminouchi 2003, 97–98.

68. Kaminouchi 2003, 119–23, 159, argues that Mark's depictions of Herod and Pilate, the only rulers in the narrative, destabilize their claim to rule.

69. So Wischmeyer 1999, 29; G. Theissen 2002, 240; Marcus 2009, 748; Winn 2014, 342–44.

70. Ps. 10:9 (9:31 LXX); 119:13 (118:14 LXX). It indicates wartime conquest in Num. 21:24 LXX; 1 Macc. 15:30; Diodorus Siculus 14.64.1.

71. Greco-Roman discussions of the good practices of rulers include negative examples, but in much greater detail than the two verbs in Mark 10:42 (e.g., Dio Chrysostom 1.12–13). Kaminouchi 2003, 127, argues that the broader representation of rulers like Herod and Pilate in the Gospel allows for the acts of ruling here to be interpreted as oppressive; see also Boring 2006, 302; Yarbro Collins 2007, 498–99; Goodrich 2018, 171.

72. On the second option, see, e.g., K. Clark 1976, 103–4; Santos 2003, 204 (noting that Jesus the κύριος is associated with ἐξουσία in Mark); Camacho Acosta 2004, 141–43.

διάκονος on its own does not indicate an individual's status, only the commissioning of an agent for a particular task. But when διάκονος and δοῦλος appear together, the significance of enslavement affects the use of διάκονος. In Mark 10:43–44, to be διάκονος means to serve (or take orders from) one another (ὑμῶν), and to be δοῦλος means to accept the authority of and labor for all (πάντων). These are the roles of a person without status, authority (except as exercised on behalf of someone else), or social honor.[73] In the absence of the descriptors that allow ideal rulers to maintain their masculinity as they care for and serve their subjects, the inversion of greatness in service and being first in enslavement implicates the disciples with Jesus's un-masculinity.

Somewhat surprisingly, the exhortation to become an enslaved person is the first explicit reference to slavery in Mark's Gospel.[74] The next references come in the parable of the tenants, as the "lord" (κύριος) of the vineyard sends enslaved people to collect the harvest. Like the vineyard owner's son, the enslaved people are beaten, insulted, and killed—abuse that compounds the tenants' usurpation of the owner/enslaver's rights over his property, which includes both the land and the living people (12:2–5).[75] The surprising violence (surprising in that the tenants, not the enslaver, enact it) and the shared experience of suffering reflect the connection between the disciples as διάκονος and δοῦλος and Jesus's mission statement in 10:45 (note also verse 39; and 8:31–38). The Son of Humanity came to serve, that is, to take orders, rather than be served, that is, to give orders (using διακονέω in the active and passive).[76] Specifically, his orders are to give his life as a ransom (λύτρον) for the lives of many.[77] The biblical concept of redemption includes freedom for enslaved people.[78] Across Greco-Roman antiquity, captives of war could be ransomed before they were

73. Cf. the conjunction of διάκονος with ταπεινόω in Matt. 23:11–12. See also Collins 1990, 247–48; Kinuwaka 2001, 183–84; Kaminouchi 2003, 134–38; Camacho Acosta 2004, 147–49; Marcus 2009, 755; Mayordomo 2013, 371; Asikainen 2018, 94. However, Winn 2014, 345, suggests the language of slavery is hyperbole that simply indicates significant service.

74. There are ten references to enslaved people (δοῦλος) plus two uses of δουλεύω by the equivalent point in Matthew's narrative (1:1–20:23), and nineteen references to δοῦλος plus three uses of δουλεύω in Luke (1:1–18:34). Of course, there are "invisible" enslaved people in Mark (the people carrying the paralytic in 2:3; the swineherds in 5:14; the mourners in 5:38; the servers at Herod's party in 6:21). The absence of explicit references deserves further study.

75. Other explicit references to slavery come in the parable in Mark 13:34–36 and the scenes of Jesus's arrest (δοῦλος in 14:47) and trials (παιδίσκη in 14:66, 69).

76. My translation of ὁ υἱὸς τοῦ ἀνθρώπου, "Son of Humanity," follows Carroll 2012, 13, to reflect the use of the phrase as a title parallel to "Son of God" and to capture the meaning of ἄνθρωπος better than "man" does.

77. See Collins 2014, 80; Shively 2021, 175.

78. Ransoming a life is part of the torah (Exod. 21:30; 30:12; Num. 3:12; 18:15; 35:31–32). Twice, it is used in reference to manumission from enslavement (Lev. 19:20; 25:51–52). This use is also attested in Diogenes Laertius 1.2.45, 2.5.31, 5.4.72. Shively 2021, 175–76, also notes the

sold into slavery.[79] Fernando Camacho Acosta consequently suggests that, as Jesus's purpose is liberation of the oppressed, so the disciples' service and slavery represents their solidarity with and work on behalf of the oppressed.[80]

Neither διακονέω nor giving up one's life are un-masculine. Rather, as the discourses of ideal kingship indicate, some manly rulers serve and sacrifice their lives for their people (an ideal disrupted by the reality that the people die for the emperor in war; cf. Seneca, *Clem.* 1.3.3–4).[81] In this respect, Peter-Ben Smit argues that διακονέω as a voluntary action interprets Jesus's death as manly.[82] While this is possible, the inclusion of enslavement in Mark 10:44 shapes the "service" of the disciples and Jesus around the un-masculinity of slavery. Moreover, the emphatic un-manliness of Mark 10:33–34 is not entirely undone by the two active verbs in verse 45.

The third passion prediction colors the ensuing conversation between Jesus and the disciples. James and John speak for the Twelve as they express their desire for status, power, and authority in line with hegemonic masculine values. Jesus in response challenges them to adopt his own model of taking orders, specifically expressed by giving his life as a ransom for many. The disciples should give up their desire for status and authority over others, represented in the narrative by their separation from the masculine arenas of household and kinship, and even, as they become "slaves," over their own lives. In a first-century context, Jesus challenges his male disciples to redefine the masculinity they desire around the un-masculinity of enslavement.

Greatness and Slavery in the Dining Room: Luke 22:24–27

Luke's version of Mark's third passion prediction occurs in the same location in the narrative, just before Jesus and his followers enter Jericho.[83] Among other modifications, Luke adds a reference to the Scriptures to indicate that

identification of God as redeemer (λυτρόω) in, e.g., Isa. 41:14; 43:1; 44:24; she argues that this redemption is accomplished by the servant's death (53:12).

79. E.g., Polybius 6.52.2; Diodorus Siculus 16.17.5; Josephus, *Ant.* 12.28, 14.371; Plutarch, *Cim.* 9.4.

80. Camacho Acosta 2004, 147–52 (cf. Kaminouchi 2003, 139, 151). See also Watts 1997, 286–87; Yarbro Collins 2007, 500–504; Marcus 2009, 750; and M. Thiessen 2016, 457–58, on the potential meanings of "ransom."

81. For the ideal ruler sacrificing (him)self for the people, see Collins 1990, 251–52; Winn 2014, 345–46; Smit 2018, 291–93 (noting that Jesus is the active agent in Mark 10:45, in contrast to the passive object in vv. 33–34). For the people dying to "ransom" the life of the emperor, see M. Thiessen 2016, 456–62.

82. Smit 2018, 299–300, 303.

83. See further Bovon 2013, 573–74, and Wolter 2017, 336, on Luke's adaptation of Mark 10:32–34.

what happens to Jesus is fulfillment of prophecy (18:31).[84] Rather than the third-person plural active verbs with Jesus as the object in Mark 10:33–34, Luke uses third-person singular passive verbs, with Jesus as the subject (παραδοθήσεται, ἐμπαιχθήσεται, ἐμπτυσθήσεται; Luke 18:32). A fourth insult is added to those in Mark's list: Jesus will be subject to ὑβρίζω, which in the context of being beaten and spat on indicates abusive mistreatment that shames its victim.[85] These shifts in Luke 18:31–34 maintain (or even heighten) the sense of un-masculinity in Mark 10:32–34.[86]

Despite Jesus's clarity, Luke's disciples do not understand; his meaning is hidden from them (18:34).[87] This reaction echoes the lack of understanding evident in Jesus's conversation with James, John, and the rest of the disciples in Mark 10:35–45. However, Luke's narrative omits James and John's request for positions of status in Jesus's kingdom, and the conversation with the disciples concerning greatness is moved from the journey toward Jerusalem to the Passover and Jesus's last meal with his followers before his arrest, trials, and execution.

While the basic structure of Mark 10:41–45 is discernible in Luke 22:24–27, a number of differences in the details create a distinctive narrative.[88] The conversation occurs during the Passover meal. Instead of James and John's search for positions of authority, in Luke all twelve disciples engage in a debate (φιλονεικία) with one another over their relative greatness. Mark's "rulers" and "great ones" are "kings" and "benefactors" (εὐεργέτης) in Luke. The compound verbs with their potentially pejorative significance in Mark 10:42 are replaced in Luke with "rule over" (κυριεύω) and "have authority over" (ἐξουσιάζω). The reference to Jesus giving his life as a ransom is missing in Luke's version (though the significance is retained by the context of the commemoration of Israel's salvation from slavery and Jesus's impending death). The language of service and slavery for the disciples and Jesus also shifts significantly:

84. Luke's Gospel and Acts repeatedly connect the story of Jesus and his earliest followers with Israel's Scriptures. See Luke 3:4; 4:17–20; 24:44; Acts 7:42; 15:15; 24:14; L. Johnson 1991, 15–20; Bovon 2013, 575–76.

85. Cf. Acts 14:5; 1 Thess. 2:2; Aristotle, *Eth. eud.* 2.1221b; Diodorus Siculus 14.107.4; Josephus, *Ant.* 4.238, 5.315 (and ὕβρις in 2 Macc. 8:17; 3 Macc. 3:25; 2 Cor. 12:10; Aristotle, *Pol.* 1315a15–28). In 2 Macc. 14:41–43, the experience of abuse (ὑβρίζω) in defeat contrasts with the manliness of suicide (though in Plutarch, *Fab.* 10.2, and Epictetus, *Diatr.* 3.22.100, manliness consists of ignoring abuse). See further Cohen 1991, 172–74; Bovon 2013, 574; and the discussion of ὕβρις in connection with sexual assault in chap. 2, above.

86. See Wilson 2015, 209–35, on un-masculinity in Luke's passion story.

87. The lack of understanding is corrected in the resurrection narrative (Luke 24:28–32, 42–49); see Carroll 2012, 368; Wolter 2017, 338.

88. Bovon 2012, 171, suggests Luke's story comes from a different source. Cf. Nelson 1994, 125–31.

> Whoever wants to be great [μέγας] among you will be your servant [διάκονος], and whoever wants to be first among you will be slave [δοῦλος] of all. For also the Son of Humanity did not come to be served [to give orders], but to serve [to take orders; διακονέω] and to give his life as a ransom for many. (Mark 10:43–45)

> The greatest [μείζων] among you must become like the youngest [ὡς ὁ νεώτερος], and the leader [ἡγέομαι] like a server [ὡς ὁ διακονῶν]. For who is greatest, the one who reclines to dine or the one who serves? The one who reclines, right? But I am among you as a server [ὡς ὁ διακονῶν]. (Luke 22:26)

In some ways, Luke's version emphasizes power and authority. Instead of being great, the disciples can be the greatest. Instead of being first, the disciples can be leaders (and, as the conversation continues, the disciples sit on thrones, judging Israel; 22:30). The introduction of ὡς as a word of comparison, "like" or "as," distinguishes Luke's version from Mark's more direct language of being a servant or slave.[89] The omission of Mark's vocabulary of enslavement (δοῦλος) alleviates the sense of social dishonor in Luke's account.[90] The differences in Luke's narrative seem to re-masculinize Jesus and the disciples in contrast with Mark's less-manly portrayal. This reading corresponds with the interpretation of Luke's Jesus as an exemplary Roman man.[91]

The apparent masculinization of Jesus and the twelve disciples in Luke 22:24–27 is complicated by the setting. The dining room was space in which masculinity could be demonstrated, enacted, and amplified. As introduced at the beginning of the chapter, masculinity was visible in the contrast between the manly men who reclined around the table with the enslaved servers who stood and moved among them. Although the vocabulary of enslavement is absent from Luke 22:24–27, Jesus and the disciples as "servers" embody enslaved people. The intersections of masculinity and slavery in the dining room in the Gospel of Luke suggest that, as in Mark 10:41–45, the challenge to become as "servers" redefines masculinity around enslavement.

Masculinity and Slavery in the Gospel of Luke

Both the development of normative masculinity and its instability are apparent in the story of Jesus, a Roman centurion, and an enslaved person in Luke 7:1–10. The centurion is characterized as a model man. He exhibits patriarchal masculinity in his authority over and care for his household. He

89. Collins 1990, 246–47; Hentschel 2007, 285–88.

90. So Asikainen 2018, 93–94.

91. E.g., D'Angelo 1999, 187; and 2002, 58–62; Scaer 2005, 45–53; Conway 2008, 132, 142 (arguing this masculinization continues in Acts, pp. 133–35; and 2017, 19–25).

holds military command; as part of the occupying force, his physical presence in Capernaum signifies Roman militarized masculinity. He acts as a benefactor in the local community. His support for the synagogue in particular demonstrates his piety. The elders of Capernaum honor him for his patronage.[92] At the end of the story, Jesus expresses amazement at his faith. The centurion is a man of status and power.[93]

The centurion's masculinity in turn masculinizes Jesus.[94] This manly man sends his clients and friends to Jesus to request his help, indicating his appraisal of Jesus as an equal or (given his description of himself as "unworthy") his superior.[95] The centurion's message to Jesus emphasizes authority. He obeys the authority over him in the military command structure, and his soldiers and slaves in turn obey his commands, going where he tells them and doing what he wants (Luke 7:8). The obedience of the soldiers and slaves signifies the centurion's masculine authority. The centurion recognizes that Jesus has the same sort of authority. If Jesus commands, the centurion's sick slave will be healed (v. 7). That the enslaved person is healed without Jesus even entering the home proves Jesus's manly power.

The enslaved person is identified as δοῦλος and παῖς, a designation used for slaves of all ages (as noted in chap. 2, above, this was a way of un-manning adult men). His illness is the reason for the interaction between the centurion and Jesus. In a story that is putatively about him, however, he is barely visible behind the focus on the centurion's patronage and authority. His virtual absence reflects the invisibility of enslaved people in the literature of the time.[96] The centurion's reference to his authority over the enslaved people in his household categorizes the dying slave with all the others as his property to command. The enslaved person's obedience is one signifier of the centurion's masculinity, but as a slave he has no masculine status of his own.

These elements in Luke 7:1–10 reflect standard aspects of masculinity in the Roman world. The characterization of Jesus throughout the Gospel incorporates masculine values.[97] So, for instance, Jesus is a man of power and

92. See J. Green 1997, 284–85; Carroll 2012, 161.

93. The centurion's masculinity would have been more ambiguous in Rome, given the attempts to limit and control the militarized masculinity of non-elite soldiers in the early empire (see Reeder 2019, 38–40). The location of this story in a provincial setting allows the centurion to be more "manly" than elites in the center of the empire would allow. The characterization of the centurion draws attention to the non-elite context of the Lukan community.

94. See Conway 2008, 132.

95. So Carroll 2012, 162.

96. Apart from Mary in 1:38 and 48 and Simeon in 2:29, this is the first enslaved person in Luke's Gospel.

97. Conway 2008, 127–42, concludes that Luke and Acts present Jesus and the apostles as "achieving their own ideal manly status in the Roman Empire" (p. 142). See also D'Angelo 2002,

authority (4:14–22; 8:22–25). He receives public recognition as a teacher, speaker, and healer (7:36; 13:10–17; 14:1; 19:36–38). At the end of the book, Jesus is acclaimed as "a prophet man powerful in action and word" (24:19). But this apparent acclamation of masculinity is ironic. It comes from two disciples who, as their speech continues, imply that the crucified Jesus has proven to be a failed prophet man, powerless to redeem Israel (vv. 20–21). The same gendered ambiguity noted in Philippians and Mark is present in Luke's portrayal of Jesus (and other characters).[98]

With respect to Jesus himself, the poverty of his family is evident in Luke 2:1–24, countering the potentially noble or heroic elements of the birth story. As in Mark, Jesus does not enact masculinity by exercising patriarchal authority over a household, and he calls people away from their own households (Luke 9:57–62; 12:49–53; 14:25–26; 18:28–30).[99] Luke's Jesus is known (and critiqued by people of status) for associating with people who lacked social status or power (5:29–32; 15:1–2; 19:5–7).[100] He is derided as a "glutton and a drunk," someone who has no control over his own bodily desires (7:34).[101] In his public speaking and private teaching, he repeatedly challenges the hierarchies of status, wealth, and power that define normative masculinity (e.g., 6:20–26; 14:7–24; 20:45–47).[102] As in the third passion prediction in 18:31–34, Luke's narrative of Jesus's death includes signifiers of un-masculinity in expanded scenes of mockery and references to flogging (23:11, 17, 22).[103]

The ambiguity of masculinity in Luke is present in the story of the centurion's dying slave.[104] Though the enslaved person disappears through most of the story, references to him frame and center the narrative (7:1, 7, 10). Moreover, the story introduces the enslaved person as ἔντιμος to the centurion. This term is not often applied to enslaved people.[105] Given the economic realities of

58–62; on Luke 1–2, Talbert 2003, 67–70, and King 2019, 409–10; and on the passion story as a "noble death," Scaer 2005, 45–53, 90–116; Eklund 2015, 30–31, 45–46. Though not using the language of masculinity, Danker 1988, 3–9, argues that Luke characterizes God and Jesus as benefactors who exemplify ἀρετή (both virtue and manliness).

98. See Carroll 2014, 372; esp. Wilson 2015, 21, chaps. 3 and 6 (on the destabilized masculinity of Zechariah and Jesus in Luke); 2017, 30, 42–46; and Solevåg and Kartzow 2023, 279–80.

99. Cf. Moxnes 2016, 334–37; Wilson 2015, 193–94; Asikainen 2018, 90–91.

100. Wilson 2015, 194–95.

101. So also Moxnes 2003, 102–3. The accusation echoes Deut. 21:18–21, but the descriptors signify a lack of manliness in, e.g., Philo, *Somn.* 2.51; Suetonius, *Vit.* 17.2; and Plutarch, [*Lib. ed.*] 4b.

102. Esp. A. C. Miller 2014b, 9, 12.

103. See esp. Wilson 2015, 203–41; 2019, 28–29.

104. A. C. Miller 2014b, 50, 185, additionally notes the centurion's questionable performance of masculinity in his reliance on non-Roman systems for help.

105. In Diodorus Siculus 16.87.2, ἔντιμος is applied to a person only after being freed from slavery. Dio Chrysostom argued that all people, including "shameful enslaved bodies," are

slavery, the descriptor may indicate the enslaved person's value as property (cf. Aristotle, *Pol.* 1.1255b25). In the only other use of ἔντιμος in Luke, however, it indicates the honorable status of an elite man (14:8), a common meaning for the term in Greco-Roman literature.[106] In military contexts, ἔντιμος describes the honor of manly men who fight courageously.[107] Applied to the enslaved person, ἔντιμος opens an unexpected wedge in the story's representation of normative masculinity. A particular example of the alternative masculinity developed in Luke is the identification of the disciples with enslaved people in the parables of 12:35–48 and 17:7–10.[108]

Luke 12:35–48

The first in the series of parables in Luke 12:35–48 is directed to a broad audience of all the people who are following Jesus (vv. 35–38). In the story world of the parable, they are enslaved people awaiting the return of their enslaver (κύριος), a scene that would doubtless have been familiar to the enslaved people in Luke's audience. Even in the enslaver's absence, the enslaved people's actions center on him: They stay awake, alert, and prepared at all times as they await his return.[109] They must maintain, in Clarice Martin's words, "constant vigilance."[110] Their obedience is rewarded when their enslaver arrives. He puts on the clothing of slavery (note περιζώννυμι in vv. 35 and 37[111]), has them recline to dine, and serves (διακονέω) them. The enslaver assumes the identity and labor of his enslaved people, and they assume his position of privilege.[112]

---

honorable (ἔντιμος) before the gods, though he then immediately limited ἔντιμος to free elites (7.138–39).

106. Aristotle, *Eth. nic.* 1122b15, 1124a19; Diodorus Siculus 19.86.2; Lucian, *Merc. cond.* 12; Athenaeus, *Deipn.* 4.146a.

107. Hyperides 6.30, 6.37; Plutarch, *Cor.* 4.3; *Marc.* 30.1–2. See also Aristotle, *Eth. nic.* 1116a13.

108. J. Strong 2021, 6–7, and passim, categorizes Jesus's parables as fables on the basis of literary structure, vocabulary and catch phrases, and messages. As discussed in the introduction, above, fables were associated with slavery; enslaved and freed people used fables to acknowledge, navigate, and protest the domination of slavery. Strong argues that the presence of fables in the Synoptic Gospels identifies the audience with a low social status (pp. 280–81).

109. Cf. Phaedrus, *Fables*, Perotti's Appendix 20; Moss 2024, 85. The imagery of Luke 12:35 echoes Exod. 12:11 (see Edwards 2015, 378).

110. C. Martin 2005, 239. Her discussion of "eye service" in Ephesians and Colossians also illuminates this parable (pp. 236–39). See also Glancy 2006, 109; Moss 2024, 29.

111. As noted in the introduction, above, belting a tunic around the waist signified enslavement (Horace, *Sat.* 2.8.10; Petronius, *Sat.* 60.8; Philo, *Contempl.* 51, 72; Suetonius, *Cal.* 26.2; Roller 2006, 29, 85). I am reading the actions described in v. 35 as part of the depiction of enslavement in vv. 36–38. Bovon 2013, 231–32, identifies v. 35 as a separate message (see also J. Green 1997, 500–501).

112. See esp. J. Green 1997, 499; Martinsen 2015, 321.

Role reversal in the context of dining is not unique to Luke. During Saturnalia, enslavers served their enslaved people a meal, though what specific tasks were included is not entirely clear. Lucian and Athenaeus both simply summarized the work with the vocabulary of service (διακονέω and διακονία).[113] Seneca used the example of Saturnalia to encourage enslavers to invite enslaved people to dine with them regularly in order to inculcate manly reason and virtue in the (un-manly) slaves. The meal service in this imagined dinner comes from other enslaved people, perhaps those who are not worthy enough (in Seneca's perception) to be invited to dine. The purpose and practice of the shared meal consequently reinforce the status distinctions between free and enslaved people (*Ep.* 47.14–16).[114] In this respect, it is notable that Pliny escaped the festivities altogether in search of quiet space to work (presumably taking his enslaved scribes and readers away from the party; *Ep.* 2.17.22).[115] Insofar as the enslaver's change of clothing signifies a change in status, the role reversal in Jesus's parable seems slightly more extreme than the special feast of Saturnalia or Seneca's paternalistic meals.[116]

The parable's apparent message is that Jesus's followers should adopt the "constant vigilance" of enslaved people, ready for their enslaver's (their "lord's") return.[117] The eschatological overtones are emphasized by the example of a thief who, like the enslaver in the first story, comes at an unexpected time. So, like the enslaved people—but unlike the "master of the house" (οἰκοδεσπότης), who is unprepared for a thief—Jesus's followers should always be ready for the Son of Humanity (Luke 12:39–40).[118] This transition introduces a second parable directed more precisely toward the twelve disciples (note v. 41). A new character features in this second parable: the enslaved (or freed) manager (οἰκονόμος) who has authority over the other people enslaved in the

113. Lucian, *Sat.* 17–18, 22–25 (the reference to enslavers serving the meal is in 18; the rest of the discussion concerns equality in quantity and quality of food for guests of all statuses); Athenaeus, *Deipn.* 14.639b. D'Arms 1991, 176, and Zelnick-Abramovitz 2012, 101–6, review the probable practices of Saturnalia.

114. Seneca's letter suggests enslavers would object to his exhortation, as is narrated in Petronius, *Sat.* 70.10–13. See Roller 2006, 20; Bradley 2008, 338–42.

115. Dionysius of Halicarnassus, *Ant. rom.* 4.14.3–4, claimed the purpose of Saturnalia and Compitalia was to make enslaved people more ready to labor for their enslavers. See further D'Arms 1991, 176, and Zelnick-Abramovitz 2012, 97–100, on the use of role reversal to enforce enslavement.

116. Cf. Schottroff 2005, 228–29; Martinsen 2015, 319–21; Cobb 2019, 30. Hentschel 2007, 267, however, suggests the parallel with Saturnalia supports the enslaver's retention of status even in meal service in Luke 12:37.

117. The elision of the parabolic enslaver with Jesus as κύριος is unavoidable in Luke 12:35–38. See also J. Green 1997, 498.

118. J. Green 1997, 497; Bovon 2013, 231–36.

household.[119] While the enslaver is away, the manager provides the enslaved people with their food.[120] If the enslaver returns to find the manager completing this task, the manager is rewarded with greater authority.

However, the enslaved manager may abuse his (or her) position by acting like an enslaver (a role reversal of a different sort than the one in Luke 12:37).[121] First, the manager beats enslaved women and men in the household.[122] A manager caught beating an enslaved person in *Life of Aesop* 9–10 fears demotion; the right to command such abuse belonged to the enslaver.[123] Second, the manager (over)indulges in food and wine. Enslavers accused enslaved people of being greedy, drunk, and gluttonous.[124] But as Seneca's contrast of silent, hungry slaves with drunk, bloated diners indicates, the ability to behave in these ways generally rested with the enslavers (*Ep.* 47.2–3, 5).[125] The enslaver in Jesus's story executes the abusive manager by chopping him (or her) in half (διχοτομέω).[126] The graphic punishment is remarkably similar to an illustration found in Epictetus: An enslaved person who appoints himself (or herself) as manager (οἰκονόμος), taking on the privilege of ordering other enslaved people around, is cut apart by the enslaver (with ἕλκω and τέμνω; *Diatr.* 3.22.3). In Luke's parable, the

119. For the οἰκονόμος of a household (and the Latin equivalent, *dispensator*) as an enslaved person, see Chariton, *Call.* 2.1–2, 7; Martial 11.39; Suetonius, *Aug.* 67.1; Plutarch, *Cat. Min.* 39.3; Lucian, *Tim.* 14, *Sat.* 26; Beavis 1992, 45; Glancy 2006, 111; Baergen 2006, 28, 30–33; Martinsen 2015, 354.

120. The "food allowance," σιτομέτριον, is a civic provision of food in Diodorus Siculus 13.58.3; Plutarch, *Cat. Maj.* 8.1. More often, it appears in military contexts as the food allowance for soldiers (e.g., Polybius 6.39.13; Diodorus Siculus 19.49.2–50.1; Josephus, *Ag. Ap.* 1.79). The term may also have been used in household settings, but given Luke's interest in war, it is an interesting term to choose.

121. The enslaved manager in Luke 12:42–46 is gendered male by masculine pronouns and the address to the male twelve disciples, but note that women also could hold this role (cf. *CIL* 3.2118, 6.9715, 8.5384, 10.5081; Bain 2014, 151–54).

122. Note that Kartzow 2010, 97–99, questions whether the παῖς and παιδίσκη are enslaved adults, free children, or enslaved children. I am reading these people as enslaved people (including adults and children) because of the situation established in Luke 12:42, but the vocabulary alone is not clear.

123. See also Achilles Tatius, *Leuc. Clit.* 5.17.9–10. In Plutarch, *Cohib. ira* 463b, the enslaved manager is subject to his enslaver's beating (along with enslaved women).

124. See Horace, *Sat.* 1.3.80–83; Columella, *Rust.* 13–14 (warning against a farm manager's overindulgence); Plutarch, *Quaest. conv.* 678e–f; Martinsen 2015, 377.

125. S. Elliott 2018, 94, notes that the worst sin of an enslaved person was to take on their enslaver's identity. She refers to enslaved people enacting masculinity or moral virtue, but her point also works for the enslaved manager's usurpation of enslavers' rights to indulgence and domination in Luke 12:45.

126. Διχοτομέω, a military term, describes dismemberment as a terror tactic (Polybius 10.15.5; Plutarch, *Pyrrh.* 24.3). Beavis 1992, 42–43, and Martinsen 2015, 410–11, compare Luke 12:46 with a litany of outrageous violence against enslaved bodies in Roman literature.

body parts are tossed out with the unfaithful—that is, removed from the boundaries of the community.

The violence continues through the conclusion of the parable. All enslaved people (managers or not) are beaten.[127] Those who deliberately disobey are beaten more than those who did not know what was required, but the enslaved people in both categories face physical violence (Luke 12:46–47). As noted in chapter 2, the ability to protect one's own bodily boundaries was a privilege of masculinity that enslaved people did not share. They were objects of casual violence on a daily basis as well as more serious, targeted punitive violence, whether (by the logic of enslavers) they had done something to deserve a beating or not.[128] The violence faced by the enslaved people in Luke's parable offers an insistent reminder of the dehumanizing un-manliness of enslavement. For Jesus's followers to be "slaves" is neither honorable nor desirable. The metaphor carries bodily consequences.[129]

The shocking violence of Luke 12:46 overwhelms the story for contemporary readers. Audiences in antiquity may also have found the violence surprising. A variety of instructions to elite enslavers discourage excessive acts of violence disproportionate to the perceived offense (for instance, crucifixion to punish an enslaved person for eating leftovers; Horace, *Sat.* 1.3.80–83).[130] While I would not want to justify the violence in Luke 12:46, it is important to note that the excessive response operates to censure the abuse of authority. The enslaved manager has beaten his (or her) fellow enslaved people and consumed their resources.[131] As a message directed at the twelve disciples, men who (in the continuing story of Acts) held authority in the community of Jesus's followers, the warning is significant.[132] The enslaved manager left in charge in the enslaver/lord's absence does not have the right to weaponize the power of normative masculinity. By extension, the disciples cannot abuse their position or center their own interests at the expense of others (see

127. As Carroll 2012, 275, notes, Luke 12:47–48 shifts between the disciples and the larger audience in vv. 35–40.

128. Illustrated by Plautus, *Merc.* 414–16; Phaedrus, *Fables*, Perotti's Appendix 20; Juvenal, *Sat.* 6.219–23, 475–94; and the texts discussed in chap. 2, above.

129. Powery and Sadler 2016, 156–58, note that enslavers in the United States used Luke 12:47 to justify their abuse of enslaved people (rightly identified as blasphemy by Frederick Douglass). See also Dowling 2008, 63–64, and Kartzow 2010, 96–99, on the problem of violence in this parable.

130. See also Demosthenes 54.4; Seneca, *Clem.* 1.18.2; Plutarch, *Cohib. ira* 459d; Martinsen 2015, 466; Lenski 2016, 281.

131. Cf. Bovon 2013, 239.

132. The history of abuse in the church demonstrates just how important the message is (see, e.g., Reeder 2022, 7–17, on the crisis of sexual abuse by priests, pastors, and other authority figures in the church).

also Luke 17:1–2). Their responsibility is to care and provide for their fellow enslaved people.

Luke 17:7–10

The parable in Luke 17:7–10 begins by identifying the twelve disciples with an enslaver whose slaves labor in agricultural tasks in addition to household work (cooking and serving meals).[133] The parable reflects life in a non-elite household with a few enslaved people carrying out all the necessary labor, rather than a wealthy household with specialized tasks for enslaved people. Standard assumptions concerning enslavement and masculinity are evident in the parable's focus on enslavers, their interests, and their perspectives on the "slaves" they owned.

Jesus asks the twelve disciples if, as such an enslaver, they would invite their slaves to dine after they had labored all day at plowing and shepherding. Despite the example of the enslaver serving enslaved people in Luke 12:37, the question in 17:7 anticipates the negative response voiced in verse 8: The enslaver tells his slaves to serve (διακονέω) him a meal, putting off their own bodily needs for this purpose.[134] This scene is, as noted above on Luke 12:45, reflected in numerous literary depictions of Roman dining rooms. The work of slavery, Jesus reminds the disciples, does not deserve a generous return (μὴ ἔχει χάριν τῷ δούλῳ). The term χάρις distinguishes enslavement from the exchange of favor or honor for benefaction among free and freed people.[135] Enslaved people were (dehumanized) tools for their enslavers' use, not (honorably masculine) agents of benefaction to their enslavers.

So far, the twelve disciples have been identified with the enslaver who gives orders to and demands the slaves' work on his behalf (Luke 17:7–9). Assuming the disciples were all free men, they might be expected to share the enslaver's perspective in the story. But the ending of the parable redefines the disciples as the enslaved: "In the same way, when you have done all you were commanded to do, say, 'We are useless [ἀχρεῖος] slaves. We have done what we were supposed to do'" (v. 10). Uselessness or worthlessness emphasizes the distinction between the enslaver and the enslaved person.[136] The disciples'

133. The twelve disciples are introduced as Jesus's specific conversation partners in Luke 17:5 ("apostles" refers to the twelve specifically in 6:13 and 9:10; see Nelson 1994, 44).

134. Glancy 2006, 110, notes that the difference between the enslaver in Luke 12:37 and 17:7–8 offers a reminder of the "caprice of the slaveholder" to govern the experiences of enslavement. See also Beavis 1992, 41–42.

135. J. Green 1997, 614; cf. Bradley 2008, 336–37, on Seneca's consideration of the possibility of a slave offering *beneficium* to an enslaver.

136. Ἀχρεῖος is not a common descriptor of enslaved people. Rather, in war narratives the term describes noncombatants and ill-prepared soldiers (as in Josephus, *Ant.* 5.28, 13.240). Among the elite, it refers to the inability to contribute to society or to be an economic resource

sudden demotion to the status of enslaved people makes them "worthless" from the perspective of enslavers (or indeed "worth less" by the social standards of the first century), disrupting their association with the masculine status of the enslaver in the first part of the parable.[137]

The values and characteristics of normative masculinity are woven through Luke's Gospel, as is evident in the masculine authority of the centurion and Jesus in 7:1–7. But, as the ascription of masculine honor to the enslaved person in that story indicates, normative masculinity is accompanied by challenges to masculine power, authority, honor, and status.[138] Luke's identification of Jesus's followers and especially the twelve disciples as enslaved people develops an alternative masculinity around the identity and other-centered behaviors of enslaved people (12:35–38), responsibility to provide for and protect the community of enslaved people without abuse of masculine privilege (12:41–48), and the social abasement of "worthless slaves" (17:7–10). The honor of the centurion's slave and the role reversal of 12:35–38, in turn, complicate the social denigration of enslaved people (though the normative oppression of enslavement is also present in 12:45–48; 17:7–10).

Masculinity and Slavery in the Dining Room

The intersections of discipleship, slavery, and serving food in Luke 12:35–48 and 17:7–10 provide important context for the conversation concerning greatness and service in 22:24–27. That conversation occurs in the context of the Passover meal commemorating Israel's salvation from the oppression of slavery. The celebration of Passover provides a fitting conclusion to Jesus's mission of liberation (announced in 4:16–21).[139] But as the scene progresses, it becomes clear that freedom from oppression does not mean freedom to oppress. Instead, as Jesus reclines around the table with his (male) disciples, he tells them to take on the status of the youngest and the server. He offers himself as an example. The development of an alternative definition of masculinity

---

(Aristotle, *Eth. nic.* 1163a; Josephus, *Ant.* 19.151); the single New Testament use reflects economic value (Matt. 25:30). It has a negative moral connotation in reference to free people in Aristotle, *Eth. nic.* 1095b, 1128b; Dio Chrysostom 7.110–12; Athenaeus, *Deipn.* 6.261d, 10.444e (cf. Rom. 3:12). Cf. enslaved people as ἄχρηστος in Philem. 11; Dio Chrysostom 10.13–14; Plutarch, *Cat. Maj.* 4.4; Epictetus, *Diatr.* 1.19.19; Martinsen 2015, 295–300.

137. See also L. Johnson 1991, 259.

138. Cf. Dowling 2007, 96–97. Noting the conflict between Jesus's proclamation of freedom for captives (Luke 4:18–21) and the lack of freedom for enslaved people in these parables, Dowling suggests that the themes of reversal and the ways enslaved people derail their enslavers' plans offer ways to resist oppression (pp. 109–11); see also Baergen 2006, 33–34, on Luke 16:1–8.

139. On the intersection of liberation with Passover in Luke, see esp. Nelson 1994, 57–58; A. C. Miller 2014b, 149–52, 159; Ramelli 2016, 116; M. Smith 2022, 55.

around the un-manliness of enslavement in the parables informs the message to the disciples concerning status and authority.

Meals are a common literary motif in Luke's Gospel. As already noted, Jesus is disparaged as "a glutton and a drunk" who spends his time with people who lack social status (7:34).[140] Echoing elements of Greco-Roman symposium narratives, the dining room often provides a literary framework for Jesus's teaching (6:1–5; 7:36–50; 11:37–41).[141] In addition, Jesus's teaching frequently concerns food, including warnings directed against those who have an abundance and promises of food for those who are hungry (reflections of the Gospel's theme of wealth and poverty).[142] The dinner party in 14:1–24 portrays Luke's use of meals to convey key concerns of social reversal, adopting a low social status, and the inclusion of socially marginalized peoples.[143]

The enslaved people who invited the guests, acquired the food, cooked and served the meal, entertained, and cleaned the leftover detritus are barely visible or entirely absent from these scenes (enslaved servers are made visible only in the parables in Luke 12:35–48; 14:15–24; and 17:7–10). The intersection of slavery and dining in Greco-Roman antiquity adds a significant layer to the interpretation of meals in Luke, particularly the conversation between Jesus and the (male) disciples concerning status and authority at the last supper. The vocabulary of slavery is missing from Luke 22:26–27, but the implications of enslavement in the spaces of dining bring the concerns of masculinity to the forefront. The function of meals to define, establish, and indulge masculinity in the Roman world clarifies this aspect of Luke 22:24–27.

Practicing Masculinity in the Dining Room

As established in chapter 2, above, the definitions of elite masculinity in the Roman Empire incorporated wealth and social position, the exercise of authority over other people, and self-discipline. These attributes

140. See Luke 5:29–32; 15:1–2; D. Smith 1987, 636–38; Snodgrass 1998, 196–97; Moxnes 2003, 102–4; Gleason 2004, 325; Schottroff 2005, 71.

141. So, e.g., D. Smith 1987, 614–23; J. Green 1997, 244–45, 540–41; Bartchy 2002, 180. Snodgrass 1998, 190–91, instead identifies Jesus's teaching with Jewish traditions of the eschatological banquet.

142. E.g., Luke 1:53; 4:25–26; 6:20–21, 25; 9:3; 10:7; 11:3, 5–8; 12:22–31; 16:19–21; D. Smith 1987, 625; Schottroff 2005, 71; Dowling 2007, 103–5; Crabbe 2011, 250–51; A. C. Miller 2014a, 416–17, 420.

143. See further Nelson 1994, 63–67; J. Green 1997, 247–48, 542, 550–62; Bartchy 2002, 175, 180; A. C. Miller 2014a, 420–24; Barreto 2018, 177–78 (identifying meals in Luke as symbolic of belonging).

of masculinity were performed publicly to be judged by onlookers. Dinners provided a key space for the demonstration and acknowledgment of masculinity.[144]

From the perspective of a host, a dinner brought the opportunity to show off household wealth and fashion with the furnishings of the dining room (the triclinium), the tableware, and the quality and quantity of food.[145] The quality and quantity of the guests also demonstrated the host's status (Plutarch, *Quaest. conv.* 679b). Guests with significant social or political positions offered opportunities for gaining influence or loyalty.[146] Guests of lower social status, including the host's clients, signified the host's generosity (Juvenal, *Sat.* 5.24–173).[147] From the guests' perspective, the seating order put their relative status on display (Plutarch, *Quaest. conv.* 616b, 617a, 619d). Proximity to the host signified social greatness, and conversely, distance from the host demonstrated a relative lack of status.[148]

The use of dinners to display wealth and status offers one intersection with elite masculinity. The conversation and education at a dinner also gave opportunities to practice masculine ideals. Plutarch credited Cato the Elder with directing dinner conversations toward exemplars of good citizenship (*Cat. Maj.* 25.2–3). Valerius Maximus similarly encouraged entertainment intended to teach freeborn young men how to be manly through poetry and music that celebrated the great deeds of Roman ancestors (2.1.10).[149] Pliny valued good conversation, philosophical debate, and cultural performances at dinners (*Ep.* 1.15.1–4, 3.12.1–2, 6.31.13–14). For Cicero, dining in company

144. The focus here is on dinners in personal homes, with invitations extended to guests from outside the household, rather than family meals or formal dinners in ceremonial spaces (cf. Roller 2006, 7–8). As Hudson 2010, 663–65, notes, some elements in literary descriptions reflect practices of dining, but some are constructed to reflect Roman social ideals.

145. Cicero, *Att.* 353.1–2; *Verr.* 2.27.62; Valerius Maximus 7.5.1; Philo, *Contempl.* 48–49; Seneca, *Ep.* 78.23–24, 114.9; Pliny, *Ep.* 1.15.1–4; Plutarch, *Quaest. conv.* 629c, 678e–f. The physical elements of dining rooms, including furnishings and tableware, are discussed by, e.g., Dunbabin 2003, 38–43; Hudson 2010, 665–93; Joshel and Petersen 2014, 40–67.

146. Cicero, *Att.* 346.2, 407A.2; *Fam.* 13.3; Suetonius, *Cal.* 39.2; Plutarch, *Quaest. conv.* 619d. Plutarch particularly identified the development of relationships as an important element of dinners (*Quaest. conv.* 617d, 621c, 660b).

147. Fitzgerald 2023, 135–46, explores dining and patronage (esp. in Martial).

148. In a very wealthy household, there might be separate dining areas or distinct qualities of food and wine for different categories of guests, though this latter practice was subject to critique (e.g., Cicero, *Att.* 353.1–2; Plutarch, *Cleom.* 13.3; Suetonius, *Jul.* 48; Pliny, *Ep.* 2.6.1–6). A poor position in the dining room, inadequate food, and being ignored by enslaved servers are frequent subjects of complaint (Martial 3.60, 6.11, 10.49; Juvenal, *Sat.* 5.1–173; Lucian, *Merc. cond.* 26; *Sat.* 22). On the use of dining to reinforce social hierarchies, see D'Arms 1994, 308–9, 318–19; Garnsey 1999, 134–37; Roller 2001, 135–39; Clarke 2003, 226; Dunbabin 2003, 83–84; on Jewish practices, see Nelson 1994, 57.

149. See Roller 2006, 159–62.

maintained a man's mental and social agility, ensuring his ability to represent himself well to others (*Fam.* 362.2–3).

Valerius Maximus contrasted the manly potential of dinners with their dangers: A young man was lured into utter debauchery by the excesses of food, wine, and pleasure at dinner parties, only to be saved by the philosophical values of modesty and self-control (6.9, ext. 1). Self-discipline, physical strength, physique, and control over bodily functions were central to elite masculinity. Consequently, as Valerius Maximus's story indicates, rich foods, freely flowing wine, and highly sexualized entertainment, along with the sexual availability of enslaved bodies, presented significant dangers.[150] Seneca's lengthy diatribe against the injury to bodies from gluttony and drunkenness depicted the emasculating potential of a dinner. His solution was to teach masculine virtue to prevent men from being enslaved to lust, desire, and luxury (*Ep.* 95.15–38).[151] There was a fine line between demonstrating masculinity at a dinner and losing it.

In another letter, Seneca addressed the use of the body to display masculine values in posture, clothing, and dining habits (*Ep.* 92.11). One particular concern at a dinner was the act of reclining.[152] To recline to dine was itself a demonstration of rank and status, as the tombstone of Aulus Caprilius Timotheos indicates. Timotheos was a formerly enslaved slave trader. His tombstone depicts his masculine status as a freed man with an image of himself reclining at a funerary banquet. He is attended by a standing slave, with a row of chained enslaved men, women, and children in a lower register (*SEG* 36.587).[153] In literature and visual art, the contrast between freeborn men of status who recline to dine and the enslaved servers who stand, walk, bend, crawl, or crouch under tables composes a landscape of masculinity.[154]

150. E.g., Caesar, *Bell. gall.* 1.1, 2.15; Cicero, *Cat.* 2.22–23; Columella, *Rust.* 1, pref. 16–17; Valerius Maximus 2.6.1; Livy 5.6.4–5, 23.4.4–5, 23.18.10–12; Seneca, *Ep.* 95.15–18, 23–24, 32–33; Tacitus, *Hist.* 3.2; Booth 1991, 105; Corbeill 1997, 107–10; Roller 2006, 65–79 (analyzing the frescoes depicting drinking parties and dinners at Pompeii).

151. Cf. Quintilian, *Inst.* 1.2.8; Valerius Maximus 2.5.5; Pliny, *Ep.* 2.6.5, 3.12.1–2; Plutarch, *Dion* 52.3; *Quaest. conv.* 629c.

152. Women also attended dinners (e.g., Valerius Maximus 2.1.3; Seneca, *Ep.* 95.20–21; Juvenal, *Sat.* 11.162–66; Plutarch, *Quaest. conv.* 619d), and at least in parts of the empire they likely reclined to dine. See Leyerle 1999, 30–31, 43–45; Clarke 2003, 223–43; Dunbabin 2003, 22–23; Roller 2006, 96–105.

153. The tombstone is discussed by Finley 1968, 162–63; Koester 2008, 772–75; Chaniotis 2023, 183–85.

154. Cf. Aristophanes, *Vesp.* 1210–13; Columella, *Rust.* 11.1.19; Phaedrus, *Fables*, Perotti's Appendix 20; Livy 24.16.11–13; Seneca, *Ep.* 47.2; Suetonius, *Cal.* 26.2; Plutarch, *Mor.* 201c. See further Booth 1991, 108–9; D'Arms 1991, 177; Leyerle 1999, 31; Dunbabin 2003, 11–13; Roller 2006, 9–10, 15–22.

Slavery in the Dining Room

A fresco from the House of the Triclinium in Pompeii pictures adult male diners surrounded by enslaved people. All the enslaved people are male, represented with childishly small figures. Their size relative to the free men in the scene may be artistic convention rather than an indication of their age, but depictions of dinners in literature also express a preference for beautiful young enslaved boys and men as servers.[155] One diner sits as his feet are washed by a slave. Another leans over in a standing position, supported by a slave, to vomit. Several other diners recline as slaves offer food and wine; one diner, possibly the host, fondles a Black slave (the other figures in the scene are White).[156] The scene is complicated. The vomiting diner is guilty of overindulgence, which could (as common as this occurrence apparently was) signify a failure in his masculine discipline. But the stature, positioning, and dishonorable work of the enslaved people in the fresco emphasize their un-masculine status.

Literary and visual depictions of dinners identify the enslaved servers as boys and men.[157] Their tasks included washing diners' bodies (hands and feet).[158] They passed around food and cared for diners during the meal (e.g., by waving off flies).[159] They observed diners' behavior to report back to the host (Lucian, *Merc. cond.* 15, 28–29). They cleaned the dining space as diners ate, crawling around on the floor with the dogs (Martial 7.20.16–17).[160] Some of the work of enslaved people was particularly intimate, including assisting inebriated diners to urinate and cleaning up their vomit.[161] Enslaved people, male and female, also entertained diners with music; visual performance; clowning; displays of their bodily disabilities; and, at the enslavers' desire, sex.[162]

155. See further Laes 2008, 253.

156. See Dunbabin 2003, 58–59; Joshel and Petersen 2014, 28; Levin-Richardson 2021, 190–91.

157. Enslaved women also served in the dining room, as in Horace, *Sat.* 2.8.10, and in the frescoes in the House of the Triclinium and the House of Casti Amanti in Pompeii. The conventional preference for enslaved men as servers connects with the sexualization of the male form; see Roller 2006, 34, 64, 72.

158. Plato, *Symp.* 175a–b, 213b; Plautus, *Most.* 308–9; *Pers.* 791–93; Petronius, *Sat.* 31.3–5; *Life of Aesop* 40, 61.

159. Horace, *Sat.* 2.6.107–9; Petronius, *Sat.* 35.6; Seneca, *Ep.* 47.6, 95.24; Martial 3.82.8–14.

160. See also Horace, *Sat.* 2.8.10; Petronius, *Sat.* 34.4; Seneca, *Ep.* 47.5; Epictetus, *Diatr.* 3.26.21–23.

161. Demosthenes 54.4; Seneca, *Ben.* 3.26.2; *Ep.* 47.5; Martial 3.82.15–17; Athenaeus, *Deipn.* 6.262d.

162. Demosthenes 54.4, 59.33–34; Xenophon, *Hell.* 5.4.6; Valerius Maximus 9.1.8; Pliny, *Ep.* 9.17.2–4; Suetonius, *Tib.* 61.6; Lucian, *Symp.* 18–19. On the general work of enslaved people and their sexual labor at a dinner, see D'Arms 1991, 172–73; Leyerle 1999, 39–41; Dunbabin 2003, 150–55; Joshel and Petersen 2014, 37–40; Levin-Richardson 2021, 189–95.

As these examples indicate, much of the work that enslaved people performed at a dinner was perceived to be humiliating. The humiliation is explicit in Seneca's depiction of enslaved people crouched under a table, eating what has fallen to the floor. He compares the shame of this position with that of a freeborn man being beaten, tortured, or mocked in public (*Const.* 2.15.1). While these examples were intended to encourage elite men to endure such terrible events with fortitude, the comparison of the posture and position of enslaved people in a dining room with the abuse and humiliation of an elite man is striking. Similarly humiliating images of enslaved people at dinners include a "greedy" slave licking up the sauce left on a plate (Horace, *Sat.* 1.3.80–83); the abuse of enslaved people for imperfectly cooked food, broken crockery, or spills (Plutarch, *Cat. Maj.* 21.3[163]); a nude enslaved man with a hunched back or spinal curvature on display for the mockery of the guests (Pliny, *Nat.* 34.11–12); and a host's desire to avoid the touch of "disgusting slaves" (Petronius, *Sat.* 34.5).

The shameful un-manliness imposed on enslaved servers slipped into intentional emasculation. Some enslaved boys and men who worked as servers in dining rooms had been forcibly castrated.[164] In *Ep.* 47.7, Seneca described an enslaved man who served wine as deliberately womanized: shaved so that he looked like a boy, dressed in women's clothing, and subjected to the owner's sexual penetration. Philo pictured a similar scene of younger male slaves carefully coiffed and made up for guests' visual enjoyment, and slightly older male slaves accustomed to sexual use by diners (*Contempl.* 50–52). Both Seneca and Philo included these scenes to critique such customs. As common elements in descriptions of dinners, however, the enforced sexualization and, consequently, assault of enslaved boys and men un-manned them for the entertainment and enjoyment of "manly" male diners.[165]

There are indications that enslaved people resisted the disempowerment and humiliation of the dining room. Juvenal suggested that enslaved servers at a dinner for their enslaver's impoverished clients would mistreat the diners (a frequent complaint, as noted above). Their tasks provided opportunities for them to exercise power over the guests (*Sat.* 5.24–173).[166] A different means of resistance comes from the philosopher Epictetus, himself a freed slave, who

163. See also *Life of Aesop* 58, 62; Petronius, *Sat.* 34.2; Seneca, *Ira* 3.35.2; Plutarch, *Cohib. ira* 461b; Athenaeus, *Deipn.* 10.420e; D'Arms 1991, 174–76.

164. E.g., Seneca, *Ep.* 95.24; Juvenal, *Sat.* 11.145–58 (cf. 6.373a–b); Lucian, *Merc. cond.* 29.

165. Diodorus Siculus 5.40.3–4; Petronius, *Sat.* 41.6–8, 74.8–9; Seneca, *Ep.* 95.24; Martial 10.66, 10.98; Juvenal, *Sat.* 5.56, 60–62; Lucian, *Merc. cond.* 16; *Sat.* 24, 37. Roller 2006, 143, addresses the intersections of dining and sex.

166. Leyerle 1999, 40, suggests enslaved people's different service for people of lower social status was a means of upholding the hierarchies of society.

critiqued elite masculinity for its reliance on enslaved labor for basic bodily tasks like eating (*Diatr.* 3.26.21–23). Especially at a dinner with philosophical readings meant to inculcate masculine virtue, enslaved servers had a prime location from which to judge their enslavers' enactments of masculinity. The reference to a server's protest against serving a drunk, gluttonous, "beardless little boy" preserves just such a judgment (Athenaeus, *Deipn.* 6.262d).

Despite these potential avenues of resistance, elite authors' depictions of dining consistently denigrate enslaved people (even when, as in Seneca, *Ep.* 47, the author is critiquing the elite denigration of enslaved people). The humiliation, powerlessness, and emasculation of enslavement in these scenes offer a vivid, bodily contrast to the manliness of the diners. In this sense, the elite diners' performances of masculinity in the dining room depend on the emasculation of the enslaved men in the same space.

Luke 22:24–27

In Luke 22:14, Jesus and the twelve disciples recline together to share the Passover meal. Whether they were enslaved or elite, a first-century audience in the Roman Empire might imagine the scene in a dining room with its couches or benches, low tables, and enslaved servers. If they were familiar with Greco-Roman elite dining customs, the scene would prompt concerns about status and honor.[167] Some dining customs in the eastern Mediterranean (Luke's probable context) differed from the west. For instance, Plutarch encouraged egalitarian seating without reference to relative status among diners of the same social class.[168] But both the luxurious excesses of dining and the (ideal) limitation of dining to men were prevalent across the empire.[169] For Luke's authorial community, men reclining together to dine encourages considerations of masculinity.

Status, honor, and masculinity have already been associated with dining in Luke's narrative. At dinner with a leading Pharisee, Jesus warned the guests against taking the more honorable positions for themselves. They should instead take the least honorable position, and perhaps the host would honor them by reseating them in a better space: "For everyone who exalts themself

167. Bashaw 2019, 237, suggests the conflict of social norms within communal dining (including people of very different social statuses) in Luke's community may explain the narrative device of meals as a site of conflict in the Gospel.

168. Plutarch, *Sept. sap. conv.* 149a–f; *Quaest. conv.* 615d–18e. On the variations in dining rooms, couches, and practices between the Greek east and Latin west, see Leyerle 1999, 30–31; Dunbabin 2003, 37–41.

169. Paul 1991, 161–62, 166; Leyerle 1999, 43–45 (concluding that women probably were present at dinners in the east, though they remain invisible in the sources); Dunbabin 2003, 19–22.

will be humiliated [ταπεινόω], but everyone who humiliates themself will be exalted" (14:7–11). Jesus also encouraged hosts to invite people without the status to raise the host's status or the ability to repay the meal (vv. 12–14).[170] This dinner scene challenges the common cultural concerns of self-promotion, reciprocity, and the centrality of masculine status, reflecting Luke's interest in questions of wealth and poverty, privilege and (humiliated) marginality.[171]

The disciples apparently did not learn this lesson. As they recline with Jesus in Luke 22:24–27, the question of their relative status, perhaps sparked by their positions around the dining room (and likely influenced by the theme of status in Greco-Roman literary traditions of the symposium), becomes a serious argument (φιλονεικία).[172] In 4 Maccabees 1:26–27, the rivalry expressed by φιλονεικία appears in a vice list alongside pride, covetousness, the search for glory, and greed—the sorts of attitudes Jesus challenged in Luke 14:7–14. The disciples' fight over their relative greatness represents a significant failing in their understanding of Jesus's message.[173] It also offers another opportunity to disrupt the cultural value of status and honor.

"The kings of the nations rule over them, and their authorities are called benefactors" (Luke 22:25). While Mark's κατακυριεύω and κατεξουσιάζω might imply tyrannical oppression, Luke's references to ruling, κυριεύω and ἐξουσιάζω, represent normative practices. The inclusion of benefaction, εὐεργέτης, reflects the economic practices of people who held wealth, political power, and social status.[174] As attested by the praise of the centurion by the elders of Capernaum (7:3–5), the benefactor received public honor, social support, and political power in return for their financial support.[175]

Benefaction aligns with core elements of elite masculinity. Aristotle identified benefactors as virtuous (ἀρετή), a term associated with both morality and masculinity (*Eth. nic.* 1168a). Polybius included benefaction in his

170. Solevåg and Kartzow 2023, 275–79, explore the intersections of masculinity and disability in this text.

171. A. C. Miller 2014a, 422–24, emphasizes that these messages challenged both elites and non-elites who sought to use the systems of the elite to gain status or wealth for themselves. See also J. Green 1997, 552–53; Bartchy 2002, 178–80; Carroll 2012, 299–301.

172. Cf. φιλονεικία in 2 Macc. 4:4; Philo, *Spec.* 3.28; Josephus, *Ant.* 20.176–77.

173. Cf. Carroll 2012, 438. Sloan 1993, 64, connects the disciples' disagreement with the preceding conversation about Jesus's betrayal.

174. Benefactors are superior to the people who receive the benefaction, as the parallels with patronage indicate. See Aristotle, *Eth. eud.* 7.1238b; *Eth. nic.* 1124b; Cicero, *Mur.* 70–71; Philo, *Decal.* 165–67; *Spec.* 2.226–27; Pliny, *Ep.* 1.19; Sloan 1993, 66–68.

175. Inscriptions across the empire commemorate benefactors like Flavia Publicia Nicomachis (Pleket 19). See also, e.g., *CIL* 2.1956, 8.2630, 11.2702; Aristotle, *Eth. nic.* 1163b; Diodorus Siculus 11.26.6; Josephus, *Ant.* 15.190, 19.184; *J.W.* 7.71; Danker 1988, 5–6; Sloan 1993, 67; Hoyer 2018, 24–30; and on Luke 7:1–10, Runesson 2023, 149.

memorial for a manly man (ἀγαθὸς ἀνήρ) known for ἀρετή. This man's example should inspire young men to develop their own masculinity (6.54.2). Military heroes—the most manly of all—could be praised as benefactors for their generosity to those they conquered (Plutarch, *Aem.* 39.4; *Flam.* 1.2). In the setting of the dining room and the context of rivalry for greatness, the collocation of ruling, exercising authority, and benefaction in Luke 22:25 reinforces masculinity as a key concern in the scene.

Jesus's disciples should not adopt the practices of rulers, authorities, and benefactors: ὑμεῖς δὲ οὐχ οὕτως (Luke 22:26).[176] Instead, the greatest must be "like the youngest" (ὡς ὁ νεώτερος) and the leader "like the server" (ὡς ὁ διακονῶν). The first time the disciples debated their relative greatness, Jesus told them to welcome little children as Jesus himself, for the least (ὁ μικρότερος) is the greatest (9:46–48). As a little child is equivalent to "the least" in society, the youngest in 22:26 signifies immaturity, inexperience, and the lack of masculine attributes like courage, wisdom, and self-control (see chap. 2, above).[177] As the story of the disciples shooing children away from Jesus indicates, children lacked social status (18:15–17). They were under the control and command of parents, nurses, and pedagogues (e.g., Philo, *Decal.* 165–67). To become like the youngest means adopting a low, un-manly status.[178]

In the space of a dining room, the position of a server is likewise inferior to those who are served.[179] The δοῦλος of Mark 10:44 does not appear in Luke 22:26, but the context of a meal and the contrast between serving and reclining in verse 27 identify the servers as enslaved people. The use of the διακον- word group to indicate the work and experience of enslaved people at meals—from cooking to serving the food to experiencing abuse—is well attested.[180] The connection of meal service with enslavement in Luke 12:35–48 and 17:7–10 confirms the definition of servers as enslaved people in 22:26.

176. So Nelson 1991, 118–19; 1994, 149–53; Bovon 2012, 174; A. C. Miller 2014b, 85–86. Hentschel 2007, 284, however, suggests the disciples retain power but without the titles or honors associated with ruling (see also Lull 1984, 293–97, who argues the disciples should act as rulers and benefactors; as Nelson 1991, 120, notes, however, the negative and the contrasts in v. 26 do not support this reading).

177. E.g., Seneca, *Const.* 12.2; Philo, *Her.* 294; Tacitus, *Ann.* 13.6; Suetonius, *Claud.* 2.1–2; Cassius Dio 50.17. "Childishness" was an insult for adult men: Polybius 16.12.6; Livy 7.17.3–5, 41.20.3–4; Appian, *Bell. civ.* 5.1.8.

178. See also Carroll 2008, 188–91, on the image of a child as a challenge to "status or power" in Luke.

179. Contra Hentschel 2007, 285–88.

180. Aristophanes, *Ach.* 1015–17; Plato, *Gorg.* 517d; *Theaet.* 175e; Herodotus 9.82; Polybius 30.26.5; Diodorus Siculus 5.40.3; Philo, *Contempl.* 70, 75 (the Therapeutae reject the normal practices of enslaved servers); Plutarch, *Quaest. conv.* 628c; Pausanias 1.27.7; Cassius Dio 54.23.2–5; Collins 1990, 150–53; Hentschel 2007, 286–88. Sometimes free family members serve meals (Diodorus Siculus 4.36.2; Dio Chrysostom 7.65; Plutarch, *Mor.* 301e).

The "slavishness" of service in the dining room is evident in Polybius's accounts of Antiochus IV Epiphanes. Antiochus regularly welcomed his guests to the dining room, seated them, and led in the enslaved servers—tasks that would generally be carried out by enslaved people. Antiochus's posture as he moved around the room and bent down to guests rather than reclining further associated him with slavery. Polybius claimed that Antiochus's guests fled his dinners from the shame of his behavior (30.26.4–9; cf. 26.1.4).[181] The contrast between the "one who reclines" and the "one who serves" in Luke 22:27 reflects this cultural background. When Jesus asks the disciples if the one who reclines is greater than the one who serves, the answer is obvious. The one who reclines is the free person, the diner, a man with the status and privilege to enjoy the leisure of a meal. The enslaved person who serves demonstrates the manliness of the reclining diners by his embodied un-masculinity.

Reflecting the role reversal in Luke 12:37, Jesus identifies himself with the enslaved server.[182] And, as the "worthless slaves" of 17:7–10, the disciples should follow his example (22:27). There is a certain tension in the comparison. Jesus and the disciples are reclining, after all, and Jesus is represented in the story as the host of the meal.[183] Moreover, immediately after challenging the disciples to be like the youngest and like the enslaved servers, Jesus promises them privilege and power: the right to eat and drink at his table in his kingdom, and the authority to judge Israel (vv. 28–30). Colleen Conway suggests the "service" of Jesus and the disciples simply reflects the discourses of ideal kingship (see above, on Mark 10:41–45).[184]

But as Polybius's account of Antiochus indicates, the stark contrast between reclining and serving, especially given the un-manly construction of enslaved servers, does not easily fit into Greco-Roman cultural values. Together with the "least" in Luke 9:48, the youngest and the server in 22:27–28 represent people who lack status, honor, and power—those who are, in effect, un-manned. The comparisons redefine greatness and leadership (and thus the disciples' position as judges in the kingdom) around the absence of privilege, social humiliation, and labor for the benefit of others.[185]

181. In Cicero, *Verr.* 2.3.53–63, and Livy 24.16.11–13, standing to dine is punishment for elite men (see further Roller 2006, 85–87).

182. L. Johnson 1991, 206.

183. There are several proposed solutions to this narrative gap. D. Smith 1987, 632; and Hentschel 2007, 215, connect the meal service in Luke 22:24–27 with the picnic in 9:12–17. L. Johnson 1991, 345, 349, points to Jesus offering the disciples bread and wine. Nelson 1994, 166–69, suggests Jesus's service reflects his general lifestyle of benefiting others.

184. Conway 2008, 142.

185. See esp. Nelson 1991, 118, 122; Carroll 2012, 438–39; Moxnes 2016, 338–39.

Jesus and the Twelve as Un-Manned Slaves

Masculinity and slavery represent a significant binary of gender in Greco-Roman antiquity. The normative constructions of masculinity are evident in Mark and Luke as the male disciples seek greatness and the power and authority that accompanied elite status. In both Gospels, Jesus exhorts the disciples to instead adopt the identity and social position of the least, the youngest, and enslaved people. To rule or exercise authority consequently looks nothing like the everyday practices of the political leaders of the time. The deliberate use of the language and imagery of enslavement in Mark 10:41–45 and Luke 22:24–27 redefines what authority might mean when it is decoupled from masculinity.[186]

Luke's parables are instructive. A position of authority does not erase enslaved identity, nor does it give one the right to oppress and abuse the people under one's authority (12:41–48). Even as the male disciples are invited to adopt the privileged position of enslavers, they are reminded that they are "worthless slaves" (17:7–10). The disciples cannot use power to place themselves above others, benefit from the work of others, or privilege themselves at the expense of others. Rather, they must embody social humiliation as they labor for the good of others without self-interest.[187] Within the world constructed in the Gospels, the un-manned disciples can nonetheless be accorded honor (like the enslaved person in the centurion's household) and greatness. But their greatness does not map onto the cultural conceptions of the first century. Outside the world constructed in the Gospels, the disciples' enslavement is dishonorable and shameful. The contrast emphasizes the un-manning of status and power.[188]

This chapter has focused attention on the twelve disciples, all men, and the particular significance of enslavement for normative masculinity. The parable in Luke 12:35–40, however, identifies all Jesus's followers (both men and women) with enslaved people. In both Mark and Luke, women are the agents of the "service" of the διακον- lexical group. Peter's mother-in-law, Mary Magdalene, Mary the mother of James and Joses, and Salome "serve" in Mark 1:31 and 15:40–41. In Luke 8:3 and 10:40, Joanna, Susanna, and Martha are added to the list of women who "serve," and Mary the mother of Jesus identifies herself as a humiliated slave (1:38, 48). The twelve disciples are only told to serve as enslaved people. The women actually do it. The next chapter explores the significance of these women, particularly Mary the mother of Jesus, for understanding the un-masculinity of enslavement in Luke.

186. Though they do not incorporate gender in their analyses, see Nelson 1994, 240–49; and Kamanouchi 2003, 204. See also Mayordomo 2013, 375.

187. Glancy 2010, 146, emphasizes their embodiment as "a despised slave."

188. Cf. Asikainen 2018, 92–98, 105.

5

Mary the Slave

And Mary proclaimed, "My soul magnifies the Lord/Enslaver [κύριος], and my spirit rejoices in God my Savior, because God has looked at the humiliation of his slave woman. Look, from now all generations will consider me blessed, because the Mighty One has done great things for me."

—Luke 1:46–49

The despot had two daughters, still unmarried, most beautiful to look upon, of marriageable age. These the conspirators seized and dragged out, having resolved to do away with them, but to torture and insult them first. . . . [Following the pleas of an honorable woman,] they decided to omit the violence, and permit the daughters to die by their own hand. When, therefore, they had returned the maidens to the house and ordered their death immediately, the elder, Myro, loosing her girdle and making a noose of it, bade farewell to her sister and urged her to take note and do exactly what she saw her do, "so that," she said, "we may not end our lives in any humiliating way, unworthy of ourselves."

—Plutarch, *Mulier. virt.* 253c–d (LCL)

As I have argued in this study, one common gender binary of the Roman Empire contrasted masculinity with enslavement. Manliness required authority over one's own body, emotions, desires, and decisions; legal rights over possessions; and the exercise of power over other people, whether they were in the man's household, larger community, or enemy forces. Enslavement was defined by the absence of personal authority and bodily autonomy. In this context, in the Christ hymn in Philippians 2:6–11 Jesus embodies a humiliated, obedient, crucified slave. As someone who is ordered around as an enslaved person was, he gives his life as a ransom to free others (Mark 10:45). He enacts the status and labor of enslaved servers in the dining room, providing food for other slaves and washing diners' feet (Luke 12:37; 22:27; John 13:1–17). His body bears the scars of unjust abuse (1 Pet. 2:22–25). The Christology of enslavement developed across these texts un-mans Jesus, with implications for the followers of Jesus who also experience unjust abuse, humiliate themselves, set aside their interests for the needs of others, and labor without rest (Luke 12:35–36; 17:7–10; Phil. 2:1–5; 1 Pet. 2:18–21).

The twelve (male) disciples are particularly singled out as recipients of this message in Mark and Luke. Precisely at the moment they seek masculine power and status, Jesus challenges them to call themselves "worthless slaves" and take on the identity and status of enslaved people and of enslaved servers in the dining room (Mark 10:43–44; Luke 22:26). Given the gendered dimensions of this challenge, it is important to notice who enacts the work of "serving" (διακονέω, διακονία) in the narratives of the Gospels: Peter's nameless mother-in-law (Mark 1:31; Luke 4:39); Martha (10:38–42); and the women who travel with Jesus, including Mary of Magdala, Mary the mother of James and Joses, Salome, Joanna, and Susanna (Mark 15:40–41; Luke 8:1–3). The association of the διακον- lexical group with discipleship identifies these women as disciples.[1]

The first reference to enslavement in Luke's Gospel also concerns a woman. Mary's humiliated enslavement is obscured in most English translations behind "humble" or "lowly" servanthood.[2] However, the vocabulary clearly indicates enslavement: "Behold, the slave [δούλη] of the lord/enslaver [κύριος]. May (everything) happen to me according to your word" (1:38). The identifier repeats in verse 48 in association with humiliation (ταπείνωσις). Mary, the mother of the lord (κύριος, v. 43), is also the lord's slave.[3] Arguably, the women who "serve" and "slave" model the discipleship of slavery for the twelve disciples within Mark and Luke and for the audiences of the two Gospels. For Luke specifically,

1. Kinuwaka 2001, 178, 190; Carey 2023, 1–6; Brobst-Renaud 2024, 27–28 (though Krause 2001, 44–49, suggests the women's "service" is subordinate).

2. Translations of Luke 1:48 include "low estate of his handmaiden" (KJV), "humble estate of his servant" (ESV), and "lowly servant girl" (NLT). Apart from the NASB 1995, which uses "bondslave," I am unaware of any English translations of δούλη and ταπείνωσις in Luke 1:38 and 48 that use the vocabulary of enslavement and humiliation.

3. As discussed in chap. 1, above, κύριος is both a divine title and an identifier for enslavers. The overlap in meaning is emphasized in Luke 1–2 by the pairing of Mary with Simeon, slave of the master (δεσπότης; 2:29).

the representation of Mary as "slave" shapes the meaning of enslavement for the (male) disciples addressed in 12:35–48; 17:7–10; and 22:24–27.

The comparison of Mary with the freeborn elite women in Plutarch's story clarifies the embodiment of enslavement in Luke 1. Plutarch's two sisters, caught up in political violence following the assassination of their father, are most likely going to be raped before they are executed.[4] Their decision to kill themselves saves their bodily honor, allowing them to avoid the humiliation (ταπεινῶς) of assault. Chastity, the protection of bodily boundaries, was a crucial concern of freeborn femininity (at least according to elite men like Plutarch).[5] The use of the ταπειν- lexical group to signify rape suggests that the violation of a freeborn woman's body brought personal trauma and social humiliation.[6] In sharp contrast to freeborn elite women, enslaved women lacked the privilege of bodily integrity. Enslavers did not ascribe chastity to them. As a slave, Mary's body is used by her lord/enslaver to bear a child. Her humiliation, indicative of social abasement and often synonymous with enslavement (see chap. 3, above), is visible in her pregnancy. But as Mary's song indicates, her humiliation is also her exaltation.

Arguably, the characterization of Mary in the infancy narrative is foundational to Luke's call for Jesus's followers, including the twelve disciples, to identify as enslaved people. That is, Mary's dramatic embodiment of enslavement in pregnancy and social humiliation informs the definition of enslavement for the Twelve. Enslavement was coded as un-masculine and, accordingly, feminine in the Roman Empire (and beyond). Luke's Gospel develops the ungendering of enslavement by presenting Mary as the ideal enslaved disciple, and (as is also the case in Mark) women as model "servers" who take orders rather than give them (διακονέω and διακονία).

This chapter begins with a review of the common interpretations of Mary and the women who serve in Luke before turning to women's experience of slavery in the Roman Empire. The rhetoric and realities of women's experience of enslavement largely mapped onto men's experience, as noted in chapter 1. However, as the comparison of Mary with the two sisters in Plutarch's story indicates, enslavement affected women in particular ways. The experiences specific to women's enslavement help to decode Luke's characterization

4. In narratives concerning freeborn women, καθυβρίζω indicates rape (Euripides, *El.* 697–98; Dionysius of Halicarnassus, *Ant. rom.* 11.2.2; Plutarch, *Comp. Demetr. Ant.* 4.2–3; *Dion* 3.1). Cf. the discussion of ὕβρις in Cole 1984, 98–99; Robson 2013, 102–3; and chap. 2, above.

5. The concept of chastity was complicated. While it was a key virtue and expectation for women (see below), narratives like this one indicate the vulnerability to violation that accompanied chastity.

6. This sense of the ταπειν- word group is particularly evident in the LXX (Gen. 34:2; Deut. 22:24, 29; Judg. 19:29; Lam. 5:11; see also Philo, *Mut.* 194).

of Mary as "slave" and women as "servers" and thus to suggest how early audiences—enslaved and free—may have responded to these representations.

Interpreting Women as Slaves and Servers in Luke

In the parable in Luke 12:45–46, enslaved men and women, παῖς and παιδίσκη, are beaten by the abusive enslaved manager. Presumably, women are among the enslaved people who populate other narratives and parables in the Gospel, carrying out agricultural work, food preparation and service, and other labor. But as enslaved people, and especially enslaved women, were generally invisible in society, enslaved women also disappear into anonymity in the background of Luke's stories.

Three enslaved women do have significant roles in Luke and Acts. As in the parable, each is identified by the term παιδίσκη, the feminine form of παῖς. The use of the same terms for freeborn children creates some ambiguity in the texts; whether a reference is to a freeborn child, enslaved child, or enslaved adult is not always clear. Παῖς and παιδίσκη infantilize enslaved adults by imposing on them a childish inability to reason or exert self-control. The use of παῖς to describe Jesus as God's agent who, in turn, works through his followers (Acts 3:13, 26; 4:27, 30) also allows for a sense of honorable enslavement. As Christy Cobb demonstrates, the enslaved women in Luke 22:56 and Acts 12:13–15 and 16:16–19 each give true testimony concerning Jesus's followers.[7]

The first reference comes in Luke's passion story, as an enslaved woman interacts with Peter outside the home of the high priest. Her identification of Peter as a disciple, someone who was with Jesus (σὺν αὐτῷ), condemns his faithless, un-manly denial of Jesus (22:56).[8] In Acts, Rhoda, enslaved by Mary of Jerusalem, announces Peter's unexpected arrival from prison. The people gathered in Mary's household do not accept her testimony (12:13–15). Finally, the unnamed enslaved diviner in Philippi proclaims Paul and his companions to be "enslaved people [δοῦλος] of the Most High God."[9] Overcome by irritation at her testimony, Paul exorcises the spirit

7. Cobb 2019, 2–3, and passim.

8. Bovon 2012, 230; Cobb 2019, 81–88, 104–21. Dowling 2007, 170–71, suggests the connection of the enslaved woman with Satan's testing of Peter in Luke 22:31–34 discredits her as a (woman) character. But the testing of "Satan" reflects Luke 4:1–13, rather than marking the woman as Satan's emissary. The woman is joined by two men who also correctly identify Peter with Jesus (an identification Peter again denies). The contrast of the woman's witness with Peter's denial discredits Peter, not the woman.

9. In addition to the identification of Jesus's followers in general and the twelve disciples in particular with enslavement in Luke's parables, see also the use of δοῦλος to identify (all) Jesus's followers as prophets in Acts 2:18 and as witnesses who speak God's word in 4:29.

of divination from her (16:16–19).[10] Of these, only Rhoda is part of the community of Jesus's followers. The fact that the unnamed enslaved women who provide true testimony in Luke 22:56 and Acts 16:16–19 are outsiders highlights the un-masculine behavior of Peter and Paul—Peter's cowardice and Paul's failure of equanimity.[11]

The function of these three women in their narratives, the relative scarcity of references to enslaved women in Luke and Acts, and the identification of Jesus's followers (including the twelve disciples) as "slaves" draw attention to the language of slavery and humiliation describing Mary in Luke 1:26–56. An initial reading suggests several key components of her identity as "slave." First, Mary calls herself δούλη (vv. 38, 48). This identity is not imposed on her by others; she claims it for herself. Second, Mary is enslaved to God, who is identified as κύριος ("lord/enslaver"). This specification connects her with the biblical metaphor of "slave of God." Third, her enslavement is embodied: She bears a child for her enslaver. And fourth, her enslavement is defined by the statuslessness of humiliation (v. 48). As explored in chapter 4, the combination of the identification of "slave" and the embodied experience of enslavement in the characterization of Mary carries over to the twelve disciples as "slaves." As Mary is the first example of this kind of "slave" in Luke's narrative, her story shapes the content of enslavement for the disciples.

Mary is accompanied by women who "serve" Jesus and his followers. Διακονέω is used with reference to Peter's mother-in-law and the women "with Jesus," including Mary of Magdala, Joanna, and Susanna (Luke 4:39; 8:3). Both διακονέω and διακονία describe Martha's work (10:40). In addition, an unnamed woman washes and anoints Jesus's feet during a meal (7:36–50). The vocabulary of enslavement and service do not appear in the story, but the woman's action echoes the labor of enslaved people (see the introduction, above). Though the story centers on the Gospel's themes of forgiveness and inclusivity, the woman can also be interpreted as enacting the enslavement of discipleship.[12] Just as Mary's example establishes what the disciples' enslavement should be, so these women's examples define the disciples' identity as servers in 22:24–27.[13]

10. Paul's irritation (διαπονέω) does not reflect well on him. The only other use of the term in the New Testament is in Acts 4:1–2, where it describes temple officials' response to Peter and John's teaching.

11. Cf. Cobb 2019, 110–11, 114, on Luke 22:56.

12. Cosgrove 2005, 687–91 (comparing this woman with the group of women in Luke 8:1–3).

13. See also Kinuwaka 2001, 183 (on διακον- in Mark's Gospel); Brobst-Renaud 2024, 30 (on Luke).

The association of the διακον- lexical group with women adds another gendered component to the broader discussion in chapter 4.[14] The basic significance of the terms—to indicate an official commissioning—is apparent in the identification of Phoebe as διάκονος in Romans 16:1–2.[15] In other texts, women's διακονέω and διακονία indicate labor with the explicit connotations of slavery: an enslaved woman's household management in Xenophon, *Oec.* 7.41; free women whose agricultural tasks are compared with enslaved people's labor in Plato, *Leg.* 7.805e; young elite women washing feet as enslaved people do in Plutarch, *Mulier. virt.* 249d; a free woman caring for her sick brother in Josephus, *Ant.* 7.165 (work carried out by an enslaved person in 13.314).[16] For both enslaved and free women, the διακον- word group also indicates sex labor.[17]

In John 12:2, Martha serves a meal (διακονέω). Reflecting the association of the διακον- word group with dinners (see chap. 4, above), free women occasionally cook and serve food alongside family members and enslaved people.[18] For most interpreters, these examples define the "service" of Peter's mother-in-law and Martha in their respective households in Luke 4:39 and 10:40 as the work of hospitality, particularly the preparation and service of food for guests.[19] In this respect, Martha's welcome is comparable with the welcoming of Jesus's followers with food and drink in 10:8–11. Within Luke, it signifies her commitment to the kingdom of God (cf. Zacchaeus in 19:1–10).[20]

The location of the women in Luke 8:1–3 outside the household and their financial support for the community distinguishes their service from that of Martha and Peter's mother-in-law. Their patronage may be their act of service.[21]

14. Hentschel 2007, 434, notes that the διακον- lexical group is rarely used specifically for women alone.

15. Collins 1990, 225; Hentschel 2007, 171–72. Cf. Bathsheba as the agent of διακονέω in Josephus, *Ant.* 8.5–6.

16. Neither Hentschel nor Collins discuss the association of women's "service" with the labor of enslaved people.

17. Xenophon, *Oec.* 10.12; Josephus, *Ant.* 18.74, 77 (see also 10.242, 12.187–88); Hentschel 2007, 80.

18. Aristophanes, *Ach.* 1015–17 (wives and enslaved people); Diodorus Siculus 5.28.4 (young girls and boys); Dio Chrysostom 7.65 (a daughter at the age of marriage and sons). See also family members (without indication of gender or age) serving meals in Strabo 16.4.26; Plutarch, *Mor.* 301e.

19. E.g., L. Johnson 1991, 84, 175; J. Green 1997, 225–26, 436–37; Hentschel 2007, 203–4, 246; Edwards 2015, 327–28.

20. Brobst-Renaud 2024, 29–31, draws a parallel between Luke 10:38–42 and Acts 6:1–3, arguing that Martha is an early example of negotiating the tension between teaching and meal service.

21. See J. Green 1997, 318–19; Corley 2001, 196; Bovon 2002, 301–2; Hentschel 2007, 232; Carroll 2012, 182.

However, Richard Bauckham notes the correlation of the women with the twelve disciples: They are on the road with Jesus (σὺν αὐτῷ). As the women's reappearance in 23:49 indicates, they witness Jesus's entire ministry. Consequently, the seventy followers sent out to heal and announce the kingdom in 10:1–12 would naturally have included women.[22] Bauckham defines their service as the same work carried out by male disciples.[23]

Luke's Gospel incorporates more female characters than Matthew or Mark, and many interpreters have consequently identified Luke as supportive of women's significance within the early Christian community.[24] But interpreters also note Luke's curtailment of women's presence and contributions. Peter's mother-in-law and Martha are both located in domestic space. Their "service" is apparently limited to the feminine-coded work of hospitality.[25] The association of women with demon possession in 4:39 and 8:1–3 disempowers their service.[26] Jesus critiques Martha's anxiety over her extensive διακονία.[27] The interaction seems to discredit Martha as "server" in favor of Mary's silent passivity.[28] Anni Hentschel in particular argues that in Luke and Acts, only men are allowed to perform the official leadership, teaching, and preaching represented by διακονία and διακονέω. Unlike the male disciples, who are only "like" (ὡς) table servers in Luke 22:26, women are restricted to domestic labor in the Lukan community.[29]

Jesus's challenge to Martha's many concerns and the absence of the commissioning of women as witnesses of the resurrection point to significant ambiguities concerning women's activity among Jesus's followers in Luke. But too sharp a distinction between women's and men's activity in Luke and Acts is also problematic. The women identified as "with Jesus" in Luke 8:1–3 are

22. Edwards 2015, 233, argues women could not have been among the group sent out in Luke 10 because a woman could not travel alone with a man. But if social norms were a concern, the women could have partnered with a male relative or another woman. The presence of women in Jesus's traveling community is already scandalous, as Edwards also notes (see "Freeborn Women: Definitions, Privileges, and Limitations," below). For women to preach and heal with a male or female partner is a negligible scandal by comparison. Corley 2001, 196–97, explores the intersections of honor, status, and gender in the analysis of women disciples.

23. Bauckham 2002, 111–15. See also Edwards 2015, 232; Carey 2023, 117; Brobst-Renaud 2024, 28; and on Mark, Kinuwaka 2001, 178, 188–90.

24. E.g., Demel 1991, 52–86; Arlandson 1997, 193, and passim.

25. Reid 1996, 101; Hentschel 2007, 199–204.

26. So Dowling 2007, 156 (connecting Luke 4:38–39 with demon possession because of ἐπιτιμάω). See also Hentschel 2007, 228–34. Overall, Hentschel contrasts Mark and Luke on the discipleship of women, arguing that Mark (e.g., 1:29–31; 15:40–41; and 16:7) preserves a more positive portrayal of women as disciples who preach about Jesus than Luke does.

27. Cf. Luke 12:11–12, 22–31.

28. So Reid 1996, 155–58; Dowling 2007, 164; Hentschel 2007, 243–45.

29. Hentschel 2007, 249–52, 374–75, 439; cf. Krause 2001, 47.

still present in 23:49. They are among Jesus's followers who hear the parable comparing them with enslaved people in 12:35–38. Given the parallel of the women with the twelve disciples in 8:1–3, Peter's question in 12:41 may also include these women in the audience of the parable in 12:42–48. Moreover, the male disciples are explicitly told to identify as "worthless slaves" who carry out household labor, including meal service (17:7–10; 22:24–27).[30] The first characters in the Gospel to model this work are women.

The story of Martha in Luke 10:38–42 is the last time that a woman is explicitly connected to "service" in Luke. In the remainder of the Gospel and into Acts, men are the agents of service (e.g., Luke 17:8; 22:27; Acts 1:25; 6:1–4; 12:25). As the narrative progresses through the two books, then, women seem to disappear as the activity of men becomes more prominent. But an alternative interpretation of this progression is also possible: The women's stories early in Luke model discipleship for the men who are challenged to adopt the identity of those who "serve" later in the Gospel. That is, by the (narrative) time the male disciples are told to become like table servers, the women have demonstrated what this service means. Moreover, if men's engagement in the work of διακονία and διακονέω in Acts includes teaching, preaching, and other leadership, then that meaning further informs the content of women's διακονία and διακονέω.[31] The narrative at least allows for this movement, and perhaps women in the audience would have drawn these connections.

The alliance of women and men as followers and "servers" corresponds with the definition of discipleship around enslavement. As I argued in chapter 4, Luke's Gospel develops the un-masculinity of enslavement for male disciples. The normative masculine practices of seeking status and exercising authority over self and others are replaced with the social humiliation, powerlessness, and labor of the enslaved. Mary as "slave," Peter's mother-in-law, the women who follow Jesus, and Martha consequently offer positive and, in the case of Martha's anxiety, negative models of the work of enslaved service.[32]

As is the case with the portrayals of masculinity, the representations of women in Luke both reflect normative social roles and disrupt them. The location of Peter's mother-in-law and Martha in the home is standard; that Mary, Mary of Magdala, Joanna, and Susanna leave their homes contrasts with

30. If the audience of the parable in Luke 17:7–10 is the entire group of disciples (as in v. 1), rather than the (twelve male) apostles (as in vv. 5–6), the women would also hear the challenge to be "worthless slaves" who work without ceasing.

31. So, e.g., J. Green 1997, 319–20; Carroll 2012, 182; Edwards 2015, 147; Carey 2023, 119–20; Brobst-Renaud 2024, 29–30. See also the discussion of the ambiguities in Luke 4:38–39 and 10:38–42 in Reid 1996, 101, and Dowling 2007, 152–53, 161–62.

32. Cf. Bauckham 2002, 164–65 (particularly comparing Luke 8:1–3 with Acts 6:1–4).

the ideal behavior for women. The representation of Mary as a humiliated, pregnant enslaved woman calls attention to the construction of freeborn elite femininity, the daily experiences of women in different social and legal positions, and the realities and rhetoric of slavery for women in the first century.

Freeborn Women: Definitions, Privileges, and Limitations

"This wasn't a pure army, able to battle manfully [ἀνδρεῖος] against the violence of necessity; rather, their courage [γενναῖος] was corrupted by the crowd of children and women, too weak [ἀσθενής] to respond to reason [ἡ ἐκ λόγων διδασκαλία]" (Josephus, *Ant.* 3.5). As discussed in chapter 2, (freeborn) femininity was defined in a binary relationship with (freeborn) masculinity. Josephus's description of women assigns them stereotypical qualities representing the absence of manly virtue: Lacking courage, women were cowardly. Lacking self-discipline, they fell prey to indulgence in luxuries and vice. Their bodies were weak, so they could not withstand physical deprivation. Without the manly ability to reason, they were undone by their emotions and desires.[33] According to Josephus, women's natural un-masculinity threatened men's ability to perform manliness (see also *J.W.* 3.263).

As a consequence of elite men's construction of feminine identity, freeborn and freed women were legally and socially subordinated to men's authority.[34] Elite men considered marrying a very young woman advantageous because they could mold the woman's developing character.[35] The virtue of marital harmony was defined by women's agreement with and emulation of their

33. Women's inability to reason is evident in, e.g., Plato, *Resp.* 4.431c–d; Livy 3.48.8; Philo, *QG* 1.33; and Plutarch, *Conj. praec.* 7. For women's physical weakness, see Plato, *Resp.* 5.455e–456a; Tacitus, *Ann.* 3.33; Artemidorus, *Onir.* 1.50. The problem of women's desire for luxury (and consequent tendency to vice) is apparent in *Life of Aesop* 32, 109; Valerius Maximus 9.1, ext. 7; 9.6.1; and Plutarch, *Conj. praec.* 12, 26, 30. See also the sources cited in chap. 2, above; Demand 1998, 70–71; Briggs 2003, 178.

34. Among other sources, note Cato, *Agr.* 143; Dionysius of Halicarnassus, *Ant. rom.* 2.25; *PSI* 1.64 (a marriage contract detailing the wife's obedience to her husband); Bryson 82; P.Fay. 91 (a woman's legal guardian guarantees a business arrangement she has made); Josephus, *Ag. Ap.* 2.201; Plutarch, *Conj. praec.* 33; Gaius, *Inst.* 1.144–45. Though their legal statuses were not the same, the subordination of free women as wives created comparisons with enslaved people (see P. Clark 1998, 118–19).

35. See esp. Hesiod, *Op.* 695–705; Plutarch, *Conj. praec.* 48. There is evidence of women who were as young as eleven years old when they were married (*CIL* 3.3572; cf. Pliny, *Ep.* 5.16), though around age sixteen was more common (*ISIS* 321). See also *CIL* 6.18817 (a wife's memorial to her husband, identifying them as "boy and girl" at the time they married) and 6.9499 (a freed woman identifies her husband, a fellow freed person, as her "father" who cared for her since she was seven years old); Parkin 2011, 283; Lieber 2012, 339 (on Jewish tradition); Caldwell 2015, 3–4, 106–16; Garnsey and Saller 2015, 155–56.

husbands.[36] Masculine ideals situated women in the home. The interior of the household was considered to be women's space, with access protected or limited (though note that the household was not private space).[37] According to a variety of sources, women were ideally restricted from appearing in political arenas like the forum or lawcourts (e.g., Valerius Maximus 3.8.6, 8.3.2); enjoying public entertainment (Suetonius, *Aug*. 44.5–7); and forming friendships with other women (Plutarch, *Conj. praec*. 40). As wives, women were responsible for bearing and raising sons and daughters to be honorable Roman citizens.[38] As discussed in chapter 2, elite women were encouraged to adopt masculine control over their physical desires and emotions.[39]

A major concern behind the limitations placed on women by elite Greek and Roman men was the maintenance of women's bodily boundaries and sexual fidelity, a concern shared by Jewish communities.[40] This concern is evident in funerary inscriptions: "To the Spirits of the Deceased Aelia Tryphera, an exceptional wife, pure and chaste beyond what can be expected of the average female; she lived for 24 years 7 months 10 days. Aelius Proximus put this up" (*ILS* 8456).[41] According to men, moving from the home into public spaces exposed a freeborn woman's body to the gaze of men who were not part of her father's or husband's households. Likewise, freeborn women were discouraged from forming friendships with other women, especially with women who were not honorable elites, as such friendships were thought to encourage immoral behavior.[42] Chastity entailed engaging in erotic activities (from kissing to intercourse) only with a man approved by a woman's father or other male authority.[43] Moreover, for a freeborn woman, the purpose of sexual intercourse in marriage was restricted to procreation.[44] Consequently,

36. Valerius Maximus 2.1.6; Plutarch, *Conj. praec*. 1–3, 11, 14, 19–20, 22, 45; Pliny, *Ep*. 4.19.2–4.

37. Bryson 80; Philo, *Spec*. 3.169–170; Plutarch, *Conj. praec*. 9, 30–32. See further Scheidel 1995, 205–6; Saller 2011, 116; Hylen 2015, 15, 21–24; Reeder 2022, 116.

38. E.g., Josephus, *Ag. Ap*. 2.202–4; Tacitus, *Dial*. 28; Plutarch, *Ti. C. Gracch*. 1.4–5; *CIL* 8.8123; Cohick 2009, 143–46; Myers 2017, 114–18. Note that mothers' tenderness could also endanger boys' ability to perform masculinity (Seneca, *Prov*. 2.5).

39. E.g., Seneca, *Helv*. 16.2–7; *Marc*. 1.1, 11.1; Plutarch, *Cons. ux*. 609a.

40. E.g., Deut. 22:13–21; Sir. 42:9–14; Philo, *Spec*. 3.65–71, 79–82; Josephus, *Ag. Ap*. 2.199–201.

41. Translation from Gardner and Wiedemann 1991, 53–54.

42. So Phintys, *On Chastity* 208; Valerius Maximus 6.3.10–12; Plutarch, *Conj. praec*. 31, 40.

43. This expectation is clear in Valerius Maximus's stories of fathers killing their daughters either to punish them or protect them from unchastity (6.1.2–4, 6.1.6). See further Parker 2004, 564, 588–92 (on the intersection of control over women's sexuality and civic stability); Cohick 2009, 69–71; Hallett 2012, 377–84; Harper 2013, 38–45; Caldwell 2015, 45–52.

44. Valerius Maximus 7.7.4; Philo, *Ios*. 43–44; Josephus, *Ag. Ap*. 2.199; Plutarch, *Conj. praec*. 18, 42, 47. This ideal is also evident in elite men's concern for elite women's sexual infidelity in, e.g., *Life of Aesop* 16; Valerius Maximus 2.1.5b; Juvenal, *Sat*. 11.183–93.

Plutarch argued that a husband's use of enslaved women for sex protected his wife's chastity (*Conj. praec.* 16). A woman who married only once, staying loyal to her first husband even after his death, was honored as a *univira*.[45] The worst kind of woman attempted to usurp her husband's authority, unmanning him by her power.[46]

The ideals of the public transcript restricted and limited freeborn women, especially elite women, but they did not necessarily reflect the entirety of women's lived experience. By the first century, most marriages were *sine manu*. In this type of marriage, the woman (and her property) remained under her father's legal authority, resulting in more freedom for the woman.[47] In one marriage contract from Egypt, the wife (Apollonia) agreed to live with and obey her husband (a normal stipulation), but remarkably, he was limited from sexual liaisons in and out of the household. The wife's economic investment in the marriage (her dowry) was also protected from misappropriation (P.Tebt. 1.104). Wives held significant authority over the household economy and enslaved laborers, indicating (as Bryson makes clear) their thoughtful intelligence.[48] Women owned property and managed businesses with little or no oversight by male guardians.[49] A woman named Valeria Maxima owned a farm; her funerary inscription names her mother but no father, husband, or any other man (*CIL* 6.3482). Wealthy women's benefaction in their communities brought them political and social power.[50]

As these examples indicate, women participated in public life in spite of elite men's ideals or preferences. Non-elite women owned, managed, and worked for businesses that required interaction with neighbors, business partners, and strangers. Their activities raised suspicions of immoral behavior among elite men. Non-elite populations, however, recognized their work as normative, necessary for the household's survival, and praiseworthy. A funerary inscription for a woman who ran a tavern recognized her honorable character, for instance.[51] Personal letters and funerary inscriptions commemorate women's

45. Valerius Maximus 2.1.3, 4.3.3; Plutarch, *Ti. C. Gracch.* 1.4; *CIL* 3.3572; Cohick 2009, 104–5.

46. *Life of Aesop* 109; Plutarch, *Conj. praec.* 6, 33; Cassius Dio 50.5, 50.27.

47. See Cohick 2009, 42–43, 100–101; Witzke 2016, 256.

48. Bryson 82, 91–92, 96–97. Cf. Xenophon, *Oec.* 7.35–37, 9.16–17; Aristotle, [*Oec.*] 3.1. See P. Clark 1998, 118, on the ambivalence of women's authority and subordination.

49. *CIL* 4.3340.24; P.Oxy. 1467 (noting a woman's right to dispense with male guardianship in return for bearing three children); *BGU* 4.22; P.Yadin 19; Saller 1998, 87; 2011, 120; Hylen 2015, 21–22.

50. Examples of benefaction are preserved in Pleket 5, 8, 15, 19; *FD* 4.79; *CIL* 10.6328. Women's ability to exercise political power can be seen in Cornelius Nepos, *Fr.* 1.1–2; Sallust, *Bell. Cat.* 24.25; Valerius Maximus 8.3.1; *CIL* 4.171, 4.207, 10.810; Cassius Dio 65.14.1–5. See also Cohick 2009, 285–301; Lieber 2012, 335–36; Hylen 2015, 26–28, 77.

51. *CIL* 14.3709. Note also *InscrAqu* 1.69 (Hemelrijk 2021, 150); *CIL* 6.9801, 6.9683, 8.24678, 9.4721; Scheidel 1995, 206–7; 1996, 5–6; Saller 2011, 121–23.

friendships.[52] Pliny knew of a grandmother who loved attending theatrical performances (*Ep.* 7.24). Women across the Greco-Roman Mediterranean ably negotiated cultural expectations, social existence, and masculine authority. But the realities of women's lives also included violence: "Restutus Picenesis and Prima Restuta made this for Prima Florentia, their dearest daughter, who was deprived of her life by Orfeus, her husband, and thrown into the Tiber."[53] As in the case of this sixteen-year-old wife, elite and non-elite women faced casual assault and punitive violence in their households, including the potential threats of (legal) execution and (illegal) murder.[54]

The complex interactions of the ideals and experiences of women's lives in the first century are apparent in Luke's narratives and parables. Women often appear in household settings, as in the stories of Elizabeth, Peter's mother-in-law, and the homeowner Martha with her sister Mary (1:24–25, 39–45; 4:38–39; 10:38–42). The Gospel incorporates non-elite women who held vulnerable positions in society: a widow from a small village mourning her only son (7:11–15); a woman cleaning her house as she searched for a lost coin (15:8–9[55]); and an impoverished widow who demonstrates her piety by contributing to the temple treasury (21:1–4). Anna's choice to remain a widow after her husband's death marks her as a *univira* (2:36–38). Elizabeth is a faithful, devoted wife who is blessed with a son (1:5–7, 24–25). Some women speak in Luke's stories and parables, but often women are silent or silenced (e.g., 2:19; 7:12–16; 10:39–42; 24:6–11). These representations of women fit within Greco-Roman social ideals.[56]

But, reflecting women's lived experiences, there are also women who act outside elite social expectation. A widow demands justice from a judge (Luke 18:1–6).[57] A woman identified as a sinner invades a Pharisee's household to wash Jesus's feet while he dines (7:36–50). A woman with a uterine disorder steals healing from Jesus (8:43–48). The twelve male disciples are joined by several named and many more unnamed women in 8:1–3. Mary of Magdala, Joanna (whose husband was Herod Antipas's steward), Susanna, and the

52. Vindolanda 291; *AE* 1968.100, 2001.317; *CIL* 6.18524.

53. *ISIS* 321 (*AE* 1987.0177k), translation from Hemelrijk 2021, 38.

54. Valerius Maximus 6.3.9; Seneca, *Ben.* 4.27; *BGU* 4.1105; Pliny, *Nat.* 14.14; P.Oxy. 2758; Plutarch, *Conj. praec.* 8, 37; Aulus Gellius 10.23.4–5. On violence against (free) women in antiquity, see P. Clark 1998, 109–22; Reeder 2015a, 527–29; Witzke 2016, 256–58.

55. According to the narrative logic of the parables in Luke 15, the woman represents God. Note also Jesus as mother hen in Luke 13:34.

56. See further Seim 1994, 249; D'Angelo 1999, 187–88; Dowling 2007, 138–78, 189–98; Hentschel 2007, 206–7, 255–56; Menéndez Antuña 2013, 490–95.

57. Dowling 2007, 183–85, suggests the woman (not the judge) represents God in the parable.

other women leave their homes (and husbands, at least in Joanna's case[58]) to be disciples (σὺν αὐτῷ in v. 1). They support the group with their economic resources.[59] These women remain with Jesus, in public sight (albeit at a distance), through his crucifixion (23:49). They provide verbal witness to his resurrection, despite the male disciples' disbelief of their report (24:1–11).[60] These references to women's presence, actions, and speech disrupt the ways Luke adheres to social norms.

This disruption is also evident in Luke's depiction of Mary the mother of Jesus. Mary is young, unmarried, and alone (i.e., without male protection) when she converses with a stranger and becomes pregnant. Although artistic depictions of the annunciation often picture Mary in her home or a walled garden, Luke's story does not locate Mary in domestic space (or any particular space). Moreover, she travels by herself to visit Elizabeth, apparently on her own initiative.[61] These features of the narrative distinguish Mary from the ideal of a woman confined to the household, avoiding friendships with other women, and subordinate to male authority. Whether the identification of Mary as an enslaved woman is a metaphor or (as argued by Winsome Munro and Mitzi Smith[62]) a representation of her legal status, her behavior in Luke 1:26–40 associates her more closely with non-elite populations, including enslaved and freed women.

Women and Enslavement

A number of funerary inscriptions provide glimpses into the experiences of enslaved women who lived and died in the Roman Empire:

> "Hedone, spinning-woman, lived thirty years" (*CIL* 6.341).
> "Rufa, foot-servant, lies here" (*CIL* 6.9781).
> "Melitine, physician, (slave) of Appuleius" (*CIL* 6.6851).

58. Bauckham 2002, 117–19, suggests Joanna may have been widowed because women would have to be single in order to leave their homes and travel with Jesus (p. 118). However, on the analogy of the male disciples abandoning their wives, parents, children, households, and businesses (Luke 5:11, 28; 14:26, 33; 18:28–29), it is not impossible to imagine that Luke's narrative represents women leaving their husbands to follow Jesus.

59. Cf. J. Green 1997, 318–21; Carroll 2012, 182–83; Carey 2023, 115–16.

60. The disciples' disbelief reflects men's stereotypical suspicion of women's testimony. In this respect, the story indicates the male disciples' failure rather than the silencing of women. The women are the first (and only, until Luke 24:35) characters to believe and announce the resurrection. Cf. Dowling 2007, 173–77, on the gendered tensions within the story.

61. See esp. Reid 2011, 57–58.

62. See "Personal Experience with Enslavement" in the introduction, above. Cf. Munro 1998; M. Smith 2022.

"Flavia Marcella, freedwoman of the emperor, made this for herself and for her [first] husband Alcimus, freedman of the emperor, and for Martialis, (slave) of our Caesar, her excellent [second] husband, and for her freedmen and freedwomen and their descendants" (*CIL* 14.2469).

"Chrematine, slave of Numisia, hairdresser" (*CIL* 10.1935).

"Saturnina, estate manager of Tiberius Claudius Caesar, lived thirty years, and Venusta, her daughter, lived fifteen years" (*CIL* 8.5384).

"Statilia Tyrannis, freedwoman of Titus, pedagogue of Statilia" (*CIL* 6.6331).[63]

As the occupations represented in the inscriptions indicate, enslaved women engaged in the same kinds of labor as enslaved men, including household tasks, production of goods for trade, education, and personal services to their enslavers. Like men, women managed household businesses and agricultural estates. Women were gladiators.[64] Women and men entered enslavement in the same ways, and they had the same routes out of enslavement: manumission (though manumission generally happened later for women than for men) or death (whether of natural causes, from accidental or intentional execution by their enslavers, or by suicide).[65] Enslaved women faced the same rhetorical denigration and bodily violations—including casual and punitive physical violence, branding, and crucifixion—as enslaved men.[66] They also participated in the same acts of resistance, including running away and, as the inscriptions commemorate, forming personal relationships in defiance of imposed natal alienation and enslavers' control over their relationships.[67]

There were some differences between women's and men's experiences of enslavement. Particular jobs were limited to women (and as far as the evidence indicates, women did not work in mines).[68] Because of the reproductive consequences, the common sexualization and sexual use of enslaved people were uniquely embodied for women. Women had options for freedom that

63. Translations from Hemelrijk 2021, 69, 71, 95, 125, 140, 177.

64. Suetonius, *Dom.* 4.2; *CIG* 6855.

65. For women's entry into enslavement, see Diodorus Siculus 12.73.3; Josephus, *J.W.* 7.208; *CIL* 6.8958; *BGU* 4.1058. Plutarch, *Mor.* 242d, discussed in chap. 1, above, tells of the Spartan woman who took her own life in enslavement. Scheidel 1997, 160, discusses the practice of delaying manumission for women until menopause. Note also Scheidel 2005, 72–73, identifying relatively even numbers of women and men in slavery.

66. Ovid, *Am.* 1.14.16–18; Josephus, *Ant.* 6.41; Suetonius, *Aug.* 69; Plutarch, *Cohib. ira* 463b; *AE* 1971.88; Witzke 2016, 260–64.

67. The evidence for enslaved women fleeing enslavement is slimmer than for men, but in addition to *CIL* 6.20905 (discussed in chap. 1, above), note that at least one iron collar (fastened around the necks of recaptured slaves) names an enslaved woman (*ILS* 9455).

68. Women did participate in agricultural labor and public works projects (ditch digging in Strabo 3.4.17). See Scheidel 1995, 207; and 1996, 1–7.

were not shared by men. Nonetheless, in many ways the gender distinctions advanced by the elite were erased by slavery (and poverty).

Just as enslaved men were not ascribed masculinity by enslavers, so enslaved women were not ascribed the characteristics, responsibilities, or virtues of femininity allotted to elite freeborn women. The construction of enslavement for women in turn reinforced freeborn femininity, an intersection particularly evident with respect to chastity. All enslaved people were denied the bodily autonomy on which the virtue of chastity depended. Consequently, freeborn elites denigrated enslaved people, including women, as lustful and licentious.[69] According to Plutarch, men's use of enslaved women's bodies for sexual pleasure protected freeborn women's bodily boundaries and virtue (*Conj. praec.* 16).[70] The complexities of enslavement for women provide a valuable framework for understanding Mary as "slave" in Luke's Gospel.

A number of manumission inscriptions preserved on the walls of ancient Delphi record the lives of enslaved and freed women. The inscriptions follow similar patterns, including the representation of manumission as a sale of the enslaved person to a god and, often, the requirement that the freed slave remain with the enslaver for a certain period of time.[71] The story of Onasiphoron is representative:

> On the following conditions Sophrona, acting with the consent of her son Sosandros, hands over to the Pythian Apollo to be free the female house-born body named Onasiphoron, priced at three silver mina, and has received the whole price. Onasiphoron has entrusted the sale to the god, with the aim of becoming free and not to be claimed by anybody at any future time, and to have no obligations of any kind whatever to anyone. . . . And if anyone touches Onasiphoron in order to enslave her, then she who has sold her and the guarantor together are to ensure that the sale to the god is valid. . . . Onasiphoron is to remain with Sophrona for the whole period of Sophrona's life, doing whatever she is ordered to do without giving cause for complaint. If she does not do so, then Sophrona is to have the power to punish her in whatever way she wishes to. And Onasiphoron is to give Sosandros a child. (*FD* 3.6.36)[72]

69. This is evident in enslavers' (fantastical) descriptions of enslaved people inviting sexual attention (as depicted with respect to enslaved women in Xenarchus, *The Pentathlete*, quoted in Athenaeus, *Deipn.* 13.569b–c; Philo, *Spec.* 3.51; and enslaved men in Lucian, *Merc. cond.* 16); Parker 1998, 155; Flemming 1999, 41.

70. Note also the terrifying story of Maximilla, a Christian convert, forcing an enslaved woman to have sex with her husband so that she could pursue celibacy in *Acts of Andrew*. See further Joshel and Murnaghan 1998, 4–5, 7; Briggs 2003, 180–81; Witzke 2016, 264; Valentine 2017, 23–37; Levin-Richardson 2021, 189; Cobb 2025, 123.

71. Tucker 1982, 225–26; Kamen 2012, 180–82: Nasrallah 2014, 67–70.

72. Translation from Wiedemann 2005, 47.

Onasiphoron was born into slavery. She was, accordingly, raised and trained into the life of enslavement by the enslaved and free members of the household. That her female enslaver is named in the manumission inscription suggests a particular relationship between the two women. The son's involvement fulfills the legal requirements surrounding the release of a living person who was also part of the household's wealth.

For Onasiphoron, freedom looked much like a continuation of her enslavement. She was required to remain in the household as long as her enslaver Sophrona lived, continuing to obey Sophrona's commands. An act of disobedience (as judged by her enslaver) brought whatever punishment the enslaver wanted. The possibilities plausibly include being whipped, the loss of privileges, and re-enslavement. The specification of Sophrona as the authority over Onasiphoron reflects the particular association of (some) enslaved women with their female enslavers.[73] Juvenal's satirical representation of such a relationship describes an enslaved woman fixing her enslaver's hair only to face violence for not meeting expectations: "Unlucky Psecas will be arranging her [enslaver's] hair with her own strands torn, with her shoulders and her breasts stripped bare. 'Why is this curl sticking up?' The bullhide strap is the immediate punishment for the wicked crime of the twisting ringlet" (*Sat*. 6.490–93 [LCL]).[74]

Onasiphoron's story also highlights a fundamental distinction between enslaved men and enslaved women: the uniquely embodied experiences of procreation, pregnancy, and childrearing. The requirement for Onasiphoron to give Sosandros a child could be interpreted in two ways. First, since she is manumitted before giving birth, her child would legally be freeborn. It is possible that Onasiphoron is being freed so that Sosandros can use her body to produce a freeborn child for himself.[75]

Male enslavers (sometimes themselves former slaves) freed enslaved women for the purpose of marriage and the birth of legitimate heirs. If the standard descriptions of marital fidelity and love in funerary inscriptions bear any relation to reality, (some of) these marriages may have developed from or into

73. Enslaved women who worked as hairdressers and tailors in *CIL* 6.3732, 8958, 8959, 9037, and 9980 are associated with women enslavers (note also the funerary relief depicting a free woman surrounded by enslaved women helping her to dress in the Rheinisches Landesmuseum Trier; Cobb 2019, 20–23). See P. Clark 1998, 122–25 (and on Augustine's narrative of Monica's relationship with her enslaved women, pp. 110–16).

74. See further P. Clark 1998, 122–25.

75. As in *FD* 3.3.329; and 3.3.333; see Tucker 1982, 230–31. Enslavers might also free their own enslaved children, born to enslaved women, in order to officially recognize them as their children. This was possibly the case for Steia Fortuna, a home-born slave who was manumitted and named as one of her enslaver's heirs (*CIL* 14.1641).

close relationships.[76] The authenticity of declarations of love or affection is most plausible in cases where both partners had been enslaved, giving them a more equal status. The unequal power differential between a freeborn husband and a formerly enslaved wife makes such declarations suspect, as the story of Acte in chapter 1, above, indicates.[77] The women who were manumitted for marriage benefited somewhat from free status. However, they had fewer rights than freeborn wives. Their consent was not needed for the marriages to begin or end, and they could not divorce their enslavers/husbands. They also could not own property independently of their enslavers/husbands.[78] Essentially, as freed slaves, these women paid the cost for their own lives through marriage. As in other practices of manumission, this system ultimately benefited the enslavers much more than the (formerly) enslaved women.[79]

There is no indication in Onasiphoron's manumission inscription that she is marrying Sosandros or that her child will be acknowledged as Sosandros's freeborn child. The second interpretation reflects a common theme in the Delphi manumission inscriptions: Enslaved women were freed with the expectation that they would replace their own enslaved lives with new slaves—their own children.[80] The fact of reproduction made enslaved women's bodies one of the sources of slaves across the Roman Empire.[81] Since Onasiphoron was a "house-born body," her mother also was (or had been) enslaved in the household of Sophrona and Sosandros. It is possible that Onasiphoron was her mother's replacement. Onasiphoron and her mother were "mothers" only until the babies were born. The enslaved infants they bore belonged not to them but to their enslavers.[82] Even their access to their infants might have been limited following birth if there was an enslaved wet nurse available in the household.

A very few sources suggest enslavers sometimes manumitted children with their mothers. In P.Oxy. 3.494, an enslaver promises the manumission of a woman and her daughter, along with three other enslaved people (two men and a woman), in his will. However, the will explicitly excludes any

76. E.g., *ILS* 1519, 1552, 1763. See also the sources discussed by Huemoller 2020, 135–36.

77. See esp. Huemoller 2020, 135–37.

78. Kleijwegt 2012, 117; Huemoller 2020, 129–33; Bonar 2025, 70.

79. See esp. Huemoller 2020, 127–29.

80. Tucker 1982, 233; Marshall and Kamen 2021, 7–8.

81. The use of enslaved women for the production of more enslaved bodies is addressed by Scheidel 1997, 156, 167; 2011, 306–7; Wessels 2010, 152–53; Perry 2021, 257, 259–63.

82. As with the infants of free women, the infants of enslaved women were sometimes exposed rather than raised in the household. The decision belonged to the enslaver, not to the pregnant woman (see Tucker 1982, 235). Perry 2021, 265–66, suggests enslaved women may have attempted reproductive control and abortion to prevent bearing children for their enslavers (see Dio Chrysostom 15.8).

and all other children born to the enslaved women who were to be freed upon the enslaver's death. As seems to have been the case for Onasiphoron, the children of enslaved women generally remained in slavery if the women who bore them were freed. The only notice given to the trauma of these experiences comes from the emotional distress of freeborn women in novels and plays who mourn the births of children into slavery.[83] To lose access to her infant at birth, witness her own child forced into hard labor and abused, and pay for her own freedom with the enslavement of her child would certainly have physical, affective, and psychological consequences for an enslaved woman.[84] These consequences, however, go unrecorded and unrecognized.

Onasiphoron might have had a longstanding, committed relationship with another slave in the household, one that could result in pregnancy. But there is also a strong possibility that Sosandros was, or would be, the father of Onasiphoron's baby.[85] As discussed in chapters 1 and 2, enslavers used the bodies of their male and female slaves for their own benefit, including sexual pleasure and (in the case of women) the potential economic advantage of adding to the living possessions of the household. The sexual use of enslaved women by male enslavers is well attested, so much so that enslaved women's involvement in (coerced) intercourse is identified as a necessity from Xenophon, in the fifth century BCE, to Seneca the Elder, in the first century CE.[86] In addition, enslaved women were used as sex laborers within enslavers' households. Cato the Elder forced enslaved men to pay to use enslaved women for sex (Plutarch, *Cat. Maj.* 21.2), and graffiti on homes and businesses in Pompeii offer up enslaved women (and men) to passersby.[87] Enslavers also staffed public-facing brothels with enslaved women.[88]

83. E.g., Virgil, *Aen.* 3.388–93; Seneca, *Tro.* 556–67; Chariton, *Call.* 2.9.6–7. In Tacitus, *Ann.* 1.59, it is the father who expresses emotional distress upon the capture of his pregnant wife.

84. The narratives of enslaved Americans illustrate the consequences of the separation of children from parents; see H. Williams 2012, 23–34.

85. Cf. Marshall and Kamen 2021, 6–7, on the expectation that freed women remaining in their enslavers' homes would continue to be used for sex.

86. Xenophon, *Oec.* 10.12; Seneca the Elder, *Controv.* 4, pref. 10. See also Horace, *Sat.* 1.2.116–19; Valerius Maximus 6.7.1; Juvenal, *Sat.* 11.162–70; Artemidorus, *Onir.* 1.78; Golden 2011, 146–51; Baird 2015, 163–64; Levin-Richardson 2021, 189–200. Perry 2015, 58, 63–70, addresses Roman legal traditions concerned with illicit sex—that is, sex with an enslaved person that the enslaver did not permit or desire. These laws focus on the violation of the enslaver's rights over the bodies of enslaved people and the potential damage to the enslaver's property.

87. A room located off the kitchen in the House of the Vettii at Pompeii is decorated with erotic artwork, and a graffito identifying the cost for using an enslaved woman named Euthychis is located at the entry to the home. Graffiti on the wall of a bakery lists the price for sex with two enslaved women and one man. See *CIL* 4.4023, 4024, 4025; Severy-Hoven 2012, 563–64.

88. *PSI* 4.406; Seneca the Elder, *Controv.* 1.2.9–10; Artemidorus, *Onir.* 1.56; Flemming 1999, 40–45; Harper 2013, 48–50; Witzke 2016, 262; Levin-Richardson 2021, 197–202; Perry 2021, 258.

Coerced intercourse did not carry moral or legal implications for the male enslavers (as long as they exercised self-control, of course). The enslaved bodies were household possessions for their use, regardless of the man's own marital status or the age, relational status, or consent of the enslaved woman.[89] As mentioned above, the forced participation of enslaved women in sex corresponded with enslavers' characterization of enslaved women as unchaste and licentious. While narratives of freeborn women taken into slavery emphasize their distress at the prospect of being used for sex, the same is rarely true for women born into slavery. The sources that do acknowledge the concern focus on men's perspective and privilege: Xenophon, for example, commented that sex with a consenting wife was better than sex with an unwilling slave (*Oec.* 10.12), and Petronius's freed slave purchases the life of his partner so that he can protect her body from being used by other men (*Sat.* 57.6). There is, as far as I am aware, no serious recognition that enslaved women who were not freeborn would also experience trauma from forced sex.[90]

The coerced involvement of enslaved women in producing more slaves for their enslavers connects with several other uniquely female occupations. Enslaved women are attested as midwives, an essential profession given the dangers of childbirth.[91] Enslaved women also worked as wet nurses for the freeborn and enslaved infants of the household, and sometimes for those of other households (through rental agreements between enslavers).[92] As an extension of nursing, enslaved women provided childcare for infants and young children.[93] They might have had primary responsibility for feeding, bathing, and comforting children; teaching them to speak, walk, and play; and also providing the enslavers' children's first experiences of interacting with (and commanding) enslaved people. These jobs required significant emotional labor for enslaved women.[94]

The freeborn children raised by enslaved nurses sometimes expressed deep care for these women, and a few inscriptions also record the nurses' affection for the freeborn children in their care.[95] As always, it is important to remember

89. See further in chap. 2, above; and Marshall and Kamen 2021, 4; Perry 2021, 257–58; A. Strong 2021, 179.

90. A. M. Miller 2019, 157–77, surveys the various ways sexual assault and rape traumatize. Cf. Hartman 2008, 11–12; Marshall 2013, 182–83, 193.

91. See Soranus, *Gyn.* 1.3–4, on the work of midwives. For enslaved or freed women working as midwives, see, e.g., *CIL* 6.6325, 6647, 8947, 8949, 9723.

92. *BGU* 4.1058; P.Oxy. 91; *CIL* 5.3950, 6.12023; Soranus, *Gyn.* 2.19.

93. E.g., *CIL* 6.4352, 5201, 36353.

94. As marked by Soranus, *Gyn.* 2.19. Plutarch, [*Lib. ed.*] 3c, however, decries nurses' affection as false. See further Edmondson 2011, 358–59; Golden 2011, 141–42; Seesengood 2019, 147–54; Chaniotis 2023, 202–4.

95. Free people's affection for enslaved nurses is apparent in *CIL* 6.16450, 10.6432, 11.6345; Pliny, *Ep.* 6.3. For enslaved or freed nurses' affection for the children, see *CIL* 6.18032, 25808.

that any such affection occurred in the context of an unequal relationship. The freeborn children the nurses raised were also their enslavers, and the enslaved children were their fellow slaves. The "mothering" labor of enslaved women excluded the rights and privileges of motherhood. The children they bore and the children they raised did not belong to them. In light of this situation, it is possible that the various warnings of elite men against using enslaved women to nurse or care for infants and young children indicate resistance on the part of enslaved women.[96]

Onasiphoron's experience of slavery and freedom framed her relationships with other members of the household. Her body may have provided a sexual outlet for Sosandros or other free or enslaved men in the household, but there is no expectation of emotional attachment. Rather, if Sosandros were married, his wife might respond to his use of Onasiphoron with jealousy or abuse.[97] Onasiphoron's intimate work of bodily care for Sophrona might encourage close ties between the women. Any such ties would be imbalanced, as Sophrona's authority over Onasiphoron even in freedom indicates. Onasiphoron might have been a nurse or caregiver for the children of the household, including those she herself bore. But equally, she might have had relatively limited contact with any children, even her own. Perhaps the most significant relationships for Onasiphoron were with other enslaved people—her friends and family, whether by choice or circumstance. However, the manumission inscription does not provide any information on her relationships beyond those with her enslavers. Onasiphoron's own identity is eclipsed by her enslavers' desires.

In a famous funerary inscription, a freed woman named Aurelia Philemation is praised for her chastity: "Chaste, modest, unfamiliar with the common crowd, faithful to my husband" (*CIL* 6.9499).[98] Aurelia Philemation gained chastity with her manumission. As is evident from this brief survey, the distinction between freeborn women (especially elite women) and enslaved women was vast. Freeborn elite women were expected to maintain their bodily boundaries, control their appetites, and exercise manly reason and emotional restraint. They should manage their households and raise their children to be productive citizens. Enslaved women lacked such privileges or responsibilities. As slaves, their bodies were permeable and unprotectable. They were not ascribed the virtue of chastity. Enslaved women were, like enslaved men, accused of vice

96. Quintilian, *Inst.* 1.1.4–5; Plutarch, [*Lib. ed.*] 3d–f; Aulus Gellius 12.1.4–9, 17–23. Elite men's preference for freeborn women to breastfeed their own infants related to their understanding that the nurse's character would be passed on to the child through breastmilk.

97. See Valerius Maximus 6.7.1; Seneca, *Ep.* 123.10; Plutarch, *Conj. praec.* 16; Perry 2021, 255–56.

98. Translation in Hemelrijk 2021, 24–25.

(especially apparent in the instructions for wet nurses). Even if they bore, nursed, and raised their own children, they were not honored as mothers. They could not protect their own children from deprivation, hard labor, or violence. The embodiment of enslavement was both particularly apparent and particularly horrifying in the sexual and reproductive labor of women like Onasiphoron. These experiences of enslavement contextualize Mary's story in Luke 1–2.

Mary the Slave in Luke's Gospel

The annunciation stories at the beginning of Luke's Gospel follow biblical literary patterns by centering the women.[99] Hannah's annunciation in 1 Samuel 1:1–20 is particularly influential for Luke's narrative of Mary. God's observation of Mary's humiliation in Luke 1:48 echoes Hannah's prayer in 1 Samuel 1:11 LXX (note ἐπιβλέπω, ταπείνωσις, and δούλη). Mary's prophetic song in Luke 1:46–55 incorporates elements of Hannah's song in 1 Samuel 2:1–10. Mary's song also echoes the celebrations of victory voiced by Miriam (Exod. 15:20–21), Deborah and Jael (Judg. 5:1–31), and Judith (Jdt. 16:1–17).[100] These connections enable the interpretation of Mary's enslavement as a representation of her faithfulness to God, vindicated by God's actions.[101] Against this background, Mary's enslavement has (though rarely) been interpreted as honorable and authoritative, on the model of biblical kings and prophets.[102]

Mary's song introduces Luke's key concern of social reversal: the blessing of a humiliated slave, the dethroning of powerful rulers (δυνάστης) and the exaltation of the humiliated (ταπεινός), the emptying of the wealthy and feeding of the hungry.[103] In Roman context, these reversals reverberate with Mary's identification as δούλη. Accordingly, Mitzi Smith describes Mary's song as the song of a slave woman.[104] In this respect, the characterization of Mary in Luke 1 associates her with Hagar in Genesis 16. The vocabulary of enslavement is different for each woman (Hagar is שִׁפחה, translated in the LXX with παιδίσκη), but both are described with the language of humiliation. Specifically, as God observes Mary's humiliation (ταπείνωσις), so God hears

99. Bauckham 2002, 50–55.

100. Esp. Wilson 2006, 436–56. See also J. Green 1997, 101–2; Bauckham 2002, 60–66; Carroll 2012, 49–52; and A. C. Miller 2014b, 96–100.

101. So Dowling 2007, 125; Reid 2011, 52–55; and Peeler 2022, 78, 87.

102. Bauckham 2002, 66; Peeler 2022, 78–80.

103. Esp. A. C. Miller 2014b, 90–92. See also Danker 1988, 44–45; Nelson 1994, 87–91; Carter 2011, 30–40; Reid 2011, 49–58.

104. M. Smith 2022, 61. On Mary's song among the poets and protestors against political and economic oppression, see A. C. Miller 2014b, 92–94; and Edwards 2015, 54.

Hagar's (v. 11).[105] The thematic and lexical connections are not as strong as with Hannah, Deborah and Jael, and Judith. But the connection of Mary with Hagar draws attention to the ways that the intersection of slavery, humiliation, and pregnancy in Luke 1:38 and 48 reflects the distinction between honorable, freeborn womanhood and enslavement.

First, Mary's response to the announcement of her pregnancy indicates her lack of bodily autonomy: "May (everything) happen to me according to your word." As with the implication of Jesus's volition in Philippians 2:6–8, the inclusion of Mary's verbal assent distinguishes her somewhat from other enslaved women.[106] At the beginning of Hagar's story, for instance, Sarai is the only speaker; Hagar remains the object of her enslavers' actions until she becomes pregnant, and she does not speak in response to God's commands (Gen. 16:1–4, 7–13). The contrast with Hagar and other enslaved women emphasizes Mary's voiced assent to the announcement of her enslaver's plan (note κύριος and ῥῆμά in Luke 1:38). Her assent does not indicate that she had another option, however.[107] Mary shares the common experience of enslaved people as her enslaver uses her body for their own purposes or desires.

Second, the specific use made of Mary the slave is reproductive.[108] While her pregnancy is attributed to divine intervention in Luke 1:34–35 (see under "Slavery, Sex, and Mary's Story," below), the angel's announcement in verse 31 has an uncomfortable resonance with Onasiphoron's manumission inscription: "Onasiphoron is to give Sosandros a child." Like Onasiphoron and countless other enslaved women through the centuries, Mary knew the physical and emotional labor of enslaved women in becoming pregnant, giving birth, nursing infants, and raising small children. The ambiguity surrounding Mary's identity as mother in Luke 2:48–50; 8:19–21; and 11:27–28 makes sense in the context of enslavement. Her child belongs to her enslaver, eliminating the potential rights or privileges of her own relationship with him.

Third, Mary the slave is humiliated (ταπείνωσις). The reappearance of the descriptor ταπεινός in Luke 1:52 indicates the low social status associated with political and economic oppression, and this significance affects the meaning of ταπείνωσις in verse 48.[109] But, as is evident in Plutarch's story of the two sisters in *Mulier. virt.* 253c–d, the ταπειν- lexical group can express the social

105. See Munro 1998, 593; Moss and Baden 2015, 160–62; Kartzow 2025, 141–42.

106. Mary's speech contrasts with Zechariah's inability to speak in Luke 1:20. Peeler 2022, 76–77, 81–84, stresses the significance of Mary's speech as active consent to her pregnancy.

107. M. Smith 2022, 59, comments that Mary is "notified—not asked—that she has been impregnated." Note that the vocabulary of Luke 1:38 connects Mary's assent with Simeon's similar statement in 2:29.

108. See also Munro 1998, 548–52; Kartzow 2018, 49–51; Peeler 2022, 23.

109. E.g., Bauckham 2002, 71–76; Bovon 2002, 61; A. C. Miller 2014b, 115, 118.

humiliation and trauma of sexual assault with respect to freeborn women.[110] Enslaved women lacked the privilege of chastity, but the consistent association of the ταπειν- word group with enslavement (established in chap. 3, above) enables a correlation between the two lexical fields. Given the overlapping contexts of the value of chastity for freeborn women and Mary's embodied enslavement, Mary's pregnancy exemplifies her humiliation.[111]

Although English translations identify Mary as a humble or lowly servant, an audience in the Roman Empire would likely see Mary as a humiliated slave whose enslaver uses her body. As discussed in the introduction, some interpreters have argued that Mary, and consequently Jesus, were (literally) enslaved.[112] Though I see the influence of the biblical identification of God's people as "slaves" in Mary's self-description, the overlap of metaphor with embodied reality blurs the distinctions.[113] In this sense, Mary's enslavement is developed by the setting of the narrative in occupied Roman Palestine and the historical setting of the Gospel in the aftermath of the First Jewish Revolt. The siege of Jerusalem in 70 CE and the consequences of defeat echo in Jesus's warnings concerning the slaughter and enslavement of women and children (Luke 13:34–35; 19:41–44; 21:20–24; 23:27–31); Mary's enslavement and the sword thrust through her in 2:35 connect her with these women.[114]

Across the ancient Mediterranean, war was a contest for masculinity.[115] Victors claimed superior manliness on the basis of courage, daring, endurance, and strength. As is evident in the portrayal of defeated Judea as a woman seated at the feet of a powerful Roman warrior on the Flavian Judea Capta coins, the emasculation of defeat was embodied by the enslavement of women and children.[116] Josephus emphasized the danger of enslavement: A man who should, according to the normative expectations of masculinity, protect his wife and children from assault is forced in defeat to see and hear them dragged

110. As in Gen. 34:2; Deut. 21:14; 22:24, 29; Judg. 19:29; 20:5; 2 Sam. 13:12, 14, 22, 32; Job 31:10; Lam. 5:11; Ezek. 22:10–11; Philo, *Mut.* 194. See also Schaberg 1990, 99–100.

111. See also Moss and Baden 2015, 160. Bauckham 2002, 72, argues instead that Mary's pregnancy is what raises her out of her humble or low status. This is theologically true in Luke 1, in the sense that Mary participates in God's salvation of Israel by bearing and giving birth to Jesus, but the gendered connotations of the ταπειν- lexical group at least complicate Mary's humiliation.

112. Munro 1998, 548, 593–94; M. Smith 2022, 59–62.

113. Cf. Kartzow 2018, 49–51; 2025, 138–45.

114. The Roman military occupation is represented in, e.g., Luke 2:1–2; 7:2–10; 13:1; 23:13–25. See further Reeder 2019, 1–25; 2021, 459–61.

115. Reeder 2019, 32–35.

116. Comparable imagery is represented in, e.g., the Gemma Augustea; the reliefs at the Sebasteion in Aphrodisias; and the column of Marcus Aurelius in Rome. See further Ferris 2000, 27–38, 56–58, 93–94, 106–10; Dillon 2006, 259–67; Reeder 2019, 53.

off to the shame of slavery. As the vocabulary of ὕβρις, αἰσχύνη, and βία indicates, enslavement realizes the loss of freeborn chastity to the enslavers' demands for sexual labor (*J.W.* 7.380–88). Portrayals of defeat emphasize the sexual danger to freeborn women and children as a particular horror of war.[117] As exemplified by Diodorus Siculus 13.58.1–2, the women in these stories often express a preference for death for themselves and their children. While the stories are told from the perspective of men, their portrayal of trauma is quite easily an imaginable reality.

Luke's representation of the destruction of Jerusalem with the pathos of suffering women and children performs a similar rhetorical function. The imagery indicates the utter destruction of Jerusalem as the children who represent the city's future are killed (19:41–44) and the women who could bear descendants are enslaved (21:20–24; 23:28–29). Mary's song celebrates God's victory over Israel's enemies (1:54–55). The angelic birth announcement contrasts the *pax Romana*, instituted and maintained by Rome's military, with God's peace for all, represented by a mother and newborn infant (2:8–14).[118] But in the next scene of the story, Mary is threatened by a sword (2:33–35), connecting this new mother with the women who face death and enslavement in 21:23–24.[119] Mary's slavery places her in a community of enslaved captives for whom wartime defeat brought the loss of kinship, cultural identity, and bodily autonomy.

Mary's slavery is multivalent. She is God's slave, an honorable identity in the biblical context. But despite the themes of salvation and the overturning of imperial power in Luke's infancy narrative, her enslavement also represents military defeat. As happened to women enslaved in human households, her body is used by her enslaver for reproductive labor. Mary's intimately embodied experience of enslavement intersects with the question of sex and slavery in the New Testament.

Slavery, Sex, and Mary's Story

Luke's birth story presents Mary's pregnancy as a unique occurrence. She is first introduced as παρθένος, a term for a young unmarried woman (1:27). In response to the angel's annunciation, she proclaims that she has not had sex with a man, further clarifying her status (v. 34). Rather than resulting from sexual intercourse, Mary's pregnancy happens by divine intervention: The Holy Spirit "comes over" her, and the power of the Most High "overshadows"

117. See Polybius 10.38.1; Diodorus Siculus 13.58.1–2, 17.35.3–7; Livy 26.13.14–15. In relation to Roman occupation, see Livy 29.17.11–16; Tacitus, *Agr.* 15; *Ann.* 14.31, 35; *Hist.* 4.14; and 4 Ezra 10:22.

118. On war and peace in Luke, see Reeder 2019, 154–91.

119. Reeder 2021, 462–65.

her (ἐπέρχομαι and ἐπισκιάζω in v. 35).[120] Neither verb indicates sexual intercourse. The descriptions instead reflect God's presence filling the tent of meeting (Exod. 40:35 LXX), promises of divine salvation (Isa. 32:15 LXX; Bar. 4:24), Jesus's transfiguration (Luke 9:34), and the Holy Spirit filling Jesus's followers (Acts 1:8).[121] The contrast between Mary's pregnancy and Elizabeth's, which was dependent on the participation of her husband (Luke 1:13, 23–24), further marks the uniqueness of Mary's situation.

Despite the unusual nature of Mary's conception, the narrative portrays an unmarried woman becoming pregnant. As Matthew 1:18–19 indicates, for a free woman such an occurrence is reason for social shame, divorce (if the woman is legally contracted to a marriage), and other negative consequences. The connection of Mary's enslavement with pregnancy and humiliation in Luke 1:38 and 48 classifies her as a woman without honor. Her pregnancy embodies her inability (as a "slave") to maintain her own bodily boundaries or live within the standards of freeborn women's chastity. As noted above, the loss of the privilege of chastity is consistently represented as an immediate bodily consequence and psychological horror of enslavement for free women.[122]

The sexual availability of enslaved people—women and men, adults and children—was a core expectation of the dehumanizing violence of enslavement in the ancient Mediterranean. Mary's embodied enslavement associates her with enslaved people whose bodies were used by enslavers for sexual labor, sexualized entertainment, and the specific labor of prostitution. For some enslaved women, sexual labor offered an opportunity to escape from slavery through manumission for the purpose of marriage with their enslavers. In general, enslaved people had little ability to resist sexual labor other than by hiding from or avoiding enslavers.[123] A short letter from two men to "beloved Epaphroditos" suggests he had managed to keep his body away from them. They threaten him with physical violence (a beating, δέρω) for his avoidance of their sexual desire (P.Oxy. 42.3070).

Epaphroditos's situation is comparable with a story told by Dionysius of Halicarnassus: A freeborn young man forced into debt slavery was whipped

120. See, e.g., R. Brown 1993, 314; J. Green 1997, 90; and esp. Peeler 2022, 23.

121. Ἐπισκιάζω and σκιάζω are consistently used to portray God's presence and protection (in addition to Exod. 40:35 LXX and Luke 9:34, see LXX Num. 9:18; Ps. 90:4; 139:8; Isa. 4:5). Ἐπέρχομαι is most commonly used to indicate negative situations, including divine punishment (Josh. 24:20 LXX; Isa. 13:13 LXX; 2 Macc. 9:18) and military action (2 Sam. 17:2 LXX; 1 Macc. 8:4); Luke's other uses of the term fit into these categories (11:22; 21:26).

122. In addition to the sources above, see Dionysius, *Ant. rom.* 4.82.1; Virgil, *Aen.* 3.320–29; Chariton, *Call.* 2.8.1; Livy 3.44.6–7, 3.47.1–2; Philo, *Virt.* 110–14. Cf. Glancy 2010, 149.

123. Levin-Richardson 2021, 204. A. Strong 2021, 184, suggests the murder of enslavers by enslaved people in Tacitus, *Ann.* 14.42–45, and Pliny, *Ep.* 3.14, may have been motivated by the enslavers' sexual abuse of the enslaved people involved.

for refusing his enslaver's sexual advances. Because of his freeborn status, he was able to seek help. His display of the lash marks on his body led to the enslaver's execution (*Ant. rom.* 16.5.1–3). A woman takes Epaphroditos's place in a similar scene in Achilles Tatius's novel *Leucippe and Clitophon*. Leucippe was beaten, chained, and forced into strenuous labor for refusing to enslave herself to the enslaved overseer's bed (πρός εὐνὴν δουλεύω). When her enslaver, a woman, visits the farm where Leucippe is laboring, Leucippe begs for help, stripping off her clothing to display the scars of the beatings she has endured. Since she is a freeborn woman, she is saved from sexual labor and the loss of her chastity (5.17.3–6). This example of a woman's successful resistance is unusual. In other stories, freeborn women taken into slavery protect their chastity by taking their own lives.[124] Enslaved women are not even accorded the privilege of protest in elite sources.[125]

The rarity of examples of enslaved people avoiding or refusing sexual labor corresponds with the consistent expectation of enslavers' access to enslaved bodies. Across the Roman Empire in the first century, male enslavers, including those who became part of the communities of Jesus's followers, assumed their right to use their enslaved people for sex.[126] For free men, sex with enslaved people was not considered immoral. The conjunction of the involuntary sexual availability of enslaved people, the legality and accepted morality of male enslavers' sexual use of enslaved bodies in Roman society, and the high standards of sexual morality proclaimed across the New Testament therefore presents a serious conundrum concerning the location of enslaved people among the followers of Jesus.[127]

The problem has two key facets. First, Jennifer Glancy notes that Paul's prohibition of men's use of sex laborers in 1 Corinthians 6:15–20 does not address the enslaved sex laborers themselves.[128] She suggests that enslaved sex laborers were excluded from Paul's communities because their labor necessarily involved them in sexual immorality.[129] Second, although Paul identified the use of sex laborers as immorality (πορνεία), his letters do not explicitly

124. Valerius Maximus 6.1, ext. 1, 3; Chariton, *Call.* 2.8.1. See further A. Strong 2021, 176–79, on the difference between enslaved freeborn men and women in stories of their sexualization.

125. Harper 2013, 49, points out that some sales contracts for enslaved people include the provision that the person cannot be forced into sexual labor (prostitution), possibly indicating enslaved people's ability to protest or resist.

126. Hezser 2005, 198–99; and Labovitz 2010, 98, note that rabbinic sources suggest similar assumptions and practices in Jewish populations. See, however, Harper 2012, 371–74, on Second Temple expectations of restrictive sexual morality.

127. Addressing Paul's rhetoric of sexual morality, see D. Martin 1997, 202–6; Knust 2006, 51–86. See also Neutel 2012, 143–46; de Wet 2018, 3–4.

128. Cf. Briggs 2010, 159–60; Cobb 2025, 131.

129. Glancy 2006, 65–67. See also Nasrallah 2014, 59.

condemn sex with household slaves. Since male enslavers' use of enslaved bodies for sex in Greco-Roman society was socially and morally condoned, Glancy argues that the male enslavers in Paul's communities would have identified enslaved people as legitimate "vessels" for their sexual desires (cf. 1 Thess. 4:3–8).[130]

Glancy leaves open the question of whether enslaved people used for sex by enslavers in the household (rather than in brothels) would be able to participate in Paul's communities.[131] If sex with these women was not *porneia* for the enslavers, the women would not necessarily be excluded as she argues is the case for enslaved sex laborers. However, the essential inability of enslaved people to practice sexual chastity may also effectively prevent their participation. Following Glancy's reasoning, if the standards of Greco-Roman society were used to judge male enslavers' sex with enslaved people in the household as moral, then since these standards denied enslaved people the virtue of chastity, they could exclude enslaved women and men from Christian communities. After all, marriage, Paul's solution to the problem of *porneia* in 1 Corinthians 7:9, was not available to enslaved people (nor, if they were in long-term partnerships with other enslaved people, could they maintain marital fidelity).[132]

Of course, enslaved people were part of the early church, including Paul's communities. Some (if not many, or all) enslaved people among Jesus's followers would have experienced forced sex regardless of their own choice or desire, either from enslavers who were not part of the community or, if Glancy is correct, from enslavers who were part of the community. There are several options for the inclusion of enslaved people who lacked the capability of sexual morality. First, it is possible to interpret the absence of any instructions concerning the woman whose body was used by her stepson for sex (1 Cor. 5:1–5[133]), enslaved sex laborers (6:15–20), or enslaved people whose

130. Glancy 2006, 59–62; and 2010, 146–48; Marchal 2015, 157–59; and 2023, 141–43. See also Briggs 2010, 160; Cobb 2025, 128. As noted by Glancy 2010, 150–51; de Wet 2015, 224–25, 231–32; and 2018, 3–4; and McKeown 2012, 296, early Christian writings attest to Christian men's use of enslaved bodies for sex into the fourth century CE (citing, e.g., Acts of Andrew; Basil of Caesarea, *Ep.* 199; Augustine, *Serm.* 296; John Chrysostom, *Hom. Col.* 12.3).

131. Glancy 2006, 69–70. However, the line between sex labor in households and in prostitution was not always clear, as evident in Plutarch's reference to an in-house brothel for enslaved men to use (*Cat. Maj.* 21.2) and in the graffiti on the walls of houses and the room apparently set aside for household prostitution in the House of the Vettii in Pompeii (see under "Women and Enslavement," above; see also Severy-Hoven 2012, 545–64).

132. Neutel 2012, 142, notes that anyone who was not an elite man, with full legal and moral control of his own person, would struggle with Paul's instructions.

133. The father's "woman" may be enslaved, rather than a (free) wife (see Knust 2006, 76). If the woman was enslaved, the condemnation of the son for using her for sex would indicate Paul did not approve of the use of enslaved people for sex. But the claim that what the son has

enslavers used their bodies for sex as an implicit recognition that they were not responsible for what happened to them.[134] The philosophical internalization of freedom and slavery provides a parallel conceptualization. The people who were used for sex could maintain chastity in mind, spirit, and will, even if they were unable to prevent their enslavers' violation of their bodies.[135] Enslaved people could also use Paul's theology of enslavement to sin and exhortations to practice self-control to critique enslavers' abuse of their bodies, enlisting what Niall McKeown calls the "moral force" of the community on their behalf.[136]

Second, enslaved people could resist. Addressing the implications of 1 Peter 2:18–21 for enslaved women, Betsy Bauman-Martin argues that enslaved people could abstain from fleshly desires (v. 11) by refusing to be used by their enslavers for sex. Their resistance would almost certainly be futile, resulting in physical abuse and rape. But their experience of unjust suffering in turn identifies them with Jesus.[137] With respect to 1 Corinthians 6:15–20, Tyler Schwaller points out that the verb φεύγω in the command to "flee *porneia*" was commonly used to describe runaway slaves. One possible interpretation, then, would be for enslaved people to "flee *porneia*" by escaping enslavement.[138] Paul's reminder that his audience had been purchased by God to be holy (6:19–20), particularly in connection with 7:22, subversively separates enslaved people from their (human) enslavers. When their enslavers misused their bodies, escape from slavery was a potential response.

Third, the story of Mary provides an example of a woman who, though her body was used by her (divine) enslaver for reproductive purposes, was not thereby excluded from the Christian community.[139] Luke's association

done is not even practiced in wider society suggests the woman was the father's (free or freed) wife, not his slave.

134. Cf. MacDonald 2007, 98–100; and Neutel 2012, 138 (discussing the different regulations for sexual morality of free and enslaved cult members in SIG 3.985); Shaner 2018, 52–53 (with the reminder that Paul's letters are only part of larger conversations). Harper 2013, 371–74, however, notes that Second Temple Jewish texts ascribe moral agency (and responsibility for *porneia*) to sex laborers.

135. While the philosophical metaphors center elite men, they at least offer the opportunity to consider how enslaved people could use similar metaphors to redefine their own experiences. Cf. Schaberg 1990, 138; Knust 2004, 170–72; and 2006, 65–70 (noting the intersections of sexual immorality and enslavement to sin in Romans); Nasrallah 2014, 59–60 (on 1 Cor. 6:20).

136. Rom. 6:5–14; 1 Cor. 7:9; 9:24–27; Gal. 5:23; McKeown 2012, 293–94. See further MacDonald 2007, 101–2.

137. Bauman-Martin 2004a, 70–72; 2004b, 269–71.

138. Schwaller 2017, 35, 76. See also Valentine 2017, 323–39, on the potential to use 1 Cor. 7:21–23 to seek manumission as an escape from "sexual exploitation."

139. Seal 2025, 211–13, makes a similar argument with respect to Jesus's bodily violation as justification for the inclusion of enslaved people in the Corinthian churches. Cobb 2025,

of Mary's pregnancy with slavery and humiliation demonstrates the acceptability of enslaved people whose bodies were involuntarily vulnerable to the desires and actions of their enslavers. Mary's story provides space for enslaved people who were raped and assaulted to participate in the communities of Jesus's followers, to be seen by God in their embodied humiliation, and to receive God's merciful help (Luke 1:46–55).[140]

Glancy's query concerning male enslavers' use of enslaved people for sex is important to consider. The absence of any explicit prohibition in Paul's letters and the assumption of morality in larger society, including (according to rabbinic texts) among Jews, make the issue a significant concern.[141] However, I am not convinced that Paul would condone or encourage enslavers to use enslaved people for sex. Looking more broadly at his understanding of the transformation of life in Christ, in Romans 13:8–10 loving a neighbor means not abusing them. In Galatians 5:13, freedom is defined not by the rights or privileges of the body (σάρξ) but by enslaving oneself to others in love. In 1 Corinthians 6, the prohibition of men's use of enslaved sex laborers follows a prohibition of lawsuits; it is better to be wronged than to wrong someone else (v. 7).[142] These concepts should have implications for enslavers' interactions with enslaved people. Arguably, the prohibition of men's use of enslaved sex laborers outside the household, itself a normative practice in Roman society, informs life inside the household as well.[143]

The development of both discipleship and, especially, the exercise of authority around enslavement reinforces this message. The exhortation to be enslaved to one another in Philippians 2:1–4 requires self-humiliation, the setting aside of personal ambitions or desires to care for the needs of others. The un-masculinity of enslavement in Mark 10:41–45 and Luke 22:24–27, coming at the moment when the male disciples seek power and authority, challenges the oppressive violence associated with normative masculinity. The punishment of the enslaved manager who abuses the enslaved people under his authority in Luke 12:45–46 offers a deadly warning. To identify as and with

131, also points to the inclusion of enslaved sex laborers (prostitutes) in Jesus's kingdom in Matt. 21:31–32. Note that Rahab, the "prostitute" from Jericho, is a model of faith in Heb. 11:31 and James 2:25.

140. Cf. Schaberg 1990, 125, 135; Reid 1996, 84; and 2011, 55.

141. Enslavers' sexual use of enslaved women is also present in biblical narratives (Gen. 16:1–4; 30:10–13), though in Sir. 41:20–22, looking at a sex laborer or someone else's wife and using an enslaved woman for sex are all deemed dishonorable (see further Harper 2012, 372).

142. See Robinson 2019, 172–79, on the un-manliness of the instructions in 1 Cor. 6:1–8.

143. See also D. Martin 1997, 202–3; MacDonald 2007, 96; Harper 2012, 377–79; Neutel 2012, 141; Valentine 2017, 332, 337 (noting a parallel with the instructions of Musonius Rufus, diatribe 12). Cf. Cobb 2025, 131.

enslaved people demands a change in behavior to enslaved people. Mary's story of enslavement witnesses to both the recognition of the oppression of enslavement and God's saving acts on behalf of the oppressed. As a model of discipleship, Mary's story demands that those who seek to oppress others instead identify with them.

Mary as Model Slave: The Un-Manning of Discipleship

In Luke 12:35–36, Jesus exhorts his followers to adopt the identity of enslaved people awaiting their enslaver's return—dressed for labor, with lamps lit, ready to open the door upon his approach. The broad representation of discipleship as enslavement is applied more specifically to the twelve male disciples in 12:41–48; 17:7–10; and 22:24–27. Even more than the community as a whole, those who seek authority are expected to be shaped by the behavior and attitudes of enslaved people: not abusing those under their care, as enslavers did (12:45–46); assuming not the status and privilege of an enslaver but the "worthlessness" and unending labor of a slave (17:10); seeking not the greatness of ruling, exercising authority, or bestowing benefaction but the paradoxical greatness of the enslaved server (22:26).

I have argued in this chapter that the definition of discipleship and leadership around enslavement marks the women who "serve" in Luke 4:38–39; 8:1–3; and 10:38–42 as models for the twelve disciples to adopt. Like Martha, even given the complicated representation of διακονία and διακονέω in her story, they should welcome Jesus. Like Mary of Magdala, Joanna, and Susanna, they should provide for the community from their own resources. Like Peter's mother-in-law, they should care for the needs of community members. All Jesus's followers, and especially the twelve disciples, should adopt the actions and characteristics of these women.

As the first person in the narrative to be identified as a "slave," Mary is the ultimate model of discipleship in Luke.[144] Her story blurs the distinction between enslavement as a metaphor for discipleship and enslavement as an embodied experience. As an example of enslaved discipleship, Mary assents to her (divine) enslaver's authority over her body. She sacrifices the social honor dependent on bodily autonomy. To be clear, Mary's story should not be used to encourage anyone to submit to abuse. Mary does not, in Luke's narrative, experience assault or rape. Her story does, however, provide a point of contact for people who have experienced these or similar acts of violence. Mary shares the embodiment of imposed dishonor, allying her with those

144. This is not a new claim. See, e.g., Schaberg 1990, 113; Reid 1996, 69, 83; 2011, 52–58; Wilson 2006, 450–52; Dowling 2007, 139–40; Peeler 2022, 79; Carey 2023, 107.

who are oppressed by the economic and political forces that rule the world. In her prophetic song, she protests the structures of inequality and exclusion that allow a few to benefit at the expense and the humiliation of many.[145]

The disciples' competition for greatness in Luke 22:24–27 places them on the side of the powerful who, Mary proclaims, God will remove from their thrones. Jesus tells the disciples that to be great they must become as the youngest and as enslaved servers. Mary's story demonstrates this reversal of social norms. As a young woman, unmarried, pregnant, and (as evident in 2:1–24) lacking wealth or social standing, Mary's enslavement is defined by humiliation (1:48). But, just as Jesus is exalted as a humiliated slave in Philippians 2:6–11, so Mary announces that the humiliated will be raised up and the hungry filled with good things, and God enacts greatness on her behalf (Luke 1:49, 52–53). Like the victorious Jael and Judith, Mary is blessed among women (Judg. 5:24; Jdt. 13:18; Luke 1:42).

The intersections between Mary's story in Luke 1 and the disciples' disagreement in chapter 22 mark her as the model disciple, an identification confirmed by the echoes of Mary's story in Acts 1–2.[146] Mary identifies herself as an enslaved woman, δούλη, a term that appears only three times in the New Testament: in Luke 1:38 and 48 and Acts 2:18. The embodiment of Mary's enslavement in her pregnancy comes about through the Holy Spirit, the "power of the Most High" (δύναμις ὑψίστου, Luke 1:35). In Acts, the Holy Spirit, embodied in flames and linguistic ability, empowers (δύναμις) Jesus's followers, including Mary herself, to witness (1:8, 13–14; 2:1–4). Mary's "slave song" is prophetic, and in Acts 2:16–21, Jesus's followers are prophetic slaves (note v. 18). The dramatic reversal Mary announces in her song is also the story of Jesus in Acts 2:22–24. Looking back at Mary in Luke 1–2 from the perspective of Acts 1–2, her embodied, humiliated enslavement is the exemplar for discipleship.[147] Those who want to be disciples of Jesus should be like Mary.

145. See A. C. Miller 2014b, 99, 118.

146. See also Schaberg 1990, 113; Peeler 2022, 180–84 (also noting the specific inclusion of Mary in Acts 1:14 and following).

147. The representation of διακονία in Acts is beyond the boundaries of the current study. The limitation of διακον- terms to men and the reversion to the standard meaning of someone who is commissioned to act are significantly different than the enslaved "service" represented by women in Luke. But, while their work of leadership is not represented with the vocabulary of διακονία, women do continue to welcome Jesus's followers into their homes, care for the needs of community members, and teach (9:36–42; 12:12–16; 16:11–15; 18:26). As other interpreters have said, the situation of women in Luke-Acts is complicated.

Conclusions

> You call me "teacher" and "lord/enslaver." . . . Therefore, if I, the lord/enslaver and teacher, have washed your feet, you all must also wash one another's feet.
>
> —John 13:13–14

At the beginning of this book, I introduced the intersecting themes of enslavement and un-masculinity in a brief analysis of John 13:1–17. There, I noted that Jesus begins and ends the story in a position of authority as teacher and κύριος, a concept that slips between a term of respect for a social or political superior, a designation for God, and the title assumed by enslavers. Making his masculine status visible, Jesus and his (male) followers are pictured reclining in a dining room, a posture associated with elite men who had the wealth and status to enjoy the leisurely entertainment of a meal served by enslaved people. In ancient Mediterranean dining rooms, reclining diners and enslaved people on the move embodied, respectively, masculinity and un-masculinity.

As he changes his clothing, picks up the equipment used by enslaved people, and walks and crouches around the room, Jesus's status slips from manliness to un-manliness. The speech in John 13:13–14 enjoins the same un-manliness on the (male) disciples: If the lord/enslaver washes the feet of the enslaved (note v. 16), then the enslaved should surely wash one another's feet. Within the story, Jesus's act redefines masculinity, traditionally expressed by the exercise of authority, around the actions, postures, and identity of an un-manly slave. As characters in the scene, the male disciples represent the Gospel's audience of Jesus's followers. Emerson Powery suggests the story challenges them to see a slave as "an exemplar for how all Christ-followers should act toward others in service to one another." The definition of Christian identity around enslavement offers opportunities for vulnerable, marginalized peoples to use texts like John 13:13–14 for justice.[1]

The intersections of slavery and masculinity provide one such opportunity (though not unproblematically). The un-manly enslavement represented in Philippians 2:1–11; Mark 10:41–45 and Luke 22:24–27 (plus Mary's embodied enslavement in Luke 1–2); and 1 Peter 2:18–25 defines Christology, the practices of authority, and discipleship. In this study, I have argued that the un-masculinity of enslavement challenges oppressive aspects of normative masculinity. In these concluding comments, I revisit several pieces of the argument: slavery and masculinity as systems of domination in the social and cultural contexts of the New Testament; the representations of Jesus, (male) authorities in the community, and all Jesus's followers as enslaved in the New Testament; and the overlapping thought worlds of metaphor and lived experience.

Systems of Domination

Both slavery and normative masculinity operated as systems of domination in the world of the New Testament. Roman law and social practice defined enslaved people, "bodies," as possessions. By the logic of enslavement, then, enslaved people needed to be possessed by an external authority who could control, direct, command, educate, discipline, punish, and provide for them. The consistent characterization of enslaved people as incapable of reason or self-control, prey to a laundry list of vices that endangered the functioning of households and society, reveals this logic.[2] Equally, the employment of enslaved people in positions of responsibility (from operating businesses to educating enslavers' children) and the self-control and ability to reason demonstrated by enslaved people as they navigated and resisted enslavement reveal the fundamental falsehood of slavery. To counteract the basic humanity, agency, and expertise and talents of enslaved people, practices of domination—natal alienation; constant labor; surveillance; bodily, psychological, and emotional violation—enforced, protected, and inculcated the (il)logic of slavery.[3]

1. Powery 2025a, 38.
2. E.g., Bryson 56–59; Quintilian, *Inst.* 1.2.5; Pliny, *Nat.* 33.27; Josephus, *Ant.* 3.18–20.
3. Esp. J. Williams 2025, 101.

The construction of enslavement overlapped with that of masculinity. While particular constructions of masculinity varied across regions, ethnic identities, and socioeconomic statuses, normative masculinity consistently incorporated authority over self (expressed by legal and economic autonomy and self-discipline) and authority over others within the household and (depending on status) beyond. Among other factors, the elite masculinity of a Roman like Germanicus was demonstrated by posture, dress, and speaking ability. A manly man exercised control over his emotions and bodily desires (and also had the privilege of indulging his bodily desires). He enjoyed the paired rights of, first, protecting his own body and the bodies under his authority from violation and, second, violating the bodies of others.[4] The ideals of masculinity propounded by Seneca, Plutarch, and other elite Romans emphasized benevolent paternalism.[5] But as the exploration of the rhetoric regarding enslaved people and of their lived experiences in this book has shown, the practices of masculinity often equate with abuse, violence, and the denial of full humanity to anyone who could be identified as lacking in status, honor, or masculinity.

In Egypt in the early first century CE, a woman named Tryphaine brought a legal suit against her husband. Among other charges, she accused him of abuse (κακουχέω) and insult (or rape, καθυβρίζω); he treated her like a slave purchased at market (ἀργυρώνητος).[6] Tryphaine's accusation demonstrates the dangers of men's power. In addition, the comparison of free wives and enslaved people reveals the intersections of gender and slavery, and also the ways these intersections functioned to doubly oppress the enslaved. Legally, enslaved people counted as possessions. They were constructed as animalistic creatures who lacked reason and self-control. Unlike Tryphaine, they were not accorded the right or privilege of protecting themselves or of protesting the violation of their own bodies or others' bodies. The domination of masculinity and the racialization of slavery un-gendered enslaved people.

For Onasiphoron and other enslaved women, un-gendering centered on their imposed inability to practice chastity (*FD* 3.6.36). Their bodies were vulnerable to their enslavers, but the illogic of slavery defined their sexual vulnerability as unvirtuous licentiousness. Enslaved women were employed for reproductive labor, from pregnancy to breastfeeding to childcare. However,

4. Tacitus, *Ann.* 2.72–73. Cf. Philo, *Leg.* 3.202; Pliny, *Nat.* 7.139–40; Juvenal, *Sat.* 8.165–70, 14.70–74; Plutarch, *Rect. rat. aud.* 37c–e.

5. E.g., Bryson 61–63; Seneca, *Ep.* 47.15–19; Plutarch, [*Lib. ed.*] 7d–f.

6. *BGU* 4.1105 (transcription available at P. 13054 R, Berliner Papyrusdatenbank, https://berlpap.smb.museum/00490/). For ἀργυρώνητος in reference to enslavement, see Herodotus 4.72.1; Josephus, *Ant.* 6.41; Plutarch, *Rect. rat. aud.* 37e.

the women were not mothers in the same way free women were. They had no rights over the children they cared for, whether born of their own bodies or not. Their bodily and emotional labor was exploited by enslavers to advance the enslavers' (freeborn) family and (enslaved) property.

Natal alienation and the inability to contract formal marriages or create stable familial households prevented enslaved men from demonstrating the masculinity of ancestral lineage and patriarchy, vividly illustrated by Cato's control over his male slaves' sexual access to female slaves (Plutarch, *Cat. Maj.* 21.2). Enslaved men could not defend against or avenge insults to their person or body. Their postures—stooping, crouching, bending—and bodily disfigurement from hard labor and violence meant they could not look or move like men. Enslaved men were not permitted to wield the weapons of war, so they could not attain militarized masculinity. Their bodies were sexually penetrated by enslavers. Seneca's enslaved servers—"womanized" by un-masculine hairstyles, clothing, and smoothly shaved faces—embody the un-manning of slaves (*Ep.* 47.7, 95.24). The forced castration of young boys, particularly in relation to the sexualization and penetrability of male slaves, represents the ultimate un-gendering.

The structures of slavery and the rhetoric of masculinity intersect in the racialization, violation, and domination of enslaved individuals. Imperial artwork and monuments portrayed this domination to audiences across the empire. On the Gemma Augustea, the Ara Pacis, the reliefs decorating the Sebasteion at Aphrodisias, and triumphal columns and arches, emperors are depicted in the clothing of masculinity (togas and armor), with upright posture, and displaying defined musculature. They are accompanied by the wives and children who signify their patriarchal success. Their militarized masculinity is further evidenced by the cowering figures at their feet: enslaved captives of war, often pictured seated or crouched, with their clothing torn from their bodies.[7] As represented by the mourning woman at the feet of a victorious Roman in the Flavian-era Judea Capta coins, the defeated enemy was un-manned by these portrayals. The captive bodies for sale in slave markets reified the emasculation of Roman victory.

The "hidden transcripts" of slavery and masculinity complicate the domination of enslaved people in significant ways. As explored throughout this study, enslaved women and men challenged the systems of enslavement by creating their own communities and families with one another, claiming their spouses and children with the vocabulary of freeborn relationships. They resisted their enslavers' control by hiding, dallying, and deliberately

7. Cf. Ferris 2000, 27–38, 50–58.

misperforming tasks. Enslaved people used what power they had in the system of slavery. They survived; they escaped; by suicide they prevented their own dehumanization; and sometimes, by murder they avenged an enslaver's abuse.

Countering the many monuments to imperial masculinity, enslaved and freed people established their own monuments that celebrated their resistance and reclamation of social identity. Funerary imagery and inscriptions proclaim the relationships of kin and friends created by enslaved people, as in the case of Alimma and her father (*CIL* 10.26). The freed person Publius Decimius Eros Merula proclaimed his masculine status as a doctor, priest of the imperial cult, and wealthy patron of the community (*CIL* 11.5400), mixing concepts that clearly demonstrated normative masculinity (priest and patron) with the professional work associated with enslavement. Jucundus, enslaved at the time of his death, was celebrated by his enslaved friends as a real man, someone who acted on behalf of himself and others (*CIL* 6.6308).

Mitzi Smith rightly insists that the status of "slave" is not shameful.[8] An enslaved person is fully human, with the human capacities for reason, social relationships, emotion, and virtue. Enslaved people in the Roman world demonstrated their humanity by their resistance, survival, and escape. But while these strategies reveal the falsehood of elite rhetoric concerning slaves, they did not (and could not) unravel the system as a whole. The intersecting dominations of the system of slavery and the construction of (elite) masculinity around the ancient Mediterranean were expressed in violent control, bodily violation, and imposed dishonor. Enslaved people were racialized, dishonored, and un-manned. The embodiment of enslavement, the damage to bodies and minds caused by enslavement, and the social humiliation of enslavement explain why the Romans understood slavery as a living death.

Slavery, Masculinity, and the New Testament

Enslaved people are listed as imperial merchandise in Revelation 18:11–13. They are beaten, dishonored, and killed in Mark 12:2–5. Their words are distrusted (Acts 12:15), their work devalued (Luke 17:7–10), and their moral character questioned (Titus 2:9–10). That they should fearfully obey their enslavers is not questioned; in fact, it is reinforced (Eph. 6:5–8). The intersecting dominations of enslavement and masculinity are evident in these texts. There are also ways in which the books of the New Testament challenge the structures of slavery and constructions of normative elite masculinity. Imagining the possibilities of, first, the involvement of enslaved and freed people

8. M. Smith 2022, 58.

in composing the texts; second, the "hidden transcripts" within the texts; and third, the reception of the texts by audiences of enslaved, freed, and free followers of Jesus opens potential spaces of resistance to the oppression and violence of the twin dominations of enslavement and masculinity.

This study has focused on a series of texts in which Jesus is depicted as an enslaved person (Mark 10:45; Luke 22:27; John 13:3–5; Phil. 2:6–11; and 1 Pet. 2:21–25); the (male) disciples and other figures of authority in the communities of Jesus's followers are exhorted to identify or act as enslaved people (Mark 10:41–44; Luke 12:41–48; 17:7–10; 22:24–27; John 13:12–15; Phil. 1:1; 2:22); and all enslaved and non-enslaved followers of Jesus are called to model themselves on Jesus the slave (Luke 12:35–40; Phil. 2:1–5; 1 Pet. 2:18–21). The story of Mary in Luke 1 illustrates the intersection of embodied experience with the descriptors of humiliating enslavement. As the first "slave" in Luke, Mary's example defines slavery and discipleship for the (male) disciples later in the narrative: She sets aside the rights and privileges of bodily integrity, social honor, and independent decision-making to obey God—who is, to her, κύριος (lord and enslaver).

Mary is also an example of the un-gendering of enslavement. Her humiliation is not clearly defined in Luke 1:46–55, though it is connected with national oppression. However, as a young, unwed woman, her humiliation overlaps with her pregnancy and the loss (or, as "slave," lack) of chastity it signifies. Mary is marginalized as a young woman and as an enslaved person in a social system built around the authority and privilege of manly men. As such, her story also exemplifies the un-masculinity of enslavement.

Assuming the identity of a slave in Luke and across the texts discussed in this study involves redefining "masculinity" around un-masculine attributes and behaviors. In 1 Peter 2:18–25, the embodiment of enslavement is represented by fear, enduring unjust violence and the resulting wounds and scars, and not defending against or avenging violation. The parallel experiences of enslaved people (men and women), Jesus, and (free) wives mark them all as un-men. The representation of Jesus as slave in Philippians 2:7–8 emphasizes un-masculinity with its descriptions of humiliation, obedience, and crucifixion. For the community that follows Jesus's model, un-masculinity is present in the exhortation to humiliation, setting aside one's own good for the good of others, and fearful obedience (vv. 1–4, 12).

In contrast to the emperors, models of imperial Roman masculinity, Jesus does not weaponize his status to abuse or dominate (Phil. 2:6). Likewise, in Mark 10:41–45 and Luke 22:24–27, Jesus upsets the (male) disciples' search for (masculine) authority and status by exhorting them to adopt the un-masculinity of slavery—an un-masculinity that, in John 13:1–17, Jesus demonstrates by serving his own disciples in a dining room. Luke's Gospel further defines the discipleship of enslavement through the parables in 12:35–48 and 17:7–10, which give examples of maintaining vigilance, laboring in a variety of tasks, enduring violence, and claiming the descriptor "worthless." Beyond the humiliating and agonizing public exhibition of crucifixion, Jesus's self-identification as an enslaved server (Luke 22:27) and his example of washing the feet of the disciples (John 13:3–16) instruct his followers in the un-masculinity of mutual enslavement.

These texts clearly reflect the domination and oppression of enslavement. I have argued in this book that it is also possible to discern strategies for survival, resistance, and potential options for justice within these texts. In 1 Peter 2:18–25, the direct address to enslaved people acknowledges their moral capability. They "do good," which, in 1 Peter, centers on obedience to God, not a human enslaver. They endure violence like men, without the sorts of reactions judged as "slavish" by the enslavers who, in this text, are characterized as perverse and unjust un-men. Precisely in their obedience to God and endurance of suffering, the enslaved people become primary models of following Jesus's footsteps. Their enslavement is paradigmatic for the identity of Jesus's followers as "free slaves" (2:16).

The exhortation to humiliation and to work for the good of others in Philippians 2:1–5 undermines the culture of status seeking in Philippi. The redefinition of being human around the characteristics of enslavement, modeled by Jesus who is a human slave (vv. 6–8), extends the possibility of glory to non-elites while calling into question the kind of glory typically sought by elites. Moreover, the Christ hymn and its implications for the community could be used to critique and restrict elites in the community who abused others for their own advantage.[9] This precise message is evident in Mark and Luke: At the moment the twelve disciples seek the power and status of elite masculinity, Jesus challenges them to become slaves of all. For Luke specifically, assuming the identity of servers in a dining room decenters elite assumptions and values. The normative masculine privilege of commanding and exploiting the labor and bodies of others is replaced by (freely given) service to others.

The communities that created, preserved, and interpreted the books of the New Testament included enslaved and freed people. Emerson Powery and Candida Moss imagine the work of enslaved scribes and readers as spaces for resistance.[10] They suggest that enslaved people who participated in the

9. Cf. M. Smith 2022, 57–58.
10. Powery 2022, 81–84; Moss 2024, 57–58, 63–69, and passim.

process of composing the letters and narratives could draw attention to enslaved characters, suggest ways to represent enslavement, or express their own experiences of enslavement to their coauthors. Enslaved people who read letters or Gospels aloud during community gatherings could use their voices and gestures to emphasize elements of the texts that pointed toward justice or, alternatively, to de-emphasize elements that pointed toward oppression. Perhaps, as happened in community gatherings in the context of slavery in the United States, enslaved people in the audience would walk out on, refuse to hear, or protest certain texts.[11]

In the mixed-status communities of the followers of Jesus in the first century, enslaved people and enslavers together heard discipleship defined around mutual enslavement.[12] They heard that being like Christ requires being like a slave. They also heard strong warnings against the abuse of power in 1 Peter 2:19's recognition of the violence experienced by enslaved people as injustice (the same sort of injustice experienced by Jesus) and in Luke 12:45–46's punishment of the enslaved manager who beat and starved other enslaved people (perhaps a story of justice for the enslaved people in the audience). It is at least imaginable that community members could use these texts to pressure authority figures and enslavers to adopt the un-masculinity of slavery in their relationships, including in their relationships with enslaved people in the community.[13] As is often highlighted by interpreters, the metaphor of enslavement to God acts to doubly oppress enslaved people.[14] But the overlapping arenas of the legal status and the metaphor of enslavement could also work in the opposite direction—to develop enslavement to God and one another around the embodied, lived experiences of enslaved people to (at least spiritually and perhaps also socially) liberative effect.

Embodied Metaphors: Real Slaves of Christ?

For people who lived within the slave system of the Roman Empire, the vocabulary, imagery, and experiences of enslavement were common currency. The pervasive presence of the economic, legal, and social structures of slavery

11. H. Thurman 1996, 20; Johnson-DeBaufre and Nasrallah 2011, 161–62; Powery and Sadler 2016, 120–21, 127.

12. I am assuming enslaved participants in the community were present for the readings of letters and narratives, for worship, and for other activities, as is suggested by the direct addresses to enslaved people in various letters. But note that S. Elliott 2018, 241, among others, imagines enslaved people were instead put to work cooking, serving, cleaning, and performing other "slavish" tasks during community gatherings.

13. Cf. MacDonald 2007, 101–2; McKeown 2012, 293–94.

14. E.g., de Wet 2018, 19–21; Kartzow 2018, 3.

and of enslaved individuals, both as their own persons and as perceived and constructed through the enslavers' gaze, resulted in the common use of the language of slavery to describe, analyze, critique, and motivate social life. So, as I have noted in this study, defeat in war was defined as enslavement, a connection that recognizes the consequences of captivity and derides the un-masculinity of the defeated in contrast to the militarized masculinity of the victors (Josephus, *J.W.* 2.355–56, 7.382–86). For an emperor, the ultimate exemplar of masculinity in the Roman Empire, the language of slavery marked the limitations of personal freedom to enact whatever he might desire (Seneca, *Clem.* 1.8.1–5). A person might be "enslaved" to the responsibilities of public office or, more problematically, to the lure of luxury, emotion, and bodily desire (Publilius Syrus, *Sent.* 40, 50, 519). "Slavishness" and enslavement were insults used to discredit and demean opponents (Cassius Dio 50.5, 62.6).

A pervasive use of the language and imagery of enslavement internalized slavery and freedom with respect to the exercise of reason and self-control. Regardless of legal, economic, or social status, an individual could express manly freedom by adopting austerity in response to luxury or physical need, disciplined displays of emotion, and equanimity in the face of misfortune. Moral laxity, indulgence in luxury or physical pleasure, and expressions of excessive emotionality, on the other hand, indicated un-manly enslavement.[15] The internalization of slavery and freedom theoretically allowed for an enslaved person to be a "free man." However, the descriptions of internal enslavement corresponded with the racialization of enslaved people as lacking reason and self-control, prey to vices that undermined elite social norms, and consequently less human than elite men. The definition of slavery as un-masculinity and the correlation of self-control and reason with elite status effectively limited the attainment of internal freedom to elite men.[16]

As is evident in these examples, the boundaries between the metaphors and realities of enslavement are ambiguous. Juvenal's satire concerning an impoverished free man who seeks the patronage of a wealthy man is illustrative. At a dinner hosted by the patron, the client is seated in a low-status position near the kitchen, signifying that the patron categorizes the client as a slave. The client waits silently (like Seneca's silent enslaved servers) for his portion of the meal. In order to eat, Juvenal says, the client will even transform himself into a slave, volunteering to be beaten with a whip (*Sat.* 5.161–73). This metaphor

15. As noted throughout this study, the internalization of slavery and freedom run through Greek and Roman literature. See, e.g., Plato, *Gorg.* 483a–b; Xenophon, *Mem.* 2.1.15–19; Seneca, *Ep.* 47.15–17, 77.14–15, 85.27; Dio Chrysostom 15.29–32; Epictetus, *Diatr.* 3.22.45–49, 3.26.23–24.

16. For instance, Plato, *Resp.* 4.431c–d; Seneca, *Ep.* 47.15–16; Philo, *Leg.* 3.202; Plutarch, *Rect. rat. aud.* 37c–e; Joshel 2011, 233–34.

of slavery builds on and extends the domination of enslavement, and the lived realities of enslavement affect the meaning made by the metaphor.[17] The intersections of status, wealth, masculinity, position and behavior, and bodily vulnerability in Juvenal's satire offer a salient reminder of the undesirability of "slavishness," of being assessed and treated as a slave, for a free Roman man.[18]

The representation of Christology, authority, and discipleship with the imagery and vocabulary of enslavement in the New Testament reflects the blurring of metaphor and reality. Some New Testament texts fit quite easily within the common discourses of the Greco-Roman world. Paul's metaphor of sin as an enslaver in Romans 6:16–23, for instance, corresponds with philosophic conceptions of the enslaving powers of wealth, luxury, and physical desire. However, the prevalence of New Testament metaphors describing and encouraging slavery to God and, especially, to other community members diverges from Greek and Roman traditions.[19]

The few uses of slavery as a positive or constructive metaphor by Greco-Roman authors, Sandra Joshel points out, omit the racialization, un-gendering, and violation of enslavement.[20] But in the New Testament, slavery to God is a living death (e.g., 2 Cor. 2:14–16), and slavery to one another requires labor, setting aside personal freedom, and social humiliation (e.g., Phil. 2:1–4). Jesus's embodied experience of slavery in Philippians 2:7–8 and 1 Peter 2:21–25 includes obedience, humiliation, physical abuse that scarred his body, and crucifixion. In Mark 10:41–45 and Luke 22:24–27, the exhortation to become slaves and servers explicitly contrasts with the elite masculinity of exercising authority. The use of women's work to define serving and of Mary to model the slavery of discipleship in Luke's Gospel drives the point home: The "metaphor" of slavery is realized by a pregnant woman whose body belongs to her enslaver.

The representation of Jesus, the twelve disciples, and Paul and his colleagues as enslaved people elevates the un-masculinity of slavery as a defining identity for Jesus's followers. For people in positions of authority, especially men, to adopt the identity, characteristics, or behaviors of enslaved people challenges the dominating forces of masculine privilege and power. The centrality of enslavement for the New Testament's depiction of discipleship redefines masculinity around being controlled by external forces (God, Jesus, the Holy Spirit[21]). It demands giving up seeking one's own good at the expense

17. See Joshel 2011, 230; de Wet 2018, 10–13; Kartzow 2018, 1–4, 26.

18. So Combes 1998, 46–47; Roller 2001, 223, 227; Joshel 2011, 232.

19. Cf. Combes 1998, 68–69; Glancy 2011, 459–60; Moss 2024, 111–12, 205–6.

20. See Joshel 2011, 234.

21. The overlapping domains of enslavement and possession by the Holy Spirit are explored by Glancy 2023, 156–58 (drawing on the work of Denise Kimber Buell); and Moss 2024, 208–14.

of others to instead seek the good of others. It asks all members of the community to demonstrate the intimate bodily care and the provision of basic needs enslavers expected of enslaved people. These attitudes and behaviors were likely the norm for many people in the communities of Jesus's followers. That enslaved people and wives (in 1 Pet. 2:18–3:7) and women (in Luke) exemplify discipleship reflects their (socially constrained) inhabitation of the values and behaviors these texts enjoin. It is free men, especially those who aspire to the masculinity of status and power, who are most challenged by the un-manning of enslavement to God and one another.

The Afterlife of a Living Metaphor

I have argued in this book that the exhortation to be enslaved to God and to one another offered a significant challenge to the paired dominations of enslavement and masculinity in the ancient Mediterranean. Those in positions of power—including elite men, household patriarchs, and (male and female) enslavers—were called to give up their status and the work required to maintain it, their ability to control and violate the bodies of others, and even their control over themselves. They had narrative examples and living people around them to teach them how to embody the identity of an enslaved person. The enslaved and freed people in the communities were part of the production, commemoration, and interpretation of the slavery of discipleship. They could employ strategies for surviving and resisting enslavement in their interpretation and use of parables, narratives, and letters. They could reject interpretations that encouraged domination and oppression. They could emphasize the condemnation of abuse and injustice and hold enslavers in the community accountable to the ideals of mutual enslavement. There is potential, even if fleeting, for employing the construction of Christian identity around enslavement for justice in opposition to the normative practices of privilege and power.[22]

As the history of interpretation indicates, the texts addressed in this study have rarely been used for justice.[23] The burden of decentering personal needs or ambitions for the sake of others is most often placed on marginalized peoples rather than on those with social, economic, or legal power and privilege. Authority figures may perform "service" by a ceremonial footwashing, but the radical challenge of enslavement is often reduced to platitudes concerning "servant leadership" as a way to exercise authority. The un-masculinity

22. Cf. McKeown 2012, 293–96, 300; Moss 2024, 205–7.
23. See esp. Kartzow 2018, 160, on the danger of slavery-based metaphors.

of Christian identity was almost entirely lost in favor of manly men worshiping a manly Christ, as is evident in Clement of Alexandria's integration of Philippians 2:1–11 and 1 Peter 2:18–25 into an exhortation to normative masculinity—an exhortation that echoes through the centuries to contemporary Christian preaching and teaching.[24] The history of interpretation and appropriation of the texts is a history of domination and oppression.

Another "Clement," however—First Clement, a letter credited to the church of Rome—suggested an alternative way to masculinize enslavement. Instead of adopting the standard features of elite masculinity for the followers of Jesus, in 1 Clement 55 willing enslavement exemplifies masculinity. This text claims that many people imprisoned themselves to ransom (λυτρόω) others and that many enslaved themselves to use the proceeds from the sale of their lives to feed the hungry (55.2).[25] Their actions compare with the manliness (ἀνδρεῖος) of Judith and of Esther, who humiliated (ταπείνωσις, ταπεινός) herself to save her people. The comparison with Judith and Esther is facilitated by the domination of enslavement. Those who enslave themselves "betray themselves into danger" (παραδίδωμι . . . τῷ κινδύνῳ) just as much as someone who infiltrates an enemy camp to assassinate the commander (55.3–6). Here the un-masculinity of enslavement is redefined as the ultimate expression of manly courage.

As Ilaria Ramelli carefully documents, Gregory of Nyssa offers another example of the interpretation of the texts addressed in this study for justice.[26] Gregory distinguishes the kind of enslavement endured by Jesus from the standard experience of humiliation endured by enslaved people (though he doesn't cite Phil. 2:7–8, the representation of Jesus there underlies his comments in *Contra Eunomium* 3.8.52–57). Similar to 1 Clement 55, Gregory identifies Jesus's assumption of humanity as taking on enslavement in order to save others from it (cf. Mark 10:45). Consequently, Easter becomes a feast of freedom. Gregory's theological exposition of the church's celebration of Jesus's resurrection emphasizes the practical effects: This is the day for enslaved people to be freed, for enslavers to be generous and merciful, and for restoring the living dead to life (*Discourse on the Holy Pascha* 250–51).

As these varied efforts to rewrite the dishonorable un-masculinity of enslavement indicate, the language, imagery, and structures of enslavement in

24. The history of the masculinization of Christianity is traced by Brown 1988; Bendroth 1993; and Du Mez 2020.

25. On this text, see esp. Downs 2022, 400–403. Downs does not comment on the connection with masculinity, but he does suggest the representation of self-enslavement as honorable and exemplary of Christian love challenges the dishonorable conception of slavery as social death.

26. Ramelli 2016, 172–92.

Mark 10:41–45; Luke 22:24–27 (and Luke's parables); Philippians 2:6–11; and 1 Peter 2:18–25 are troubling reflections of the experiences of enslavement in the Roman world. The lived, embodied metaphors of enslavement to Christ and one another were developed by authorial communities that lived in a world structured by hierarchies of domination. For this reason, it is difficult to escape metaphors of domination in the New Testament. In John's Gospel, there is a shift from the metaphor of enslavement to the metaphor of friendship, and the latter may be better suited for shaping understandings of the Christian life that lead to just outcomes—especially if friendship is modeled not on elite men's exploitation of friendship to exercise status and power but, rather, on non-elite and enslaved people's relationships of care and support for one another.[27]

Recognizing the intersections of slavery and masculinity opens opportunities to resist their dominating forces and to develop alternative ways of structuring communal relationships and identities. The texts I have explored in this book center enslaved people as living examples of what it means to follow Jesus. Their experiences of enslavement inform the representations of Jesus in Philippians 2:5–11 and 1 Peter 2:18–25; the story of Mary, the model disciple and humiliated "slave," in Luke 1; and the challenge to Jesus's followers to adopt his "slavish" way of life in the Gospels, Philippians, and 1 Peter. Jesus's way is defined by the refusal to exploit or abuse status, the willingness to set aside status or (social) honor on behalf of others, and the embrace of the mutuality and solidarity enabled by un-masculinity. The exhortation to assume the identity of an enslaved person decenters normative masculinity in both personal and communal identity.

27. Marchal 2006a, 35–45, addresses friendship as a hierarchical system. On John 15:15, see Powery 2025a, 38.

Works Cited

Primary Sources

Achilles Tatius. *Leucippe and Clitophon*. 1969. Translated by S. Gaselee. LCL. Harvard University Press.

Aeneas Tacticus, Asclepiodotus, and Onasander. 1923. Translated by Illinois Greek Club. LCL. Harvard University Press.

Appian. *Roman History*. 1912–13. Translated by Horace White. 4 vols. LCL. Harvard University Press.

Apuleius. 1989–2017. Translated by J. Arthur Hanson and Christopher P. Jones. 3 vols. LCL. Harvard University Press.

Aristophanes. 1998–2008. Translated by Jeffrey Henderson. 5 vols. LCL. Harvard University Press.

Aristotle. 1926–2011. Translated by H. Rackham et al. 23 vols. LCL. Harvard University Press.

Artemidorus. 1975. *The Interpretation of Dreams*. Translated by Robert J. White. Noyes.

Athenaeus. 2007–12. Translated by S. Douglas Olson. 8 vols. LCL. Harvard University Press.

Aulus Gellius. 1927. Translated by J. C. Rolfe. 3 vols. LCL. Harvard University Press.

The Babylonian Talmud. 1935–48. Edited by Isidore Epstein. Soncino.

Bathrellou, Eftychia, and Kostas Vlassopoulos. 2022. *Greek and Roman Slaveries*. Blackwell Sourcebooks in Ancient History. Wiley & Sons.

Bowman, Alan K., and J. David Thomas. 1994. *The Vindolanda Writing-Tablets (Tabulae Vindolandenses II)*. British Museum Press.

Bryson. 2013. *Management of the Estate*. In *Economy, Family, and Society from Rome to Islam: A Critical Edition, English Translation, and Study of Bryson's "Management of the Estate,"* edited by Simon Swain. Cambridge University Press.

Caesar. 1917–2016. Translated by H. J. Edwards et al. 3 vols. LCL. Harvard University Press.

Callistratus. 1931. Translated by Arthur Fairbanks. LCL. Harvard University Press.

Cassius Dio. 1914–27. Translated by Herbert B. Foster and Earnest Cary. 9 vols. LCL. Harvard University Press.

Cato. 1934–2023. Translated by William Davis Hooper and Gesine Manuwald. 3 vols. LCL. Harvard University Press.

Chariton. 1995. *Callirhoe*. Translated by G. P. Goold. LCL. Harvard University Press.

Charlesworth, James H., ed. 1983–85. *The Old Testament Pseudepigrapha*. 2 vols. Anchor Bible Reference Library. Doubleday.

Cicero. 1913–2010. Translated by Walter Miller et al. 30 vols. LCL. Harvard University Press.

Clement of Alexandria. 1954. *Christ the Educator*. Translated by Simon P. Wood. Fathers of the Church 23. Catholic University of America Press.

Columella. 1941–55. Translated by Harrison Boyd Ash et al. 3 vols. LCL. Harvard University Press.

Cornelius Nepos. 1929. Translated by J. C. Rolfe. LCL. Harvard University Press.

Demosthenes. 1926–49. *Orations*. Translated by J. H. Vince et al. 7 vols. LCL. Harvard University Press.

Dio Chrysostom. 1932–51. Translated by J. W. Cohoon and H. Lamar Crosby. 5 vols. LCL. Harvard University Press.

Diodorus Siculus. 1933–67. Translated by C. H. Oldfather et al. 12 vols. LCL. Harvard University Press.

Diogenes Laertius. 1925. Translated by R. D. Hicks. 2 vols. LCL. Harvard University Press.

Dionysius of Halicarnassus. 1937–85. Translated by Earnest Cary. 9 vols. LCL. Harvard University Press.

Epictetus. 1925. Translated by W. A. Oldfather. 2 vols. LCL. Harvard University Press.

Euripides. 1994–2010. Translated by David Kovacs et al. 8 vols. LCL. Harvard University Press.

Florus. 1929. *Epitome of Roman History*. Translated by E. S. Forster. LCL. Harvard University Press.

Gregory of Nyssa. 1981. *The Easter Sermons of Gregory of Nyssa: Translation and Commentary*. Edited by Andreas Spira and Chrisoph Klock. Patristic Monograph 9. Philadelphia Patristic Foundation.

———. 2014. *Contra Eunomium III: An English Translation with Commentary and Supporting Studies*. Edited by Johan Leemans and Matthieu Cassin. VCSup 124. Brill, 2014.

Hemelrijk, Emily A. 2021. *Women and Society in the Roman World: A Sourcebook of Inscriptions from the Roman West*. Cambridge University Press.

Herodotus. 1920–25. Translated by A. D. Godley. 4 vols. LCL. Harvard University Press.

Hesiod. 2018. Translated by Glenn W. Most. 2 vols. LCL. Harvard University Press.

Homer. 1919–25. Translated by A. T. Murray. 4 vols. LCL. Harvard University Press.

Horace. 1926–2004. Translated by H. R. Fairclough and Niall Rudd. 2 vols. LCL. Harvard University Press.

Hoyland, Robert. 2007. "A New Edition and Translation of the Leiden Polemon." In *Seeing the Face, Seeing the Soul: Polemon's "Physiognomy" from Classical Antiquity to Medieval Islam*, edited by Simon Swain. Oxford University Press.

Hyperides. 1954. Translated by J. O. Burtt. LCL. Harvard University Press.

Isocrates. 1928–45. Translated by George Norlin and La Rue Van Hook. 3 vols. LCL. Harvard University Press.

Jerome. 2010. *St. Jerome's Commentaries on Galatians, Titus, and Philemon*. Translated by Thomas P. Scheck. University of Notre Dame Press.

Josephus. 1926–65. Translated by H. St. J. Thackeray et al. 10 vols. LCL. Harvard University Press.

Juvenal. 2004. *Satires*. Translated by Susanna Morton Braund. LCL. Harvard University Press.

Karla, Grammatiki A. 2024. *Life of Aesop the Philosopher: Introduction, Text, and Commentary*. Translated by David Konstan. Texts from the Greco-Roman World 50. SBL.

Lefkowitz, Mary R., and Maureen B. Fant, eds. 2005. *Women's Life in Greece and Rome: A Source Book in Translation*. 3rd ed. Johns Hopkins University Press.

Livy. 1919–59. Translated by B. O. Foster et al. 14 vols. LCL. Harvard University Press.

Lucan. 1928. *The Civil War*. Translated by J. D. Duff. LCL. Harvard University Press.

Lucian. 1915–67. Translated by A. M. Harmon et al. 7 vols. LCL. Harvard University Press.

Martial. 1993. Translated by D. R. Shackleton Bailey. 3 vols. LCL. Harvard University Press.

Ovid. 1914–31. Translated by Grant Showerman et al. 6 vols. LCL. Harvard University Press.

Pausanias. 1918–35. Translated by W. H. S. Jones et al. 5 vols. Loeb Classical Library. Harvard University Press.

Petronius. 2020. *Satyricon*. Translated by Gareth Schmeling. LCL. Harvard University Press.

Phaedrus. 1965. *Fables*. Translated by Ben Edwin Perry. LCL. Harvard University Press.

Philo. 1929–53. Translated by F. H. Colson et al. 12 vols. LCL. Harvard University Press.

Philostratus. 2023. *Lives of the Sophists*. Translated by Graeme Miles. LCL. Harvard University Press.

Plato. 1921–2025. Translated by Harold North Fowler et al. 13 vols. LCL. Harvard University Press.

Plautus. 2011–13. Translated by Wolfgang de Melo. 5 vols. LCL. Harvard University Press.

Pleket, H. W. 1969. *Texts on the Social History of the Greek World*. Vol. 2 of *Epigraphica*. Brill.

Pliny the Elder. 1938–63. Translated by H. Rackham et al. 10 vols. LCL. Harvard University Press.

Pliny the Younger. 1969. Translated by Betty Radice. 2 vols. LCL. Harvard University Press.

Plutarch. 1914–2003. Translated by Bernadotte Perrin et al. 28 vols. LCL. Harvard University Press.

Polybius. 2010–12. Translated by W. R. Paton and S. Douglas Olson. 6 vols. LCL. Harvard University Press.

Publilius Syrus. 1934. Translated by J. Wight Duff and Arnold M. Duff. LCL. Harvard University Press.

Quintilian. 2002–6. Translated by Donald A. Russell. 7 vols. LCL. Harvard University Press.

Repath, Ian. 2007a. "Anonymous Latinus, *Book of Physiognomy*." In *Seeing the Face, Seeing the Soul: Polemon's* Physiognomy *from Classical Antiquity to Medieval Islam*, edited by Simon Swain. Oxford University Press.

———. 2007b. "The *Physiognomy* of Adamantius the Sophist." In *Seeing the Face, Seeing the Soul: Polemon's* Physiognomy *from Classical Antiquity to Medieval Islam*, edited by Simon Swain. Oxford University Press.

Rowlandson, Jane, ed. 1998. *Women and Society in Greek and Roman Egypt: A Sourcebook*. Cambridge University Press.

Sallust. 2013. *The War with Catiline. The War with Jugurtha*. Translated by J. C. Rolfe. LCL. Harvard University Press.

Scott, Samuel P., trans. 1932. *The Digest or Pandects of Justinian*. https://droitromain.univ-grenoble-alpes.fr/Anglica/digest_Scott.htm.

Select Papyri. 1932–41. Translated by A. S. Hunt et al. 3 vols. LCL. Harvard University Press.

Seneca. 1917–2004. Translated by Richard M. Gummere et al. 10 vols. LCL. Harvard University Press.

Seneca the Elder. 1974. Translated by Michael Winterbottom. 2 vols. LCL. Harvard University Press.

Shelton, Jo-Ann. 1998. *As the Romans Did: A Sourcebook in Roman Social History*. 2nd ed. Oxford University Press.

Soranus. 1991. *Gynecology*. Translated by Oswei Temkin. Johns Hopkins University Press.

Strabo. 1917–32. Translated by Horace Leonard Jones. 8 vols. LCL. Harvard University Press.

Suetonius. 1914. Translated by J. C. Rolfe. 2 vols. LCL. Harvard University Press.

Tacitus. 1914–37. Translated by M. Hutton, W. Peterson, et al. 5 vols. LCL. Harvard University Press.

Tertullian. 1885–87. *On the Apparel of Women*, *To His Wife*, *Exhortation to Chastity*, *On Monogamy*, *On Modesty*. In vol. 4 of *Ante-Nicene Fathers*, edited by Alexander Roberts and James Donaldson. T&T Clark.

Thucydides. 1919–23. *History of the Peloponnesian War*. Translated by C. F. Smith. 4 vols. LCL. Harvard University Press.

Valerius Maximus. 2000. *Memorable Doings and Sayings*. Translated by D. R. Shackleton Bailey. 2 vols. LCL. Harvard University Press.

Varro. 1934–38. Translated by William Davis Hooper and Roland G. Kent. 3 vols. LCL. Harvard University Press.

Virgil. 1999–2001. Translated by H. Rushton Fairclough. 2 vols. LCL. Harvard University Press.

Wiedemann, Thomas. 2005. *Greek and Roman Slavery*. Routledge.

Xenophon. 1914–2013. Translated by Walter Miller et al. 7 vols. LCL. Harvard University Press.

Xenophon of Athens. 2009. *Anthia and Habrocomes*. Translated by Jeffrey Henderson. LCL. Harvard University Press.

Zulueta, Francis de. 1946–1953. *Institutes of Gaius*. 2 vols. Clarendon.

Secondary Sources

Aageson, James W. 2004. "1 Peter 2.11–3.7: Slaves, Wives and the Complexities of Interpretation." In *A Feminist Companion to the Catholic Epistles and Hebrews*, edited by Amy-Jill Levine and Maria Mayo Robbins. T&T Clark.

Achtemeier, Paul J. 1996. *1 Peter*. Hermeneia. Fortress.

Alimi, Toni. 2024. *Slaves of God: Augustine and Other Romans on Religion and Politics*. Princeton University Press.

Alston, Richard. 1998. "Arms and the Man: Soldiers, Masculinity, and Power in Republican and Imperial Rome." In *When Men Were Men: Masculinity, Power and Identity in Classical Antiquity*, edited by Lin Foxhall and John Salmon. Routledge.

Anderson, Janice Capel, and Stephen D. Moore. 2004. "Matthew and Masculinity." In *New Testament Masculinities*, edited by Stephen D. Moore and Janice Capel Anderson. SBL SemeiaSt 45. Brill.

Arlandson, James Malcolm. 1997. *Women, Class, and Society in Early Christianity: Models from Luke-Acts*. Hendrickson.

Arzt-Grabner, Peter. 2010. "How to Deal with Onesimus? Paul's Solution Within the Frame of Ancient Legal and Documentary Sources." In *Philemon in Perspective: Interpreting a Pauline Letter*, edited by D. Francois Tolmie. BZNW 169. De Gruyter.

Ascough, Richard S. 2003. *Paul's Macedonian Associations: The Social Context of Philippians and 1 Thessalonians*. WUNT 2.161. Mohr Siebeck.

Asikainen, Susan. 2018. *Jesus and Other Men: Ideal Masculinities in the Synoptic Gospels*. Biblical Interpretation Series 159. Brill.

Baergen, Rene A. 2006. "Servant, Manager or Slave? Reading the Parable of the Rich Man and His Steward (Luke 16:1–8a) Through the Lens of Ancient Slavery." *SR* 35 (1): 25–38.

Bain, Katherine. 2014. *Women's Socioeconomic Status and Religious Leadership in Asia Minor in the First Two Centuries C.E.* Emerging Scholars. Fortress.

Baird, J. A. 2015. "On Reading the Material Culture of Ancient Sexual Labor." *Helios* 42: 163–75.

Bakke, O. M. 2005. *When Children Became People: The Birth of Childhood in Early Christianity*. Fortress.

Barclay, John M. G. 1997. "The Family as the Bearer of Religion in Judaism and Early Christianity." In *Constructing Early Christian Families: Family as Social Reality and Metaphor*, edited by Halvor Moxnes. Routledge.

Barreto, Eric D. 2018. "A Gospel on the Move: Practice, Proclamation, and Place in Luke and Acts." *Interpretation* 73: 175–87.

Barrier, Jeremy W. 2008. "Marks of Oppression: A Postcolonial Reading of Paul's *Stigmata* in Galatians 6:17." *BibInt* 16: 336–62.

Bartchy, S. Scott. 2002. "The Historical Jesus and Honor Reversal at the Table." In *The Social Setting of Jesus and the Gospels*, edited by Wolfgang Stegemann, Bruce J. Malina, and Gerd Theissen. Fortress.

Bashaw, Jennifer Garcia. 2019. "Finding Common Ground in God's Story: Experiencing Luke 7:36–50 with the First-Century Hearers." *RevExp* 116: 233–39.

Bauckham, Richard. 2002. *Gospel Women: Studies of the Named Women in the Gospels*. Eerdmans.

Bauman-Martin, Betsy J. 2004a. "Feminist Theologies of Suffering and Current Interpretations of 1 Peter 2.18–3.9." In *A Feminist Companion to the Catholic Epistles and Hebrews*, edited by Amy-Jill Levine and Maria Mayo Robbins. T&T Clark.

———. 2004b. "Women on the Edge: New Perspectives on Women in the Petrine *Haustafel*." *JBL* 123: 253–79.

Beavis, Mary Ann. 1992. "Ancient Slavery as an Interpretive Context for the New Testament Servant Parables with Special Reference to the Unjust Steward (Luke 16:1–8)." *JBL* 111: 37–54.

———. 2021. *The First Christian Slave: Onesimus in Context*. Cascade.

Beers, Holly. 2013. "Servant of Yahweh." In *Dictionary of Jesus and the Gospels*, edited by Joel B. Green and Scot McKnight. InterVarsity Press.

———. 2015. *The Followers of Jesus as the 'Servant': Luke's Model from Isaiah for the Disciples in Luke-Acts*. LNTS 535. Bloomsbury.

Bell, Sinclair W., Dorian Borbonus, and Rose MacLean. 2024. "Introduction." In *Freed Persons in the Roman World: Status, Diversity, and Representation*, edited by Sinclair W. Bell, Dorian Borbonus, and Rose MacLean. Cambridge University Press.

Bell, Sinclair, and Teresa Ramsby. 2012. Introduction to *Free at Last! The Impact of Freed Slaves on the Roman Empire*, edited by Sinclair Bell and Teresa Ramsby. Bristol Classical Press.

Bendroth, Margaret Lamberts. 1993. *Fundamentalism and Gender: 1875 to the Present*. Yale University Press.

Berkowitz, Beth. 2023. "Udders, Queer Nests, and Animal Family Trees: Kinship as Keyword in Animal Studies in the Bible." *Biblical Interpretation* 31: 635–51.

Bermejo-Rubio, Fernando. 2018. "Did Jesus the Galilean Redefine the Concept of Kingship? Apologetic Agendas from Ancient Texts to Modern Scholarship." *ASE* 35: 51–82.

Bieberstein, Sabine. 2000. "Disrupting the Normal Reality of Slavery: A Feminist Reading of the Letter to Philemon." *JSNT* 79: 105–16.

Bird, Jennifer G. 2011. *Abuse, Power and Fearful Obedience: Reconsidering 1 Peter's Commands to Wives*. LNTS 442. T&T Clark International.

Blake, Sarah. 2012. "Now You See Them: Slaves and Other Objects as Elements of the Roman Master." *Helios* 39: 193–211.

———. 2016. "*In Manus*: Pliny's Letters and the Arts of Mastery." In *Roman Literary Cultures: Domestic Politics, Revolutionary Poetics, Civic Spectacle*, edited by Alison Keith and Jonathan Edmondson. University of Toronto Press.

Bloomquist, L. Gregory. 2007. "Subverted by Joy: Suffering and Joy in Paul's Letter to the Philippians." *Interpretation* 61: 270–82.

Boatwright, Mary T. 2011. "Women and Gender in the Forum Romanum." *TAPA* 141: 105–41.

Bodel, John. 2011. "Slave Labour and Roman Society." In *The Cambridge World History of Slavery*. Vol. 1, *The Ancient Mediterranean World*, edited by Keith Bradley and Paul Cartledge. Cambridge University Press.

Bonar, Chance, and Christy Cobb. 2025. "The Rhetoric and Ethic of Translating and Representing Enslaved Persons in the New Testament and Early Christian Studies." *JSNT* 48: 5–32.

Bonar, Chance Everett. 2025. "Manumission." In *Ancient Slavery and its New Testament Contexts*, edited by Christy Cobb and Katherine A. Shaner. Eerdmans.

Bond, Sarah E. 2022. "Maintaining the City: Enslaved Labor and Trade in Roman Philippi." In *Philippi, from* Colonia Augusta *to* Communitas Christiana*: Religion and Society in Transition*, edited by Steven J. Friesen, Michalis Lychounas, and Daniel N. Schowalter. NovTSup 186. Brill.

Booth, Alan. 1991. "The Age for Reclining and Its Attendant Perils." In *Dining in a Classical Context*, edited by William J. Slater. University of Michigan Press.

Borbonus, Dorian. 2024. "*Permissu decurionum*: Freed Persons and Burial Management in the Collective Tomb of the *Volusii*." In *Freed Persons in the Roman World: Status, Diversity, and Representation*, edited by Sinclair W. Bell, Dorian Borbonus, and Rose MacLean. Cambridge University Press.

Borg, Barbara E. 2012. "The Face of the Social Climber: Roman Freedmen and Elite Ideology." In *Free at Last! The Impact of Freed Slaves on the Roman Empire*, edited by Sinclair Bell and Teresa Ramsby. Bristol Classical Press.

Boring, M. Eugene. 2006. *Mark: A Commentary*. NTL. Westminster John Knox.

Bosworth, A. B. 2002. "Vespasian and the Slave Trade." *CQ* 52: 350–57.

Bovon, François. 2002. *Luke 1: A Commentary on the Gospel of Luke 1:1–9:50*. Translated by Christine M. Thomas. Fortress.

———. 2012. *Luke 3: A Commentary on the Gospel of Luke 19:28–24:53*. Translated by James Crouch. Fortress.

———. 2013. *Luke 2: A Commentary on the Gospel of Luke 9:51–19:27*. Translated by Donald S. Deer. Hermeneia. Fortress.

Bradley, Keith. 1994. *Slavery and Society at Rome*. Key Themes in Ancient History. Cambridge University Press.

———. 2000. "Animalizing the Slave: The Truth of Fiction." *JRS* 90: 110–25.

———. 2004. "On Captives Under the Principate." *Phoenix* 58: 298–318.

———. 2008. "Seneca and Slavery." In *Seneca*, edited by John G. Fitch. Oxford Readings in Classical Studies. Oxford University Press.

———. 2011a. "Resisting Slavery at Rome." In *The Cambridge World History of Slavery*. Vol. 1, *The Ancient Mediterranean World*, edited by Keith Bradley and Paul Cartledge. Cambridge University Press.

———. 2011b. "Slavery in the Roman Republic." In *The Cambridge World History of Slavery*. Vol. 1, *The Ancient Mediterranean World*, edited by Keith Bradley and Paul Cartledge. Cambridge University Press.

Briggs, Sheila. 2000. "Paul on Bondage and Freedom in Imperial Roman Society." In *Paul and Politics: Ekklesia, Israel, Imperium, Interpretation*, edited by Richard A. Horsley. Trinity Press International.

———. 2003. "Slavery and Gender." In *On the Cutting Edge: The Study of Women in Biblical Worlds*, edited by Jane Schaberg, Alice Bach, and Esther Fuchs. Continuum.

———. 2010. "Gender, Slavery, and Technology: The Shaping of the Early Christian Moral Imagination." In *Beyond Slavery: Overcoming Its Religious and Sexual*

Legacies, edited by Bernadette Brooten and Jacqueline L. Hazelton. Black Religion / Womanist Thought / Social Justice. Palgrave MacMillan.

Brobst-Renaud, Amanda. 2024. "Women as Patterns for Ministry in the Gospel of Luke." *Currents in Theology and Mission* 51: 27–32.

Brooten, Bernadette. 2010. Introduction to *Beyond Slavery: Overcoming Its Religious and Sexual Legacies*, edited by Bernadette Brooten and Jacqueline L. Hazelton. Black Religion / Womanist Thought / Social Justice. Palgrave MacMillan.

Brown, Peter. 1988. *The Body and Society: Men, Women, and Sexual Renunciation in Early Christianity*. Lectures on the History of Religions. Columbia University Press.

Brown, Raymond E. 1993. *The Birth of the Messiah: A Commentary on the Infancy Narratives in the Gospels of Matthew and Luke*. Updated edition. Anchor Bible Reference Library. Doubleday.

Brown, Vincent. 2009. "Social Death and Political Life in the Study of Slavery." *American Historical Review* 114: 1231–49.

Brownlow, William C. 1857. *A Sermon on Slavery; A Vindication of the Methodist Church, South: Her Position Stated*. Kinsloe & Rice.

Brueggemann, Walter. 1998. *Isaiah 40–66*. Westminster Bible Companion. Westminster John Knox.

Buell, Denise Kimber. 2005. *Why This New Race: Ethnic Reasoning in Early Christianity*. Columbia University Press.

Bühner, Ruben A. 2023. "Die paulinische Rede von der Selbstversklavung in 1 Kor. 9, 19 vor dem Hintergrund jüdischer Identität im Sklavenstand." *NTS* 69: 195–209.

Burgett, Katherine Heather. 2022. "In Slavery with God's Children: The Law as Enslaved Agent in Galatians." PhD diss., Duke University.

Burke, Sean D. 2013. *Queering the Ethiopian Eunuch: Strategies of Ambiguity in Acts*. Fortress.

Burrus, Virginia. 2009. "The Gospel of Luke and the Acts of the Apostles." In *A Post Colonial Commentary on the New Testament Writings*, edited by Fernando F. Segovia and R. S. Sugirtharajah. Bloomsbury T&T Clark.

Butler, Shane. 1998. "Notes on a *Membrum Disiectum*." In *Women and Slaves in Greco-Roman Culture: Differential Equations*, edited by Sandra R. Joshel and Sheila Murnaghan. Routledge.

Caldwell, Lauren. 2015. *Roman Girlhood and the Fashioning of Femininity*. Cambridge University Press.

Callahan, Allan Dwight. 2022. "God's Only Begotten Thug." In *Bitter the Chastening Rod: Africana Biblical Interpretation After "Stony the Road We Trod" in the Age of BLM, SayHerName, and MeToo*, edited by Mitzi J. Smith, Angela N. Parker, and Ericka S. Dunbar Hill. Fortress Academic.

Callahan, Allan Dwight, Richard A. Horsley, and Abraham Smith. 1998. "Introduction: The Slavery of New Testament Studies." In *Semeia 83/84: Slavery in Text and*

Interpretation, edited by Allen Dwight Callahan, Richard A. Horsley, Abraham Smith, and David Jobling. SBL.

Callender, Dexter E. 1998. "Servants of God(s) and Servants of Kings in Israel and the Ancient Near East." In *Semeia 83/84: Slavery in Text and Interpretation*, edited by Allen Dwight Callahan, Richard A. Horsley, Abraham Smith, and David Jobling. SBL.

Camacho Acosta, Fernando. 2004. "Poder y Servicio: Análisis de Mc 10, 42–45." *Isd* 25: 139–54.

Carey, Holly J. 2023. *Women Who Do: Female Disciples in the Gospels*. Eerdmans.

Carroll, John T. 2008. "'What Then Will This Child Become?': Perspectives on Children in the Gospel of Luke." In *The Child in the Bible*, edited by Marcia J. Bunge. Eerdmans.

———. 2012. *Luke: A Commentary*. NTL. Westminster John Knox.

———. 2014. "The Gospel of Luke: A Contemporary Cartography." *Interpretation* 68: 366–75.

Carter, Warren. 2004. "Going All the Way? Honoring the Emperor and Sacrificing Wives and Slaves in 1 Peter 2.13–3.6." In *A Feminist Companion to the Catholic Epistles and Hebrews*, edited by Amy-Jill Levine and Maria Mayo Robbins. T&T Clark.

———. 2011. "Singing in the Reign: Performing Luke's Songs and Negotiating the Roman Empire (Luke 1–2)." In *Luke-Acts and Empire*, edited by David Rhoads, David Esterline, and Jae Won Lee. Princeton Theological Monograph Series. Pickwick.

———. 2015. "Cross-Gendered Romans and Mark's Jesus: Legion Enters the Pigs (Mark 5:1–20)." *JBL* 134: 139–55.

Chaniotis, Angelos. 2023. "Slavery and the History of Emotions: The Greek Epigraphic Evidence." *Proceedings of the American Philosophical Society* 164: 183–214.

Charles, Ronald. 2020. *The Silencing of Slaves in Early Jewish and Christian Texts*. Routledge Studies in the Early Christian World. Routledge.

Clark, Kenneth Willis. 1976. "The Meaning of [kata]kyrieyein." In *Studies in New Testament Language and Text*, edited by George Dunbar Kilpatrick and J. K. Elliott. NovTSup 44. Brill.

Clark, Patricia. 1998. "Women, Slaves, and the Hierarchies of Domestic Violence: The Family of St. Augustine." In *Women and Slaves in Greco-Roman Culture: Differential Equations*, edited by Sandra R. Joshel and Sheila Murnaghan. Routledge.

Clarke, John R. 2003. *Art in the Lives of Ordinary Romans: Visual Representation and Non-Elite Viewers in Italy, 100 B.C.–A.D. 315*. University of California Press.

Clines, David J. A. 2004. "Paul, the Invisible Man." In *New Testament Masculinities*, edited by Stephen D. Moore and Janice Capel Anderson. SBL SemeiaSt 45. Brill.

Cobb, Christy. 2019. *Slavery, Gender, Truth, and Power in Luke-Acts and Other Ancient Narratives*. Palgrave Macmillan.

———. 2025. "Gender and Sexuality." In *Ancient Slavery and Its New Testament Contexts*, edited by Christy Cobb and Katherine A. Shaner. Eerdmans.

Cohen, David. 1991. "Sexuality, Violence, and the Athenian Law of 'Hubris.'" *Greece & Rome* 38: 171–88.

Cohick, Lynn H. 2009. *Women in the World of the Earliest Christians*. Baker Academic.

Cole, Susan Guettel. 1984. "Greek Sanctions Against Sexual Assault." *CP* 79: 97–113.

Coleman, Javal A. 2025. "Enslavement in the Roman World." In *Ancient Slavery and Its New Testament Contexts*, edited by Christy Cobb and Katherine A. Shaner. Eerdmans.

Collins, John N. 1990. *Diakonia: Re-Interpreting the Ancient Sources*. Oxford University Press.

———. 2012. "A Monocultural Usage: διακον-words in Classical, Hellenistic, and Patristic Sources." *VC* 66: 287–309.

———. 2014. *Diakonia Studies: Critical Issues in Ministry*. Oxford University Press.

———. 2018. "The Rhetorical Value of Διακον- in Matthew 25:44." In *Deacons and Diakonia in Early Christianity: The First Two Centuries*, edited by Bart J. Koet, Edwina Murphy, and Esko Ryökäs. WUNT 479. Mohr Siebeck.

Combes, I. A. H. 1998. *The Metaphor of Slavery in the Writings of the Early Church: From the New Testament to the Beginning of the Fifth Century*. JSNTSup 156. Sheffield Academic.

Connolly, Joy. 1998. "Mastering Corruption: Constructions of Identity in Roman Oratory." In *Women and Slaves in Greco-Roman Culture: Differential Equations*, edited by Sandra R. Joshel and Sheila Murnaghan. Routledge.

Conway, Colleen M. 2008. *Behold the Man: Jesus and Greco-Roman Masculinity*. Oxford University Press.

———. 2017. "Taking the Measure of Masculinities in Acts." In *Reading Acts in the Discourses of Masculinity and Politics*, edited by Eric D. Barreto, Matthew L. Skinner, and Steve Walton. LNTS 559. Bloomsbury.

Cook, John Granger. 2014. *Crucifixion in the Mediterranean World*. WUNT 327. Mohr Siebeck.

Corbeill, Anthony. 1997. "Dining Deviants in Roman Political Invective." In *Roman Sexualities*, edited by Judith P. Hallett and Marilyn B. Skinner. Princeton University Press.

Corley, Kathleen E. 2001. "Slaves, Servants and Prostitutes: Gender and Social Class in Mark." In *A Feminist Companion to Mark*, edited by Amy-Jill Levine and Marianne Blickenstaff. Pilgrim Press.

Cosgrove, Charles H. 2005. "A Woman's Unbound Hair in the Greco-Roman World, with Special Reference to the Story of the 'Sinful Woman' in Luke 7:36–50." *JBL* 124: 675–92.

Cousar, Charles B. 2007. "The Function of the Christ-Hymn (2.6–11) in Philippians." In *The Impartial God: Essays in Biblical Studies in Honor of Jouette M. Bassler*, edited by Calvin J. Roetzel and Robert L. Foster. Sheffield Phoenix.

———. 2009. *Philippians and Philemon: A Commentary*. NTL. Westminster John Knox.

Crabbe, Kylie. 2011. "A Sinner and a Pharisee: Challenge at Simon's Table in Luke 7:36–50." *Pacifica* 24: 247–66.

Crowther, Steven. 2018. *Biblical Servant Leadership: An Exploration of Leadership for the Contemporary Context*. Christian Faith Perspectives in Leadership and Business. Palgrave Macmillan.

Cuvillier, Élian. 2014. "Abaissement et exaltation en Philippians 2,5–11: Une poétique de la foi." *ETR* 89: 373–85.

D'Angelo, Mary Rose. 1999. "Women in the Gospel of Matthew and Luke-Acts." In *Women and Christian Origins*, edited by Ross Shepard Kraemer and Mary Rose D'Angelo. Oxford University Press.

———. 2002. "The ANHP Question in Luke-Acts: Imperial Masculinity and the Deployment of Women in the Early Second Century." In *A Feminist Companion to Luke*, edited by Amy-Jill Levine. Sheffield Academic.

———. 2004. "'Knowing How to Preside over His Own Household': Imperial Masculinity and Christian Asceticism in the Pastorals, *Hermas*, and Luke-Acts." In *New Testament Masculinities*, edited by Stephen D. Moore and Janice Capel Anderson. SBL SemeiaSt 45. Brill.

Danker, Frederick W. 1988. *Jesus and the New Age: A Commentary on St. Luke's Gospel*. Rev. ed. Fortress.

D'Arms, John H. 1991. "Slaves at Roman Convivia." In *Dining in a Classical Context*, edited by William J. Slater. University of Michigan Press.

———. 1994. "The Roman *Convivium* and the Idea of Equality." In *Sympotica: A Symposium on the* Symposium, edited by Oswyn Murray. Clarendon.

Demand, Nancy. 1998. "Women and Slaves as Hippocratic Patients." In *Women and Slaves in Greco-Roman Culture: Differential Equations*, edited by Sandra R. Joshel and Sheila Murnaghan. Routledge.

Demel, Sabine. 1991. "Jesu Umgang mit Frauen nach dem Lukasevangelium." *BibNot* 57: 41–95.

Dench, Emma. 1998. "Austerity, Excess, Success, and Failure in Hellenistic and Early Imperial Italy." In *Parchments of Gender: Deciphering the Bodies of Antiquity*, edited by Maria Wyke. Clarendon.

de Vos, Craig Stephen. 1999. *Church and Community Conflicts: The Relationships of the Thessalonian, Corinthian, and Philippian Churches with Their Wider Civic Communities*. SBLDS 168. SBL.

de Wet, Chris L. 2015. *Preaching Bondage: John Chrysostom and the Discourse of Slavery in Early Christianity*. University of California Press.

———. 2018. *The Unbound God: Slavery and the Formation of Early Christian Thought*. Routledge Studies in the Early Christian World. Routledge.

Dillon, Sheila. 2006. "Women on the Columns of Trajan and Marcus Aurelius and the Visual Language of Roman Victory." In *Representations of War in Ancient Rome*, edited by Sheila Dillon and Katherine E. Welch. Cambridge University Press.

Dowling, Elizabeth V. 2007. *Taking Away the Pound: Women, Theology and the Parable of the Pounds in the Gospel of Luke*. LNTS 324. T&T Clark.

———. 2008. "Slave Parables in the Gospel of Luke—Gospel 'Texts of Terror'?" *Australian Biblical Review* 56: 61–68.

Downs, David J. 2022. "'Many Have Sold Themselves into Slavery': Voluntary Imprisonment and Slavery, Survival Strategies Among Associations, and the Reception of 1 Corinthians in 1 Clement 55." In *Greco-Roman Associations, Deities, and Early Christianity*, edited by Bruce W. Longenecker. Baylor University Press.

Du Mez, Kristen Kobes. 2020. *Jesus and John Wayne: How White Evangelicals Corrupted a Faith and Fractured a Nation*. Liveright.

Dunbabin, Katherine M. D. 1991. "*Triclinium* and *Stibadium*." In *Dining in a Classical Context*, edited by William J. Slater. University of Michigan Press.

———. 2003. *The Roman Banquet: Images of Conviviality*. Cambridge University Press.

Dunn, James D. G. 1998. *The Theology of Paul the Apostle*. Eerdmans.

du Toit, Sean. 2021. "Practicing Idolatry in 1 Peter." *JSNT* 43: 411–30.

Edmondson, Jonathan. 2011. "Slavery and the Roman Family." In *The Cambridge World History of Slavery*. Vol. 1, *The Ancient Mediterranean World*, edited by Keith Bradley and Paul Cartledge. Cambridge University Press.

Edwards, James R. 2015. *The Gospel According to Luke*. Pillar New Testament Commentary. Eerdmans.

Eklund, Rebekah. 2015. *Jesus Wept: The Significance of Jesus' Laments in the New Testament*. LNTS 515. Bloomsbury T&T Clark.

Elliott, Neil. 2004. "The Apostle Paul's Self-Presentation as Anti-Imperial Performance." In *Paul and the Roman Imperial Order*, edited by Richard Horsley. Trinity Press International.

Elliott, Susan M. 2018. *Family Empires, Roman and Christian*. Vol. 1, *Roman Family Empires: Household, Empire, Resistance*. Polebridge.

El Mansy, Aliyah. 2013. "Interreligiöse Ehen im literarischen Diskurs des I./2. Jahrhunderts. Plutarch und der Erste Petrusbrief im Vergleich." In *Doing Gender—Doing Religion: Fallstudien zur Intersektionalität im frühen Judentum, Christentum und Islam*, edited by Ute E. Eisen, Christine Gerber, and Angela Standhartinger. Mohr Siebeck.

Engberg-Pedersen, Troels. 2003. "Radical Altruism in Philippians 2:4." In *Early Christianity and Classical Culture: Comparative Studies*, edited by John T. Fitzgerald, Thomas H. Olbricht, and L. Michael White. NovTestSup 110. Brill.

Fairchild, Mark R. 2025. *Paul's Enslavement: The Early Life of Saul the Zealot*. Hendrickson.

Fee, Gordon D. 1995. *Paul's Letter to the Philippians*. NICNT. Eerdmans.

Feldmeier, Reinhard. 2008. *The First Letter of Peter: A Commentary on the Greek Text*. Translated by Peter H. Davids. Baylor University Press.

———. 2013. "'Basis des Kontaktes unter Christen': Demut als Schlüsselbegriff der Ethik des Ersten Petrusbriefes." In *Bedrängnis und Identität: Studien zu Situation, Kommunikation und Theologie des 1. Petrusbriefes*, edited by David S. du Toit. BZNW 200. De Gruyter.

Feník, Juraj, and Róbert Lapko. 2021. "Jesus's Inverse Transfiguration in John 13." *Neot* 55: 347–64.

Ferris, I. M. 2000. *Enemies of Rome: Barbarians Through Roman Eyes*. Sutton.

Finley, M. I. 1968. *Aspects of Antiquity: Discoveries and Controversies*. Viking.

———. 1998. *Ancient Slavery and Modern Ideology*. Expanded edition. Edited by Brent D. Shaw. Markus Wiener.

Fitzgerald, John T. 2007. "Christian Friendship: John, Paul, and the Philippians." *Interpretation* 61: 284–96.

———. 2010. "The Stoics and the Early Christians on the Treatment of Slaves." In *Stoicism in Early Christianity*, edited by Tuomas Rasimus, Troels Engberg-Pedersen, and Ismo Dunderberg. Baker Academic.

———. 2023. "Dining in Martial's World." In *The Social Worlds of Ancient Jews and Christians*, edited by Jaimie Gunderson, Tony Keddie, and Douglas Boin. NovTestSup 189. Brill.

Fitzmyer, Joseph A. 1981. *The Gospel According to Luke (I–IX): Introduction, Translation, and Notes*. AB 28. Doubleday.

Flemming, Rebecca. 1999. "*Quae Corpore Quaestum Facit*: The Sexual Economy of Female Prostitution in the Roman Empire." *JRS* 89: 38–61.

Flexsenhar, Michael. 2019. *Christians in Caesar's Household: The Emperor's Slaves in the Makings of Christianity*. Inventing Christianity. Pennsylvania State University Press.

Friedman, David A. 2014. "Josephus on the Servile Origins of the Jews." *JSJ* 45: 523–50.

Gäckle, Volker. 2021. "Jesus, the Slaves, and the Servant(s) in 1 Peter 2:18–25." In *Isaiah's Servants in Early Judaism and Christianity*, edited by Michael A. Lyons and Jacob Stromberg. WUNT 554. Mohr Siebeck.

Galvao-Sobrinho, Carlos R. 2012. "Feasting the Dead Together: Household Burials and the Social Strategies of Slaves and Freed Persons in the Early Principate." In *Free at Last! The Impact of Freed Slaves on the Roman Empire*, edited by Sinclair Bell and Teresa Ramsby. Bristol Classical Press.

Gardner, Jane F. 2011. "Slavery and Roman Law." In *The Cambridge World History of Slavery*. Vol. 1, *The Ancient Mediterranean World*, edited by Keith Bradley and Paul Cartledge. Cambridge University Press.

Garland, Robert. 2010. *The Eye of the Beholder: Deformity and Disability in the Graeco-Roman World*. 2nd ed. Bristol Classical Press.

Garnsey, Peter. 1996. *Ideas of Slavery from Aristotle to Augustine*. W. B. Stanford Memorial Lectures. Cambridge University Press.

———. 1999. *Food and Society in Classical Antiquity*. Key Themes in Ancient History. Cambridge University Press.

Garnsey, Peter, and Richard Saller, with Jaś Elsner, Martin Goodman, Richard Gordon, and Greg Woolf. 2015. *The Roman Empire: Economy, Society and Culture*. 2nd ed. University of California Press.

Gaventa, Beverly Roberts. 2007. *Our Mother Saint Paul*. Westminster John Knox.

George, Michele. 2011. "Slavery and Roman Material Culture." In *The Cambridge World History of Slavery*. Vol. 1, *The Ancient Mediterranean World*, edited by Keith Bradley and Paul Cartledge. Cambridge University Press.

Gevaert, Bert, and Christian Laes. 2013. "What's in a Monster? Pliny the Elder, Teratology and Bodily Disability." In *Disabilities in Roman Antiquity: Disparate Bodies A Capite ad Calcem*. Mnemosyne Sup 356. Brill.

Giannella, Nicole. 2024. "The Cost of Ingratitude: Freed Persons, Patrons, and Re-Enslavement." In *Freed Persons in the Roman World: Status, Diversity, and Representation*, edited by Sinclair W. Bell, Dorian Borbonus, and Rose MacLean. Cambridge University Press.

Glancy, Jennifer A. 2006. *Slavery in Early Christianity*. Fortress.

———. 2010. "Early Christianity, Slavery, and Women's Bodies." In *Beyond Slavery: Overcoming Its Religious and Sexual Legacies*, edited by Bernadette Brooten and Jacqueline L. Hazelton. Black Religion / Womanist Thought / Social Justice. Palgrave MacMillan.

———. 2011. "Slavery and the Rise of Christianity." In *The Cambridge World History of Slavery*. Vol. 1, *The Ancient Mediterranean World*, edited by Keith Bradley and Paul Cartledge. Cambridge University Press.

———. 2023. "Master Jesus and the Enslaved Apostles." In *Divided Worlds? Challenges in Classics and New Testament Studies*, edited by Caroline Johnson Hodge, Timothy A. Joseph, and Tat-Siong Benny Liew. SBL SemeiaSt 100. SBL.

Gleason, Maud W. 1995. *Making Men: Sophists and Self-Presentation in Ancient Rome*. Princeton University Press.

———. 2004. "By Whose Gender Standards (If Anybody's) Was Jesus a Real Man?" In *New Testament Masculinities*, edited by Stephen D. Moore and Janice Capel Anderson. SBL SemeiaSt 45. SBL.

Golden, Mark. 2011. "Slavery and the Greek Family." In *The Cambridge World History of Slavery*. Vol. 1, *The Ancient Mediterranean World*, edited by Keith Bradley and Paul Cartledge. Cambridge University Press.

González, Justo L. 2015. *The Story Luke Tells: Luke's Unique Witness to the Gospel*. Eerdmans.

Gooder, Paula. 2006. "*Diakonia* in the New Testament: A Dialogue with John Collins." *Ecclesiology* 3: 33–56.

Goodrich, John K. 2018. "Rule of the Congregation and Mark 10:32–52: Glory and Greatness in Eschatological Israel." In *Reading Mark in Context: Jesus and Second Temple Judaism*, edited by Ben C. Blackwell, John K. Goodrich, and Jason Maston. Zondervan.

Gorman, Michael J. 2009. *Inhabiting the Cruciform God: Kenosis, Justification, and Theosis in Paul's Narrative Soteriology*. Eerdmans.

Green, F. Mira. 2025. "Roman Law and Material Culture." In *Ancient Slavery and Its New Testament Contexts*, edited by Christy Cobb and Katherine A. Shaner. Eerdmans.

Green, Joel B. 1997. *The Gospel of Luke*. NICNT. Eerdmans.

———. 2007. *1 Peter*. Two Horizons. Eerdmans.

Grubbs, Judith Evans. 2002. "*Stigmata Aeterna*: A Husband's Curse." In *Vertis in Usum*, edited by John F. Miller, Cynthia Damon, and K. Sara Myers. Beiträge zur Altertumskunde 161. Saur.

Gruca-Macaulay, Alexandra. 2016. *Lydia as a Rhetorical Construct in Acts*. Emory Studies in Early Christianity 18. SBL.

Gundry, Judith M. 2008. "Children in the Gospel of Mark, with Special Attention to Jesus' Blessing of the Children (Mark 10:13–16) and the Purpose of Mark." In *The Child in the Bible*, edited by Marcia J. Bunge. Eerdmans.

Gupta, Nijay K. 2010. "To Whom Was Christ a Slave (Phil. 2:7)? Double Agency and the Specters of Sin and Death in Philippians." *HBT* 32: 1–16.

Haenchen, Ernst. 1984. *John 2: A Commentary on the Gospel of John Chapters 7–21*. Hermeneia. Fortress.

Hall, Edith. 1993. "Asia Unmanned: Images of Victory in Classical Athens." In *War and Society in the Greek World*, edited by John Rich and Graham Shipley. Routledge.

Hallett, Judith P. 2012. "Women in Augustan Rome." In *A Companion to Women in the Ancient World*, edited by Sharon L. James and Sheila Dillon. Blackwell Companions to the Ancient World. Wiley-Blackwell.

———. 2015a. "Fulvia: The Representation of an Elite Roman Woman Warrior." In *Women & War in Antiquity*, edited by Jacqueline Fabre-Serris and Alison Keith. Johns Hopkins University Press.

———. 2015b. "Making Manhood Hard: Tiberius and Latin Literary Representations of Erectile Dysfunction." In *Sex in Antiquity: Exploring Gender and Sexuality in the Ancient World*, edited by Mark Masterson, Nancy Sorkin Rabinowitz, and James Robson. Rewriting Antiquity. Routledge.

Hansen, G. Walter. 2009. *The Letter to the Philippians*. Pillar New Testament Commentary. Eerdmans.

Hanson, Paul D. 1995. *Isaiah 40–66*. IBC. Westminster John Knox.

Harley-McGowan, Felicity. 2020. "The Alexamenos Graffito." In *The Reception of Jesus in the First Three Centuries*. Vol. 3, *From Celsus to the Catacombs: Visual, Liturgical, and Non-Christian Receptions of Jesus in the Second and Third Centuries CE*, edited by Chris Keith, Helen K. Bond, Christine Jacobi, Jens Schröter. T&T Clark.

Harper, Kyle. 2012. "*Porneia*: The Making of a Christian Sexual Norm." *JBL* 131: 363–83.

———. 2013. *From Shame to Sin: The Christian Transformation of Sexual Morality in Late Antiquity*. Revealing Antiquity 20. Harvard University Press.

Harris, Edward M. 2015. "'Yes' and 'No' in Women's Desire." In *Sex in Antiquity: Exploring Gender and Sexuality in the Ancient World*, edited by Mark Masterson, Nancy Sorkin Rabinowitz, and James Robson. Rewriting Antiquity. Routledge.

Harris, Murray J. 1999. *Slave of Christ: A New Testament Metaphor for Total Devotion to Christ*. New Studies in Biblical Theology 8. Apollos.

Harris, William V. 1980. "Towards a Study of the Roman Slave Trade." *MAAR* 36: 117–40.

———. 1999. "Demography, Geography and the Sources of Roman Slaves." *JRS* 89: 62–75.

Hartman, Saidiya. 2007. *Lose Your Mother: A Journey Along the Atlantic Slave Route*. Farrar, Straus & Giroux.

———. 2008. "Venus in Two Acts." *Small Axe* 26: 1–14.

Hawthorne, Gerald F. 1983. *Philippians*. WBC 43. Word.

Heen, Erik M. 2004. "Phil 2:6–11 and Resistance to Local Timocratic Rule: *Isa theō* and the Cult of the Emperor in the East." In *Paul and the Roman Imperial Order*, edited by Richard Horsley. Trinity Press International.

Hellerman, Joseph H. 2005. *Reconstructing Honor in Roman Philippi:* Carmen Christi *as* Cursus Pudorum. SNTS Monograph 132. Cambridge University Press.

Hengel, Martin. 1977. *Crucifixion in the Ancient World and the Folly of the Message of the Cross*. Fortress.

Hentschel, Anni. 2007. *Diakonia im Neuen Testament*. WUNT 226. Mohr Siebeck.

Hezser, Catherine. 2005. *Jewish Slavery in Antiquity*. Oxford University Press.

———. 2011. "Slavery and the Jews." In *The Cambridge World History of Slavery*. Vol. 1, *The Ancient Mediterranean World*, edited by Keith Bradley and Paul Cartledge. Cambridge University Press.

Holloway, Paul. 2017. *Philippians: A Commentary*. Hermeneia. Fortress.

Holmes, Brooke. 2012. *Gender: Antiquity and Its Legacy*. Ancients and Moderns. Oxford University Press.

Hooker, Morna D. 2003. "Philippians." In *The Cambridge Companion to St. Paul*, edited by James D. G. Dunn. Cambridge University Press.

Horrell, David G. 2007. "Between Conformity and Resistance: Beyond the Balch-Elliott Debate Towards a Postcolonial Reading of First Peter." In *Reading First Peter with New Eyes: Methodological Reassessments of the Letter of First Peter*, edited by Robert L. Webb and Betsy Bauman-Martin. LNTS 364. T&T Clark.

Horsley, Richard A. 1998. "The Slave Systems of Classical Antiquity and Their Reluctant Recognition by Modern Scholars." In *Semeia 83/84: Slavery in Text and Interpretation*, edited by Allen Dwight Callahan, Richard A. Horsley, Abraham Smith, and David Jobling. SBL.

Hoyer, Daniel. 2018. *Money, Culture, and Well-Being in Rome's Economic Development, 0–275 CE*. Mnemosyne Sup 412. Brill.

Huber, Lynn R. 2008. "Sexually Explicit? Re-Reading Revelation's 144,000 Virgins as a Response to Roman Discourses." *Journal of Men, Masculinities and Spirituality* 2: 3–28.

Hudson, Nicholas F. 2010. "Changing Places: The Archaeology of the Roman 'Convivium.'" *AJA* 114: 663–95.

Huemoller, Katharine P. D. 2020. "Freedom in Marriage? Manumission for Marriage in the Roman World." *JRS* 110: 123–39.

———. 2024. "Doubling Up: Patronal and Familial Designations on Epitaphs." In *Freed Persons in the Roman World: Status, Diversity, and Representation*, edited by Sinclair W. Bell, Dorian Borbonus, and Rose MacLean. Cambridge University Press.

Hunsinger, George. 2020. *Philippians*. Brazos Theological Commentary. Brazos.

Hunt, Peter. 2011. "Slaves in Greek Literary Culture." In *The Cambridge World History of Slavery*. Vol. 1, *The Ancient Mediterranean World*, edited by Keith Bradley and Paul Cartledge. Cambridge University Press.

———. 2018. *Ancient Greek and Roman Slavery*. Wiley Blackwell.

Hylen, Susan E. 2015. *A Modest Apostle: Thecla and the History of Women in the Early Church*. Oxford University Press.

———. 2022. "Malleable Masculinity: Rethinking Paul's Masculinity in Light of Valerius Maximus." *JSNT* 45: 157–76.

Isaac, Benjamin. 2004. *The Invention of Racism in Classical Antiquity*. Princeton University Press.

Jobes, Karen H. 2013. "'Foreigners and Exiles': Was 1 Peter Written to Roman Colonists?" In *Bedrängnis und Identität: Studien zu Situation, Kommunikation und Theologie des 1. Petrusbriefes*, edited by David S. du Toit. BZNW 200. De Gruyter.

———. 2022. *1 Peter*. Baker Exegetical Commentary on the New Testament. 2nd ed. Baker Academic.

Jodoin, Daniella. 2009. "Au cœur de la dispersion, un appel personnel á la suite du Christ: Lecture narratologique de 1 P 2,18–25." *LTP* 65: 515–30.

Johnson, Luke Timothy. 1991. *The Gospel of Luke*. SP 3. Liturgical Press / Michael Glazier.

Johnson, Walter. 2003. "On Agency." *Journal of Social History* 37: 113–24.

Johnson-DeBaufre, Melanie, and Laura S. Nasrallah. 2011. "Beyond the Heroic Paul: Toward a Feminist and Decolonizing Approach to the Letters of Paul." In *The Colonized Apostle: Paul Through Postcolonial Eyes*, edited by Christopher D. Stanley. Paul in Critical Contexts. Fortress.

Joly, Fábio Duarte. 2024. "Between Moral Slavery and Legal Freedom: Freed People and Aristocratic Behavior in Neronian Literature." In *Freed Persons in the Roman World: Status, Diversity, and Representation*, edited by Sinclair W. Bell, Dorian Borbonus, and Rose MacLean. Cambridge University Press.

Jones, Christopher P. 1991. "Dinner Theater." In *Dining in a Classical Context*, edited by William J. Slater. University of Michigan Press.

Joselow, Maxine. 2025. "Park Service Is Ordered to Take Down Some Materials on Slavery and Tribes." *New York Times*, September 17, 2025. https://www.nytimes.com/2025/09/16/climate/trump-park-service-slavery-photo-tribes.html.

Joseph, Abson Prédestin. 2012. *A Narratological Reading of 1 Peter*. LNTS 440. T&T Clark.

Joshel, Sandra R. 2010. *Slavery in the Roman World*. Cambridge Introduction to Roman Civilization. Cambridge University Press.

———. 2011. "Slavery and Roman Literary Culture." In *The Cambridge World History of Slavery*. Vol. 1, *The Ancient Mediterranean World*, edited by Keith Bradley and Paul Cartledge. Cambridge University Press.

Joshel, Sandra R., and Lauren Hackworth Petersen. 2014. *The Material Life of Roman Slaves*. Cambridge University Press.

Joshel, Sandra R., and Sheila Murnaghan. 1998. "Introduction: Differential Equations." In *Women and Slaves in Greco-Roman Culture: Differential Equations*, edited by Sandra R. Joshel and Sheila Murnaghan. Routledge.

Jung, Jaewoong. 2022. "1 Peter 2:18–25." *Interpretation* 76: 57–59.

Kamen, Deborah. 2012. "Manumission, Social Rebirth, and Healing Gods in Ancient Greece." In *Slaves and Religions in Graeco-Roman Antiquity and Modern Brazil*, edited by Stephen Hodkinson and Dick Geary. Cambridge Scholars.

Kaminouchi, Alberto De Mingo. 2003. *"But It Is Not So Among You": Echoes of Power in Mark 10.32–45*. JSNTSup 249. T&T Clark.

Kanno-Youngs, Zolan. 2025a. "In Trump's Ideal Picture of America, Diversity Is Taboo." *New York Times*, August 22, 2025. https://www.nytimes.com/2025/08/21/us/politics/trump-diversity-black-americans.html.

———. 2025b. "Trump Slams Smithsonian Over View of Slavery." *New York Times*, August 21, 2025. https://www.nytimes.com/2025/08/19/us/politics/trump-smithsonian-slavery.html.

Kartzow, Marianne B. 2010. "Striking Family Hierarchies: Luke 12:35–48, Gender and Slavery." *Acta Patristica et Byzantina* 21: 95–108.

———. 2018. *The Slave Metaphor and Gendered Enslavement in Early Christian Discourse: Double Trouble Embodied*. Routledge.

———. 2025. "Metaphors of Enslavement." In *Ancient Slavery and Its New Testament Contexts*, edited by Christy Cobb and Katherine A. Shaner. Eerdmans.

Käsemann, Ernst. 1968. "A Critical Analysis of Philippians 2:5–11." *JTC* 5: 45–48.

Kelley, Robert L. 1995. "Meals with Jesus in Luke's Gospel." *HBT* 17: 123–31.

Keown, Mark. 2012. "The Christ-Pattern for Social Relationships: Jesus as Exemplar in Philippians and Other Pauline Epistles." In *Paul and His Social Relations*, edited by Stanley E. Porter and Christopher D. Land. Brill.

———. 2017. *Philippians 1:1–2:18*. Evangelical Exegetical Commentary. Lexham.

King, Karen L. 2019. "Jesus." In *The Oxford Handbook of New Testament, Gender, and Sexuality*, edited by Benjamin H. Dunning. Oxford University Press.

Kinuwaka, Hisako. 2001. "Women Disciples of Jesus (15.40–41; 15.47; 16.1)." In *A Feminist Companion to Mark*, edited by Amy-Jill Levine and Marianne Blickenstaff. Pilgrim Press.

Kittredge, Cynthia Briggs. 1998. *Community and Authority: The Rhetoric of Obedience in the Pauline Tradition*. HTS. Trinity Press International.

Klassen, William. 1998. "Normative Self-Definitions of Christianity in the New Testament." In *Common Life in the Early Church*, edited by Julian V. Hills. Trinity Press International.

Kleijwegt, Marc. 2012. "Deciphering Freedwomen in the Roman Empire." In *Free at Last! The Impact of Freed Slaves on the Roman Empire*, edited by Sinclair Bell and Teresa Ramsby. Bristol Classical Press.

———. 2024. "Fitting in by Decree: Freed Slaves, Euergetism, and Local Politics." In *Freed Persons in the Roman World: Status, Diversity, and Representation*, edited by Sinclair W. Bell, Dorian Borbonus, and Rose MacLean. Cambridge University Press.

Knapp, Robert. 2011. *Invisible Romans*. Harvard University Press.

Knust, Jennifer Wright. 2004. "Paul and the Politics of Virtue and Vice." In *Paul and the Roman Imperial Order*, edited by Richard Horsley. Trinity Press International.

———. 2006. *Abandoned to Lust: Sexual Slander and Ancient Christianity*. Columbia University Press.

Koester, Craig R. 2008. "Roman Slave Trade and the Critique of Babylon in Revelation 18." *CBQ* 70: 766–86.

Koops, Egbert. 2020. "The Practice of Manumission Through Negotiated Conditions in Imperial Rome." In *Roman Law and Economics*. Vol. 2, *Exchange, Ownership, and Disputes*, edited by Giuseppe Dari-Mattiacci and Dennis P. Kehoe. Oxford Studies in Roman Society and Law. Oxford University Press.

Kraftchick, Steven J. 2008. "Self-Presentation and Community Construction in Philippians." In *Scripture and Traditions: Essays on Early Judaism and Christianity*, edited by Patrick Gray and Gail R. O'Day. *NovTSup* 129. Brill.

Krause, Deborah. 2001. "Simon Peter's Mother-in-Law—Disciple or Domestic Servant? Feminist Biblical Hermeneutics and the Interpretation of Mark 1.29–31." In *A Feminist Companion to Mark*, edited by Amy-Jill Levine and Marianne Blickenstaff. Pilgrim Press.

Krentz, Edgar. 1998. "Order in the 'House' of God: The *Haustafel* in 1 Peter 2:11–3:12." In *Common Life in the Early Church*, edited by Julian V. Hills. Trinity Press International.

Krull, Waltraud. 1998. "Sur un lien entre la 1ére épître de Pierre et la theologie de la liberation: La question do rapport entre souffrance et identité Chrétienne." *Théophylon* 3: 481–96.

Kyrtatas, Dimitris J. 2011. "Slavery and Economy in the Greek World." In *The Cambridge World History of Slavery*. Vol. 1, *The Ancient Mediterranean World*, edited by Keith Bradley and Paul Cartledge. Cambridge University Press.

Labovitz, Gail. 2010. "The Purchase of His Money: Slavery and the Ethics of Jewish Marriage." In *Beyond Slavery: Overcoming Its Religious and Sexual Legacies*, edited by Bernadette Brooten and Jacqueline L. Hazelton. Black Religion / Womanist Thought / Social Justice. Palgrave MacMillan.

Laes, Christian. 2008. "Child Slaves at Work in Roman Antiquity." *Ancient Society* 38: 235–83.

Larson, Jennifer. 2004. "Paul's Masculinity." *JBL* 123: 85–97.

Lateiner, Donald. 2009. "Tears and Crying in Hellenic Historiography: Dacyrology from Herodotus to Polybius." In *Tears in the Graeco-Roman World*, edited by Thorsten Fögen. Walter de Gruyter.

Lendon, J. E. 2007. "War and Society." In *The Cambridge History of Greek and Roman Warfare*. Vol. 1, *Greece, the Hellenistic World and the Rise of Rome*, edited by Philip Sabin, Hans van Wees, and Michael Whitby. Cambridge University Press.

Lenski, Noel. 2016. "Violence and the Roman Slave." In *The Topography of Violence in the Greco-Roman World*, edited by Werner Riess and Garrett G. Fagan. University of Michigan Press.

Levine, Amy-Jill. 2019. "The Gospels and Acts." In *The Oxford Handbook of New Testament, Gender, and Sexuality*, edited by Benjamin H. Dunning. Oxford University Press.

Levin-Richardson, Sarah. 2021. "Sex and Slavery in the Pompeian Household." In *Slavery and Sexuality in Classical Antiquity*, edited by Deborah Kamen and C. W. Marshall. University of Wisconsin Press.

Leyerle, Blake. 1999. "Meal Customs in the Greco-Roman World." In *Passover and Easter: Origins and History to Modern Times*, edited by Paul F. Bradshaw and Lawrence A. Hoffman. Two Liturgical Traditions 5. University of Notre Dame Press.

Lieber, Laura S. 2012. "Jewish Women: Texts and Contexts." In *A Companion to Women in the Ancient World*, edited by Sharon L. James and Sheila Dillon. Blackwell Companions to the Ancient World. Wiley-Blackwell.

Liew, Tat-Siong Benny. 1999. "Tyranny, Boundary and Might: Colonial Mimicry in Mark's Gospel." *JSNT* 73: 7–31.

———. 2004. "Re-Mark-Able Masculinities: Jesus, the Son of Man, and the (Sad) Sum of Manhood?" In *New Testament Masculinities*, edited by Stephen D. Moore and Janice Capel Anderson. SBL SemeiaSt 45. Brill.

Luciani, Franco. 2024. "Freed Public Slaves in Roman Italy and the Western Provinces: Legal Status and Social Integration." In *Freed Persons in the Roman World: Status, Diversity, and Representation*, edited by Sinclair W. Bell, Dorian Borbonus, and Rose MacLean. Cambridge University Press.

Lull, David John. 1984. "The Servant-Benefactor as a Model of Greatness (Luke 22:24–30)." *NovT* 28: 289–305.

MacDonald, Margaret Y. 2007. "Slavery, Sexuality and House Churches: A Reassessment of Colossians 3.18–4.1 in Light of New Research on the Roman Family." *NTS* 53: 94–113.

Machado, Dominic. 2023. "Freedom, Slavery, and Beyond: A Reflection." In *Divided Worlds? Challenges in Classics and New Testament Studies*, edited by Caroline Johnson Hodge, Timothy A. Joseph, and Tat-Siong Benny Liew. SBL SemeiaSt 100. SBL.

MacLean, Rose. 2018. *Freed Slaves and Roman Imperial Culture: Social Integration and the Transformation of Values*. Cambridge University Press.

Marchal, Joseph A. 2006a. *Hierarchy, Unity, and Imitation: A Feminist Rhetorical Analysis of Power Dynamics in Paul's Letter to the Philippians*. SBL AcBib 24. SBL.

———. 2006b. "With Friends Like These . . . : A Feminist Rhetorical Reconsideration of Scholarship and the Letter to the Philippians." *JSNT* 29: 77–106.

———. 2007. "Expecting a Hymn, Encountering an Argument: Introducing the Rhetoric of Philippians and Pauline Interpretation." *Interpretation* 61: 245–55.

———. 2011. "The Usefulness of an Onesimus: The Sexual Use of Slaves and Paul's Letter to the Philippians." *JBL* 130: 749–70.

———. 2015. "Slaves as Wo/men and Unmen: Reflecting upon Euodia, Syntyche, and Epaphroditus in Philippi." In *The People Beside Paul: The Philippian Assembly and History from Below*, edited by Joseph A. Marchal. ECL 17. SBL Press.

———. 2023. "Wayward and Willful Members: Twisting Figures Past *Porneia* in Paul's Letters." In *Divided Worlds? Challenges in Classics and New Testament Studies*, edited by Caroline Johnson Hodge, Timothy A. Joseph, and Tat-Siong Benny Liew. SBL SemeiaSt 100. SBL.

Marcus, Joel. 2000. *Mark 1–8: A New Translation with Introduction and Commentary*. AB 27. Yale University Press.

———. 2009. *Mark 8–16: A New Translation with Introduction and Commentary.* AB 27A. Yale University Press.

Marshall, C. W. 2013. "Sex Slaves in New Comedy." In *Slaves and Slavery in Ancient Greek Comic Drama*, edited by Ben Akrigg and Rob Tordoff. Cambridge University Press.

Marshall, C. W., and Deborah Kamen. 2021. "Mere Sex Objects?" In *Slavery and Sexuality in Classical Antiquity*, edited by Deborah Kamen and C. W. Marshall. University of Wisconsin Press.

Martin, Clarice J. 2005. "The Eyes Have It: Slaves in the Communities of Christ-Believers." In *A People's History of Christianity*. Vol. 1, *Christian Origins*, edited by Richard A. Horsley. Fortress.

Martin, Dale B. 1990. *Slavery as Salvation: The Metaphor of Slavery in Pauline Christianity*. Yale University Press.

———. 1997. "Paul Without Passion: On Paul's Rejection of Desire in Sex and Marriage." In *Constructing Early Christian Families: Family as Social Reality and Metaphor*, edited by Halvor Moxnes. Routledge.

Martin, Ralph P. 1967. *Carmen Christi: Philippians ii.5–11 in Recent Interpretation and in the Setting of Early Christian Worship*. Cambridge University Press.

———. 1976. *Philippians*. NCB. Oliphants.

Martinsen, Anders. 2015. "Men and Unmen in the Parables of Luke: Reception, Slavery, Masculinity." PhD diss., Oslo Metropolitan University.

Mason, John Edwin. 2003. *Social Death and Resurrection: Slavery and Emancipation in South Africa*. Reconsiderations in South African History. University of Virginia Press.

Matuszewski, Rafał. 2021. "Same-Sex Relations Between Free and Slave in Democratic Athens." In *Slavery and Sexuality in Classical Antiquity*, edited by Deborah Kamen and C. W. Marshall. University of Wisconsin Press.

Mayor, Adrienne. 2016. "Warrior Women: The Archaeology of Amazons." In *Women in Antiquity: Real Women Across the Ancient World*, edited by Stephanie Lynn Budin and Jean MacIntosh Turfa. Rewriting Antiquity. Routledge.

Mayordomo, Moisés. 2013. "Jesu Männlichkeit im Markusevangelium: Eine Spurensuche." In *Doing Gender—Doing Religion: Fallstudien zur Intersektionalität im frühen Judentum, Christentum und Islam*, edited by Ute E. Eisen, Christine Gerber, and Angela Standhartinger. Mohr Siebeck.

McCarthy, Kathleen. 1998. "*Servitium Amoris*: *Amor Servitii*." In *Women and Slaves in Greco-Roman Culture: Differential Equations*, edited by Sandra R. Joshel and Sheila Murnaghan. Routledge.

McCoskey, Denise Eileen. 1998. "'I, Whom She Detested So Bitterly': Slavery and the Violent Division of Women in Aeschylus' *Oresteia*." In *Women and Slaves in Greco-Roman Culture: Differential Equations*, edited by Sandra R. Joshel and Sheila Murnaghan. Routledge.

———. 2024. "Seeing Subjection: Tiro, Cicero, and the Pernicious Sentimentality of Classical Studies." *TAPA* 154: 63–75.

McDonnell, Myles. 2006. *Roman Manliness: Virtus and the Roman Republic*. Cambridge University Press.

McInerney, Jeremy. 2003. "Plutarch's Manly Women." In *Andreia: Studies in Manliness and Courage in Classical Antiquity*, edited by Ralph M. Rosen and Ineke Sluiter. Mnemosyne Sup. Brill.

McKeown, Niall. 2007. "Had They No Shame? Martial, Statius and Roman Sexual Attitudes Towards Slave Children." In *Children, Childhood and Society*, edited by Sally Crawford and Gillian Shepherd. IAA Interdisciplinary Series: Studies in Archaeology, History, Literature and Art 1. BAR International Series 1696. Archaeopress.

———. 2011. "Resistance Among Chattel Slaves in the Classical Greek World." In *The Cambridge World History of Slavery*. Vol. 1, *The Ancient Mediterranean World*, edited by Keith Bradley and Paul Cartledge. Cambridge University Press.

———. 2012. "Magic, Religion, and the Roman Slave: Resistance, Control and Community." In *Slaves and Religions in Graeco-Roman Antiquity and Modern Brazil*, edited by Stephen Hodkinson and Dick Geary. Cambridge Scholars.

Menéndez Antuña, Luis. 2013. "Male-Bonding, Female Vanishing: Representing Gendered Authority in Luke 23:26–24:53." *Early Christianity* 4: 490–506.

Merk, Otto. 1968. *Handeln aus Glauben: Die Motovierungen der Paulinischen Ethik*. Marburger Theologishche Studien 5. N. G. Elwert.

Merz, Annette. 2018. "Believers as 'Slaves of Christ' and 'Freed Persons of the Lord.'" *NTT* 72: 95–110.

Miller, Amanda C. 2014a. "Bridge Work and Seating Charts: A Study of Luke's Ethics of Wealth, Poverty, and Reversal." *Interpretation* 68: 416–27.

———. 2014b. *Rumors of Resistance: Status Reversals and Hidden Transcripts in the Gospel of Luke*. Fortress.

Miller, Anne Marie. 2019. *Healing Together: A Guide to Supporting Sexual Abuse Survivors*. Zondervan Reflective.

Moessner, David P. 2009. "Turning Status 'Upside Down' in Philippi: Christ Jesus' 'Emptying Himself' as Forfeiting Any Acknowledgement of His 'Equality with God' (Phil. 2:6–11)." *HBT* 31: 122–43.

Moore, Stephen D. 2004. "'O Man, Who Art Thou . . . ?': Masculinity Studies and New Testament Studies." In *New Testament Masculinities*, edited by Stephen D. Moore and Janice Capel Anderson. SBL SemeiaSt 45. Brill.

Moore, Stephen D., and Janice Capel Anderson. 1998. "Taking It Like a Man: Masculinity in 4 Maccabees." *JBL* 117: 249–73.

Moore, Will. 2021. "A Godly Man and a Manly God: Resolving the Tension of Divine Masculinities in the Bible." *Journal for Interdisciplinary Biblical Studies* 2: 71–94.

Morley, Neville. 2011. "Slavery Under the Principate." In *The Cambridge World History of Slavery*. Vol. 1, *The Ancient Mediterranean World*, edited by Keith Bradley and Paul Cartledge. Cambridge University Press.

Morris, Ian. 1998. "Remaining Invisible: The Archaeology of the Excluded in Classical Athens." In *Women and Slaves in Greco-Roman Culture: Differential Equations*, edited by Sandra R. Joshel and Sheila Murnaghan. Routledge.

Moss, Candida. 2024. *God's Ghostwriters: Enslaved Christians and the Making of the Bible*. Little, Brown and Co.

Moss, Candida R., and Joel S. Baden. 2015. *Reconceiving Infertility: Biblical Perspectives on Procreation and Childlessness*. Princeton University Press.

Moxnes, Halvor. 2003. *Putting Jesus in His Place: A Radical Vision of Household and Kingdom*. Westminster John Knox.

———. 2008. "Body, Gender and Social Space: Dilemmas in Constructing Early Christian Identities." In *Identity Formation in the New Testament*, edited by Bengt Holmberg and Mikael Winninge. WUNT 227. Mohr Siebeck.

———. 2014. "The Beaten Body of Christ: Reading and Empowering Slave Bodies in 1 Peter." *R&T* 21: 125–41.

———. 2016. "Placing Men in the Double Message of Luke's Gospel." In *Bodies, Borders, Believers: Ancient Texts and Present Conversations*, edited by Anne Hege Grung, Marianne Bjelland Kartzow, and Anna Rebecca Solevåg. Lutterworth.

Munro, Winsome. 1998. *Jesus, Born of a Slave: The Social and Economic Origins of Jesus' Message*. Studies in the Bible and Early Christianity 37. Edwin Mellen.

Myers, Alicia D. 2017. *Blessed Among Women? Mothers and Motherhood in the New Testament*. Oxford University Press.

Myles, Robert. 2010. "Dandy Discipleship: A Queering of Mark's Male Disciples." *Journal of Men, Masculinities and Spirituality* 4: 66–81.

Nasrallah, Laura Salah. 2014. "'You Were Bought with a Price': Freedpersons and Things in 1 Corinthians." In *Corinth in Contrast: Studies in Inequality*, edited by Steven J. Friesen, Sarah A. James, and Daniel N. Schowalter. NovTSup 155. Brill.

———. 2019. *Archaeology and the Letters of Paul*. Oxford University Press.

Nelson, Peter K. 1991. "The Flow of Thought in Luke 22.24–27." *JSNT* 43: 113–23.

———. 1994. "The Unitary Character of Luke 22.24–30." *NTS* 40: 609–19.

Neutel, Karin. 2012. "Slaves Included? Sexual Regulations and Slave Participation in Two Ancient Religious Groups." In *Slaves and Religions in Graeco-Roman Antiquity and Modern Brazil*, edited by Stephen Hodkinson and Dick Geary. Cambridge Scholars.

Nielsen, Anders E. 2000. *Until It Is Fulfilled: Lukan Eschatology According to Luke 22 and Acts 20*. WUNT 126. Mohr Siebeck.

Nordling, John G. 2009. "A More Positive View of Slavery: Establishing Servile Identity in the Christian Assemblies." *BBR* 19: 63–84.

North, J. A. 2012. "The Ritual Activities of Roman Slaves." In *Slaves and Religions in Graeco-Roman Antiquity and Modern Brazil*, edited by Stephen Hodkinson and Dick Geary. Cambridge Scholars.

Oakes, Peter. 2001. *Philippians: From People to Letter*. SNTS Monograph 110. Cambridge University Press.

———. 2022. "Popular Heroization in Philippian Funerary Epigraphy and Paul's Letter to the Philippians." In *Philippi, from* Colonia Augusta *to* Communitas Christiana*: Religion and Society in Transition*, edited by Steven J. Friesen, Michalis Lychounas, and Daniel N. Schowalter. NovTSup 186. Brill.

O'Brien, Peter T. 1991. *The Epistle to the Philippians: A Commentary on the Greek Text*. NIGTC. Eerdmans.

Okantey, Peter Carlos. 2013. "Jesus, the Originator of Servant Leadership: A Narrational Texture Analysis of John 13:1–17." *American Journal of Biblical Theology* 14. https://biblicaltheology.com/Research/OkanteyPC01.pdf.

Olson, Kelly. 2014. "Masculinity, Appearance, and Sexuality: Dandies in Roman Antiquity." *Journal of the History of Sexuality* 23: 182–205.

Osiek, Carolyn. 2000. *Philippians, Philemon*. ANTC. Abingdon.

Owens, William M. 2024. "Novel Evidence for Ancient Freed People: Xenophon of Ephesus' *Ephesiaca* and the *Cena Trimalchionis*." In *Freed Persons in the Roman World: Status, Diversity, and Representation*, edited by Sinclair W. Bell, Dorian Borbonus, and Rose MacLean. Cambridge University Press.

———. 2025. "Literary Constructions and Stereotypes of Slavery." In *Ancient Slavery and Its New Testament Contexts*, edited by Christy Cobb and Katherine A. Shaner. Eerdmans.

Padilla Peralta, Dan-el. 2024. "The Affects of Manumission: Racial Melancholy and Roman Freed Persons." In *Freed Persons in the Roman World: Status, Diversity, and Representation*, edited by Sinclair W. Bell, Dorian Borbonus, and Rose MacLean. Cambridge University Press.

Park, M. Sydney. 2007. *Submission Within the Godhead and the Church in the Epistle to the Philippians: An Exegetical and Theological Examination of the Concept of Submission in Philippians 2 and 3*. LNTS 361. T&T Clark.

———. 2024. "Letter to the Philippians." In *The New Testament in Color: Multiethnic Bible Commentary*, edited by Esau McCaulley, Janette H. Ok, Osvaldo Padilla, and Amy Peeler. IVP Academic.

Parker, Holt. 1998. "Loyal Slaves and Loyal Wives: The Crisis of the Outsider-Within and Roman *Exemplum* Literature." In *Women and Slaves in Greco-Roman Culture: Differential Equations*, edited by Sandra R. Joshel and Sheila Murnaghan. Routledge.

———. 2004. "Why Were the Vestals Virgins? Or the Chastity of Women and the Safety of the Roman State." *AJP* 125: 563–601.

Parkin, Tim. 2011. "The Roman Life Course and the Family." In *A Companion to Families in the Greek and Roman Worlds*, edited by Beryl Rawson. Blackwell Companions to the Ancient World. Wiley-Blackwell.

Patterson, Orlando. 1982. *Slavery and Social Death: A Comparative Study*. Harvard University Press.

Paul, George. 1991. "*Symposia* and *Deipna* in Plutarch's *Lives* and in Other Historical Writings." In *Dining in a Classical Context*, edited by William J. Slater. University of Michigan Press.

Peeler, Amy L. B. 2022. *Women and the Gender of God*. Eerdmans.

Perry, Matthew J. 2015. "Sexual Damage to Slaves in Roman Law." *JAH* 3: 53–75.

———. 2021. "Control of Roman Slave Sexuality: Authority, Profit, and Resistance." In *Slavery and Sexuality in Classical Antiquity*, edited by Deborah Kamen and C. W. Marshall. University of Wisconsin Press.

Peterlin, Davorin. 1995. *Paul's Letter to the Philippians in the Light of Disunity in the Church*. NovTSup 79. Brill.

Phang, Sara Elise. 2008. *Roman Military Service: Ideologies of Discipline in the Late Republic and Early Principate*. Cambridge University Press.

Porter, Jason Douglas. 2021. "The Sexual Agency of Slaves in Classical Athens." In *Slavery and Sexuality in Classical Antiquity*, edited by Deborah Kamen and C. W. Marshall. University of Wisconsin Press.

Powery, Emerson B. 2022. "Reading with the Enslaved: Placing Human Bondage at the Center of the Early Christian Story." In *Bitter the Chastening Rod: Africana Biblical Interpretation After "Stony the Road We Trod" in the Age of BLM, SayHerName, and MeToo*, edited by Mitzi J. Smith, Angela N. Parker, and Ericka S. Dunbar Hill. Lexington Books / Fortress Academic.

———. 2025a. "Placing Human Bondage at the Center of the Johannine Community." *Interpretation* 79: 30–39.

———. 2025b. "The Language of 'Enslavement' in the New Testament." In *Ancient Slavery and Its New Testament Contexts*, edited by Christy Cobb and Katherine A. Shaner. Eerdmans.

Powery, Emerson B., and Rodney S. Sadler, Jr. 2016. *The Genesis of Liberation: Biblical Interpretation in the Antebellum Narratives of the Enslaved*. Westminster John Knox.

Punt, Jeremy. 2013. "Pauline Brotherhood, Gender and Slaves: Fragile Fraternity in Galatians." *Neot* 47: 149–69.

———. 2022. "Manly Suffering: Trauma, Masculinity, and Paul." *Neot* 56: 109–28.

Quigley, Jennifer, and Laura Nasrallah. 2022. "Cost and Abundance in Roman Philippi: The Letter to the Philippians in Its Context." In *Philippi, from* Colonia Augusta *to* Communitas Christiana*: Religion and Society in Transition*, edited by Steven J. Friesen, Michalis Lychounas, and Daniel N. Schowalter. NovTSup 186. Brill.

Rabinowitz, Nancy Sorkin. 2011. "Greek Tragedy: A Rape Culture?" *EuGeStA* 1: 1–21.

Ramelli, Ilaria L. E. 2016. *Social Justice and the Legitimacy of Slavery: The Role of Philosophical Asceticism from Ancient Judaism to Late Antiquity*. Oxford Early Christian Studies. Oxford University Press.

Ramin, Jacques, and Paul Veyne. 1981. "Droit Romain et société: Les hommes libres qui passent pour esclaves et l'esclavage volontaire." *Historia* 30: 472–97.

Ramsby, Teresa. 2012. "'Reading' the Freed Slave in the *Cena Trimalchionis*." In *Free at Last! The Impact of Freed Slaves on the Roman Empire*, edited by Sinclair Bell and Teresa Ramsby. Bristol Classical Press.

Reeder, Caryn A. 2015a. "1 Peter 3:1–6: Biblical Authority and Battered Wives." *BBR* 25: 519–35.

———. 2015b. "Gender, War, and Josephus." *JSJ* 46: 65–85.

———. 2017. "Wartime Rape, the Romans, and the First Jewish Revolt." *JSJ* 48: 363–85.

———. 2019. *Gendering War and Peace in the Gospel of Luke*. Cambridge University Press.

———. 2021. "Mary's Sword: Women and War in the Gospel of Luke." *CBQ* 83: 446–65.

———. 2022. *The Samaritan Woman's Story: Reconsidering John 4 after #ChurchToo*. IVP Academic.

Reese, Ruth Anne. 2022. *1 Peter*. New Cambridge Bible Commentary. Cambridge University Press.

Rei, Annalisa. 1998. "Villains, Wives, and Slaves in the Comedies of Plautus." In *Women and Slaves in Greco-Roman Culture: Differential Equations*, edited by Sandra R. Joshel and Sheila Murnaghan. Routledge.

Reid, Barbara E. 1996. *Choosing the Better Part? Women in the Gospel of Luke*. Collegeville: Liturgical.

———. 2011. "Women Prophets of God's Alternative Reign." In *Luke-Acts and Empire*, edited by David Rhoads, David Esterline, and Jae Won Lee. Princeton Theological Monograph Series. Pickwick.

Reinhartz, Adele. 1993. "Parents and Children: A Philonic Perspective." In *The Jewish Family in Antiquity*, edited by Shaye J. D. Cohen. Brown Judaic Studies 289. Scholars Press.

Reumann, John. 2008. *Philippians: A New Translation with Introduction and Commentary*. AB 33B. Yale University Press.

Rhee, Helen. 2022. *Illness, Pain, and Healthcare in Early Christianity*. Eerdmans.

Richlin, Amy. 2015. "Reading Boy-Love and Child-Love in the Greco-Roman World." In *Sex in Antiquity: Exploring Gender and Sexuality in the Ancient World*, edited by Mark Masterson, Nancy Sorkin Rabinowitz, and James Robson. Rewriting Antiquity. Routledge.

Riesner, Rainer. 1998. *Paul's Early Period: Chronology, Mission Strategy, Theology*. Eerdmans.

Rihll, T. E. 2011. "Classical Athens." In *The Cambridge World History of Slavery*. Vol. 1, *The Ancient Mediterranean World*, edited by Keith Bradley and Paul Cartledge. Cambridge University Press.

Rinehart, Nicholas. 2022. "Reparative Semantics: On Slavery and the Language of History." *Common Place*. https://commonplace.online/article/reparative-semantics/.

Ripley, C. Peter, ed. 1991. *The Black Abolitionist Papers*. Vol. 4, *The United States, 1847–1858*. University of North Carolina Press.

Ripley, Jason J. 2015. "'Behold the Man'? Subverting Imperial Masculinity in the Gospel of John." *JBRec* 2: 219–39.

Rizakis, Athanasios. 2022. "Reconstructing the Religious Landscape of the Roman Colony of Philippi." In *Philippi, from* Colonia Augusta *to* Communitas Christiana*: Religion and Society in Transition*, edited by Steven J. Friesen, Michalis Lychounas, and Daniel N. Schowalter. NovTSup 186. Brill.

Robertson, Bruce. 2008. "The Slave-Names of *IG* i^3 1032 and the Ideology of Slavery at Athens." In *Epigraphy and the Greek Historian*, edited by Craig Hooper. Phoenix Sup 47. University of Toronto Press.

Robinson, Brian J. 2019. *Being Subordinate Men: Paul's Rhetoric of Gender and Power in 1 Corinthians*. Lexington Books / Fortress Academic.

Robson, James. 2013. *Sex and Sexuality in Classical Athens*. Debates and Documents in Ancient History. Edinburgh University Press.

———. 2015. "Fantastic Sex: Fantasies of Sexual Assault in Aristophanes." In *Sex in Antiquity: Exploring Gender and Sexuality in the Ancient World*, edited by Mark Masterson, Nancy Sorkin Rabinowitz, and James Robson. Rewriting Antiquity. Routledge.

Roller, Matthew B. 2001. *Constructing Autocracy: Aristocrats and Emperors in Julio-Claudian Rome*. Princeton University Press.

———. 2006. *Dining Posture in Ancient Rome: Bodies, Values, and Status*. Princeton University Press.

Roth, Ulrike. 2010. "Peculium, Freedom, Citizenship: Golden Triangle or Vicious Circle? An Act in Two Parts." In *By the Sweat of Your Brow: Roman Slavery in Its Socio-Economic Setting*, edited by Ulrike Roth. Bulletin of the Institute of Classical Studies Supplement 109. Oxford University Press.

———. 2021. "Speaking Out? Child Sexual Abuse and the Enslaved Voice in the *Cena Trimalchionis*." In *Slavery and Sexuality in Classical Antiquity*, edited by Deborah Kamen and C. W. Marshall. University of Wisconsin Press.

———. 2025. "Slave Labor and Trade." In *Ancient Slavery and Its New Testament Contexts*, edited by Christy Cobb and Katherine A. Shaner. Eerdmans.

Ruiz, Delio. 2023. "'By His Wounds You Have Been Healed': A Christological Portrait in 1 Pet 2:18–25." *Revista Teología* 60: 9–34.

Runesson, Rebecca. 2023. "Centurions in the Jesus Movement? Rethinking Luke 7:1–10 in Light of the Gaianus Inscription at Kefar 'Othnay." *JBL* 142: 129–49.

Saller, Richard P. 1998. "Symbols of Gender and Status Hierarchies in the Roman Household." In *Women and Slaves in Greco-Roman Culture: Differential Equations*, edited by Sandra R. Joshel and Sheila Murnaghan. Routledge.

———. 2011. "The Roman Family as Productive Unit." In *A Companion to Families in the Greek and Roman Worlds*, edited by Beryl Rawson. Blackwell Companions to the Ancient World. Wiley-Blackwell.

Santos, Narry F. 2003. *Slave of All: The Paradox of Authority and Servanthood in the Gospel of Mark*. JSNTSup 237. Sheffield Academic.

Satlow, Michael L. 1996. "'Try to Be a Man': The Rabbinic Construction of Masculinity." *Harvard Theological Review* 89 (1): 19–40.

Scaer, Peter J. 2005. *The Lukan Passion and the Praiseworthy Death*. New Testament Monographs 10. Sheffield Phoenix.

Schaberg, Jane. 1990. *The Illegitimacy of Jesus: A Feminist Theological Interpretation of the Infancy Narratives*. Crossroads.

Scheidel, Walter. 1995. "The Most Silent Women of Greece and Rome: Rural Labor and Women's Life in the Ancient World (I)." *G&R* 42: 202–17.

———. 1996. "The Most Silent Women of Greece and Rome: Rural Labor and Women's Life in the Ancient World (II)." *G&R* 43: 1–10.

———. 1997. "Quantifying the Sources of Slaves in the Early Roman Empire." *JRS* 87: 156–69.

———. 2005. "Human Mobility in Roman Italy, II: The Slave Population." *JRS* 95: 64–79.

———. 2011. "The Roman Slave Supply." In *The Cambridge World History of Slavery*. Vol. 1, *The Ancient Mediterranean World*, edited by Keith Bradley and Paul Cartledge. Cambridge University Press.

———. 2012. "Slavery." In *The Cambridge Companion to the Roman Economy*, edited by Walter Scheidel. Cambridge University Press.

Schertz, Mary H. 2004. "Radical Trust in the Just Judge: The Easter Texts of 1 Peter." *WW* 24: 430–41.

Schipper, Jeremy. 2011. *Disability & Isaiah's Suffering Servant*. Biblical Refigurations. Oxford University Press.

Schottroff, Luise. 2005. *Die Gleichnisse Jesu*. Gütersloh.

Schüssler Fiorenza, Elisabeth. 2009. "Slave Wo/men and Freedom: Some Methodological Reflections." In *Postcolonial Interventions*, edited by Tat-siong Benny Liew. Sheffield Phoenix.

Schwaller, Tyler M. 2017. "The Use of Slaves in Early Christianity: Slaves as Subjects of Life and Thought." PhD diss., Harvard Divinity School, Harvard University.

———. 2021. "Picturing the Enslaved Christ: Philippians 2:6–8, Alexamenos, and a Mockery of Masculinity." *Journal of Early Christian History* 11: 38–65.

Seal, Darlene M. 2025. "The Intersectionality of Gender and Slavery: Paul's Social Creativity Within an Unchangeable System." *JSNT* 48: 197–218.

Sechrest, Love Lazarus. 2022. *Race & Rhyme: Rereading the New Testament*. Eerdmans.

Seeley, David. 1993. "Rulership and Service in Mark 10:41–45." *NovT* 35: 234–50.

Seesengood, Robert Paul. 2019. "'Not Grudgingly, nor Under Compulsion': Love, Labor, Service, and Slavery in Pauline Rhetoric." In *Reading with Feeling: Affect Theory and the Bible*, edited by F. C. Black and J. L. Koosed. SBL.

Seim, Turid Karlsen. 1994. *The Double Message: Patterns of Gender in Luke-Acts*. Studies of the New Testament and Its World. T&T Clark.

Sève, Michel. 2022. "The Forum at Philippi: The Transformation of Public Space from the Establishment of the Colony to the Early Byzantine Period." In *Philippi, from* Colonia Augusta *to* Communitas Christiana*: Religion and Society in Transition*, edited by Steven J. Friesen, Michalis Lychounas, and Daniel N. Schowalter. NovTSup 186. Brill.

Severy-Hoven, Beth. 2012. "Master Narratives and the Wall Painting of the House of the Vettii, Pompeii." *Gender & History* 24: 540–80.

Shaner, Katherine A. 2017. "Seeing Rape and Robbery: Ἁρπαγμός and the Philippians Christ Hymn (Phil. 2:5–11)." *BibInt* 25: 342–63.

———. 2018. *Enslaved Leadership in Early Christianity*. Oxford University Press.

———. 2025. "Household Codes." In *Ancient Slavery and its New Testament Contexts*, edited by Christy Cobb and Katherine A. Shaner. Eerdmans.

Sheckler, Allyson Everingham, and Mary Joan Winn Leith. 2010. "The Crucifixion Conundrum and the Santa Sabina Doors." *HTR* 103: 67–88.

Shively, Elizabeth E. 2021. "The Servant(s) in the Gospel of Mark and the Textual Formation of Early Christian Identity." In *Isaiah's Servants in Early Judaism and Christianity*, edited by Michael A. Lyons and Jacob Stromberg. WUNT 554. Mohr Siebeck.

Sloan, Ian. 1993. "The Greatest and the Youngest: Greco-Roman Reciprocity in the Farewell Address, Luke 22:24–30." *SR* 22: 63–73.

Smit, Peter-Ben. 2018. "Servant Leadership Revisited: Διακονία, Masculinity and Martyrdom in Mark 10:42–45." *Ecclesiology* 14: 284–305.

Smith, Abraham. 2023. "Visualizing Oppression: Slavery and the Arts of Domination." In *Divided Worlds? Challenges in Classics and New Testament Studies*, edited by Caroline Johnson Hodge, Timothy A. Joseph, and Tat-Siong Benny Liew. SBL SemeiaSt 100. SBL.

Smith, Clint. 2020. "Telling the Truth About Slavery Is Not 'Indoctrination.'" *The Atlantic*, September 24, 2020. https://www.theatlantic.com/ideas/archive/2020/09/real-stakes-fight-over-history/616455/.

———. 2025. "Actually, Slavery Was Very Bad." *The Atlantic*, August 22, 2025. https://www.theatlantic.com/ideas/archive/2025/08/trump-attack-smithsonian-slavery/683969/.

Smith, Dennis E. 1987. "Table Fellowship as a Literary Motif in the Gospel of Luke." *JBL* 106: 613–38.

Smith, Mitzi J. 2022. "Abolitionist Messiah: A Man Named Jesus Born of a *Doulē*." In *Bitter the Chastening Rod: Africana Biblical Interpretation After "Stony the Road We Trod" in the Age of BLM, SayHerName, and MeToo*, edited by Mitzi J. Smith, Angela N. Parker, and Ericka S. Dunbar Hill. Lexington Books / Fortress Academic.

———. 2023. *Chloe and Her People: A Womanist Critical Dialogue with First Corinthians*. Cascade.

Smith, Shively T. J. 2016. *Strangers to Family: Diaspora and 1 Peter's Invention of God's Household*. Baylor University Press.

Snodgrass, Klyne. 1998. "Common Life with Jesus: The Parable of the Banquet in Luke 14:16–24." In *Common Life in the Early Church*, edited by Julian V. Hills. Trinity Press International.

Soards, Marion L. (1987) 2015. *The Passion According to Luke: The Special Material of Luke 22*. Biblical Studies: Gospel Narrative. Bloomsbury Academic Collections. JSNTSup 14. JSOT. Reprint, Bloomsbury Academic.

Solevåg, Anna Rebecca, and Marianne Bjelland Kartzow. 2023. "The Ideal Meal: Masculinity and Disability Among Host and Guests in Luke." *BTB* 53: 272–82.

Sommer, Michael. 2021. "Freiheit und Intellekt: Der 1.Petrusbrief und römisch-hellenistiche Gelehrtendiskurse über Sklaverei." *Early Christianity* 12: 471–92.

Steetskamp, Jisk. 2020. *Autorschaft und Sklavenperspektive im Ersten Petrusbrief*. Mohr Siebeck.

Stewart, Roberta. 2008. "Who's Tricked: Models of Slave Behavior in Plautus's *Pseudolus*." In *Role Models in the Roman World: Identity and Assimilation*, edited by Sinclair Bell and Inge Lyse Hansen. MAARSup 7. University of Michigan Press.

Strong, Anise K. 2021. "Male Slave Rape and Victims' Agency in Roman Society." In *Slavery and Sexuality in Classical Antiquity*, edited by Deborah Kamen and C. W. Marshall. University of Wisconsin Press.

Strong, Justin David. 2021. *The Fables of Jesus in the Gospel of Luke: A New Foundation for the Study of Parables*. Studies in Cultural Contexts of the Bible 5. Brill Schöningh.

Stroup, Christopher. 2017. "Making Jewish Men in a Greco-Roman World: Masculinity and the Circumcision of Timothy in Acts 16.1–5." In *Reading Acts in the Discourses of Masculinity and Politics*, edited by Eric D. Barreto, Matthew L. Skinner, and Steve Walton. LNTS 559. Bloomsbury.

Stubbs, Monya A. 2007. "Philippians." In *True to Our Native Land: An African American New Testament Commentary*, edited by Brian K. Blount. Fortress.

Swain, Simon, ed. 2007. *Seeing the Face, Seeing the Soul: Polemon's "Physiognomy" from Classical Antiquity to Medieval Islam*. Oxford University Press.

Talbert, Charles H. 2003. *Reading Luke-Acts in Its Mediterranean Milieu*. NovTSup 107. Brill.

Tamez, Elsa. 2017. "Philippians." In *Philippians, Colossians, Philemon*, by Elsa Tamez, Cynthia Briggs Kittredge, Claire Miller Colombo, and Alicia J. Batten. Wisdom Commentary 51. Liturgical.

Tan, Kim Huat. 2016. *Mark*. New Covenant Commentary. Lutterworth.

Thalmann, William G. 1998. "Female Slaves in the *Odyssey*." In *Women and Slaves in Greco-Roman Culture: Differential Equations*, edited by Sandra R. Joshel and Sheila Murnaghan. Routledge.

Theissen, Gerd. 2002. "The Political Dimensions of Jesus' Activities." In *The Social Setting of Jesus and the Gospels*, edited by Wolfgang Stegemann, Bruce J. Malina, and Gerd Theissen. Fortress.

Thiessen, Matthew. 2016. "The Many for One or One for the Many? Reading Mark 10:45 in the Roman Empire." *HTR* 109: 447–66.

Thomas, John Christopher. 2014. *Footwashing in John 13 and the Johannine Community*. 2nd ed. CPT.

Thompson, Dorothy J. 2011. "Slavery in the Hellenistic World." In *The Cambridge World History of Slavery*. Vol. 1, *The Ancient Mediterranean World*, edited by Keith Bradley and Paul Cartledge. Cambridge University Press.

Thompson, Marianne Meye. 2015. *John: A Commentary*. NTL. Westminster John Knox.

Thurman, Eric. 2004. "Looking for a Few Good Men: Mark and Masculinity." In *New Testament Masculinities*, edited by Stephen D. Moore and Janice Capel Anderson. SBL SemeiaSt 45. Brill.

———. 2007. "Novel Men: Masculinity and Empire in Mark's Gospel and Xenophon's *An Ephesian Tale*." In *Mapping Gender in Ancient Religious Discourses*, edited by Todd Penner and Caroline Vander Stichele. BibInt 84. Brill.

Thurman, Howard. (1949) 1996. *Jesus and the Disinherited*. Abingdon. Reprint, Beacon.

Tiede, David L. 1980. *Prophecy and History in Luke-Acts*. Fortress.

Tsang, Sam. 2005. *From Slaves to Sons: A New Rhetorical Analysis on Paul's Slave Metaphors in His Letter to the Galatians*. Studies in Biblical Literature 81. Peter Lang.

Tuck, Steven L. 2005. "The Origins of Roman Imperial Hunting Imagery: Domitian and the Redefinition of *Virtus* Under the Principate." *G&R* 52 (2): 221–45.

———. 2016. "Imperial Image-Making." In *A Companion to the Flavian Age of Imperial Rome*, edited by Andrew Zissos. John Wiley & Sons.

Tucker, C. Wayne. 1982. "Women in the Manumission Inscriptions at Delphi." *Transactions of the American Philological Association* 112: 225–36.

Vahrenhorst, Martina. 2013. "Leiden als Gnade: Zum realen Hintergrund einer theologischen Deutung." In *Bedrängnis und Identität: Studien zu Situation, Kommunikation und Theologie des 1. Petrusbriefes*, edited by David S. du Toit. BZNW 200. De Gruyter.

Valentine, Katy E. 2017. *"For You Were Bought with a Price": Sex, Slavery and Self-Control in a Pauline Community*. GlossaHouse.

Vander Stichele, Caroline, and Todd Penner. 2009. *Contextualizing Gender in Early Christian Discourse: Thinking Beyond Thecla*. T&T Clark.

Velden, Nina Müller van. 2019. "When Gender Performance Is Not Straightforward: Feet, Masculinity and Power in John 13:1–11." *Neot* 53: 291–309.

Verboven, Koenraad. 2012. "The Freedman Economy of Roman Italy." In *Free at Last! The Impact of Freed Slaves on the Roman Empire*, edited by Sinclair Bell and Teresa Ramsby. Bristol Classical Press.

Vermote, Kristof. 2024. "Framing the Freed Person: (De)Contextualizing the Representation of Freed Peoples' Voices in the Literary Record." In *Freed Persons in the Roman World: Status, Diversity, and Representation*, edited by Sinclair W. Bell, Dorian Borbonus, and Rose MacLean. Cambridge University Press.

Via, E. Jane. 1985. "Women, the Discipleship of Service, and the Early Christian Ritual Meal in the Gospel of Luke." *Saint Luke's Journal of Theology* 29: 37–60.

Vlassopoulos, Kostas. 2011. "Greek Slavery: From Domination to Property and Back Again." *JHS* 131: 115–30.

Vouga, François. 2013. "'Auch Christus hat für uns gelitten': Christologie und Soteriologie im 1. Petrusbrief." In *Bedrängnis und Identität: Studien zu Situation, Kommunikation und Theologie des 1. Petrusbriefes*, edited by David S. du Toit. BZNW 200. De Gruyter.

Walters, Jonathan. 1997. "Invading the Roman Body: Manliness and Impenetrability in Roman Thought." In *Roman Sexualities*, edited by Judith P. Hallett and Marilyn B. Skinner. Princeton University Press.

Ware, James P. 2021. "The Servants of the Servant in Isaiah and Philippians." In *Isaiah's Servants in Early Judaism and Christianity*, edited by Michael A. Lyons and Jacob Stromberg. WUNT 554. Mohr Siebeck.

Watts, Rikki E. 1997. *Isaiah's New Exodus in Mark*. Biblical Studies Library. Baker Academic.

Wees, Hans van. 1998. "A Brief History of Tears: Gender Differentiation in Archaic Greece." In *When Men Were Men: Masculinity, Power and Identity in Classical Antiquity*, edited by Lin Foxhall and John Salmon. Routledge.

Wehus, Glenn Øystein. 2019. "Freedom, Slavery, and Self in Epictetus." *Teologisk Tidsskraft* 8: 227–42.

Wessels, G. Francois. 2010. "The Letter to Philemon in the Context of Slavery in Early Christianity." In *Philemon in Perspective: Interpreting a Pauline Letter*, edited by D. Francois Tolmie. BZNW 169. De Gruyter.

Westfall, Cynthia Long. 2016. *Paul and Gender: Reclaiming the Apostle's Vision for Men and Women in Christ*. Baker Academic.

Whipple, Karri L. 2021. "White Folx at the Border: Trauma-Informed Preparations for Intercultural Biblical Encounters." *Bible & Critical Theory* 17: 14–26.

Wilcox, Amanda. 2006. "Exemplary Grief: Gender and Virtue in Seneca's Consolations to Women." *Helios* 33: 73–100.

Williams, Craig A. 1999. *Roman Homosexuality: Ideologies of Masculinity in Classical Antiquity*. Ideologies of Desire. Oxford University Press.

Williams, Demetrius K. 2002. *Enemies of the Cross of Christ: The Terminology of the Cross and Conflict in Philippians*. JSNTSup 223. Sheffield Academic.

Williams, H. H. Drake. 2012. "Honouring Epaphroditus: A Suffering and Faithful Servant Worthy of Admiration." In *Paul and His Social Relations*, edited by Stanley E. Porter and Christopher D. Lamb. Brill.

Williams, Heather Andrea. 2012. *Help Me to Find My People: The African American Search for Family Lost in Slavery*. University of North Carolina Press.

Williams, Jeremy L. 2024. *Criminalization in Acts of the Apostles: Race, Rhetoric, and the Prosecution of an Early Christian Movement*. Cambridge University Press.

———. 2025. "Race and Ethnicity." In *Ancient Slavery and Its New Testament Contexts*. Edited by Christy Cobb and Katherine A. Shaner. Eerdmans.

Williams, Travis B. 2011. "Reconsidering the Imperatival Participle in 1 Peter." *WTJ* 73: 59–78.

Williams, Travis B., and David G. Horrell. 2023a. *A Critical and Exegetical Commentary on 1 Peter*. Vol. 1, *Commentary on 1 Peter 1–2*. T&T Clark.

———. 2023b. *A Critical and Exegetical Commentary on 1 Peter*. Vol. 2, *Commentary on 1 Peter 3–5*. T&T Clark.

Wilson, Brittany E. 2006. "Pugnacious Precursors and the Bearer of Peace: Jael, Judith, and Mary in Luke 1:42." *CBQ* 68: 436–56.

———. 2015. *Unmanly Men: Refigurations of Masculinity in Luke-Acts*. Oxford University Press.

———. 2017. "Contextualizing Masculinity in the Book of Acts: Peter and Paul as Test Cases." In *Reading Acts in the Discourses of Masculinity and Politics*, edited by Eric D. Barreto, Matthew L. Skinner, and Steve Walton. LNTS 559. Bloomsbury.

———. 2019. "Masculinity in Luke-Acts: The Lukan Jesus and Muscular Christianity." In *Luke-Acts*, edited by James P. Grimshaw. Texts@Contexts. Bloomsbury Academic.

Winn, Adam. 2014. "Tyrant or Servant? Roman Political Ideology and Mark 10:42–45." *JSNT* 36: 325–52.

Wire, Antoinette Clark. 2015. "Response." In *The People Beside Paul: The Philippian Assembly and History from Below*, edited by Joseph A. Marchal. ECL 17. SBL Press.

Wischmeyer, Oda. 1999. "Herrschen als Dienen—Mk 10,41–45." *ZNW* 90: 28–44.

Witherington, Ben. 1994. *Friendship and Finances in Philippi: The Letter of Paul to the Philippians*. New Testament in Context. Trinity Press International.

Witzke, Serena S. 2016. "Violence Against Women in Ancient Rome: Ideology Versus Reality." In *The Topography of Violence in the Greco-Roman World*, edited by Werner Riess and Garrett G. Fagan. University of Michigan Press.

Wolter, Michael. 2017. *The Gospel According to Luke*. Vol. 2, *Luke 9:15–24*. Translated by Wayne Coppins and Christoph Heilig. Baylor-Mohr Siebeck Studies in Early Christianity. Baylor University Press.

Wood, Graeme. 2022. "Just Say 'Slavery.'" *The Atlantic*, July 11, 2022. https://www.theatlantic.com/ideas/archive/2022/07/slavery-involuntary-relocation-texas-schools/670470/.

Wright, Benjamin C. 1998. "*'Ebed/Doulos*: Terms and Social Status in the Meeting of Hebrew Biblical and Hellenistic Roman Culture." In *Semeia 83/84: Slavery in Text and Interpretation*, edited by Allen Dwight Callahan, Richard A. Horsley, Abraham Smith, and David Jobling. SBL.

Wright, Tom F., ed. 2020. *Transatlantic Rhetoric: Speeches from the American Revolution to the Suffragettes*. Edinburgh University Press.

Yamada, Frank M. 2008. *Configurations of Rape in the Hebrew Bible: A Literary Analysis of Three Rape Narratives*. StBibLit 109. Peter Lang.

Yarbro Collins, Adela. 2007. *Mark: A Commentary*. Hermeneia. Fortress.

Zelnick-Abramovitz, Rachel. 2012. "Slaves and Role Reversal in Ancient Greek Cults." In *Slaves and Religions in Graeco-Roman Antiquity and Modern Brazil*, edited by Stephen Hodkinson and Dick Geary. Cambridge Scholars.

Index of Scripture and Other Ancient Sources

Scripture

Old Testament

John

Acts